JEWISH WRITING IN THE CONTEMPORARY WORLD

Series Editor: Sander L. Gilman, University of Chicago

Contemporary Jewish Writing in Britain and Ireland

An Anthology

Edited by Bryan Cheyette

PETER HALBAN
LONDON

FIRST PUBLSHED IN GREAT BRITAIN BY
PETER HALBAN PUBLISHERS
42 SOUTH MOLTON STREET
LONDON WIY IHB
1998

British Library Cataloguing-in-Publication Data.

A catalogue record for this book is available from the British Library.
ISBN 1 870015 68 1 (cased)
ISBN 1 870015 67 3 (paperback)

Acknowledgements for the use of copyrighted material appear on page 335, which constitutes an extension of the copyright page.
Copyright © 1998 by the University of Nebraska Press.

To Susan and Jacob

Contents *in chronological order*

Series Editor's Introduction

This volume inaugurates a new way of reading literature across cultures. The title of this series is 'Jewish Writing in the Contemporary World.' Each volume will focus on one culture and the writing of Jews in that culture today. The complexity of this project is that in moving from time to time, from language to language, from culture to culture, all of these terms take on fine differentiations.

The series will appear over years and thus the definition of 'today' will, of course, change. We will bring not only established writers but also writers at the very beginning of their careers, represented by unpublished materials. What a 'culture' is will also change. The volume on the United Kingdom includes writers from Ireland, Scotland, and Wales, all writing in English. A volume on Switzerland would include texts from four different languages in one national culture. And yet the volumes will not necessarily be 'national' in their construction. We hope to have a volume on 'Jewish Writing in the Arab World' which would include the diaspora of these Jews into the greater world. Such a volume would not have a single linguistic denominator and certainly not come from a single national space, and yet would have the coherence of memory.

The litmus test for the series is the editor's answer to the perennial and unanswerable question: what is 'Jewish'? In fact, many of the texts wrestle with this question. In this series the definition of 'Jewish' writer and 'Jewish' text is left open. Neither the Halachic definition of the religious community nor the self-constructed self-representation of the Jew will dominate. Each volume editor needs to struggle with this as a problem of his or her own confrontation with the 'now' of Jews and Jewish culture. A South African volume will need to confront this question in the New South Africa; an Australian volume, in the new multicultural Australia. Are Jews part of the dominant culture or are they peripheral? Do they set the tone or do they follow the fashion? Such questions will have different answers in different volumes.

My purpose as the initiator and general editor of 'Jewish Writing in the Contemporary World' is to make writing by young and notable Jewish writers available to an American reading public that recognizes only a few categories of 'Jewish' writing. Readers in the United States understand Jewish writing as American Jewish writing (such as Philip Roth and Cynthia Ozick), modern Israeli Jewish writing (such as Amoz Oz and Yael Dyan), and the ghost of Yiddish writing in the still present voice of I. B. Singer. That there are major writers who identify themselves as Jewish and write on what they consider Jewish themes from Argentina to New Zealand is largely unknown. Part of the reason they remain unknown is the language problem. What is a 'Jewish' language? Hebrew (of course—even though there are now Arab writers publishing work in modern Hebrew); Yiddish (a secular language of ghosts, though the Rabbinic literature in Yiddish is booming in Brooklyn); and American (that most Jewish of languages—the language of Leo Rosten and Lionel Trilling). But there are multitudes of other Jewish languages from Ladino to Hungarian, from Judeo-Arabic to French. All languages in which 'Jews' contest and represent their place in their culture come to be Jewish languages. And we in our provincial, monolingual world read few of them. Thus, this series will also provide a place for the translation of Jewish writers into English. It is the place where, I hope, new readers will be captured by these texts and help provide a broader reading public (and, yes, a new market) for the authors' other works.

Welcome, enjoy—read!

SANDER L. GILMAN

Preface

This anthology is the first in a series entitled 'Jewish Writing in the Contemporary World.' I am indebted to the general editor of the series, Sander Gilman, for inviting me to put together this collection. Sander Gilman was one of the first cultural critics to take seriously British-Jewish writing, in keeping with his pioneering work in uncovering lost histories and ignored literatures in a broad range of fields. His warm encouragement and rich insights have made the task of editing this collection much easier and more pleasurable than it might have been. I am also grateful to Maren Linett, at the University of Michigan, for her editorial assistance at a crucial stage in the production of the manuscript. My copyeditor, Kim Vivier, along with the outstanding staff of the University of Nebraska Press, have all been extremely helpful and have contributed greatly to this work. The writers in this anthology have also, perhaps unusually, been models of cooperation, which in itself is an eloquent commentary on the perceived need for such a collection.

It is always a pleasure when one's individual preoccupations turn out to have a more general resonance. I have been publishing widely on British-Jewish literature for nearly two decades. As Jewish writers are thought not to exist in Britain, the common reaction to my eccentric enthusiasms has been, until recent years, incredulity. Such disbelief is shared by a surprisingly disparate group of bedfellows, from newspaper reviewers to academic critics. Workaday literary journalists, who are paid to avoid complexity, treat the Jewishness of British-born writers as a form of embarrassment, a guilty secret to be passed over with unseemly haste or ignored altogether. Jewish history, after all, is meant to take place on the battlefields of the Middle East or in the capitals of Europe or the urban centers of America, not in the heartlands of the English bourgeoisie.

The English literature academic establishment, in particular, has long since subsumed writers from most of the globe—especially the United States, Australia, Canada, Ireland, New Zealand, Scotland, and Wales—into the canon of 'English' letters. No wonder Jewish writers have been either smothered under this rubric or, more usually, simply left out in the cold. Judaic literary scholars also look for their inspiration and their canonical writers in the supposedly more authentic fields of Hebrew and Yiddish literature or, at a stretch, in the American-Jewish diaspora. From the narrow perspective of ignominious exile and national rebirth, European writers are divided retrospectively into those who published before and after the death camps, with Britain occupying a strangely untouched space on the sidelines.

The perception that Jewish writing in Britain is outlandish at best and an impossibility at worst runs deep. During a recent undergraduate course on modern Jewish literature at the University of Michigan, my students were astonished that Jews could live in Britain and, at the same time, were curious to read the literature produced by these odd creatures. In London my courses on British-Jewish writing are always full of bemused students surprised that authors they had been reading in a variety of contexts also addressed Jewish concerns. Many of these students, on both sides of the Atlantic, wished to read British-Jewish literature more deeply. This anthology is mainly for them. It is also for all those general audiences, in both Britain and America, who have sat patiently through my overeager potted histories of Jewish writers in Britain. Many kind and indulgent listeners, once my ramblings were finally over, wished to know which authors they should read first. This is my list of the imaginative prose writers to whom I personally turn for inspiration.

The work on this collection was carried out primarily between the summer of 1996 and the spring of 1997. This period coincides with the birth of my first child, Jacob Cooklin Cheyette, a time that his mother, Susan Cooklin, and I will always think of as one of the happiest in our lives. Jacob, in his first few months, has lived longer in Ann Arbor, Michigan, than in London. But this is as it should be for the latest unbounded generation of British-born citizens, to whom this volume is dedicated.

BRYAN CHEYETTE

Introduction

Many competing narratives and genres are open to the Jewish writer in Britain. My aim is to focus on one specific narrative by tracing a history of extraterritorial or diasporic British-Jewish literature from the early twentieth century to the present day. But this is just one strand. I also touch on other literary forms from the nineteenth century, including apologetic, satirical, documentary, and proletarian novels. For reasons of space, I concentrate mainly on British-Jewish fiction, although I allude to the literary history of poetry and drama, which is equally strong. My emphasis throughout is as much on the Englishness of Jewish writing as on a supposedly authentic Jewishness. One cannot understand the authors in this anthology, I believe, without taking note of the national context in which they produce their works.

I use the term Englishness, as opposed to a more inclusive Britishness, as this identity is based on a fixed and homogeneous sense of self that is rooted in the past. Although some of the writers in this volume have more autonomous Welsh, Irish, or Scottish identities, or are émigrés, most have had to write against the dominance of an oppressive Englishness. For this reason, there is a tension in the anthology between writers who aim to represent a particular British-Jewish experience and those who wish to transcend the particular. I have attempted to validate a Jewish cultural ethnicity in Britain and Ireland while trying not to reduce the plurality of a broad range of literary voices to an ethnic monolith.

Grace Aguilar and Celia and Marion Moss

Jewish writing in Britain has a long and multiple history that is only now being retold. The origins of this literary tradition at the beginning of the nineteenth century have been understood variously in relation to the Anglo-Jewish emancipation struggle, as a key aspect of Victorian women's writing, and as part of the conversionist agenda of English liberal culture.[1] Within these contexts British-Jewish writers were, above all else, mediators who in elaborate and differing ways were buffeted and bowed by the common expectations of Victorian society. Writing between the 1820s and 1850s, when Anglo-Jewry was attempting to gain full political and civil rights, these authors were called on to represent their nascent community in the best possible light. Since there were only about thirty-five thousand Jews in England and Wales in 1851, we should not underestimate the pressure the majority culture exerted on this minority literature.

Many of the earliest British-Jewish writers were women, among them Grace Aguilar (1816–47), Celia and Marion Moss (1819–73 and 1821–1907), and Charlotte Montefiore (1818–54). At this time, influential groups of evangelists were focusing on the youthful and beautiful 'Jewish daughter' as a symbol of redemptive desire, accounting, in part, for the extraordinary popularity of Sir Walter Scott's *Ivanhoe* (1819). In the decades following *Ivanhoe*, Scott's willful and exotic Rebecca was continually fetishized as a convert. This recurring preoccupation with the often sexualized figure of the Jewish woman signified, according to a recent study, a 'revisionist' shift away from Shylockian representations of 'the Jew' which eventually resulted in the national incorporation of Jewish otherness.[2]

This feminized rhetoric of acculturation also enabled the first British-Jewish women writers to draw on and write against the prevalent culture of conversion. Thus the Anglo-Jewish novel form was initially gendered feminine, but this was not, as has been argued, necessarily a progressive protofeminism. The feminization of Jewish writing had as much to do with prevalent discourses concerning the transcendent character of Jewish women as with the presumed autonomy and authenticity of their voices. What is more, the prevailing association with women and the domestic sphere, beyond the social realm, chimed perfectly with liberal constructions of Judaism as a matter of personal conscience. Far from being progressive, the privatization of Jewish identity left a homogeneous English nation unchanged and, worse still, essentially unchangeable. There was always a severe tension between the liberatory potential of Jewish women's self-representations and the dominant discourses that shaped their writing.[3]

The originating moment of British-Jewish writing indicates the continual struggle within Anglo-Jewry in the face of the enormous authority of the idea of England in the age of empire. The seductive power of a superior Englishness meant that Jews were extremely anxious to win acceptance in their adopted country. In her *History of the Jews of England* (1847), completed just before her death, Grace Aguilar makes explicit the Jewish self-denial generated by this authority: 'In externals and in all secular thought and actions, the English naturalized Jew is an Englishman, and his family is reared with the education and accomplishments of other members of the [English] community. Only in some private and personal characteristics, and in religious belief, does the Jew differ from his neighbour.'[4]

Not that all Aguilar's contemporary writers anglicized or domesticated Anglo-Jewry in quite the same way. The romances of the Moss sisters, for instance, tended to associate Jewish women with heroic national liberation. In the preface to their *Tales of Jewish History* (1843) they pointedly sought to 'awaken their reader's curiosity to know more of [Jewish] records; which were fuller of instances of fervent piety, courage, endurance and constancy under suffering than any other people.'[5] By historicizing the suffering Jewess, the Moss sisters were able to draw on the vocabulary of antislavery societies just as Aguilar was to be the perfect fictional coda for the emancipationist construction of Jews as 'Englishmen of the Mosaic persuasion.'

It is tempting to view these Victorian novelists, poets, and essayists as forming a distinct community that published a discrete and liberatory tradition of Jewish women's writing. But the countervailing processes of acculturation and accommodation inevitably qualify this attractive but flawed idealization. More accurately, British-

Jewish writing articulates a specific set of identities that are framed by the dominant culture of unremitting assimilation. As well as being a 'feminist foremother,' Aguilar raises intriguing issues about the Jewish writer's fraught relationship with English assimilationist desires. Aguilar's contemporaries did not distinguish absolutely between Christian and Jewish representations or even male and female writing, as there was a good deal of interchange between these divergent spheres.

The assumption that British-Jewish writing registered an increased sophistication and political radicalism in the end merely flattens out the complexities of this literary history into the bland arena of unfulfilled liberal aspirations.[6] A sadder truth is that the anglicizing origins of the Jewish writer in Britain became a significant element within Anglo-Jewry. Long after this originary moment many British-Jewish women writers converted to Christianity, such as Cecilly Sidgwick in the Edwardian period, G. B. Stern and Naomi Jacob in the 1940s, and Muriel Spark in the 1950s. This embrace of a supposedly superior aesthetic order indicates just how literally these writers were to internalize the assumption that Jews were profoundly materialist and outside the pantheon of culture.

THE PAST (2): INSIDERS

Israel Zangwill and Louis Golding

One conspicuous strand of British-Jewish letters has always remained a prisoner of the apologetic expectations of its origins. Postemancipationist writers such as Emily Harris, Benjamin Farjeon, and Samuel Gordon all wrote novels depicting Jews as good citizens who embodied the bourgeois ideals of the patriarchal family, entrepreneurship, and religious communalism. These liberal representations of the 'good Jew' are, to this day, upheld by the Anglo-Jewish community as the consummate set of images for the British-Jewish writer to reinforce. Until recently, the communal newspapers of Anglo-Jewry required Jewish writers to fulfill their traditional mediating role of portraying Jews 'sympathetically' according to the language of the dominant culture. Two years after Oswald John Simon—the son of the founder of the assimilationist

Anglo-Jewish Association—published his novel *The World and the Cloister* (1890), the *Jewish Chronicle* editorialized in the following terms: 'The novel is now the recognised means of those who have messages to deliver; and we welcome Oswald Simon's message to the world. It is prompted by pure and lofty thought and informed by reverence and true religious feeling.'[7]

After Jews were gradually granted full political and civil rights, in the latter half of the nineteenth century, there was still a distinct unease about whether they could accomplish the emancipationist contract and finally transform themselves into 'Englishmen of the Mosaic persuasion.' This renewed anxiety was caused especially by the influx of around one hundred fifty thousand Jewish immigrants from eastern Europe between 1881 and 1914. Historians have described this transformation of Anglo-Jewry in terms of the complex nexus of class, community, and nation. Within this fluid and constantly changing context, the anglicization of migrant Jews was given the highest priority by a centralized and homogenizing Anglo-Jewish elite.[8] Jewish writers were encouraged to reassure a British readership that Jewish difference was to be limited to the private sphere. The towering figure of Israel Zangwill (1864–1926) undoubtedly produced the best-known and most influential portraits of immigrant Jews in these communal-inspired terms.

Zangwill, from the beginning, wrote from within the dominant culture as an insider and even replicated the conversionist agenda of his early Victorian predecessors. In his important article 'English Judaism: A Criticism and a Classification' (1889) he attempted to combine, like Grace Aguilar, what he called the 'scientific morality of Moses and the emotional morality of Christ.'[9] This article persuaded Judge Mayer Sulzberger, a founder of the Jewish Publication Society of America, to commission Zangwill to write his bestselling *Children of the Ghetto: A Story of a Peculiar People* (1892). This was the first fictional account of London's East End immigrant Jewish community and quickly established Zangwill, at the age of twenty-eight, as a writer with an international readership.

Realizing the potential importance of this forthcoming novel, the *Jewish Chronicle* wrote a long editorial urging Zangwill to counteract 'unsympathetic' depictions of Jews and to act as an 'antidote' to the 'literary poison that has been [hitherto] poured in the public ear.'

But Zangwill, clearly worried by this apologetic role, only partially conformed to what was expected of him. In protracted negotiations with Judge Sulzberger over the writing of Children of the Ghetto, Zangwill repeatedly noted his misgivings at being 'shut up in the ghetto.' In February 1891 he wrote to Sulzberger that 'behind all the Jewish details, there must be a human interest which will raise it into that cosmopolitan thing, a work of art.' His chief fear, as he put it in the same letter, was that a novel based on the East End Jewish 'ghetto' would merely 'appeal exclusively to a section.'[10]

Given his view of the novel form as a means of incorporating and transfiguring the ghetto, Zangwill wanted to write in a more 'catholic' form so as to universalize his novel's 'Jewish detail.' Children of the Ghetto therefore has two contradictory impulses. On the one hand, it sets out to introduce the East End to the wider world, producing a set of domesticated images in line with communal expectations. In these terms, Zangwill reversed the stereotypes of the Jewish 'alien' or 'pauper' Jew to show that such despised individuals were really God-fearing and law-abiding citizens. On the other hand, he needed artistically to transcend the East End so that it would be of more universal interest, and he thus wished to move away from merely illuminating Anglo-Jewry.

One reason for the immediate popularity and prestige of Children of the Ghetto was its reassurance for an English bourgeois readership. As a grateful Times reviewer pointed out, it turned a 'sudden light upon the darkness' and explained the 'East End Jew' for the first time.[11] The novel's communal aspect is, however, always in tension with Zangwill's equally authoritative universalizing ideals. Despite her father's Judaic 'strenuous inner life' (66), Esther Ansell, the novel's heroine, confesses to her brother that she enjoys reading the New Testament: 'Why do I feel good when I read what Jesus said?' (174–75) she wonders. All the major characters in the novel wish to transfigure a Judaism that is described as an 'endless coil of laws winding round us and cramping our lives at every turn' (138).

Zangwill's much-loved King of Schnorrers (1894), written soon after Children of the Ghetto, was a satire on the materialism of Anglo-Jewry's leaders. In the fantasy world of the Sephardi schnorrer—

Manessah Bueno Barzillai Azevedo da Costa—the splendor of Judaism's spiritual heritage overcomes all in its wake. This use of Sephardi history to undermine the materialism of contemporary Jewry echoes the Marrano heritage of Grace Aguilar. But with the publication of *Ghetto Comedies* (1907), Zangwill, at the age of forty-three, stopped writing on explicitly Jewish themes. Instead, he chose to live in rural England near Rudyard Kipling and to write novels modeled on Thomas Hardy and Jerome K. Jerome and universalizing plays like those of George Bernard Shaw. At the same time, he devoted much of his abundant energies to saving east European Jewry from persecution, to his version of Jewish nationalism, and, in general, to modernizing the Anglo-American diaspora.

At an early stage Zangwill summed up his self-contradictions in his important and largely forgotten *Dreamers of the Ghetto* (1898). This book is a series of historical portraits of heterodox Jews—such as Baruch Spinoza, Ferdinand Lassalle, and Heinrich Heine—which suggests the extreme divisions in Zangwill's outlook. For, as well as being a writer of the 'ghetto,' Zangwill predicted the disappearance of all ethnicities in his play *The Melting-Pot* (1908). President Theodore Roosevelt saw this drama on its opening night in Washington and is reported to have shouted across the theater, 'That's a great play, Mr. Zangwill.'[12] Zangwill popularized the idea of America as an ethnic 'Melting-Pot' by proclaiming it 'God's crucible, the great Melting-Pot, where all the races of Europe are melting and re-forming!' In this brave new world a Zangwill-like Jewish immigrant from Russia argues that 'God is making the American' and that the 'feuds and vendettas' between Jews and Russians, among many other ethnic groups, will die out eventually in 'God's crucible.'[13]

This irrevocable split between English and Jewish culture, or the 'ghetto' and the 'melting-pot,' characterizes a good deal of Zangwill's writing. What is clear from his literary politics is that it was impossible for Zangwill to imagine an Englishness that could in any way accommodate a Jewish past. The severe division between the oblivion of the melting-pot and his narrow ghetto territorialism shows the dangers of conforming as an insider to the restrictive choices allowed within English national culture. But these were the choices foisted on British-Jewish writers, choices that continued to deform these writers' literary output long after Zangwill was forgotten.

The figure who most closely followed Zangwill as an Anglo-Jewish insider was the novelist Louis Golding (1895–1958). Like his predecessor, he continued to present mainly sympathetic images of Anglo-Jewry that conformed to the dominant communal expectations of him. Golding was described by the *Times* as an 'apt interpreter of British Jewry,'[14] thereby truly assuming Zangwill's mantle. In his novel *Magnolia Street* (1932), which became a bestseller, he records the clash between Jews and Gentiles in a provincial town and their eventual reconciliation. This vision of harmony clearly struck a chord at a time when the Anglo-Jewish elite was constantly embarrassed by the poor and unassimilated sons and daughters of immigrants. Nearly a century after the struggle for emancipation Anglo-Jewry was still desperately attempting to prove it was worthy of the rights and freedoms extended by the dominant society. This crushing need to present favorable images of Jews to the outside world distorted much British-Jewish writing and remained at the top of Anglo-Jewry's communal agenda throughout the interwar years.[15]

THE PAST (3): OUTSIDERS

Julia Frankau, Amy Levy, and Isaac Rosenberg

Alongside the largely conformist tradition of Zangwill and Golding were more transgressive writers such as Amy Levy (1861–89), Julia Frankau (1864–1916), and Isaac Rosenberg (1890–1914). Levy and Frankau, in their role as avowed outsiders, came close to realizing the liberatory potential of their early Victorian foremothers. Isaac Rosenberg, on the other hand, originated a diasporic British-Jewish writing that is explored at length throughout this volume. Although from very different backgrounds—Rosenberg from the poverty-stricken East End, Levy and Frankau from wealthier London households—these writers all challenged the assumptions of an English national culture and Anglo-Jewry's complacent self-image.

As the daughters of well-to-do professionals, Levy and Frankau can be brought together in relation to their class and gender along with their critique of the bourgeois values of the Jewish community. Frankau's *Dr. Phillips: A Maida Vale Idyll* (1887) and Levy's *Reuben Sachs: A Sketch* (1888) are most often compared in these terms, although there are some distinct differences between these two novels. For one thing, Frankau wrote under the pseudonym Frank Danby—a presumably non-Jewish man—which probably accounts for her emphasis on the national degeneracy of contemporary England. Her use of the genre of French naturalism also enabled her to include subject matter that was conventionally thought of not only as unladylike but also as immoral and even illegal. In contrast to Levy's fiction and poetry, in Frankau's works the gender of the protagonists was viewed through the distorting prism of either their Englishness or their Jewishness. But her description in *Dr. Phillips* of middle-class Anglo-Jewry as being 'entirely unemancipated' firmly places her novel in revisionist opposition to the earlier apologetic tradition of British-Jewish letters.[16]

As well as new accounts of Julia Frankau, there has been a huge resurgence of interest in the varied oeuvre of Amy Levy. Like Frankau, Levy engaged in a radical rewriting of the myths of English national culture, although, in contrast to Frankau, this culture was always perceived from the perspective of a marginalized woman. In particular, Levy's poem 'Magdalen' (1881), based on the New Testament figure of Mary Magdalen, is at pains to subvert the early Victorians' Christological associations with women and redemption. In Levy's transgressive reinterpretation Mary Magdalen's unanswered dramatic monologue is a sign not of faith but of faithlessness, as the Christ figure has 'neither part nor lot' in the future of Levy's Magdalen. Instead of personifying the redeemed woman, Mary Magdalen is constructed in unusually individualistic terms as a 'woman with a heart of stone.'[17]

At Levy's most accomplished, this sense of defying all the conventional methods of representing the category 'woman' also feeds into her skeptical way of portraying both Jews and the English. Her poem 'Captivity' (1889), for instance, questions the assumption of what it is to be 'tame' or 'wild,' undermining the postemancipationist basis of domesticating or taming Anglo-Jewry:

I cannot remember my country
  The land whence I came;
Whence they brought me and chained me and made me
  Nor wild thing nor tame.[18]

The cultural amnesia engendered by the process of migration from one country to another results in a form of semiacculturation, a person who is neither 'wild' nor 'tame,' neither Jewish nor English. Although 'Captivity' is located in the natural domain, Levy sets up a series of metaphors in this evocative poem which sums up the painful cost of assimilation. She goes on to apply these images of in-betweenness to herself in an article for London Society and to her persona, Alfred Lazarus Cohen, in her story 'Cohen of Trinity' (1889).[19]

Levy's novel Reuben Sachs is also about being outside both the natural and cultural realms. Here the civilizing promise of Jewish emancipation, especially as experienced by her heroine, Judith Quixano, has still to be fulfilled. Levy's novel contains a much-cited critique of Daniel Deronda (1876), George Eliot's famous account of Jewish self-discovery and migration to Palestine:

As a novel treating modern Jews, Daniel Deronda cannot be regarded as a success. . . . There has been no serious treatment of the subject; at grappling in its entirety with the complex problems of Jewish life and character. The Jew, as we know him today, with his curious mingling of diametrically opposed qualities; his surprising virtues, and no less surprising vices; leading his eager, intricate life; living, moving, and having his being both within and without the tribal limits; this deeply interesting product of our civilisation has been found worthy of none but the most superficial observations.[20]

Once again, Levy questions the inevitability of liberal advancement by stressing the incomplete process of assimilation, which places Jews both 'within and without the tribal limits.' This is in stark contrast to George Eliot's unambiguous point of closure, which sees Palestine as the site that will resolve Deronda's confusion at being both English and Jewish. Eliot's novel has recently been understood as ending the age-old evangelical association between the Jewish return to Palestine and the Second Coming of Christ. After all, when Daniel and Mirah eventually travel to Palestine, they are able to define their own Jewishness in relation to an Englishness that can, implicitly, no longer accommodate them.[21] But such easy resolutions are questioned by Amy Levy as she writes about the mass of unsituated 'modern' British Jews who are left both 'within and without' the Jewish community and Britain as a whole.

Reuben Sachs inverts Daniel Deronda so that the story is not Deronda's nascent Zionism but instead Gwendolen Harleth's marginalization in relation to this heady sense of ascendancy. Levy gently pokes fun at Eliot's novel by making her Jewish convert a feckless English aristocrat who, although from the same social class as Deronda, lacks the conviction of Eliot's hero. Gwendolen's failed and brutal marriage to the aristocratic Henleigh Mallinger Grandcourt significantly becomes the focus of Levy's novel. To this extent Reuben Sachs can be said to begin where Daniel Deronda leaves off. Levy, in other words, rewrites Daniel Deronda in the same way earlier British-Jewish women writers addressed Scott's Ivanhoe. This tradition of reworking prevalent English cultural images of Jewishness has been continued by postwar authors into the present day.

The untold and unrealized story of Judith Quixano relates directly to Gwendolen Harleth's own feeling of worthlessness at the end of Eliot's novel. Unlike Deronda, however, Reuben Sachs is merely self-destructive, and his lack of idealism reinforces Judith's own mood of isolation. The absence of historical validation in Reuben's life means that Judith, unlike Gwendolen, has only her own inadequate destiny as a feeble yardstick. Though her Sephardi heritage links Judith with the heroines of Grace Aguilar, this spiritualized Judaism remains firmly located in the past. Her unresolved sense of self cannot be contained by the corrupt values inherent in the assimilatory processes that eventually destroy Reuben. And yet Levy's novel suggests an alternative set of values that challenge the dominant culture, where Jewish men are located in the same materialistic social and political arena as their non-Jewish counterparts. Through the consciousness of Judith Quixano, Levy begins to place Jewish history outside the conventional communal and national agendas. This female other-realm is taken up by many British-Jewish women writers throughout the twentieth century.

Like the poetry and fiction of Amy Levy, the poetry and versedrama of Isaac Rosenberg can be allied to much of the best British-

Jewish writing in the twentieth century. Because both writers died young, they did not make the impact on British-Jewish letters that was justified by the quality of their work, the promise and distinction of which has only recently been recognized. These writers' premature deaths inevitably cast a shadow over their modern-day compatriots, although some, such as Jon Silkin, have courageously tried to write poetry as if Rosenberg had achieved something near his enormous potential. Unlike Israel Zangwill, who has had a deleterious effect on those coming after him, Isaac Rosenberg offers a radically different diasporic tradition of British-Jewish writing.

Interestingly, Rosenberg sent a copy of his verse-drama *Moses* (1916) to Zangwill, who replied to Rosenberg's sister, Annie Wynick, that the poem contains 'a good many beautiful and powerful lines, but that I hope his experiences of war will give his next book the clarity and simplicity which is somewhat lacking in this.' This response clearly indicates the dissimilarity in approach between the two writers. Whereas Zangwill saw the world in terms of simple, irreducible oppositions, Rosenberg undermined such oppositions in a more complex and hybrid vision. For this reason, Rosenberg was championed by Ezra Pound and other advocates of modernist writing in Britain.[22]

In one of his best-known poems, 'Break of Day in the Trenches' (1916), which he wrote as a private soldier in the British army during World War I, Rosenberg provides an ironic self-image of someone who is between cultures and who is unable to assimilate, even in wartime, into any single national identity:

> Droll rat, they would shoot you if they knew
> Your cosmopolitan sympathies.
> Now you have touched this English hand
> You will do the same to the German—
> Soon, no doubt, if it be your pleasure
> To cross the sleeping green between.[23]

Rosenberg's poetry is full of such images of subversive mergings across seemingly incongruous domains. The droll, cosmopolitan rat is a creature that is intriguingly given an attractive human consciousness, though more conventionally the rat is associated negatively with cosmopolitanism and parasitism. These images, needless to say, were in turn used to dehumanize Jews, including Rosenberg, in the British army and beyond.[24] Along with his playful self-identification, Rosenberg ironically places himself below the rat, which at least roams free while the hapless soldiers on all sides merely wait for the next wave of bloodshed.

In a letter to the poet R. C. Trevelyan, Rosenberg described his verse-drama *Moses* as 'symbolis[ing] the fierce desire for virility and original action in contrast to slavery of the most abject kind.'[25] In this quest for masculine virility in the face of powerlessness, Rosenberg's fecund words make new and indiscriminate relationships. Words often took the unlikely form of worms, bees, and fleas—as well as the ubiquitous rats—in his fertile imagination. The opposing dominions of God, man, and animal merge in Rosenberg's writing along with the temporal realms of past and present. His reaction to the horrors of trench warfare was to invoke the vibrant figure of Moses, who challenges simultaneously the slave-like position of diasporic Jews as well as the emasculated working-class soldier in the British army. That Moses was primarily a romantic visionary, not unlike Rosenberg, can be seen from the last lines of the verse-drama. As Moses decides to liberate the Jewish slaves, thus strangling the hated Egyptian Abinoah, there are unconscious echoes of Rosenberg's own promiscuous poetic method:

> Their hugeness be a driving wedge to a thing,
> Ineffable and useable, as near
> Solidity as human life can be.
> So grandly fashion these rude elements
> Into some newer nature, a consciousness
> Like naked light seizing the all-eyed soul,
> Oppressing with its gorgeous tyranny
> Until they take it thus—or die.[26]

Here the figure of Moses gives the reader a sense of visionary unity on a social as well as an aesthetic level. The all-transforming sense of an 'ineffable and useable' Jewish people—'as near solidity as human life can be'—is not unlike Rosenberg's earlier description of his poetry as being 'understandable and still ungraspable.'[27] The fashioning of 'rude elements / Into some newer nature' is exactly what Rosenberg attempted to achieve in his poetry. These 'rude elements' crossed time, were between the spiritual and physical realms, and were above all not bounded by any one national culture, whether 'Jewish' or 'English.' By definition, Moses's wish to fashion a 'newer nature, a consciousness / Like naked light seizing the all-eyed soul, / Oppressing with its gorgeous tyranny' cannot be reduced to just the Judaic tradition. At the same time, Rosenberg's evocation of the figure of Moses as a response to his own slavery and vilification in the British army shows that it was impossible for him wholly to assimilate into an English poetic tradition.

In his poem 'Chagrin' (1916) Rosenberg uses the figure of Absalom, hanging by his hair, to summarize his own diasporic condition:

> From the imagined weight
> Of spaces in the sky
> Of mute chagrin, my thoughts
> Hang like branch-clung hair
> To trunks of silence swung,
> With the choked soul weighing down
> Into thick emptiness.[28]

For Rosenberg, 'thoughts,' 'silence,' and 'emptiness' are weighty, as opposed to the weightless 'cloud-boughs' from which Absalom is 'caught and hanging still.' This topsy-turvy poem thus expands the levitating figure of Absalom so as to include Rosenberg's fellow soldiers as well as Anglo-Jewry: 'We are lifted of all we know / And hang from implacable bows.' This seemingly endless sensation of being caught in midair, neither flying nor standing still, is reminiscent of Amy Levy's sense of being neither 'wild' nor 'tame' or of being 'within and without.' Such diasporic images of in-betweenness, of simultaneously belonging and not belonging, prefigure much of the postwar British-Jewish literature of this anthology.

THE PRESENT (I): OUT OF THE GHETTO

Bernard Kops, Emanuel Litvinoff, Harold Pinter, and Arnold Wesker

At the end of 1958, in a series of articles entitled 'The Man behind the Pen,' the London-based Jewish *Chronicle* called on the 'younger

generation of Jewish writers in England' to discuss their attitudes
to 'Judaism and the Jewish community.'[29] The interviews were led
by the writer Brian Glanville, who had recently published his contro-
versial novel *The Bankrupts* (1958). Glanville's work, echoing Levy's
Reuben Sachs, portrayed North West London Jewry as materialistic
and spiritually desiccated. Like *Reuben Sachs* more than half a century
before, and Philip Roth's collection of stories *Goodbye, Columbus*
(1959), *The Bankrupts* provoked a prolonged and hostile communual
disdain. Roth, in his autobiography, described the 'bruising' public
reaction to his fiction as constituting 'not the end of my imagination's involvement with the Jews, let alone an excommunication,
but the real beginning of my thralldom. My humiliation . . . was
the luckiest break I could have had. I was branded.'[30] Glanville, on
the other hand, ended his 'imagination's involvement with the Jews'
after the publication of *Diamond* (1962), his second and last Anglo-
Jewish novel. It is ironic that, at the time, Brian Glanville was hailed
as initiating a 'new wave' of postwar Jewish writing in Britain. Today
he is a full-time sports journalist who publishes fiction primarily
about Italy.

   To the pain and chagrin of the *Jewish Chronicle* readership, all
Glanville's interviewees showed either indifference or animosity
toward Anglo-Jewry. As the only surviving European Jewish community after the war, Anglo-Jewry was four hundred fifty thousand
strong and, as we have seen, had a literary culture that went back
for more than a century. But all the authors interviewed were ignorant of writing in a continuous cultural tradition. Alexander Baron,
for instance, declared, 'I don't think there's any real cultural life in
the Jewish community.' Like many British-Jewish writers, Baron
stopped writing fiction in the 1970s after a distinguished beginning.
The playwright Peter Shaffer from the start refused to engage imaginatively with his Jewishness, as he regarded 'Yiddishkeit' as 'the
most boring thing in the world.' Even prizewinning British-Jewish
authors such as the late Gerda Charles had astonishingly short literary careers.[31]

   Roth and Glanville had virtually identical communal reactions to
their early fiction and yet responded in completely different ways.
Throughout his interviews Glanville repeated Arthur Koestler's
belief that the diaspora will eventually disappear through assimila-

tion or migration to Israel, but he added that, in the case of Anglo-Jewry, this would ensure artistic independence. When Glanville's view is set against Roth's more buoyant sense of remythologizing American Jewry, and even the diaspora as a whole, one becomes painfully aware of the malaise at the heart of British-Jewish culture.[32]

Wolf Mankowitz, who was steeped in 'Yiddishkeit,' said in his interview that it was impossible for him to write about Anglo-Jewry, as he would be forced to attune himself to the 'dead, flat rhythms of the English vernacular.'[33] As someone whose imagination was also fired by a hybrid Yiddish English, Saul Bellow, with his complex, multilayered vocabulary, stands in strong contrast to Mankowitz, with his impotent sense of 'either/or.' In short, Mankowitz's professed inability to represent Anglo-Jewry using the language of the dominant culture indicates the major differences between British and American literature. As has been rightly argued, the American novel 'tends to rest in contradictions and among extreme ranges of experience,' whereas the English novel 'gives the impression of absorbing all extremes, all maladjustments and contradictions into a normative view of life.'[34] Such is the disparity between the mobility and protean nature of American culture as opposed to a national identity based on a fixed Englishness rooted in the past.

The fact that these interviews took place in the late 1950s indicates a significant moment in the history of Britain and Anglo-Jewry as a whole. For it was at this time that a homogeneous bourgeois culture began to break down and a plurality of voices gradually moved to the center. But it should be stressed that many postwar British-Jewish writers advanced the expansion of British culture as much by their class position as by their ethnicity. The playwrights Arnold Wesker and Bernard Kops, for instance, were two new working-class voices who by moving from the drawing room to the kitchen helped reinvigorate a rather narrow theatrical culture. Both were born into poverty-stricken backgrounds in London's East End and, for the first time, brought this experience to the English stage. Kops's early plays, such as *The Hamlet of Stepney Green* (1956), *The Dream of Peter Mann* (1960), and *Change for the Angel* (1960), were distinguished by a mixture of fantasy and naturalism and by a tone of poetic exuberance and apocalyptic rejection. Like Wolf Mankowitz, Kops enabled working-class voices and Yiddish folk traditions to enter the mainstream.

In his early career Arnold Wesker was much more of an overt class warrior than Bernard Kops and strongly identified with the New Left in the 1960s. By this time he was the artistic director of Centre 42, which used trade union support in Britain to popularize the arts across a wide range of social groups. His early trilogy, *Chicken Soup with Barley* (1958), *Roots* (1959), and *I'm Talking about Jerusalem* (1960), made a considerable impact and also helped rethink a postimperial Britain. Set in the East End of London, his plays take as their subject matter the disintegration of a single politically conscious family. Starting with the Battle of Cable Street in 1936, Wesker moves from this idealistic antifascist opposition to the disillusionment, twenty years later, with the British welfare state and the Stalinist invasion of Hungary. His trilogy re-creates a community and a radical culture that had been largely destroyed in the blitz during the war.

Wesker's drama significantly records the breakup of the close-knit Jewish community in London's East End and its resulting estrangement from the mass-produced values of modern industrial society. In this way Wesker challenges one of the abiding myths of Anglo-Jewry, that the trajectory of poor immigrant Jews was, above all, away from the ghettoes and into the suburbs; that is, away from Jewishness and into Englishness. That bit of the Anglo-Jewish story which does not fit into a narrative of liberal self-improvement and embourgeoisment has, conventionally, been excluded from Anglo-Jewry's communal sense of itself.[35] Wesker, however, was aware of being overly didactic in his plays, which contrast the idealism of his characters with the harsh realities that surround them. This theme is given its most comprehensive treatment in *The Merchant* (1976), later renamed *Shylock*. Just as Amy Levy rewrote *Daniel Deronda* in her *Reuben Sachs*, Wesker's play is an impressive reworking of Shakespeare's *Merchant of Venice* from Shylock's viewpoint. This shift from class to ethnicity has a wider historical resonance with the general breakdown of univocal explanations and the location of identity outside the nation-state. The move from the modernity of liberal progress to the postmodern critique of these assumptions is repeated by many of the writers in the anthology.

As we have seen, the radical tradition of East End Jewish writing has a long history that goes back at least to Isaac Rosenberg. Along with Kops, Wesker, and Mankowitz, a significant number of interwar proletarian novelists preceded the 'new wave' of British-Jewish writers in the 1950s. Novelists such as Simon Blumenfeld and William Goldman produced hard-hitting autobiographical works that concentrated on the powerless and impoverished East End Jewish community. Goldman's *East End My Cradle* (1940), for instance, is based on his experiences in one of the poorest neighborhoods in London. His novel, like Blumenfeld's *Jew Boy* (1935), is an unremitting account of how economic deprivation can destroy even the most promising of lives. Like Wesker, both interwar writers were reacting against the previous generation of British-Jewish literature. Instead of writing about the aspirations of lower-middle-class Jews, Blumenfeld and Goldman were class warriors who stayed close to their proletarian origins. The persona in Blumenfeld's *Jew Boy* is quite explicit about not having a high opinion of the upwardly mobile Israel Zangwill. At the same time, the very fact that Blumenfeld and Goldman were writing fiction inevitably distanced them from their fellow East Enders. Their reluctance to move beyond naturalistic detail in the end limited their impact on a literary culture in which the transcendence of such detail was considered paramount.

The master chronicler of the East End in the postwar era was Emanuel Litvinoff, an excerpt from whose *Journey through a Small Planet* (1972) is included here. His preface to this work makes it clear that he is engaged primarily in an act of re-creation and memorialization in a bid to reclaim a past that has long been forgotten. He notes from the beginning that those who 'survived' the East End were 'moving eagerly into the universe of the future and had no wish to look back at the retreating past.'[36] The Jewish East End, in other words, was destroyed as much by the cultural amnesia of those who left as by the bombs of the German Luftwaffe. At the end of *Journey through a Small Planet* Litvinoff writes his first youthful poem and is aware that 'things would never be the same again' (158). This shift from the 'outer space' of his 'small planet' to the 'inner space' (158) of his imagination means he is able to transfigure his past into a timeless story. In this way his memoir lies somewhere between historical testimony and narrative storytelling.

Litvinoff covers the same territory as many other East End memoirists, but his artistry breathes new life into familiar figures. All East End memoirs evoke a street culture that challenges the conventional mores of British society. On a factual level Litvinoff's tale of impoverishment, overcrowding, sweat shops, and unemployment—and the forced repatriation of non-naturalized fathers into the Russian army—have been recounted many times before. Litvinoff's disillusionment with Orthodox Judaism and also with far left politics is the recurring fate of many Jewish intellectuals and writers. But what Litvinoff uniquely manages is to distill these common histories into succinct folktales that capture, with poetic economy, the atmosphere and feel of the Jewish East End. Thus in 'Fanya,' included in the anthology, Litvinoff explores the differential fate of women and men in the East End as well as the impact of Yiddish theater on this community. The use of a child's perspective defamiliarizes the material so that we observe it with renewed insight.

Complex issues of national identity are embodied in Litvinoff's adolescent persona and his Italian school friend, Leoni, in a chapter aptly named 'Enemy Territory.' Although both are London-born, Leoni intends to return to Italy and has no sense of belonging to England. The young Litvinoff, on the other hand, embraces an English identity that he claims should be broad enough to include Jews and Italians. Although both are victims of English schoolboy racism, Journey through a Small Planet does not bring these outsiders together in a facile way. For one thing, Leoni supports the Fascist movement in Italy and Litvinoff still believes in a communist-inspired hunger politics. In his later fiction Litvinoff was at pains to bring his characters face to face with the harsh political realities of the twentieth century. All his novels, such as The Lost Europeans (1960) and the trilogy Faces of Terror (1973–78), begin with the specificities of the East End and explore the ramifications of this 'small planet,' especially in relation to the impact of the Russian Revolution and the horrors of Stalinism and Nazism. With the disappearance of his own little world, Litvinoff, like many British-Jewish writers, was forced to write about the larger world of another generation.

Along with Alexander Baron, who wrote novels of the Second
World War, Litvinoff first gained a national readership as a chronicler of war. But, like Wesker and Baron, he gradually moved from
writing about the war from the perspective of the British working
class to representing it in explicitly post-Holocaust terms. His poem
'To T. S. Eliot' (1951), for instance, continues the tradition of radically rewriting English literary works. The following lines from this
poem rewrite, with bitter irony, Eliot's 'Burbank with a Baedeker:
Bleistein with a Cigar' (1920):

> I am not accepted in your parish.
> Bleistein is my relative, and I share
> the protozoic slime of Shylock, a page
> in Stürmer, and underneath the cities,
> a billet somewhat lower than the rats.[37]

During one recital of the poem, to the embarrassment of those
present, Eliot entered the room and heard Litvinoff deliver these
lines. Eliot's words—'The rats are underneath the piles. / The jew
is underneath the lot'[38]—had returned to haunt him.

This embrace of ethnicity and rejection of an assimilationist
modernist aesthetics is, however, only one possible reaction to the
tradition of T. S. Eliot. Other writers, although rejecting absolutely
the anti-Semitism of English literary culture, have styles and trajec-
tories that are diametrically opposed to those of Wesker or Litvinoff.
Harold Pinter, in particular, reverses the literary careers of Wesker
and Litvinoff and turns aspects of his life history into an assimilationist modernism. He was born in Hackney, also in London's East
End, and one can view the modernist deracination of Pinter's plays
as an implicit comment on his shared loss of community. His autobiographical novel The Dwarfs (1990), excerpted here, was written
between 1952 and 1956, although it belies its origins. European
literature and philosophy, as well as the fiction of James Joyce,
overwhelm this youthful bildungsroman, which shows the extent
that, from the beginning, Pinter wished to transfigure his particular
background and identity.[39] Though the novel is dotted throughout
with Yiddish jokes and references to the Talmud, circumcision, and
'the gaschamber,' Pinter is at pains not merely to reproduce the
social and cultural milieu of Hackney. Since much of the Jewish

East End was destroyed during the war, Pinter's tabula rasa has a real historical subtext. The intense seriousness of the gifted Jewish men in the novel also indicates something of the flavor of Pinter's background without simply being reduced to that background.

In The Birthday Party (1958), produced soon after The Dwarfs was written, Goldberg, Pinter's most unequivocally Jewish figure, simultaneously articulates an unreal and nostalgic Englishness and a fixed Jewishness. On the one hand, he extols the virtues of 'a little Austin, tea in Fullers, a library book from Boots' in a self-consciously artificial construction of an idealized English past. But, within a few lines, he acts as if Stanley's grotesque 'birthday party' is not unlike an Anglo-Jewish family Simchah: 'Stanley, my heartfelt congratulations. I wish you, on behalf of us all, a happy birthday. I'm sure you've never been a prouder man than you are today. Mazeltov! And may we only meet at Simchahs!'[40]

Englishness and Jewishness are, crucially, brought together in relation to a contrived and illusory past. Goldberg's underlying menace goes hand in hand with his sentimentality, and Anglo-Jewish insiders know that the phrase 'may we only meet at Simchahs' is rather ominous, as it is routinely said at funerals. Throughout the play Goldberg's blatant self-contradictions concerning his upbringing expose both his Englishness and Jewishness as specious fabrications, a refusal to come to terms with the past. As Goldberg delineates them, these cross-cultural identities are no longer opposites but mirror images. Their equally distorted sense of a flawless community ultimately threatens to overwhelm Stanley's sense of self, which explains, in part, his breakdown in the final scenes of the play. But, after The Birthday Party, Pinter did not explicitly represent his complex Jewishness again. That his oeuvre is now located at the center of English national culture contrasts with the relative isolation of his East End contemporaries in the 1950s, such as Wesker and Kops, who also helped transform a complacent English drama of reassurance. Clearly, Pinter had to leave out a great deal in order to enter the pantheon of English literature, although his latest play, Ashes to Ashes (1996), subtly evokes the Holocaust. We now explore the price of such radical assimilation, in which the British-Jewish writer can be overly preoccupied with refiguring dominant images of what it is to be a Jew in England.

Anita Brookner, Howard Jacobson, Ruth Prawer Jhabvala, Bernice Rubens, and Michelene Wandor

What the literary history of Anglo-Jewry reveals, above all, is the dual pressure on British-Jewish writers to universalize their Jewishness out of the public sphere (which takes the extreme form of conversionism) or to particularize it in preconceived images. This reductive 'either/or' has, until recently, deformed much of the literary output of Anglo-Jewry into tame satire or crude apologetics. One should not, in this regard, underestimate the extent to which Jews have been regarded as Other in Britain. In the 1990s a host of studies has explored the varying fabrications of 'the Jew' that have saturated English national identity since the medieval period.[41] The dead hand of this history has, I believe, taken its toll on postwar British-Jewish literature. This can be seen especially in the continuation of a culture of apology that attempts to portray Jews in 'positive' terms. There is, in other words, a strong sense in which English society still saps the confidence of Jewish writers. Along with other ethnic minorities, as many have argued, British Jews 'were invited to take their place, and become spectators of a culture already complete and represented for them by its trustees.' Ever since Israel Zangwill refused to be 'shut up in the ghetto,' as he put it, Jewish writers in Britain have been made to feel distinctly uncomfortable with their Jewishness.[42]

The writers Maisie Mosco and Rosemary Friedman have, in particular, written Jewish family sagas in the 1980s as a direct response to the negative stereotype of the Jew in English culture. Friedman's trilogy *Proofs of Affection* (1982) is designed to 'explain' a range of Anglo-Jewish life—aspects of Judaism, the Holocaust, contemporary Israel—to the outside world. When asked what motivates them to write their family sagas in the first place, both Mosco and Friedman invariably reply that it is to counter images of 'Shylock' or 'Fagin' or 'Svengali' that still circulate in contemporary Britain. Both see their fiction as rectifying these images by correcting an imbalanced portrait of 'the Jew.' They write, in other words, to represent Jews in a favorable manner (what Philip Roth calls, in relation to Leon Uris, 'public relations' fiction).[43]

All this, needless to say, has little to do with Jewishness and everything to do with the Englishness of the wider culture. It is almost as if Jewish writers in Britain have had to combat an all-encompassing Englishness throughout their careers, and, quite often, Englishness wins. As a consequence, there are countless numbers of British-Jewish writers, such as Gerda Charles and Alexander Baron, who lost the fight and fell into silence. These 'walking wounded' can be contrasted with the writers in this anthology, who have managed to find strategies to resist an overbearing Englishness fixed in the past. Such narrative strategies vary from the radical interrogation and rewriting of the dominant culture in Bernice Rubens, Michelene Wandor, and Howard Jacobson, to the self-conscious refusal to engage with this culture in Anita Brookner and Ruth Prawer Jhabvala.

I begin with Dannie Abse and Bernice Rubens, whose common Welsh background meant that they avoided a stultifying Englishness throughout their childhoods. These writers can be regarded as the great survivors of the defunct 'new wave' of the 1960s. They have, in particular, access to a range of ethnic, cultural, and professional identities, which enables them to explore specific aspects of their hybrid upbringing. A doctor, Abse writes as much about this part of his life as anything else, and he is equally regarded as a Welsh, Jewish, and 'Golders Green' poet.[44] Because her fiction deals with family life in general, Rubens has avoided the label 'Jewish writer.' She has, nonetheless, consistently explored her Jewish upbringing and has recently attempted to encompass the diaspora as a whole.

The claustrophobic particularity of Rubens's fiction can be contrasted with the work of other proponents of the 'new wave,' such as Frederic Raphael, who universalize their Jewishness as a form of alienation. At the same time, Rubens resists the tendency to classify Anglo-Jewry in reductive terms that can be found in other 'new wave' writers such as Gerda Charles. In The Crossing Point (1960) Charles's narrator typically describes 'the Jews' as the 'natural rentiers of society. They are suppliers rather than consumers.'[45] Rubens's fiction lies somewhere between Raphael's sense of generalized alienation and Charles's categorizing tendencies in The Crossing Point.

Instead of documentary realism, Rubens has been said to embrace a more symbolic mode, which we have already seen in the poetry of Amy Levy and Isaac Rosenberg.[46] This is an understandable reading of Rubens's prolific literary output of twenty novels, which are well known for their lack of descriptive passages. But the emphasis on the symbolic in her fiction belittles the extent to which Rubens, like her predecessors, explicitly challenges the dominant norms of both Anglo-Jewry and English national culture. Her writing takes the 'positive' stereotypes of what it is to be a respected citizen in Britain—such as upward social mobility, family values, and an untroubled sense of community—and turns them on their heads. Rubens's fiction accepts Freud's argument in *Civilization and Its Discontents* (1929) that the process of becoming civilized members of society can do more harm than good. Her subject matter is the disabling nature of family and communal expectations, which tend emotionally to cripple her fragile characters.

At her most extreme, in her grotesque *Spring Sonata* (1979), a violin-playing fetus named Buster eavesdrops on his deranged parents and decides to remain in the womb. The internecine warfare of family life, which Buster refuses to join, is in stark contrast to the bourgeois values the Jewish community is meant to embody. Rubens focuses instead on those figures, such as Norman Zweck in *The Elected Member* (1969; published in the United States as *The Chosen*), who are condemned to partial lives by their parents. *The Elected Member*, which is excerpted here, has as its epigraph a quotation from alternative psychiatrist R. D. Laing: 'If patients are disturbed, their families are very disturbing.'[47] Norman Zweck has been elected to bear the burden of his family's fervent craving for social betterment. Because he was born a brilliant linguist, his overpowering mother, Sarah Zweck, turns Norman into a child prodigy of monstrous proportions.

The Elected Member opens with Norman, who eventually becomes a lawyer, completely vanquished by his neurotic upbringing. Throughout the novel Norman's history of drug addiction, schizophrenia, and confinement to a mental institution is painfully revealed. His sisters, to a lesser degree, are also victims of the disabling intensity of their all-controlling mother and emasculated father. But it is Norman who is literally turned insane by a mother whose ferocious appetite for self-improvement is in the end sanctioned by the wider society. When Norman's father, Rabbi Zweck, first meets Sarah, her father belittles his choice of profession as an East End rabbi: "Forget already the *Rabbonischkeit*," he almost shouted. "A business you should find. Your own business" (47). For this reason, it is Sarah who runs the local grocery store, who is empowered by the values of entrepreneurship, while Rabbi Zweck remains unmanned by insisting on retaining his spiritualized Judaism.

By the end Norman is most at home with the 'cold and chosen ones' (206) of the local asylum, who have also been turned insane by the supposed civilizing aspirations of British society. But this more general framework, relating Norman's deranged form of election to the wider culture, prevents Rubens from reducing Judaism to a form of madness. Although her fiction can be divided into 'Jewish' and 'non-Jewish'—or even 'English' and 'Welsh'—motifs, there is a good deal of thematic crossover. By situating her dysfunctional families in a range of contexts, her novels critique the values of society in general and not merely those of the Jewish community. In this way Rubens both universalizes her particular Jewish identity and particularizes a supposedly universal culture.

Other authors take specific myths and fantasies or key texts—insofar as they are part of the larger national and communal narratives of Englishness and Jewishness—and radically interrogate them. From an explicitly feminist position the stories of Michelene Wandor rework or transfigure commonplace assumptions of what it is to be a Jew, or a woman, in England. Her story 'Return to Sender' (1986), included here, is a reworking of the moment in George Eliot's *Daniel Deronda* when Deronda meets his mother to discover his own Jewishness. In returning to this text Wandor is able to highlight the liberatory potential for Jewish women in Eliot's novel. After all, Daniel's mother, Princess Halm-Eberstein, is the repressed center of *Daniel Deronda* where the cosmopolitan power of art and of women's independence challenges the masculine, national narratives of Deronda. By dramatizing the autonomy and potency of Deronda's unmarried mother, Wandor is able to question the limitations inherent in the idealized Mirah, who eventually marries Deronda. Amy Levy was rightly irritated by Mirah's stereotypical beauty and nobility, which go back at least to Scott's Rebecca and Shakespeare's Jessica. But 'Return to Sender' rethinks *Daniel*

Deronda in such a way that the hitherto unrealized dramatic power of Halm-Eberstein finally comes of age.

Wandor's 'Song of the Jewish Princess' (1989), also included in the anthology, explores a common myth of Jewish femininity so as to understand its liberatory potential. Wandor's feisty 'Jewish princess,' who acts as a female counterpart to the Wandering Jew, contrasts starkly with the compliant, endlessly malleable Jewish women prevalent in conversionist rhetoric. What happens, Wandor asks, when you replace the common public images of the male Jew with their supposedly domesticated female counterparts? Although she still uses popular mythology, the location of the 'Jewish princess' in a public, historicized realm is paradoxically liberating. By situating her myth-figure at the time of the Jewish expulsion from Catholic Spain in the fifteenth century, she places Jewish women at the center of historical narratives. Wandor's reworking of the 'Jewish princess' in relation to the subversive spirituality of Lilith is also reflected in the later fiction of Bernice Rubens. Here Rubens seems to have mellowed somewhat, tempering her unremittingly bleak portrayal of traumatic family relations with a redemptive, metaphysical presence. In *Our Father* (1987), the best of her later works, she introduces the figure of 'God' into the scarred psyche of her novel's heroine. The age-old association of women and the private spiritual realm is again reimagined in iconoclastic terms.

In contrast to Michelene Wandor, Howard Jacobson is an aggressively masculine writer who has faced head-on the thorny question of Englishness. His first two comic novels, *Coming from Behind* (1983) and *Peeping Tom* (1984) (an excerpt from the latter is included here), directly resist a definition of Jewishness based on an excessive regard for the Englishness of others. Jacobson's protagonists specifically undermine the oppressive language of culture, which divides the world into the beautiful or civilized as opposed to the ugly or uncivilized 'Jew.' He especially exposes how English culture has attempted to civilize Jews, or other minorities, and make what is 'ugly' beautiful again. His subject is thus the psychic damage this causes to British Jews.

When *Coming from Behind* and *Peeping Tom* were published, Jacobson was mistakenly acclaimed as Britain's answer to Woody Allen or Philip Roth. But Jacobson, I believe, is a quintessentially English writer. He was born in Manchester, in the industrial north of England, and was educated at Cambridge University. At Cambridge he was taught by the influential literary critic F. R. Leavis, who instilled in him a respect for the great tradition of English literature. At the same time, Jacobson was an avowed outsider both from the Manchester Jewish community (he was not wealthy enough) and from English culture (he was not English enough).

As an outsider, Jacobson began his academic career at Australia's Sydney University in the early 1960s as a lecturer in English literature. Lecturing to eight hundred students on the best English novelists and poets, Jacobson described himself as the first 'alternative comedian' two decades before this became a fashionable label. His juxtaposition of reverence for English culture and irreverence as a comic outsider characterizes his fiction. This doubleness meant that *Coming from Behind* and *Peeping Tom* are not, strictly, 'Jewish' novels. More accurately, they are 'anti-Gentile novels' in which his protagonists define themselves as the opposite of English gentility (in both senses of the word). Sefton Goldberg in *Coming from Behind*, Jacobson's campus novel, is Jewish because he hates *goyische* soccer, the English countryside, small towns and midland polytechnics, British Rail, students, Cambridge, women, homosexuals, you name it. He is not Jewish because he attends a synagogue.

In *Peeping Tom* Jacobson cleverly turns this negative definition of self into the subject of his novel by directly confronting his opposite, the Victorian rural novelist Thomas Hardy. Barney Fugleman discovers that he, in the end, needs Thomas Hardy's 'goyische greenery' to exist. On the one hand, Hardy is Barney's antagonist in the novel: 'Pity the poor Jew. Let him gentrify and ruralize himself all he likes . . . he will never know what it is to take a turn around the garden.'[48] But Barney also *is* Hardy, or, at least, his reincarnation. He becomes Hardy because he is part of a culture that he feels is not really his own. In other words, Jacobson's fictional personae define themselves negatively in terms of their supposed gentile Other. The danger for Jacobson is that this turns his Jewish characters into a vacuum with nothing of positive value apart from their hatred of the outside world. His later works—*The Very Model of a Man* (1992) and *Roots Shmoots: Journeys among Jews* (1993)—attempt to fill the vacuum of his characters' acknowledged nonidentity.

Not that Barney Fugleman lacks substance. The fact that he sees himself as steeped in a culture that he also feels alienated from neatly sums up the dilemma of many British-Jewish writers. Jacobson's skill is to concentrate on Fugleman's realization that he is nothing without Hardy's alien rural community. *Peeping Tom* is, finally, a study in cultural masochism. What Jacobson highlights is the extent to which Jews, who had come to love English culture, were caught in a double bind. He argues that Jews participate in this culture, through the English language, but that they still have a precarious foothold in it. This is a particularly painful contradiction for Jacobson, as he thinks of himself as a Leavisite who is meant to be one of the custodians of culture. But as a 'Jew' he can always be expelled from that which he loves.

Although the radical interrogation and reworking of the prevalent myths of Englishness is obviously most welcome, it has some limitations. All the writers discussed in this section are, ultimately, bounded by certain dominant images of 'the Jew,' however radically they are rewritten. To avoid this limitation, Anita Brookner refuses to engage explicitly with the dominant culture in these terms and tends to set her novels on the Continent. On one level, Brookner is a prime example of a mainstream British-Jewish writer who has written out virtually any reference to her Jewishness. Only with *The Latecomers* (1988), a chapter of which is included here, and *A Family Romance* (1993) is the Jewishness of her characters made explicit. But although Brookner writes stylistically as an English insider, in the tradition of Jane Austen, George Eliot, and E. M. Forster, her protagonists are mainly cultural or ethnic outsiders. There is also a self-consciousness about Brookner's reluctance to engage directly with her Jewishness in her fiction which raises crucial questions about the nature of the silence imposed on ethnic voices.

Bringing together a disparate group of authors and categorizing them as 'British-Jewish' clearly risks reducing them to a monolithic ethnicity. Some critics have classified British-Jewish writers in terms of their relation to the East End and North West of London. But one cannot understand a writer such as Brookner in terms of these city limits, as she narrates, above all, from the outside in and thereby challenges the received cultural boundaries of Englishness.[49] Brookner writes in an ostensibly conventional mode of realism and subtly evokes the great tradition of English letters, at the same time broadening into a European context dominant images of Englishness. Her precarious position—as neither an insider nor an outsider, neither Jewish nor English—can, in this regard, be related to Harold Pinter. After *The Birthday Party* Pinter, not unlike Brookner, universalized his Jewishness so as to make it impossible to reduce it to a set of images. Until *A Family Romance* Brookner similarly refused to portray her characters openly as Jewish outsiders, although this does not apply to the way she represents herself in various interviews.

As her novel *The Latecomers* demonstrates, Brookner's reluctance to make her Jewishness usable in her fiction was a self-conscious strategy. In an article on contemporary British Jewry, she defines 'latecomers' as 1930s German-Jewish émigrés to Britain. Two such latecomers, Thomas Hartmann and Thomas Fibich, are at the heart of this novel, although their status as émigrés remains teasingly inexact. If Hartmann and Fibich are latecomers to England, then a line of earlier arrivals is assumed, but this is an immigrant story Brookner pointedly refuses to tell. Brookner's narrative method has, in this sense, been rightly described as a 'refusal of emplotment.'[50] Hartmann and Fibich are both child refugees from Nazism who lost their families during the Holocaust, but Brookner uses the word 'Jew' only once in her novel. Not unlike the painfully incomplete storytelling of the Israeli writer Aharon Appelfeld, what is left unsaid in *The Latecomers* becomes the subject of the novel. To this extent Brookner makes overt the silence that surrounds Jewishness within English national culture, as opposed to challenging it head-on in the manner of Rubens, Wandor, and Jacobson. Anticipating other émigré writers such as Eva Figes and Gabriel Josipovici, Ruth Prawer Jhabvala also refuses to particularize her Jewishness in a distinct set of images.

Prawer Jhabvala's tightly controlled aesthetic form, also in the tradition of Jane Austen, E. M. Forster, and Henry James, can be especially related to the work of Anita Brookner. Prawer Jhabvala was born in Cologne of German-Jewish parentage but emigrated to London, with her parents and brother, at the age of twelve just before the outbreak of war. Her father, Marcus Prawer, committed suicide in 1948, three years after hearing that he had lost all his family and many friends in the Shoah. 'A Birthday in London' (1962), included in this anthology, is a direct evocation of the postwar expatriate German-Jewish community living in London. This story was eventually given a more ambitious novelistic framework in *In Search of Love and Beauty* (1983) and *Poet and Dancer* (1993), both of which locate this refugee community in contemporary New York. In 1951 Prawer Jhabvala married Cyrus S. H. Jhabvala and returned with him to his home in Delhi until 1960. Since 1975 she has lived mainly in New York and London.

Prawer Jhabvala is best known as a novelist of contemporary India and as a superb screenwriter for Merchant-Ivory. But one can argue that her fiction, set in India, is a way of indirectly encompassing the loss of her family and childhood friends. All her novels emphasize themes of alienation, disinheritance, exile, and the flux of history. In the preface to her selected stories *Out of India* (1987) Prawer Jhabvala speaks of the unendurable dilemma of living and writing in a country where the majority of the population is starving. She goes on to state that the Hindu belief in reincarnation is, in the context of human misery, an understandable reaction, as one can then 'write off' this world and 'substitute something more satisfying.' But her inability to assimilate fully and to see India from the viewpoint of its religious culture brings her to the 'heart of her problem': 'To live in India and be at peace, one must to a very considerable extent become Indian and adopt Indian attitudes, habits and beliefs, assume if possible an Indian personality. But how is this possible? And even if it were possible—without cheating oneself—should it be desirable? Should one want to try to become something other than what one is?'[51]

The sense of being surrounded by the horror of millions of people needlessly dying—which makes her want to escape into spiritual obfuscation and eventually destroys her feeling of well-being—can be thought of as a way of speaking about the Holocaust. That she implicitly links the ameliorating search for 'love and beauty' to her German-Jewish background can be seen in *In Search of Love and Beauty*, in which Leo Kellerman takes the more familiar role of the mystifying Indian shaman. Her novels, such as *Heat and Dust* (1975), are full of dark secrets or forbidden topics that are eventually explicated from the position of both victim and victimizer. What is more, in the one interview in which she directly addresses the trauma of her childhood, she stresses that she regards her past as literally unspeakable. Like Brookner and also the émigré writer Eva Figes, Prawer Jhabvala surrounds an unrepresentable past with, in a postcolonial setting, a bitterly ironic English innocence.[52]

Prawer Jhabvala's refusal to 'cheat herself' or to represent India through Western eyes means that she eventually had to leave her husband's country and become a diasporic writer, spanning several continents and not easily categorized in terms of a single religion or culture. 'A Birthday in London' is an early exploration of how it is possible for her characters to find a modus vivendi in a world that has tried to push them off the edge. The supposed remedy of British naturalization or a backward-looking nostalgia is, in this story, seen to be hopelessly inadequate. At the same time, there is a redemptive optimism at the heart of the tale with the tight-knit group of refugees finally looking to the quotidian joys of the present. The absolute hope engendered by the grandiose superstructure of religious conversion is eschewed in this story. Instead, it shows that simple, everyday happiness, which includes the comforts of English literature, can also be a means of living with the horrors of the twentieth century.

THE PRESENT (3): ÉMIGRÉS

Eva Figes, Ronit Lentin, Dan Jacobson, Gabriel Josipovici, and George Steiner

It is not a coincidence that many of the Jewish writers who thrive in Britain are not British-born. As émigrés, these writers do not have to transcend an Englishness that was imbibed with their mothers' milk. Because they do not need to engage with the cultural fixity of the past in Britain, all these writers have a skeptical and detached relationship both to the past and to national cultures in general. Not that these writers have reacted in the same way to the experience of migration and exile. Some, such as George Steiner and Ronit Lentin, have directly engaged with their personal histories in both their fiction and criticism. Others, such as Gabriel Josipovici and Eva Figes, have created a more general modernist and feminist aesthetic that only implicitly addresses their particular history. Dan Jacobson's fiction, on the other hand, lies somewhere between these two polarities, as it has moved from directly embracing his specific background to creating more universalized imaginary homelands.

In his influential essay 'Our Homeland, the Text' George Steiner contends that the 'dwelling . . . ascribed to Israel is the House of the Book' and that the 'centrality of the book does coincide with and enact the condition of exile.'[53] Steiner is the émigré writer par excellence. Born in Paris to Viennese parents in 1929, he was brought to the United States in 1940, escaping the Nazi occupation of France, and has lived in Britain intermittently since 1950. He taught comparative literature mainly in Geneva, however, and he remains at home in many different European traditions. Steiner's ideal of a textual homeland has been criticized by Cynthia Ozick for giving precedence to a surface aestheticism that is defined as 'a-thing-that-subsists-for-its-own-sake-without-a-history.'[54] But Steiner is well aware of the tension between his extraterritorial homeland and the particularities of history, which he defines as 'the dialectical relations between an unhoused at-homeness in the text . . . and the territorial mystery of the native ground, of the promised strip of land.'[55] The struggle between the historical specificities of the past and a transcendent sense of exile is the theme of much of Steiner's fiction and cultural criticism.

It might be considered perverse to treat his imagination as seriously as his intellect. But Steiner has always been a writer-critic. More than four decades ago, in his twenties, he published a now forgotten anthology of verse, followed soon after by his key story, 'The Deeps of the Sea' (1956). Since then his fiction and his cultural criticism have remained intimately connected. On the one hand, he consistently belittles his stories as 'allegories of argument' or 'scripts for thought,' as if they were merely straightforward dramatizations of his intellectual endeavors. He often restates, with relish, the orthodox Jewish disdain for the merely imaginary, which is after all a form of lying or fabulation, the very opposite of genuine learning.[56] But Steiner is, above all, a self-translator. He writes philosophical essays as if they were a species of poetry, and fiction as if it was philosophy.

Many of the lifelong obsessions of his extraordinarily compelling set of essays, *Language and Silence* (1967), were imaginatively

prefigured in his early stories, *Anno Domini* (1964). The primacy of
translation, explored at length in *After Babel* (1975), has rightly been
understood as a structuring metaphor in *The Portage to San Cristobal
of A. H.* (1981).[57] With an ambiguity that still disturbs, Steiner, in
this work, puts into the mouth of an aged Hitler ('A. H.') words
that he himself had used a decade earlier in his *In Bluebeard's Castle*
(1971). In this way, Steiner is able to explore the dark side of his
own reasoning. His more recent novella and stories, *Proofs and Three
Parables* (1992), continues this pattern of self-questioning. Written
at about the same time as his *Real Presences: Is There Anything 'in' What
We Say?* (1989), these fictions make human the 'wager on transcendence' that Steiner has long since called for as an antidote to our
current 'postcultural' nihilism. His fiction, now collected into a
substantial volume, provides a persuasive internal commentary on
his more familiar critical writings.[58]

When we look back at the early stories collected in *Anno Domini*,
it is clear that Steiner's imagination has frequently been engaged in
an inner dialogue with his intellect. In 'Cake' (1964) an American-
born 'kind of survivor' (like Steiner himself) decides to stay behind
in Nazi-occupied France and begins to fantasize about being captured by the Gestapo. Only under torture can he really know himself;
otherwise, he fears, he will live 'as spinsters do, in the brittle famil-
iarity of mere acquaintance.'[59] Although this romantic masochism
is soon quashed when Steiner's narrator fearfully escapes capture,
it points to an essential subtext in *Language and Silence*. In this volume,
and ever since, Steiner is both attracted and repulsed by the horrors
he escaped, which is why the words he uses are, he insists, both
complicit with the destruction of European culture and the only
means of redeeming it.

Steiner's parable 'A Conversation Piece' (1985), included in this
anthology, subtly illustrates his inner contradictions. As a cultural
critic, Steiner tends to eschew comic writing—by, for instance,
Chaucer, Shakespeare, Sterne, Dickens, and Joyce—which indicates an overwrought and rather Germanic earnestness in his value
system. His fiction, although often using the form of tragedy, is by
contrast closer to the comic mode (and is, thus, more democratic
in its various registers), speaking with equal conviction in many
disparate voices. One cannot understand his fiction without taking

note of the fundamental tension between these two versions of George Steiner (one predominantly monovocal, one predominantly multivocal). In 'A Conversation Piece' distant 'beelike' humming distorts the transcendent Midrashic dialogue and turns everything into the 'slurred slow song of gas.'[60] Such is the uneasy alliance between the imagination and the intellect in Steiner's work.

Throughout his career Steiner has been obsessed with the unbearable ambiguity—or 'dialectic'—between the aesthetic and the barbaric, or metaphor and history, which is illustrated in 'A Conversation Piece.' In this parable we are told that 'God' and 'unnameable evil' are 'utterly alike'; the 'difference between them is only that of the sound of a rain-drop in the sea' (387). Only this kabbalistic understanding of the terrible intimacy between God and the devil enables Steiner to use the Hitler figure in The Portage to explore the underside of his own thinking. Steiner and his Hitler ('A. H.') both believe Jews are the conscience of the world and that this has caused a lethal resentment culminating in the Shoah. And yet, by embodying the redemptive homeland of the text—at its most creative and lasting in an extraterritorial central Europe—diasporic Jews have embodied a life-giving self-transcendence. In these terms Jewish transcendence is both a form of moral validation and a death warrant. The Portage and 'A Conversation Piece' take risks with such heartrending chasms of meaning so as to let the reader decide where the truth lies.

On a smaller scale the Israeli-Irish writer Ronit Lentin has also devised a narrative framework, which lies somewhere between metaphor and history, in a bid to come to terms with the trauma of the past. Lentin was born in Haifa and settled in Dublin shortly after the Six Day War. Her parents came from Romania, and her mother emigrated to Palestine in 1941. Night Train to Mother (1989), the prologue of which is included in the anthology, is a fictionalized autobiography that attempts to transfigure and reclaim her mother's history. Lentin has noted how the Israeli national identity of her childhood prevented her from coming to terms with her family's history in much the same way that Englishness has obfuscated other minority histories.[61] Her novel, therefore, attempts to capture the minutiae of four generations of Romanian-Jewish women in a bid to break down the spurious universality of a nationalized and masculinized Israeli identity. Not that Lentin replaces one fixed sense of self with another. At the end of the novel her persona states that she is 'in exile like the rest' and refuses to indulge in the myth of return.[62] Her diasporic identity, in which she 'becomes' her mother's past, thus challenges the national certainties of the Jewish state.

Lentin has described her move to Ireland as a form of 'translation' from one culture to another, and this act of self-translation is, as for Steiner, central to her fiction. Her role of translator, however, is never easy or facile, as she is always aware of the difficulties of transforming the past into the present. At the same time, this skepticism toward the past is set against her overpowering feeling of being compelled (since the age of eight or nine) to tell her mother's story. For this reason, her family saga is framed as a momentary performance that is always somewhere between autobiography and fiction. The refrain 'When did the journey begin,' which opens the novel, gives a variety of points of origin for a story that can only ever be arbitrary and capricious. Lentin, above all, does not want to create another mythologized ethnicity to replace the 'sabra arrogance' (218) of her alter ego. Just as Eliot's *Daniel Deronda* was notoriously distrustful of fixed beginnings, *Night Train to Mother* refuses the narrative a limited point of origin, which is, by definition, predicated on a continuous line of history. Defined by her inner exile, Lentin's women-centered stories are both a means of restoring the past and self-conscious and limited acts of memorialization.

Gabriel Josipovici and Eva Figes create more generalized images of displacement and loss in their modernist fiction, which is characterized by a refusal to turn past trauma into simple stories. Like Steiner and Lentin, Josipovici and Figes have a profound sense of dislocation and of writing in a language they were not born into. Born in France in 1940, Josipovici emigrated to Egypt with his mother shortly after the Nazi occupation. He was educated in Cairo and at Oxford and has taught comparative literature at Sussex University since 1963. His fiction and criticism are steeped in a European tradition of literary modernism that has been increasingly influenced by the Greek classics and the Bible. His delicate, vulnerable novellas aim to make art out of the everyday and discover a 'thousand subjects for every moment of time,' as he puts it in his *Contre-Jour: A Triptych after Pierre Bonnard* (1986).[63] Although his pointedly fluid and exilic Jewishness has always been a key aspect of his outstanding critical works—such as *The World and the Book* (1971) and *The Book of God* (1988)—it has only recently been addressed in his fiction.

The move from the cosmopolitanism of his early fiction to a more explicitly Judaic understanding of the world illustrates the limitations of a universalizing modernism that has, historically, been unable to assimilate Judaism. Not that Josipovici's Jewishness is, in any way, fixed or easily formulated.[64] The epigraph of his *In a Hotel Garden* (1993), which is excerpted in this anthology, is the Midrash on Genesis (39:7), 'Potiphar's wife too wished to belong to the history of Israel.'[65] Josipovici's 'history of Israel,' in other words, eschews well-worn images and clichés of what it is to be a Jew. For this reason, his novel is principally concerned with the difficulties of both representing and reproducing the past. Ben, the protagonist of *In a Hotel Garden*, thinks he is understanding the history of a Jewish family touched by the Holocaust, but Josipovici's fiction is never quite as certain as his rather innocent characters.

In fact, Ben eventually belongs to Josipovici's contemporary 'history of Israel' even though he is not himself Jewish. When on holiday in the Italian Alps, he meets Lily, the granddaughter of a family of Italian Jews. Lily remembers a story her grandmother told her about a rendezvous in a hotel garden with a distant cousin who, she learned later, died during the war. The cousin fell in love with the grandmother but married someone else, so she refused to answer any of his letters. In an attempt to commune with her grandmother, Lily decides to return to the garden. As the novel progresses, Ben gradually reenacts the story of Lily's grandmother, thus continuing her family's history for another generation.

To recount Josipovici's novel in these terms, however, is to ignore just how fragile and transitory is Lily's retelling of her grandmother's story. Ben relates to friends his encounter with Lily but also virtually forces her to turn her desire to visit the site of her grandmother's unrequited love affair into an oversimple story. That her grandmother's cousin was killed along with his family during the war makes *In a Hotel Garden*, on one level, a post-Holocaust novel.

But, again, it is somewhat reductive to think of the novel merely in these terms. Lily throughout is undecided about the nature of her visit to the hotel garden and the import of her grandmother's memories. She does not accept at face value that the rediscovery of the past is necessarily valuable or enlightening. At times she believes that 'everything' would be 'resolved' (107) by entering the garden, but at other times she remains skeptical of this absolute sense of past and present coming together. Here Lily, like Goldberg in Josipovici's previous novel, The Big Glass (1991), negotiates between a Christian 'ache for redemption'[66] and a Judaic uncertainty.

This markedly Hebraic imprecision concerning Lily's transcendent resolution of past, present, and future is pointedly juxtaposed with an English disdain for dwelling on Nazi atrocities. Toward the end of the novel Ben's friend, Fran, becomes exasperated with Lily's story and complains that she is 'fed up with people being obsessed by the Holocaust. It's done and we've got to move on' (125). Her husband remarks that 'it's different if you're Jewish' (125), and these competing versions of the past are highlighted throughout by Josipovici. At one point in the novel Jews are thought of primarily as a memory community, rather like the four generations in Lentin's Night Train to Mother. Speaking of her grandmother's family from Constantinople, Lily comments, 'Jewish families from that part of the world had spread all over the Eastern Mediterranean. And as they didn't own land they had memories instead, and genealogies, as Jews have always had' (110). Here Jewishness is presented as an imaginary diaspora held together by the deceptive power of memory and genealogical storytelling. Lily herself exemplifies this version of Jewishness, although Josipovici is at pains not to reduce it to a fixed myth. For this reason, Lily often quotes another Midrash, 'Absalom gloried in his hair—therefore he was hanged by his hair' (42). She purposely cites this Midrash to avoid at all costs any overly simple transfigurations of her past into easily comprehensible patterns. In this way In a Hotel Garden becomes both myth and history and is simultaneously located in the past and the present. Not unlike Isaac Rosenberg's similar use of the figure of Absalom, this sense of in-betweenness captures the spirit of Josipovici's writing.

The haunting images of displacement and plangent note of distress that characterize Josipovici's early novellas, such as Migrations

(1977), can also be found in the poetic fiction of Eva Figes. A refugee from Nazism, Figes was born in Berlin and escaped to London with her parents in 1939 after her father was imprisoned at Dachau and then released. Although most of her short novels do not directly address this history, many are suffused with a poignant sense of dislocation. Stephan Konek, in Konek Landing (1969), for instance, is a stateless war orphan whose humanity is put at risk by the need to survive in a nameless country full of victims and executioners. And the determinedly non-naturalistic Ghosts (1988) explores the consciousness of an elderly woman as she looks back over the 'ghosts' of another country and of her younger self. Like Josipovici, who is also influenced by the tradition of Kafka and Samuel Beckett, Figes has increasingly combined pained images of fragmentation with a lyric intensity. She has above all eschewed a cozy English realism as being unable to deal with her childhood experiences. Her fiction is not directly autobiographical, although it obviously relates on a deeper level to a profound sense of rupture and of having an irredeemable past.

Only in her memoir Little Eden: A Child at War (1978; excerpted in the anthology) does Figes engage directly with her childhood in Germany and her fraught migration to Britain as a seven-year-old. Outside this memoir and her first quasi-autobiographical novel, Equinox (1966), her Jewishness remains an unfigured source of anxiety. In an article written at the same time as Little Eden Figes described herself as a 'European wrestling with a different reality [to England]. A piece of shrapnel lodges in my flesh, and when it moves, I write.'[67] This crippling disruption contrasts starkly with the need for historical continuity in Britain after the war, which Figes has located in both the conventions of English political life and its artistic forms. Her influential Patriarchal Attitudes (1970) was one feminist response to a gendered conservatism in England, and her fiction can also be seen as a more subtle aesthetic reaction to an overly cautious and narrow English literary culture. She has spoken of the 'fragmentary nature of remembered experience'[68] and has thus tried to find a new poetic language and set of conventions to express her inner consciousness.

What is paradoxical about Little Eden is that it is precisely the wholesome conservatism of English society which made it such a comfort to the adolescent Figes. Her memoir tells the story of her childhood evacuation to rural England and her subsequent rite of passage when she learns of the Holocaust and of the deaths of immediate members of her family. For Figes, the discovery of her Jewishness goes together with her loss of innocence. After a particularly difficult time with her understandably preoccupied mother, the thirteen-year-old Eva is told to go to the local cinema to see a newsreel account of the liberation of the Belsen slave labor camp. Her reaction to the horrendous pictures is telling: 'At last I knew what it meant to be a Jew, the shameful secret which had been hinted at but kept from me for so many years. . . . Now I knew. I was not a child any longer.'[69]

Little Eden makes it clear that the untroubled narcissism of English society is, for those with a traumatized past, a double-edged sword. On the one hand, as Figes states elsewhere, 'England does not share the European experience. German troops did not march down Whitehall; men were not rounded up and shot or sent to labour camps.'[70] Living in England and absorbing its cheery continuity with the past can thus be a necessary relief, as Figes illustrates in Little Eden when, at the end, she desperately needs to escape back into her rural English idyll. Other childhood accounts of German émigrés growing up in Britain during the war are, however, less sanguine. In Karen Gershon's autobiographical novel, The Bread of Exile (1985), England is an alien culture that ostracizes its refugees from Nazism. An English official typically informs Gershon's persona, 'You'll never be anything but a foreigner to the English.'[71] Instead of an island refuge, England in this account is a promised land that can only be espied from afar.

Dan Jacobson left South Africa in his twenties and has since mainly lived in London, where he has worked for more than four decades as a university lecturer. He began by writing naturalistic South African novels such as The Trap (1955) and A Dance in the Sun (1956) but eventually moved toward myth and fable—in The Rape of Tamar (1970) and The Confessions of Josef Baisz (1977)—to create a world that was no longer determined by the culture of apartheid. Jacobson's move from an unproblematic realism to myth-history has culminated in The God-Fearer (1992), which is excerpted here. This novel is explicitly described as 'Another history! Another past for the human race!'[72] It is, above all, an other-world where the dominant proselytizing religion in Europe is no longer Christianity but Judaism. Unlike Steiner and Lentin, whose fiction interrogates their past histories, and Josipovici and Figes, who transcend too easy forms of representation, Jacobson spans the literary spectrum in his fiction from documentary naturalism to extraterritorial imaginary homelands.

The God-Fearer radically rewrites European history to show how the past needs to be continually remade. In this novel it is the minority 'Christer' people—'the followers of Yeshua, Jesus, the Christus, the Natzerit, whatever they liked to call him' (18)—who suffer pogroms, prejudice, and expulsions. Without the advent of Christendom, medieval Europe is governed by Old Testament God-Fearers, or followers of the one true God. This inversion of history is accompanied by a series of alternative homelands and myth-figures, such as Manasse, Sar of the Upperland, who are superimposed on more familiar historical landscapes. Although Kobus, Jacobson's octogenarian protagonist, has a good deal of trouble remembering even his deceased wife's name, the one thing he is sure of is that the past alone could not be 'forever without ambiguity' (53). Out of the 'wreckage of what was left of his mind' (68–69) Kobus spends most of the novel, like the reader, trying to make sense of his ambiguous past.

In his Story of the Stories: The Chosen People and Its God (1982) Jacobson was at pains to show that the chosenness of the biblical chosen people was a manmade myth, not a God-imposed truth. In The God-Fearer Kobus is a 'bookbinder,' not unlike Steiner's proofreader, because he embodies the theological need to canonize or fix stories that are inherently changeable. For this reason, Jacobson has a good deal of fun in the novel dramatizing a multitude of possible national stories and imagined communities that are not a part of received history. The strength of The God-Fearer is that these abiding concerns are not merely of intellectual interest. Kobus feels the 'pain of recollection' (84) throughout as he thinks of his existence as a 'kind of postscript to a life that was already concluded' (3). That he is dominated by his 'errant, grotesque, utterly absurd' (126) memories is finally realized in the ghostly young 'Christer' children, who, as the novel progresses, begin to absorb him. These 'phantom lives,' taken from Henry James's *Turn of the Screw* (1898), fatally disrupt the certainties Kobus has about himself and the chosenness of his people. By playfully sketching a fantasy world made up of 'non-historic peoples,' as he put it in his novel *Hidden in the Heart* (1991),[73] Jacobson shows how our notions of the past are both arbitrary and variable. As we have seen, although émigré writers react differently to the experience of dislocation and exile, they all crucially transcend a dominant culture and rewrite both its past and its present.

THE PRESENT (4): DIASPORAS OF THE MIND

Ruth Fainlight, Elaine Feinstein, Simon Louvish, and Clive Sinclair

What is clear from reading British-Jewish writers since about 1970 is that to succeed as a creative writer in England, one has to become, at least symbolically, an émigré or outsider. We have seen the historical precedents for this in the fiction and poetry of Isaac Rosenberg and Amy Levy, who, half a century later, have finally come of age. Because a Jewish past has been written out of British national culture, Jewish writers have had to look to the diaspora or Israel for their sites of Jewishness. This extraterritoriality might, on one level, be considered a form of postmodern fiction. But the very fact that the writers in this section want to historicize their Jewishness and not merely universalize it points to an implicit critique of a too generalized postmodernism.[74] All these British-born novelists and poets create diasporas of the mind in a bid to subvert a wide range of national certainties. They nonetheless remain wedded to their particularist identities, however fluid and capricious they may be. Clive Sinclair and Simon Louvish focus as much on Israel as the diaspora, and their masculine perspective contrasts with the women-centered fiction and poetry of Ruth Fainlight and Elaine Feinstein. But, unlike Eva Figes or Michelene Wandor, these two women writers do not have an explicitly feminist aesthetic.

Clive Sinclair has been rightly described as instigating a 'quiet but profound revolution' in Anglo-Jewish letters. His two early collections of short stories, *Hearts of Gold* (1979) and *Bedbugs* (1982), pointedly attempted to 'write fiction that owes nothing to any

English antecedents.' Sinclair has, therefore, located his 'national'
history as a Jew in Israel, America, and eastern Europe. He describes
his fiction as a self-consciously failed 'attempt to distill the essence
of other places. To make myself temporarily at home.'[75]

Continuing this theme in his *Diaspora Blues: A View of Israel* (1987),
Sinclair defines himself as having a 'dual loyalty' to 'the language
of England and the history of Israel' and argues that, for a writer,
there is 'something to be gained from having a language but no
history, a history but no language.'[76] Compared with his alienation
from England, his unrequited love affair with Israel has provided
him a 'narrative' in which to situate himself. His early story 'Wingate
Football Club' (1979), included in this anthology, is a tragicomic
treatment of this theme. Whereas this story brings together England and Israel, soccer and war, other stories move to eastern Europe
or west to America. The sources for his work are both national and
international; his characters therefore shift from place to place, and
history changes its meaning so as to remake events.[77]

The crossing of all temporal and spatial boundaries so as to
transcend his English birthplace—which is displaced onto both
the Jewish diaspora and Israel—poses an interesting dilemma for
Sinclair. On the one hand, as the story 'Bedbugs' (also in the anthology) demonstrates, the history of the Holocaust is deemed to be
outside the moral purview of his protagonists. When asked to teach
First World War poetry to German students, Joshua, Sinclair's persona, fantasizes about teaching a parallel course called 'Rosenberg's Revenge' which highlights Nazi atrocities. Rosenberg's
poem 'Louse Hunting' (1917) is evoked in this story as a metaphor
for the Shoah, as Joshua and a German student burn the bedbugs
that infect their living quarters. But all Sinclair's stories are about the
dangers of turning such historical metaphors into reality. Joshua,
finally, acts as if he has the right to exact 'revenge' on behalf of
the Nazi victims, but by the end of the story he is clearly deranged.

The reference to Rosenberg is significant here, as Sinclair is making explicit an alternative British-Jewish literary canon to that of
the insider and documentary realist Israel Zangwill. Only the poet
Jon Silkin has so explicitly written in this tradition.[78] What is crucial
here is that Sinclair is careful not to universalize Rosenberg's extraterritoriality. Sinclair's protagonists are often made delirious by

their impossible displacement of an 'English' identity onto a wider diaspora. In his story 'Ashkenazia' Sinclair takes such solipsism to its extreme by inventing a mythic 'imaginary homeland' untouched by genocide.[79] Situated somewhere in central Europe, Ashkenazia, a fictitious Yiddish-speaking country that reappears in Jacobson's *The God-Fearer*, is defined as a language community outside history: 'Many of my fellow-countrymen do not believe in the existence of God. I am more modest. I do not believe in myself. What proof can I have when no one reads what I write? There you have it; my words are the limit of my world. You will therefore smile at this irony; I have been commissioned by our government to write the official English-language *Guide to Ashkenazia*' (238).

By the end of the story, all that remains of Ashkenazia is a 'field of wooden skeletons,' and Sinclair's demented persona truly becomes bounded by his words: 'Now the world will listen to me, for I am the guide to Ashkenazia. I am Ashkenazia' (248). This conflation of selfhood with nationhood is, on one level, the necessary solipsistic response of an author who displaces the national culture of his English birthplace onto a useful fiction. For the post-Holocaust writer, however, such aestheticized imaginary homelands cannot be constituted by words alone. A purely textual Ashkenazia is an act of artistic megalomania precisely because Sinclair's narrator thinks he can bring these skeletons to life.

Sinclair's two early novels, *Blood Libels* (1985) and *Cosmetic Effects* (1989), take to its logical conclusion the insane union, in his stories, of selfhood with nationhood. Both novels, that is, are personal histories that have national consequences. As in one of Sinclair's later stories, 'Kayn Aynhoreh,' hypochondria is the natural condition of those who place the imagination at the center of nationhood. Jake Silkstone, the alter ego in this story, reappears in *Blood Libels* and describes his various Scriptophobic and Dermagraphic ailments as 'the psychosomatic approach to history': 'Just as the mind, knowing the symptoms, has no need of bacillus or virus to counterfeit an illness, so history does not need facts to proceed. What people believe to have happened is more important than what actually did.'[80] 'The psychosomatic approach to history' has especially telling consequences in *Blood Libels*, resulting in the emergence of the fascistic 'Children of Albion' in England and the 1982 Israeli

invasion of Lebanon. In this novel Sinclair deliberately undermines
the idea of history as the 'pseudo-scientific study of facts' (188) by
treating well-known political events in Israel as grotesque fantasy
and by turning grotesque fantasy in England into seemingly plausible historical narrative.

Cosmetic Effects deals with the possibility of Jonah Isaacson's being
unwittingly turned into a human bomb by his Palestinian doctor,
Said Habash, who fits him with a prosthetic arm. Whether Isaacson
is a 'Son of Ishmael' (the name of a Palestinian guerrilla group) or
the son of Isaac (an Israeli national hero) is deliberately left open
to question. Isaacson loses his memory for much of the novel and
thus has a number of competing national stories imposed on him.
His animalistic desires and domestic constraints embody this ter-
rorizing or civilizing doubleness but are also part of a conscious
narrative 'pluralism' that encourages 'a proliferation of stories and
interpretations [so that] the future won't be fascistic.'[81] For Sinclair,
the imagination 'bind[s] more strongly than kinship,' and yet he is
careful to locate his diasporic fiction within specific national stories.

In *Augustus Rex* (1992) Sinclair brings August Strindberg back to
life, after half a century in the grave, with the Faustian pact that he
will once again become an all-powerful writer and unbridled lover
of women. The novel is narrated by Beelzebub, Lord of the Flies,
who tempts the resurrected Strindberg to overreach himself (he is
turned into a fly). In the same vein as the megalomaniacal storyteller
of 'Ashkenazia,' *Augustus Rex* sets out to make ironic the supposedly
unlimited power of Strindberg's death-defying art. In this way Sinclair is able to question the limits of an extraterritorial writing that
is displaced from space and time. His most recent collection of
stories, *The Lady with the Laptop* (1996), continues to invent purely
imaginary national homelands—such as 'Ishmalyia' in his story
'The Iceman Cometh'—simultaneously subjecting his aestheticized
diaspora to the contingencies of history.

Reimagining histories and debunking received mythologies and
taboos, especially with regard to Israel, is also the subject of much
of the fiction of Simon Louvish. Louvish was born in Glasgow in
1947 and was taken to Israel at the age of two. He was educated in
Israel, serving in the Six Day War as a military camera man, and in
1968, returned to Britain where he has lived since then. Like the

Irish-Israeli Ronit Lentin, the Scottish-Israeli Louvish is a hybrid cross-cultural voice whose literary influences range from the South American novel to North American science fiction and Israeli popular satire. His uncategorizable writing not only eschews the conventional forms that stifle much fiction in Britain but also challenges the boundaries of what supposedly constitutes literary fiction. *The Days of Miracles and Wonders* (1997), part of which is included in this volume, is an endlessly mobile hodgepodge of memory, fantasy, history, graffiti, parody, and Israeli street humor. All Louvish's 'Blok-busters' have the same exuberant overflowing accretion and a central figure, Avram Blok, who seeks to contain these multiple histories, which span the 1973 Yom Kippur War and the 1991 Gulf War.

In his first Blok novel, *The Therapy of Avram Blok* (1985), which is also excerpted here, a lunatic asylum in Jerusalem has become a metaphor for a world where the line between fantasy and political reality is increasingly blurred. By the end the novel revolves around the pun of whether Israel remains an asylum—that is, a refuge— or is just plain lunatic. Louvish refuses to use a linear narrative and therefore structures his Blok novels in terms of historical cycles that encompass the First World War, the Second World War, the Shoah, the Israeli wars, and the Gulf War. In this way he leaps about in time while still, depressingly, dealing with the same themes. As well as transgressing temporal boundaries, where dead figures come back to life, Louvish crosses ever-changing spatial boundaries. His alter ego, Avram Blok, thus travels throughout the globe in a desperate but failed bid to obtain some kind of rational perspective. Although plural contexts, temporal fluidity, and filmic intercutting characterize Louvish's fiction as postmodern par excellence, this would be a reductive reading. His fiction is a roller-coaster ride through the fundamentalist politics of the postwar period, and, in these terms, Louvish remains a Swiftian political satirist whose aim is to subvert the moral certainties that have led to war and bloodshed in the first place.

In his second Blok novel, *City of Blok* (1988), which spans the election of Menachem Begin in 1977 and the Lebanon War of 1982, Louvish's protagonist is pursued by the shadowy Department of Apocalyptic Affairs. At one point the fragmented, restless, perpetually mobile Blok sums up his desperation when he states that he does not care about the future, as 'the past has taken over the present.'[82] And yet, like an inverted Dorian Gray, Blok remains pure and innocent while everyone around him becomes corrupt. Forced into the maelstrom of Middle Eastern politics, Blok encounters Jewish fascists, Palestinian resistance fighters, and Israeli peaceniks—in short, a world 'composed of a thousand splinters,' as he puts it. To show that he has the courage of his convictions, Louvish has recently published *What's Up, God?* (1995), a satirical account of the apocalyptic age after the arrival of the Messiah. He has also written comic thrillers, such as *The Death of Moishe Ganef* (1986) and *The Silencer* (1991), to give his themes a more recognizable form. His diasporic Jewishness extends the range and vocabulary of the novel in English to global concerns and a sense of morality beneath the rubble.

Elaine Feinstein, in her fiction and poetry, also locates herself in a diasporic realm beyond a restrictive Englishness. Her poetic novels are mainly situated in an imaginary but historically specific central Europe. Interestingly, when she does write directly about her British antecedents, in *The Survivors* (1982), she is unable to go beyond the restrictions inherent in the conventional family saga novel form. Her writing, in other words, needs a liberating extraterritoriality in order to eclipse the parochial representations and received images of an apologetic Anglo-Jewry. Her poetry, on the other hand, is flexible enough for her to deal directly with her immediate family and friends but also ranges through a myriad of voices and topics. I concentrate here on her fiction.[83]

When her early novels were seen as a species of contemporary 'Gothic'—along with fiction by Angela Carter, J. G. Ballard, and Emma Tennant—Feinstein was quick to differentiate herself from what she thought of as this 'steely rejection of humanism, a fashionable resistance to compassion which I believe is as much a luxury of our English innocence as the euphoria of the flower generation.'[84] Her career as a writer has gone beyond such 'English innocence,' in stark contrast to those émigré writers, such as Eva Figes and Ruth Prawer Jhabvala, who take comfort in such parochialism. Only when she became the translator of the poetry of Marina Tsvetayeva, and later of Margarita Aliger, Yunna Moritz, and Bella Akh-madulina, did Feinstein discover her voice as a 'European' writer. Her writing was thus directly opposed to that of an early influential group of Essex University poets (including Lee Harwood and Tom Pickard) who wished to foreground their common Englishness and 'de-Europeanize' themselves.

As a woman, Feinstein has situated 'magical' father-enchanters at the heart of her fiction and has principally historicized the domestic sphere. In this way her female alter egos resist assimilation into the dominant sexual values of English national culture. In contrast, Sinclair and Louvish attempt to masculinize their personae in op-position to the powerlessness of diaspora life. Far from being lib-erating, Feinstein's father-enchanters are always thoroughly am-biguous, both breathing 'life' into her female protagonists and threatening to make them 'dead with dependence.' In *The Shadow Master* (1978) the seventeenth-century Jewish false messiah Sabbatai Zevi is the ultimate historical expression of this double-edged enchantment. By the time of *The Border* (1984), excerpted here, and *Loving Brecht* (1992), Feinstein situated Walter Benjamin and Bertolt Brecht in this 'magical' role. If the source of this life-giving 'magic' is the 'music of words,' as she suggests in *The Circle* (1970), then male writers are a peculiarly disabling embodiment of this imagina-tive 'refuge' for her female personae.[85]

In *The Border* Walter Benjamin—'a Marxist who is not a material-ist'[86]—is a 'mystical' synthesizing figure whom the novel deliber-ately deconstructs. Set in Vienna before the *Anschluss*, this work is written as a triptych in diary and epistolary form, allowing for three equally passionate accounts of an erotic triangle. Far from a single male consciousness, the multiple, hallucinatory sense of reality in this novel—which turns history into the domestic and the domestic into history—is foregrounded even when the main characters are faced with the threat of Nazism. The Spanish border at Port Bou in 1940, where Benjamin actually committed suicide, by the end signifies both his tragically fixed place in history and the internal fissures that are writ large in the novel. This is acknowledged in the form of *The Border*, which reads an arbitrary version of its own story back from a contemporary perspective.

The poet and story writer Ruth Fainlight has, like Feinstein,

domesticated the political and historical realm and defamiliarized
what is usually thought to make up the domestic sphere. Born in
New York and of Austro-Hungarian and British parentage, Fainlight has lived in England since the age of fifteen. Her writing is
divided between her immediate personal concerns—of what it
means to be a 'Jew, woman, poet' in Britain—and the location of
an identity outside these categories. At one point in her *This Time of
Year* (1994) Fainlight admits:

> Half of my nature is as simple as a
>   medieval
> peasant. The other isn't and that's
>   the trouble.[87]

This split characterizes much of her poetry. She is constantly aware
of having an 'other life,' which makes her question all boundaries,
whether domestic or global. Thus, on the one hand, she is rightly
said to make 'dailiness strange, exotic and demanding' while giving conventionally domestic images a historical resonance.[88] In
'A Child's Fear of Spiders' (1968), for instance, Fainlight relates
this fear initially to the image of parents copulating and to two
swastikas, and finally to the concept of absolute power. 'Stubborn'
(1983) speaks of this abiding sense of doubleness in terms of a
'stone-age self' that scorns the veneer of civilization.[89] At the same
time, she is aware that her 'stone-age' or 'medieval' self lacks a
poetic eye, which, above all, gives shape and meaning to the world.

But these contradictions often take the form of characterizing
women, and especially her mother, as visionaries, and she has written a series of 'Sybil' poems to explore this strangeness. 'Lineage'
(1994), for instance, has a pointedly ambivalent relationship to her
mother's superstitions, which signify both the mother's absolute
power over the adolescent persona and her alluring otherness:

> Remedies and simples from the old
> country, still useful in the city,
> were passed from mother to daughter
> and not yet scorned. We rarely saw
> a doctor. When I was little
> it seemed normal to be sickly

for half of the year. I never told her
that I was proud she was a witch.[90]

Like many of Fainlight's poems in her eleven anthologies, her stories, collected in *Daylife and Nightlife (1971)* and *Dr. Clock's Last Case and Other Stories* (1994), are vignettes. In 'Another Survivor' (1978), included here, a dress like one his mother used to wear reminds Rudi of his escape to England from Germany in 1938 when he was twelve. But with this return to his lost childhood Rudi is unable to contain the violence he has kept suppressed for decades. When his non-Jewish daughter, Faith, puts on the dress, he begins to torment and victimize her for innocently assuming the identity of his dead mother. In her quasi-autobiographical 'A Wizard's Robe Patterned with Stars and Moons' (1994), also in the anthology, Fainlight locates this childlike naiveté in a New York school at the time of the Second World War. As with the memoirs of Emanuel Litvinoff and Eva Figes, Fainlight's juxtaposition of the language and outlook of childhood with the horror of war is telling.

By situating a great many different kinds of texts and local and global perspectives in their fiction and poetry, Fainlight and Feinstein, like Louvish and Sinclair, establish the possibility of refiguring a European past in terms of imaginative wordplay as well as the insurmountable borders of history. But this is not, as some have argued, merely a 'journey of self-integration' into the European past for the Jewish writer.[91] On the contrary, it is the lack of a sense of integration into another history which these British-Jewish writers highlight in their fiction. In other words, all these writers evoke an indeterminate Jewishness precisely to help us rethink the presumed certainties of the present.

THE PRESENT (5): NEW VOICES

Elena Lappin, Jonathan Treitel, and Jonathan Wilson

What is interesting about present-day British-Jewish writing is that as well as no longer conforming to the dominant expectations of English or Anglo-Jewish culture, it actively helps deconstruct these received conventions. As recent studies of the postwar English

novel have shown, British writers in general have a fraught relationship with the past. In contrast to the Victorian era, when British
history was synonymous with world history, with the advent of
postcolonialism there has been an increasingly impoverished sense
of national destiny. Because the values of imperial Britain are no
longer disseminated around the globe, mainstream British writers
lack confidence about their place in the world and are uncertain
about what constitutes English identity. In these terms, the British-
Jewish writers in this anthology have a good deal in common with
such postcolonial counterparts as Salman Rushdie, Kazuo Ishi-
guro, and Hanif Kureishi. All their work, in other words, exposes
a radically different sense of the past and rewrites an alternative
Englishness from the margins. Contemporary fiction in Britain is,
for this reason, a study in fragmentation. No longer do writers learn
from the previous generation or have a settled sense of place or
identity.[92]

In this context, even what defines a 'new voice' is peculiarly prob-
lematic. The novelist Alan Isler, for instance, published *The Prince
of West End Avenue* (1994), his prizewinning first novel, at the age of
sixty. Moving effortlessly from the comic to the tragic mode, Isler
combines raucous New York humor with the bleak undertow of
European history. Much of his family emigrated from Vienna in the
late 1930s, and Isler spent the war years with them in Harrogate in
the north of England. He then moved to postwar London and in
1952, at the age of eighteen, to New York, where he stayed to teach
English literature for nearly three decades. Isler's narrative skill is
to give his Anglo-American narrator many different cultural registers that mischievously catch the reader unawares. In these terms,
Isler is both a British and American writer as well as a welcome
'old-new' voice.

Jonathan Wilson, on the other hand, was born in London and
educated in Jerusalem and New York, and this tripartite setting is
reflected in his stories, one of which, 'From Shanghai' (1993), is
included here. Unlike Isler, Wilson writes in a multitude of contexts, reflecting the boundlessness of the English-born diasporic
writer. No longer is history contained within national territories, as
it is everywhere both local and global. His recent novel *The Hiding
Room* (1995) encompasses Jerusalem over a fifty-year period, and

'From Shanghai' brings together the Far East, Nazi Europe, and postwar Britain. In the latter tale an obsessive uncle who emigrates to Britain from Shanghai in the 1950s turns out to have lost his wife and child in the Second World War. The transformation of his collection of Hans Christian Andersen into a shrine for his family both encircles and transcends his varied histories.

Like many of the authors in this anthology, Jonathan Treitel uses a restless and unsettling narrative technique in his extraterritorial fiction and poetry. The ability to set a story off like a spinning top so that it eventually comes back to a fixed point characterizes his two stories in this volume: 'Selflessness; or Alexander and His Electric Wok' and 'Shaking Hands with Theodor Herzl.' Although London-born, Treitel was educated in California and has lived and worked in San Francisco and Tokyo. Like Wilson, Treitel can be regarded as a second-generation diasporic writer whose sense of place and identity has always been situated outside national boundaries. His first novel, The Red Cabbage Café (1990), is set in Russia in 1922, and his stories also range through personal intimacies to historical landscapes. Like many of the writers anthologized here, Treitel skillfully blends fantastical wordplay with actual events or personages. This heady combination results in a new kind of writing that reconfigures both the inner and outer world, moving in and out of both Englishness and Jewishness.

In this new writing the authenticity of experience no longer determines how we read or what is written, as it is precisely the assumption of authenticity that is being undermined. Although the Shoah has not directly touched her flesh, the playwright Julia Pascal in her Holocaust Trilogy (1996) communes wholeheartedly with it. Seen together, her three plays are an unapologetic and obsessive identification with the ghosts that, she believes, still haunt European culture. Along with Diane Samuels's more understated and subtle Kindertransport (1992), there is a strong sense in which different pasts —here the Shoah and women's history—collide to form new wholes. This can be seen especially in Linda Grant's important first novel The Cast Iron Shore (1996), which places her heroine, Sybil Ross, at the center of many of the key events of the twentieth century. The novel drifts across continents, taking in America, Vietnam, and the Balkans, as well as England, in an ambitious bid to bring together political idealism and personal commitment. No longer does the male figure assume the mock-heroic role of being buffeted by forces beyond his control. Grant, for the first time, puts a woman at the heart of the century's history.

Most recent British-Jewish writers are not merely unapologetic in their Jewishness but can be characterized as Jews 'with attitude' who disrupt all conventions. In this assertive spirit William Sutcliffe's *New Boy* (1996) makes gay Jewish identity a key motif. Equally significant, the expressionist drama of Steven Berkoff explores the extreme violence inherent in a masculine Jewish identity. Like *The Cast Iron Shore*, Elena Lappin's story 'Noa and Noah,' included in the anthology, uses material that has hitherto been thought of exclusively as subject matter for male Jewish writing. Lappin has lived in Prague, Berlin, Haifa, and New York, but, now based in London, she has written a determinedly British-Jewish story. At their most compelling, the contemporary British-Jewish writers in this book defy the authority of England and the Anglo-Jewish community and disrupt the usual categories in which they have been authenticated. Much present-day British-Jewish literature is written against fixed boundaries that are increasingly contested and more fluid than ever. All the writers in the anthology are risk-takers who are helping to replace narrow national narratives and gendered identities with a broader, more plural, diasporic culture.

Notes

1. See Michael Galchinsky, *The Origin of the Modern Jewish Woman Writer: Romance and Reform in Victorian England* (Detroit: Wayne State University Press, 1996); Nadia Valman, 'Jews and Gender in British Literature, 1815–1865,' Ph.D. dissertation, University of London (1996); and Linda Gertner Zatlin, *The Nineteenth-Century Anglo-Jewish Novel* (Boston: Twayne, 1981).

2. Michael Ragussis, *Figures of Conversion: 'The Jewish Question' and English National Identity* (Durham NC: Duke University Press, 1995), chap. 3. See also Galchinsky, *Modern Jewish Woman Writer*, chap. 1, and Valman, 'Jews and Gender in British Literature,' chap. 2.

3. My disagreement here is with Galchinsky's *Modern Jewish Woman Writer*, which, I believe, has turned the 'Jewish woman writer' into an idealized

figure outside the contingencies of history. For a more historically nuanced account, see Valman, 'Jews and Gender in British Literature.' See also Bryan Cheyette, 'And Which the Jew?' *TLS*, 11 October 1996, p. 29.

4. Grace Aguilar, 'History of the Jews in England,' in *Chambers' Miscellany of Useful and Entertaining Tracts*, vol. 18 (Edinburgh: William and Robert Chambers, 1847). For the wider context of Aguilar's history, see Geoffrey Alderman, 'English Jews or Jews of the English Persuasion? Reflections on the Emancipation of Anglo-Jewry,' in Pierre Birnbaum and Ira Katznelson (eds.), *Paths of Emancipation: Jews, States, and Citizenship* (Princeton: Princeton University Press, 1995), chap. 5.

5. Celia and Marion Moss, *Tales of Jewish History: Volume 1* (London: Miller & Field, 1843), pp. 1–3.

6. Zatlin, *Nineteenth-Century Anglo-Jewish Novel*, pp. 122–23, and Galchinsky, *Modern Jewish Woman Writer*. For a sophisticated counter to this teleology, see David Feldman, *Englishmen and Jews: Social Relations and Political Culture, 1840–1914* (New Haven: Yale University Press, 1994), and Todd Endelman, *Radical Assimilation in English Jewish History, 1656–1945* (Bloomington: Indiana University Press, 1990).

7. 'The Jew of Fiction, and the Jewess,' *Jewish Chronicle*, 20 May 1892, p. 9. See also Bryan Cheyette, 'From Apology to Revolt: Benjamin Farjeon, Amy Levy, and the Post-emancipation Anglo-Jewish Novel, 1880–1900,' *Transactions of the Jewish Historical Society of England* 29 (1982–86): 253–65.

8. See Eugene Black, *The Social Politics of Anglo-Jewry, 1880–1920* (Oxford: Blackwell, 1988), and Feldman, *Englishmen and Jews*.

9. Israel Zangwill, 'English Judaism: A Criticism and a Classification,' *Jewish Quarterly Review* 1 (1889): 403.

10. 'Jew of Fiction,' p. 9; Zangwill quoted in Harold Fisch, 'Israel Zangwill: Prophet of the Ghetto,' *Judaism* 13, no. 4 (1964): 414. See also Bernard Winehouse, 'Israel Zangwill's *Children of the Ghetto*: A Literary History of the First Anglo-Jewish Best-Seller,' *English Literature in Transition* 16 (1973): 95.

11. Joseph Udelson, *Dreamer of the Ghetto: The Life and Works of Israel Zangwill* (Tuscaloosa AL: University of Alabama Press, 1990), pp. 82–83 and chap. 5. References to Israel Zangwill, *Children of the Ghetto: A Story of a Peculiar People* (New York: Macmillan, 1895), are cited in the text by page number.

12. Neil Larry Shumsky, 'Zangwill's *The Melting-Pot*: Ethnic Tensions on Stage,' *American Quarterly* 27 (March 1975): 29. See also Bryan Cheyette, 'The Other Self: Anglo-Jewish Fiction and the Representation of Jews in

England, 1875–1905,' in David Cesarani (ed.), *The Making of Modern Anglo-Jewry* (Oxford: Blackwell, 1990), pp. 106–11.

13. Israel Zangwill, *The Melting-Pot* (London: Globe, 1925), p. 33.

14. *Times*, 11 August 1958, p. 10.

15. For a view of British-Jewish writing in terms of Anglo-Jewry's communal agenda, see Stanley Waterman and Marlena Schmool, 'Literary Perspectives on Jews in Britain in the Early Twentieth Century,' in Russell King, John Connell, and Paul White (eds.), *Writing across Worlds: Literature and Migration* (London: Routledge, 1995), chap. 12.

16. Julia Frankel, *Dr. Phillips: A Maida Vale Idyll* (London: Vizetelly, 1887), p. 192. Cheyette, 'From Apology to Revolt,' pp. 26–64, and 'Other Self,' pp. 102–6. See also Nadia Valman, 'Women and Jews in an Age of Emancipation (1845–1900),' master's thesis, University of Leeds (1991), chaps. 3 and 4, and Todd Endelman, 'The Frankaus of London: A Study in Radical Assimilation, 1837–1967,' *Jewish History* 8 (1994): 117–54.

17. Amy Levy, 'Magdalen,' in *Xantippe and Other Verse* (Cambridge: E. Johnson, 1881).

18. Amy Levy, 'Captivity,' in *A London Plane-Tree and Other Verse* (London: T. Fisher Unwin, 1889), pp. 62–63.

19. Melvyn New (ed.), *The Complete Novels and Selected Writings of Amy Levy* (Gainesville: University of Florida Press, 1993), pp. 378, 480, 478–85, 558. This volume is an excellent resource for Amy Levy's fiction, with a useful introduction, although it has a thin selection of her poetry.

20. Amy Levy, *Reuben Sachs: A Sketch* (London: Macmillan, 1888), pp. 115–16.

21. Ragussis, *Figures of Conversion*, pp. 290–300, and Bryan Cheyette, *Constructions of 'the Jew' in English Literature and Society: Racial Representations, 1875–1945* (Cambridge: Cambridge University Press, 1993), pp. 43–54.

22. Israel Zangwill to Annie Wynick, 12 June 1916, quoted in Joseph Cohen, *Journey to the Trenches: The Life of Isaac Rosenberg, 1890–1918* (London: Robson, 1975), p. 149; Jon Silkin, *Out of Battle: The Poetry of the Great War* (London: Routledge, 1972), pp. 253, 257.

23. Isaac Rosenberg, 'Break of Day in the Trenches,' in Ian Parson (ed.), *The Collected Works of Isaac Rosenberg* (London: Chatto & Windus, 1979), pp. 103–4.

24. On anti-Semitism in the British army, see Cohen, *Journey to the Trenches*, pp. 127–28; see also Adam Phillips, 'Isaac Rosenberg's English,' in *On Flirtation* (London: Faber & Faber, 1994), pp. 175–95.

25. Rosenberg to R. C. Trevelyan, 15 June 1916, in Parson, *Collected Works of Isaac Rosenberg*, p. 235.

26. Isaac Rosenberg, *Moses*, in Parson, *Collected Works of Isaac Rosenberg*, pp. 151 and 138–55.

27. Rosenberg to Gordon Bottomley, 23 July 1916, in Parson, *Collected Works of Isaac Rosenberg*, p. 238.

28. Isaac Rosenberg, 'Chagrin,' in Parson, *Collected Works of Isaac Rosenberg*, p. 95.

29. *Jewish Chronicle*, 19 December 1958, p. 19; 26 December 1958, p. 13; 2 January 1959, p. 17; 9 January 1959, p. 17; and 16 January 1959, p. 19. On the interviews, see Chaim Bermant, *Troubled Eden: An Anatomy of British Jewry* (London: Vallentine, Mitchell, 1969), pp. 162–64 and chap. 13, and David Cesarani, *The Jewish Chronicle and Anglo-Jewry, 1841–1991* (Cambridge: Cambridge University Press, 1994), chap. 8.

30. Philip Roth, *The Facts: A Novelist's Autobiography* (London: Jonathan Cape, 1988), pp. 129–30.

31. *Jewish Chronicle*, 26 December 1958, p. 13, and 2 January 1959, p. 17.

32. See Howard Cooper and Paul Morrison, *A Sense of Belonging: Dilemmas of British Jewish Identity* (London: Weidenfeld & Nicolson, 1991); see also Bryan Cheyette, 'Philip Roth and Clive Sinclair: Representations of an "Imaginary Homeland" in Post-War British and American-Jewish Literature,' in Ann Massa and Alistair Stead (eds.), *Forked Tongues? Comparing Twentieth-Century British and American Literature* (London: Longman, 1994), and Brian Glanville, 'The Anglo-Jewish Writer,' *Encounter* 24, no. 2 (1960): 62–64.

33. *Jewish Chronicle*, 19 December 1958, p. 19.

34. Richard Chase, *The American Novel and Its Tradition* (New York: Doubleday, 1957), pp. 1–2. See also Ann Massa, 'Fictions of the Ghetto: A Trans-Atlantic Comparison,' *Jewish Quarterly* (winter 1989): 21–24.

35. Cesarani, *Making of Modern Anglo-Jewry*, attempts to fill some of the gaps in the received historical record. See also Tony Kushner (ed.), *The Jewish Heritage in British History: Englishness and Jewishness* (London: Frank Cass, 1992).

36. Emanuel Litvinoff, *Journey through a Small Planet* (London: Michael Joseph, 1972), p. 9. References to this work are cited in the text by page number.

37. Emanuel Litvinoff, 'To T. S. Eliot,' in *Notes for a Survivor* (Newcastle upon Tyne: Northern House, 1973).

38. T. S. Eliot, 'Burbank with a Baedeker: Bleistein with a Cigar,' in *Poems* (New York: Knopf, 1920).

39. Martin Esslin, *Pinter: The Playwright*, expanded ed. (London: Methuen, 1977), pp. 121–30.

40. Harold Pinter, *The Birthday Party*, ed. Margaret Rose (London: Faber & Faber, 1993), p. 86.

41. See, for example, James Shapiro, *Shakespeare and the Jews* (New York: Columbia University Press, 1996); Frank Felsenstein, *Anti-Semitic Stereotypes: A Paradigm of Otherness in English Popular Culture, 1660–1830* (Baltimore: Johns Hopkins University Press, 1995); Ragussis, *Figures of Conversion*; Cheyette, *Constructions of 'the Jew'*; and Bryan Cheyette (ed.), *Between 'Race' and Culture: Representations of 'the Jew' in English and American Literature* (Stanford: Stanford University Press, 1996).

42. Philip Dodd, 'Englishness and the National Culture,' in Robert Colls and Philip Dodd (eds.), *Englishness and Culture, 1880–1920* (London: Croom Helm, 1986), p. 22.

43. Philip Roth, 'Writing about Jews,' in *Reading Myself and Others*, rev. ed. (Harmondsworth: Penguin, 1985), pp. 212 and 205–25.

44. See Joseph Cohen (ed.), *The Poetry of Dannie Abse: Critical Essays and Reminiscences* (London: Robson Books, 1983), and Daniel Weissbort, 'Startled by the Visible,' *Jewish Quarterly* (autumn 1994): 67–69.

45. Gerda Charles, *The Crossing Point* (London: Eyre & Spottiswoode, 1960), p. 78.

46. David Daiches, 'Some Aspects of Anglo-American Jewish Fiction,' in Jacob Sonntag (ed.), *Jewish Writing Today, 1953–1973* (London: Vallentine, Mitchell, 1973), pp. 88–93. See also Shifra Sharlin, 'Bernice Rubens: A Novelist of Family,' *Jewish Quarterly* (autumn 1987): 35–38, and *Jewish Chronicle*, 3 May 1991, p. 28.

47. Bernice Rubens, *The Elected Member* (London: Eyre & Spottiswoode, 1969). References to this work are cited in the text by page number.

48. Howard Jacobson, *Peeping Tom* (London: Chatto & Windus, 1984), p. 186.

49. See John Skinner, *The Fictions of Anita Brookner* (London: Macmillan, 1992), p. 6, and Ephraim Sicher, *Beyond Marginality: Anglo-Jewish Literature after the Holocaust* (New York: State University of New York Press, 1985), for a reductive reading of British-Jewish writing.

50. Skinner, *Fictions of Anita Brookner*, p. 137. See also Anita Brookner, 'Aches and Pains of Assimilation,' *Observer*, 23 April 1989, p. 44, and John Haffenden, *Novelists in Interview* (London: Methuen, 1985), p. 60, for Brookner's account of her Polish-Jewish antecedents.

51. Ruth Prawer Jhabvala, *Out of India* (Harmondsworth: Penguin, 1987), pp. 20, 21.

52. Ruth Prawer Jhabvala, 'Disinheritance,' *Blackwoods*, April 1979, p. 6, is her only published account of her childhood. See also Judie Newman, *The Ballastic Bard: Postcolonial Fictions* (London: Arnold, 1995), p. 30 and chaps. 3 and 5.

53. George Steiner, 'Our Homeland, the Text,' in *No Passion Spent: Essays, 1978–1995* (London: Faber & Faber, 1996), p. 305.

54. Cynthia Ozick, 'Toward a New Yiddish,' in *Art and Ardor: Essays* (New York: Knopf, 1984), p. 155.

55. Steiner, 'Our Homeland, the Text,' p. 305.

56. See, for example, George Steiner, 'A Responsion,' in Nathan A. Scott and Ronald A. Sharp (eds.), *Reading George Steiner* (Baltimore: Johns Hopkins University Press, 1994), pp. 275–85.

57. Ronald A. Sharp, 'Steiner's Fiction and the Hermeneutics of Transcendence,' in Scott and Sharp, *Reading George Steiner*, chap. 10.

58. George Steiner, *Extraterritorial: Papers on Literature and the Language Revolution* (Harmondsworth: Penguin, 1975), chap. 9, and *Real Presences: Is There Anything 'in' What We Say?* (London: Faber & Faber, 1989). His fiction has been collected as *The Deeps of the Sea and Other Fiction* (London: Faber & Faber, 1996).

59. George Steiner, 'Cake,' in *Deeps of the Sea*, p. 75.

60. George Steiner, 'A Conversation Piece,' in *Deeps of the Sea*, p. 393. References to this work are cited in the text by page number.

61. 'Childhood Landscapes,' *Jewish Quarterly* (summer 1990): 48–51.

62. Ronit Lentin, *Night Train to Mother* (Dublin: Attic Press, 1989), p. 218. References to this work are cited in the text by page number.

63. Gabriel Josipovici, *Contre-Jour: A Triptych after Pierre Bonnard* (Manchester: Carcanet, 1986), p. 76.

64. For Josipovici's most explicit account of his Jewishness, see his 'Going and Resting,' in David Theo Goldberg and Michael Krausz (eds.), *Jewish*

Identity (Philadelphia: Temple University Press, 1993), pp. 309–21, and his *Book of God: A Response to the Bible* (New Haven: Yale University Press, 1988).

65. Gabriel Josipovici, *In a Hotel Garden* (Manchester: Carcanet, 1993), p. 6. References to this work are cited in the text by page number.

66. Gabriel Josipovici, *The Big Glass* (Manchester: Carcanet, 1991), p. 54.

67. Eva Figes, 'The Long Passage to Little England,' *Observer*, 11 June 1978, p. 14.

68. Quoted in Peter Conradi, 'Eva Figes,' in Jay L. Halio (ed.), *Dictionary of Literary Biography: Volume 14, British Novelists since 1960* (Detroit: Gale Research, 1983), p. 301.

69. Eva Figes, *Little Eden: A Child at War* (London: Faber & Faber, 1978), p. 131.

70. Figes, 'Long Passage to Little England,' p. 14; see also Conradi, 'Eva Figes,' pp. 298–302.

71. Karen Gershon, *The Bread of Exile* (London: Gollancz, 1985), p. 22.

72. Dan Jacobson, *The God-Fearer* (London: Bloomsbury, 1992), p. 65. References to this work are cited in the text by page number.

73. Dan Jacobson, *Hidden in the Heart* (London: Bloomsbury, 1991), p. 189.

74. See Bryan Cheyette, "Ineffable and Usable": Towards a Diasporic British-Jewish Writing,' *Textual Practice* 10 (spring 1996): 295–300.

75. "On the Edge of the Imagination": Clive Sinclair Interviewed by Bryan Cheyette,' *Jewish Quarterly* (autumn–winter 1984): 26–29. See also the entry on Sinclair in *World Authors: 1985–1990* (New York: H. W. Wilson, 1995), pp. 818–20, and Antony Lerman, "Diaspora Blues": Real or Imagined,' *Jewish Quarterly* (winter 1987): 11–12.

76. Clive Sinclair, *Diaspora Blues: A View of Israel* (London: Heinemann, 1987), pp. 65, 53.

77. See Clare Hanson, *Short Stories and Short Fictions, 1880–1980* (London: Macmillan, 1985), pp. 166–69; Malcolm Bradbury, *No, Not Bloomsbury* (London: Arena, 1987), pp. 352–58; and Michael Woolf, 'Negotiating the Self: Jewish Fiction in Britain since 1945,' in A. Robert Lee (ed.), *Other Britain, Other British: Contemporary Multicultural Fiction* (London: Pluto Press, 1995), chap. 8.

78. See Sicher, *Beyond Marginality*, pp. 143–52.

79. Clive Sinclair, 'Ashkenazia,' in *For Good or Evil: The Collected Stories of Clive Sinclair* (Harmondsworth: Penguin, 1991), pp. 238–48. References to this work are cited in the text by page number.

80. Clive Sinclair, *Blood Libels* (London: Alison & Busby, 1985), p. 188. References to this work are cited in the text by page number.

81. Clive Sinclair, *Cosmetic Effects* (London: André Deutsch, 1989), p. 45.

82. Simon Louvish, *City of Blok* (London: Collins, 1988), p. 361.

83. On Feinstein's poetry, see Karen Alkalay-Gut, 'Beyond Borders,' *Jewish Quarterly* (summer 1995): 67–68, and Peter Robinson (ed.), *Liverpool Accents: Seven Accents and a City* (Liverpool: Liverpool University Press, 1996), pp. 1–34.

84. Cited in Peter Conradi, 'Elaine Feinstein: Life and Novels,' *Literary Review* (April 1982): 24–25.

85. Elaine Feinstein, *The Circle* (Harmondsworth: Penguin, 1973), p. 164. See Olga Kenyon, *Writing Women: Contemporary Women Novelists* (London: Pluto Press, 1991), pp. 39–50, and Halio, *Dictionary of Literary Biography*, 14:292–97, for this argument.

86. Elaine Feinstein, *The Border* (London: Hutchinson, 1984), p. 57.

87. Ruth Fainlight, *This Time of Year* (London: Sinclair Stevenson, 1994), and Elaine Feinstein, 'Making Dailiness Exotic,' *Jewish Quarterly* (autumn 1994): 64–65.

88. Barbara Hardy, 'Introduction,' in Fainlight, *This Time of Year.* See also Feinstein, 'Making Dailiness Exotic,' pp. 64–65, and *TLS*, 8 April 1977, p. 428, and 23 May 1980, p. 586.

89. Ruth Fainlight, 'A Child's Fear of Spiders,' in *To See the Matter Clearly and Other Poems* (London: Macmillan, 1968), and 'Stubborn,' in *Fifteen to Infinity* (London: Hutchinson, 1983).

90. Ruth Fainlight, 'Lineage,' in *This Time of Year.*

91. Mark Shechner, *The Conversion of the Jews and Other Essays* (London: Macmillan, 1990), p. 100.

92. See Steven Connor, *The English in History, 1950–1995* (London: Routledge, 1996).

Ruth Prawer Jhabvala

was born in Cologne in 1927 and emigrated
to London in 1939. She was educated at
Hendon Grammar School and Queen Mary
College, University of London, where
she achieved a master of arts degree.
Prawer Jhabvala is the author of twelve
novels, including the Booker Prize–winning *Heat and Dust* (1975), and four collections of short stories. Her scripts for
film and television include *A Room with a
View*, which won an Academy Award in
1987, and *Howards End*, which won an
Academy Award in 1993. Prawer Jhabvala
also received a Neil Gunn International
Fellowship in 1978 and a MacArthur Foun-
dation Award in 1984. Most of her parents' relatives and friends were killed
during the Holocaust, and her story 'A
Birthday in London' (1963) is about the
German-Jewish émigré community that
was part of her adolescence. This community has preoccupied much of her later
fiction since she left Delhi for New York in
1975.

Ruth Prawer Jhabvala

A Birthday in London

Mr. Lumbik was the first guest to arrive, rather too early. He had a big bunch of flowers in tissue paper and wore a tweed jacket with leather buttons, which gave him a jaunty air. 'A happy birthday and so many of them,' he said, bending over her hand to kiss it with that special tender air he had adopted towards her.

Sonia was flustered—by his early arrival, by the flowers, by the tender air which she never knew how to deal with. She blushed, and this made her seem like a lovely young girl receiving her first suitor. 'Mr. Lumbik,' she said, 'you shouldn't. An old woman like me has no birthdays.'

'Ow, ow!' he cried, clutching his ears, which stood away from his head so that the light shone through them. 'They are hurting, hearing you speak such things!'

She laughed, all young and gay—'You and your jokes, you should be ashamed, Mr. Lumbik.'

'One little birthday favour,' he begged, holding up one modest little finger. 'Just one little, little favour from the birthday child.'

She again became somewhat agitated. She hoped he wasn't going to ask for a kiss, though that was what she rather expected. She didn't want to kiss Mr. Lumbik at all—not even, bending down, to peck at his cheek, which was never shaved well enough for her liking.

'Not Mr. Lumbik,' he begged. 'Not ever again Mr. Lumbik. Karl.' He put his head to one side and looked up at her pleadingly out of pale little ageing eyes. 'All right? Karl. Such a nice name.'

She didn't reply. Instead she carried the *Apfelstrudel* from the kitchen into her room, where the table was laid for the birthday party. Mr. Lumbik followed her on soft crêpe soles. He didn't press for an answer. He prided himself on his knowledge of women: and

Sonia was the type one had to proceed with gently and tactfully, for she was of very good family and had had a romantic upbringing.

'Now I have a surprise for you,' he said. 'You will be pleased to learn from me that now they have granted me my British citizenship.'

'How nice,' said Sonia, concentrating on the last-minute touches to her table. She had been a British citizen for ten years, and the thrill had worn off.

'Yes, a special telephone call from Scotland Yard.' He dialled an imaginary telephone and held an imaginary receiver to his ear. 'Hallo, Karl Lumbik? You are now a very small member of the very big British Commonwealth. God save the Queen, Karl Lumbik! God save the Queen, Mr. Scotland Yard!' The imaginary receiver was replaced and Mr. Lumbik stood at attention.

Sonia laughed: 'How funny you are.' Everything was a joke to him. If only Otto had been a bit more like that. But Otto had always taken everything very tragically. When they became British citizens, he had taken that tragically too. 'Yes, our passports they have given us,' he had said, 'but what else have we got?' 'Ottolein!' she had cried, 'be happy!' But no need to tell Karl Lumbik to be happy.

He was using his tender voice again. 'So now I am a very eligible cavalier, I think.' But it was the wrong note, he saw at once: she had turned away from him and was adjusting Otto's framed photograph on the table by her sleeping-couch. 'I think again I have opened my big mouth too wide,' he said ruefully, so that the defensive expression went from her face and she couldn't help laughing. She never could help laughing with him, he said such comic things. She tried to be remote and dignified, but after all she was the same Sonia Wolff, née Rothenstein, she had always been. The big laughing girl, they had called her. She always had been big—large bosom, large hips, though graceful with it, a fine full-blown flower on slender stalk legs—and she had been for ever laughing, or on the brink of laughter, her short curved upper lip trembling over her healthy teeth.

There was a ring at the door-bell, and Mr. Lumbik glided out like an expert butler to open. 'Come in, come in,' he said, bowing deeply at the entrance door, 'the *Apfelstrudel* has come out very well.'

'Where is the birthday child?' cried Mrs. Gottlob in her hoarse, uninhibited voice. It was a voice Sonia knew only too well, for she had heard it often enough, screaming up the stairs about lights that had been left burning and baths that had not been cleaned after use; and Otto, on hearing it, used to grow pale and very quiet, so that Sonia had to go downstairs and be as charming as she could be, accepting and admitting everything to stop Mrs. Gottlob from shouting and upsetting Otto. But, of course, all that was over now, and Mrs. Gottlob was no longer the landlady but a friend.

She came in and gave Sonia a big smack of a kiss and a box of chocolates. 'The kiss is for love and the chocolates for eating,' she said.

The box was very large and ornate, tied with a blue satin ribbon. It was just like the ones Otto had so often brought for her in Berlin. He used to come tiptoeing into what they called the morning-room, where she would be sitting at her escritoire writing letters or answering invitations; and smiling and pleased, the box held roguishly behind his back, he would say, 'Let us see now what nice surprise there is for us today.' And she would jump up, all large and graceful and girlish: 'Oh Otto!'

'So,' said Mrs. Gottlob, sitting down with a creak and a groan, 'how does it feel like to be twenty-five?'

'Already twenty-five!' cried Mr. Lumbik, clasping his hands together in wonder.

'Even my baby, my Werner, is nearly twenty-six,' said Sonia, shining and proud as always when she spoke of either of her children.

'And where is he today, on Mutti's birthday?' demanded Mrs. Gottlob. 'Again out with the girl-friends, I think?' She shook an extremely fat forefinger: 'I know your Werner—a very bad boy.'

'If you are not a bad boy at twenty-six, then when can you be a bad boy?' said Mr. Lumbik. He gave a reminiscent smile: 'Ask them in Vienna about one Karl Lumbik at twenty-six—la, la, la,' and he swayed his head, thinking of the girls and the cafés and Karl Lumbik in a tilted hat and camel coat.

'Ask them in London about one Karl Lumbik at fifty-six,' Mrs. Gottlob retorted, 'the story will not be different, only it is an old good-for-nothing where once there was a young good-for-nothing.'

'You are giving me a bad reputation,' said Mr. Lumbik, not ill-pleased, running his hands down the lapels of his coat and rocking to and fro on his heels.

'I had a letter from my Lilo today,' Sonia said. 'My birthday letter—just think, all the way from Israel and it arrives exactly on the right day. And there are nice photos too.' She took down the letter from where it was propped proudly on the mantelpiece and showed Mrs. Gottlob the photos of Lilo and her husband—sun-burnt stocky farmworkers with open collars and rolled-up sleeves—and their blond naked baby.

'Ach, the lovely baby,' crooned Mrs. Gottlob lovingly into the photo. 'He is like your Werner, I think—I remember just like this your Werner's hair went when he was four years old and first came to live in my house.'

Mr. Lumbik peered over one of Mrs. Gottlob's shoulders and Sonia over the other. 'There is also something from my dear late Papa in him,' Sonia said, sighing for her father, a large, healthy, handsome man who had loved good living and had died at Auschwitz. 'And also, I think—you don't think so?' she asked timid and hopeful, 'of my dear late Otto—the eyes, you see, and the forehead, Otto had always such a wonderful forehead.'

Mr. Lumbik glanced towards Otto's photo by the sleeping-couch. The wonderful forehead, he thought, was mainly created by the absence of any hair on the head. He remembered Otto Wolff as a small, bald, shrinking man, very tired, very sick, very old, in an expensive German dressing-gown which had grown too big for him. Mr. Lumbik had always thought what a pity it was that a fine woman like Sonia couldn't have married something better. Though, of course, Otto Wolff had been a very wealthy factory-owner in Berlin, and it wasn't quite fair to judge him as he had been in his last years—only a poor refugee who couldn't speak English, had no work and lodged in Mrs. Gottlob's house.

'Yes, perhaps also our good Mr. Wolff,' said Mrs. Gottlob, considering the grandchild. 'What a fine gentleman he was—Lumbik, I always say, never have I had a fine gentleman like Mr. Wolff in my house.'

A little tear came into Sonia's eye, but she was smiling with pleasure. How good Mrs. Gottlob was! Sonia had always told Otto that she was a good woman, in spite of her loud voice and crude manners. But Otto was so sensitive; and, of course, he had always been used to refined people and it was difficult for him to adjust. The little tear ran down her cheek, and she wiped it away with her handkerchief monogrammed with s. 'Yes, Mrs. Gottlob,' she said, 'we will none of us see a fine gentleman like my dear late Otto again. Oh, if you had known him in Germany, when he had the factory and the villa in Charlottenburg, what a respect you would have had for him then!' Always so dapper and neat, in his well-cut suit made of the best English cloth, spats over his hand-made shoes and smelling of gentleman's eau-de-cologne. All those years in Germany—from the time when she had first met him at Marienbad, when she was seventeen and he thirty-six, right till 1938, when they had had to leave—he had always looked the same: small, bald, rosy-cheeked, fresh, elegant. Only in England had he suddenly become old and mostly worn his dressing-gown.

Mrs. Gottlob gave a big sigh, which heaved her overfed body with its ill-functioning glands: 'Yes, there we were all different people.' She thought of Gottlob's butcher-shop, where you got the finest liver-sausage in the whole of Gelsenkirchen, and sighed again. 'Still, here we all are, no bones broken, eh, Lumbik? That must be Else,' she said, as the door-bell rang again.

Tiny Else, as plump as she was short, came in, all breathless, her coat flying open, her grey bun half drooping out of its pins, an enormous old leather handbag tucked under her arm. 'See, again I am late,' she cried, 'what can I do? Always work work, rush rush, Else this, Else that—every day at five o'clock I feel like giving my notice.' She put down the handbag and fumbled at her hair, while Mr. Lumbik stood behind her and gallantly helped her out of her coat. She gave him a suspicious look: 'Are you making a joke of me again, you there, Lumbik?' but carried on again immediately—'Just think, today at half-past four she comes to me: Else, one little work, this skirt to be shortened for a very special customer. Mrs. Davis, I say to her, it is half-past four. I am today invited for a birthday party in Swiss Cottage at five-thirty sharp——'

'Enough of your blah-blah-blah,' Mrs. Gottlob interrupted her, 'and at least wish something for the birthday child.'

Else raised both her hands to her forehead: 'You see, even that

has completely gone out of my—wait, I have brought a present!'
She began to grabble in the vast interior of her handbag and brought
up wrong things like keys, a bunch of safety-pins and a bottle of
aspirin. Then she held up a letter and cried, 'Oh I must tell you,
what news!' It had a German stamp. Sonia, who always got excited
when she saw letters with foreign stamps, cried, 'I hope good news?'

'And what good news—my compensation! Ten thousand marks!'

'Else, how nice!'

Mrs. Gottlob snatched the letter and read it. 'You should have
asked for twenty thousand,' she commented. She was quite an
expert on compensation. All her friends, all her lodgers, had had
compensation from Germany for their losses; she herself had collected handsomely for the butcher-shop. Of course, Sonia had had
the most of all, for she and her family had lost the most. Sonia was
a rich woman again now, which was as it should be.

'Ten thousand is also a nice little bit,' Else said, all red with
pleasure. 'Now what shall I do with my ten thousand? I think perhaps first a nice holiday in Switzerland in a good hotel——'

'Oh Else, let's go to St. Moritz!' Sonia cried. She clapped her
hands together, her eyes shone, her big body swayed on the slender,
elegant legs. 'I was there with Papa and Mama in—when was it?
Years and years ago, when I was fifteen. Oh it was so beautiful!'

'Na, and the birthday coffee?' Mrs. Gottlob reminded. Sonia went
out into the kitchen, and soon she came back with the coffee-pot
and they all sat round the table.

'So today is a good day for us all,' Mr. Lumbik said. 'First, there
is someone's birthday.' And he languished across the table, so that
Sonia became shy and peered down into her coffee cup, and Mrs.
Gottlob gave him a sharp push and said, 'Keep your eyes to yourself,
Lumbik.' He shut them immediately and sat up, prim and sheep-
like, so that Sonia and Else burst out laughing like two schoolgirls.
'Always a success with the ladies,' he commented. 'So first this
birthday. Then Miss Else gets her compensation and goes skiing in
St. Moritz.'

'Yes,' cried Else, 'I will break my legs also for my ten thousand—
we only live once, yu-hu!'

'And Karl Lumbik is made a British citizen, Class 4.'

'So,' said Mrs. Gottlob, her mouth full of *Apfelstrudel*, 'you are also one of us now.'

'That is just what she said to me when I got mine—that Mrs. Davis,' Else said. 'So you are one of us now, Else. Yes, I said, Mrs. Davis, I am one of you.' She gave a snort of contempt: 'I would rather tear out my arms and legs—"one of us"! If she opens her mouth, at once you know what class of people she comes from.' Else herself came from a very respectable family and never forgot what was due to her. Her father, Emil Levy, had been a High School teacher and a leading citizen of Schweinfurt; he had also, till the Nazis came, been a very patriotic German and there had always been a picture of the Kaiser and his family in the Levy drawing-room.

Sonia said, 'English Jews are all so uncultured, they are not like we were in Germany.'

'Uncultured!' Else cried. 'If you say to her Beethoven, she will think you have said a bad word.'

'Do you know about Moyshe Rotblatt from Pinsk who was taken to *Tristan und Isolde*?' Mr. Lumbik said.

'None of your kind of stories now, Lumbik,' Mrs. Gottlob said. 'You are in good company.'

'The best company,' Mr. Lumbik said. 'Twenty years ago if you had said to me, Karl Lumbik, in twenty years time you will be drinking coffee with three very fine ladies in a luxury flat, with central heating and lift——'

'Well, thank God, we are all a bit better off than we were twenty years ago,' Else said.

'If only he had waited,' Sonia said. 'He never believed things could be well again one day. I would say to him "Otto, it is dark now but the sun will come again"; "no," he said, "it is all finished." He didn't want to live any more, you see.'

'There were many days I also didn't want to live any more,' Else said. 'After I had sat for ten hours at the back of the shop, sewing my eyes out for Mrs. Davis, and then come home to the furnished room where the bed wasn't made and I couldn't find a shilling for the gas to heat up a tin—I would say to myself, Else, what are you doing here? Father, mother, sisters all gone, why are you still here, finish off now.'

'Who hasn't had such days?' Mr. Lumbik said. 'But then you go to the café, you play a game of chess, you hear a new joke, and everything is well again.' He smiled and somewhere a gold tooth twinkled so merrily, so bravely, that Sonia's heart quite leaped and she thought he is a good man.

Then Werner came home, and he said, 'Oh nice—a coffee-party.'
  'What coffee-party?' Mrs. Gottlob said indignantly. 'It is a birthday party.'
  'Oh my God!' Werner said. He clapped his hand in front of his mouth and looked at his mother with large guilty eyes.
  'So he has forgotten the mother's birthday!' Mrs. Gottlob cried.
  'I thought only husbands forgot birthdays,' Mr. Lumbik said facetiously.
  'What can I say?' Werner said to his mother.
  'No no, what does it matter,' she said quickly.
  'Of course it matters. It matters terribly.' He took both her hands and kissed her cheek with a slightly condescending affection. He was the same height as she was, a handsome boy with thick brown hair and an elegant air.
  'No kissing now!' cried Mrs. Gottlob. 'You are a bad boy and should be smacked.'
  'For one kiss from Werner, I also would forgive him everything,' Else said. Werner stooped down to kiss her cheek, saying, 'How are you, Tante Else?' She shut her eyes in rapture: 'Sonia, why do you have such a son?' Sonia looked on, smiling and proud.
  'Sit down next to the old Gottlob now,' Mrs. Gottlob said, patting the seat beside her, 'and tell her all about your girl-friends.'
  'Which one would you like to hear about?' said Werner, hitching up his well-creased trousers and crossing one leg over the other to display elegant socks. 'There's the blonde, then there's the brunette, and—my favourite—the redhead——'
  'Mine come in only one colour,' said Mr. Lumbik. 'Grey.' But now that Werner was there, nobody listened to him.
  Mrs. Gottlob shook her finger at Werner. 'You can't impress me. For me you will only be little Werner Wolff who comes running down the stairs to his Tante Gottlob's kitchen and says Tante Gottlob, bake a nice cheese-cake for me! Yes yes, now you pretend you have forgotten!' She pinched his cheek, a bit harder than he liked.

'Of course not, how can we ever forget?' Sonia said. She spoke in a hearty, grateful voice, though she would have preferred to forget the years in Mrs. Gottlob's house, the bedsitting room where Otto shivered over the gas-fire and the noise of the other refugee lodgers quarrelling over whose turn it was next to use the bathroom.

'Werner,' Else cried, 'only think where we are going! To St. Moritz!'

'St. Moritz?' He lifted an eyebrow, smiled, looking charming. 'But Mutti must have been there, long ago, with Mama and Papa——'

'He is laughing at me!' Sonia wailed, stretching out a hand as if to defend herself. He caught it and kissed it and continued, 'That must have been the year after Karlsruhe, or was it the year after Bad Ems, when she had that lovely white-lace dress with a flower at her waist and played the piano by moonlight?'

'Well laugh then,' Sonia said, 'but they were beautiful times. Mama's health was delicate——'

'Of course,' Werner put in with mock solemnity.

'Shush now! And just think, Else, twice a year we would go for holidays, once in summer, once in winter, always to some very beautiful place where we lived in big hotels——'

'With red plush carpets and a winter garden and five o'clock tea à l'anglaise,' Werner said.

'All right!' Sonia cried, tossing her head in gay girlish defiance. 'So you laugh—but if we hadn't gone to Marienbad that year, where would you be now?' She looked round triumphantly, having made her forceful point.

Werner clasped his hands and swayed his head like a coy little girl. 'And whom did pretty Sonia Rothenstein, on holiday in Marienbad with Papa and Mama, whom did this well-bred, well-brought-up young lady meet in Marienbad?'

'Werner, today you are terrible,' said Sonia, glowing and happy.

'Yes yes, it is always like that,' Mrs. Gottlob said. 'They make fun of the parents.' She tried to pinch his cheek again, but he got it away in time.

'It is strange,' said Mr. Lumbik, still a few paces behind, 'I have stayed in so many hotels in my life but none has ever had a red plush carpet.'

'Tell more, Werner!' Else said. 'I want to hear the whole romance!'

Her round cheeks were glowing—she had loved romance all her life and now, at spinster fifty, was as eager and waiting for it as ever.

'Else, why do you encourage him?' Sonia protested.

'But I must hear what it is like when a young lady goes on holiday to Marienbad. Perhaps shall we go to Marienbad instead of St. Moritz, Sonia? Who knows what will happen to us—you with your looks and me with my ten thousand? We have a fine chance!' She nudged Sonia's arm and screwed her apple-round face into an expression of bliss.

'I will tell you something else strange,' Mr. Lumbik said. 'You know, I have never been away on holiday.'

This time he was taken notice of: 'Never away on holiday!' cried Sonia and Else; and Mrs. Gottlob said, 'Is there another of your jokes coming, Lumbik?'

'Really, it is quite true. In Vienna, why should I go away on a holiday? My whole life was a holiday.'

'Yes yes, we know what kind of a holiday,' Mrs. Gottlob said.

'I had my friends there, my chess, my girl-friends, the café-houses, the opera—what should I want with a holiday?'

'How silly,' said Else. 'Everyone wants a summer holiday. Every year, when the schools were closed, my father took all six of us to the mountains and we stayed there in a Pension. It was called Pension Katz, I remember it so well.'

'And then afterwards——' He spread his hands and hunched his shoulders. 'A poor refugee tries to make a living, he doesn't make holidays. But all the same, I'm a much-travelled man—Budapest, Prague, Shanghai, Bombay, London, is that bad for one lifetime?'

'What sort of travelling is that?' said Mrs. Gottlob. 'That is only tramping.'

'It is true,' Mr. Lumbik admitted, 'some people travel for pleasure, for—how does one say?'

'For kicks,' Werner said.

'For kicks, thank you, and some travel because—yes, because they are kicked. Is this a bad pun, Mr. Werner? I am being very English now, for I am making puns so that I can apologize for them.'

'There is no need to boast, you there, Lumbik,' Else said. 'We have already heard how you are a British citizen now.'

'Yes, now I am a British citizen and no one can say to me any more "Pack your bags, Lumbik! Time to move on." It is so restful, it is quite bad for my nerves.'

'Well,' Werner said, lazily stretching his legs, 'it's time for me now to do a bit of bag-packing.'

Sonia looked up with large anxious eyes: 'Werner, what for?'

'I'm off to Rome soon,' and seeing his mother's face—'oh come on, darling, I told you I might be going.'

She lowered her eyes and clenched her large white hand with the diamond ring in her lap. Mr. Lumbik looked at her with compassion and tenderness. The others were looking at Werner.

'How exciting, Werner!' Else said. 'Why are you going?'

'There are things doing there—and I'm tired of London. So, pack your bags, Werner! Time to move on.' He smiled his handsome smile at Mr. Lumbik who, however, did not respond.

'So it's not good enough for you with the mother any more,' Mrs. Gottlob scolded. 'This lovely flat, the beautiful meals she cooks for you—you leave it all and say goodbye.'

'What will you do there, Werner?' Sonia said in a small voice.

'I told you—there's lots doing there, films and, oh lots. Don't worry, darling,' he said, trying to sound light and gay, but with an edge of exasperation all the same.

'Of course I don't worry,' she said quickly. There wasn't any need to worry. There was enough money now and he could do in Rome what he did in London—a little film-work here, a little art-photography there, a lot of parties, a lot of girl-friends.

He looked at his watch. 'Heavens, I must fly! I've got a date at seven!' He disappeared into his own room which adjoined his mother's. The moment he had gone, Sonia began to cry.

'Sonia, liebchen!' Else cried. Mrs. Gottlob clicked her tongue and said in her rough way, 'Na, what is this?'

'How silly I am,' Sonia sobbed. Mr. Lumbik looked tactfully at a picture on the wall showing Sonia's parents honeymooning in Biarritz.

'You see, I keep thinking how different it would have been,' Sonia said, wiping at her eyes with her little handkerchief. 'Otto would have retired by now and Werner would be running the factory. He would be Werner Wolff, Director of SIGBO, everybody would know and respect him——'

'So who respects me here!' Else cried. 'For Mrs. Davis I am only her alteration hand, but I know I am still Else Levy, daughter of Oberlehrer Levy of Schweinfurt, so what does it matter to me what Mrs. Davis thinks?'

'But the children,' Sonia said. 'We know who we are, but what does my Werner know, and my Lilo?' At the thought of Lilo, new tears came and she clasped the handkerchief to her eyes. 'My poor Lilo—I have had such a lovely girlhood, such lovely dresses and always parties and dancing-classes and the Konservatorium in Berlin for my piano-playing. And she has had only hard work in the Kibbutz, hard work with her hands, and those horrible white blouses and shorts——' Her voice broke and she said, 'My handkerchief is quite wet.'

'The birthday present!' cried Else, snatching her large leather bag. She fumbled inside and this time came up with three lace-trimmed handkerchiefs. 'Happy birthday, Sonia, it is very good lace.'

'Oh Else, how beautiful,' Sonia said gratefully and immediately used one to wipe her eyes.

'You see, it is a very useful present,' Else said. 'But next time it is only for blowing the nose—no more tears, understand?' she said strictly.

'And I would like to know what cause for tears you have,' Mrs. Gottlob said. 'You are alive, you are healthy, the children are alive and healthy, what else matters?'

'You know sometimes I say to myself,' Mr. Lumbik said, 'Lumbik, what have you achieved in your life? And then I answer myself I have survived, I am still alive, and this is already a success story.'

'For once this Lumbik has also something sensible to say!' Mrs. Gottlob said. 'Be grateful to God for still letting you be here, Mrs. Wolff, and let your Werner and Lilo look after themselves.'

'One thing I have been asking and asking myself,' Mr. Lumbik said. 'For me it is a very serious question: shall I be offered some more *Apfelstrudel* or no?'

'Always thinking of the stomach, Lumbik,' Mrs. Gottlob said. 'Na, perhaps another cup of coffee will also do us good.'

'We will start celebrating the birthday all over again!' Else cried. 'Birthday parties are so nice, and today we'll have two!'

'For such a special birthday child,' Mr. Lumbik said in his tender voice, 'even two isn't enough.'

'Ach Mr. Lumbik,' Sonia said reproachfully, blushing.

He held up one entreating little finger: 'Remember my birthday wish from you!'

'Karl,' she said, pouring coffee with a smiling, averted face.

'This is something new now,' said Mrs. Gottlob, and Else gave Mr. Lumbik's arm a pinch and said, 'You have been making sheep's eyes at Sonia long enough—now it is my turn, I am also a nice young lady.'

'You are all three nice young ladies,' said Mr. Lumbik, and this compliment made Mrs. Gottlob laugh so much that she went quite red and had a cramp in her throat.

When Werner came out of his room, dressed for his date, he found them having a very merry party. 'Well, I'm off,' he said, but no one heard him. Mr. Lumbik was telling a story about his experiences in Shanghai. 'Bye!' called Werner. Only Sonia glanced at him. 'Are you going, Werner?' she said in an absent-minded way as she poured another cup of coffee for Mr. Lumbik. Werner smiled at their preoccupation; he was glad to see them having a good time.

Bernice Rubens

was born in Cardiff, Wales, in 1927 and
was educated at the University College
of South Wales and Monmouthshire. She
has worked as a schoolteacher in Birmingham and a documentary film writer
for the United Nations. Her prizewinning films were generally about marginal
or disadvantaged groups and individuals, themes that have subsequently fed into
her fiction. Rubens is the author of
twenty works of fiction, and *Madame Sou-
satska* (1962), her second novel, has been
made into a feature film. *The Elected Member*
(1969), published in America as *Chosen
People* (1970), won the Booker Prize. The
excerpt here is taken from the beginning
of *The Elected Member*, which is Rubens's
fourth novel. A brilliant linguist, Norman Zweck is turned into a child prodigy
of monstrous proportions by his overpowering mother, Sarah Zweck. He is
elected to bear the burden of his family's
fervent craving for social betterment.

Bernice Rubens

EXCERPT FROM The Elected Member

But at eight o'clock, as was his custom, Rabbi Zweck came into Norman's room to wake him. He hesitated as he saw him crumpled at the foot of the bed, but he did not allow the position to unnerve him. His son had had a restless night, a bad dream maybe; everybody did from time to time. Even when the smell of Dettol hit him, he tried to dismiss its known associations. He tapped his son gently on the shoulder. 'Norman,' he said, 'is eight o'clock.'

Norman responded immediately, and as he raised his head, he saw his father sniffing around the room. He jumped off the bed, wild with gratitude. 'You can smell them?' he said.

Rabbi Zweck turned pale. It was starting all over again. This was the fifth breakdown in less than a year. 'Dettol, I smell,' he shouted angrily. 'That's what I smell. Dettol.' His anxiety exploded inside him with automatic anger at the mad. 'Nothing to smell,' he screamed at him again, 'only Dettol. Get up meshuggana. Breakfast is ready.'

Rabbi Zweck slammed the door. He doubted whether he could survive if Norman collapsed again. He heard the key turn in his son's door and the sound sickened him. As he stood outside the kitchen, he shuddered at his own loneliness, but the sense of his son's isolation behind the locked door, almost killed him.

Norman waited for his father's slippered tread to die away. Then he got down on his knees, and scrambled at a loose floorboard underneath the bed for his day's supply. Wedged under the board was an old cardigan, and from its wrapping he extracted a large bottle. He held it up and looked at its level. He was frightened that it was so low. He had bought the bottle only a week ago, and he panicked at the thought of getting money for more. He poured a handful into his palm, remembering the old days, years ago it seemed, when he'd tentatively taken just one. He stuffed them into his mouth hurriedly, screwing on the cap at the same time. He replaced the floorboard, and got shakily to his feet. Then quietly he unlocked his door and opened it. He heard the whisperings of his father and sister in the kitchen. They thought he was mad. Oh not that. That couldn't happen in their family. He was just being perverse. He was breaking their hearts for want of something better to do. It was not his agony. It was theirs. 'Silver-fish,' he heard his father muttering, 'again with his silver-fish. Whoever heard of fish crawling on a carpet? Water they need. But no. My son's fish, such a clever son I have, on carpets they can live, in pillows, in sheets. Insects, he calls them. Fish are fish,' he yelled at his daughter as if she were denying it. 'On the carpet they should be. Huh.'

'Shut the door, for heaven's sake,' he heard Bella whisper, and he knew that they had begun to conspire against him. He did not bother to wash or dress. He wanted to interrupt their plotting. He threw on a dressing-gown, and tip-toed to the kitchen. Then suddenly he burst open the door. His sister stopped mid-sentence, and began to fuss over his place at the table. As he came over to sit down, she started sniffing at him.

'Can you smell something?' he asked with waning optimism.

'Dettol she smells,' his father jumped in to answer for her.

'They're all over the place,' he threatened them. 'They're on my body too. You must be a couple of blind insensitive bastards if you can't see them.' Although vulgarity always accompanied Norman's hallucinations, Rabbi Zweck could never get used to it. In the rare intervals of his son's sanity, and the accompanying good relations between them both, he forgot the crudity, he forgot the belligerence, and when they appeared, it was always as if for the first time. He looked across at his son, forcing himself to remember the boy's innate gentleness. It was not his son who was rambling on about his silver-fish; it was some devil that possessed him, some evil eye in temporary lodging. And when he saw his son as one possessed, Rabbi Zweck found it easier to forgive him. He stretched out his hand over the table, and covered his son's with his own.

Norman snatched his hand away. 'I'm going to ring up the Health Authorities.'

'Again?' Bella said wearily. 'They came,' she tried to be patient with him, 'they came two months ago. They went through the house with a tooth-comb. They took away samples you gave them. They tested them in laboratories. All they found was carpet fluff and dirt. You had their letter. In black and white. What more d'you want?'

'They were here for five minutes,' Norman shouted at her. 'What did they expect to find in five minutes? They've got to pull up the carpets and do it thoroughly. Don't you bloody well *care*,' he shouted at them, 'that you've got them crawling all over the place?'

'Eat your breakfast,' his father said gently.

Norman tapped his father's arm and grinned at him. 'I bet you've got them all over your body too.'

It was the grin that finished Rabbi Zweck. During his son's breakdown, he often had the feeling that Norman was having him on. That he was just driving him mad for the kick of it. 'You think you are so funny,' he shouted at him, and he slapped Norman's cheek with the back of his ringed hand.

'You'll be sorry for that,' Norman said quietly.

Nobody said anything for a long time. Norman rubbed his stubbled cheek, and Bella watched her father choking back his tears. Once or twice, she saw him open his mouth to speak, but his voice was not yet ready. She heard him mutter an apology. Then he tried again.

'Norman,' he said gently. He hesitated, fearful of what he knew he must ask. 'Norman,' he said again, 'where d'you get them from? How many have you taken?'

'I haven't got any,' Norman shouted. 'I haven't taken any. I haven't taken any for years.'

Rabbi Zweck lost his temper again. 'Who is the murderer who gives them to you? I'll kill him. I'll kill him,' he was crying with the agony of it. 'What for you want to take them?' he begged. 'Stop it with the pills already or I shall go mad.'

'Why d'you have to do it to him?' Bella shouted. 'Can't you see it's killing him? What are you trying to do to us?'

Rabbi Zweck buried his head in his hands. 'Stop it with the bloody pills already,' he said feebly. He hated his own unfamiliar language, but he had used it deliberately as a desperate bid for his son's confidence. 'I'll ring Dr Levy,' he said, getting up.

'You keep that bastard out of this house,' Norman said. 'I'm not having him here. What's he know about anything, that tit. You bring him here, and I'll kill him.' He pushed his unfinished breakfast away from him, and strode out of the room. They waited, listening, until they heard his key turn in the door.

'Poor, poor boy,' Rabbi Zweck muttered, and he went to the telephone.

'Dr Levy?'

'Rabbi Zweck,' the doctor said. He recognised the voice and he knew what it wanted. The calls were getting more frequent.

'It's silver-fish again,' the Rabbi said, and he hated the contempt for his son that he heard in his own voice.

'I'll come right away.'

Rabbi Zweck put down the phone. He was shivering with his son's fear. He wished to God he could see them like his son saw them, that they could go into madness together, hand in hand. It was his son's loneliness that stabbed him like a knife, his yellow-faced boy, haggard with the terror of his imaginings, no doubt at this moment sitting crouched on his infested floor, trapping his evidence. 'I'll tell him I can see them,' the Rabbi said to himself. 'Perhaps he'll stop the joke already.'

He tapped on Norman's door. 'Norman,' he called.

'What d'you want?'

'Norman,' he repeated softly. 'They still there? I should have another look?'

There was a silent suspicion behind the door.

'I should have another look?' Rabbi Zweck pleaded.

The key turned in the lock and the door opened gingerly. It was dark in the room. The curtains were drawn, and books held them down at each corner to block out the light.

'You've got to be very quiet,' Norman whispered.

His father watched his son's drawn face and the black eyes that swelled out of it. The dark and the whisperings made him ashamed and he wondered what God must think of his behaviour. He hoped He wasn't misled by it. Who was He punishing anyway, he thought, himself, or his son.

'Stand by the fire-place,' Norman was saying. 'Be quiet. You'll see plenty, if you just wait.'

But Rabbi Zweck was prepared to see without waiting. 'I can see them,' he whispered, staring at the empty carpet. He raised himself on his toes, excitedly. 'My, my,' he marvelled, 'so many, like an army they are.' He looked at his son for his gratitude.

'You think I'm mad, don't you?' Norman said quietly. 'Look here,' he opened a drawer. Inside, wedged in the corner, was a glass jar, with a few leaves that rested on red carpet fluff on the bottom. Opposite the jar was a magnifying mirror. 'Look in that mirror,' Norman said, 'you'll see them all right.'

'Leaves I see,' Rabbi Zweck said bewildered.

'I'm feeding them,' Norman laughed.

He wanted to hit his son again, but instead, he left the room quietly.

'Don't come back,' Norman almost sobbed after him. 'Leave me alone. Just leave me alone.'

The key turned again in the door, and Rabbi Zweck went back to the kitchen. 'Go down, open the shop,' he said. 'Is already nine o'clock.'

As she passed him, Bella put her hand on his shoulder. 'Don't worry,' she said, 'he'll be over it soon.'

'And then again it starts.' He clutched at her arm. ' We must find them,' he said desperately. 'We must get him out of that room and you must find them. They're there. He's getting them from someone. If ever I lay my hands on him, I'll . . . You haven't done the room thoroughly enough,' he shouted at her. He bit his lip to stem the tears. 'Go, go,' he said quickly, 'open the shop. On top of everything I should lose the business too.'

He caught sight of her white ankle-socks as she left the room. She was forty, almost, his Bella, and still in her girlhood socks. But that was another agony. He daren't give any thought to that one. He sniffed his tears away and waited for the doctor.

When the bell rang, he heard Norman shout, 'If that's that shit Levy, tell him to piss off.'

Rabbi Zweck knew that Dr Levy must have heard through the door and he began apologising on his son's behalf as he let the doctor in.

'Don't worry,' Dr Levy said, 'it's natural. Can we go into the kitchen?' he whispered. He knew Norman would be listening by his door, and he didn't want to be overheard. He followed Rabbi Zweck into the kitchen and sat at the table. He had become familiar with the room. The copper ladle that hung over the kitchen sink was always at the same angle and with the same high polish. In the cup of lemon tea that Rabbi Zweck put before him, he saw the familiar and now fading rose pattern that lined the cup. He was not their official family doctor. Dr Levy was a psychiatrist, but he was a long-standing friend of the Zweck family. As a friend, he had been in on Mrs Zweck's dying, sitting on the same chair by the kitchen table, drinking tea out of a less faded rose-patterned cup. Then he had sat with Rabbi Zweck much as he was doing now, comforting him, the truth exposed between them. 'It's only a matter of time,' he had told the Rabbi then, 'and the sooner, the better for you all.' Meanwhile, in the vast seven-footer, Mrs Zweck wondered why she was taking so long to recover from her operation. 'It takes longer when you're older,' the doctor had told her. 'Another month or so and you'll be up and about.' So she lay there, having patience, fingering the holiday brochure that Rabbi Zweck had bought her, to help her decide where to convalesce. Now, it was Norman, on the same bed, with a different illusion, but an illusion all the same, while between his father and Dr Levy in the kitchen, straddled the same uneasy truth.

'How long has he been like this?' Dr Levy asked.

'How should I know,' Rabbi Zweck said helplessly. 'For many days now he doesn't eat. Breakfast he has, a big breakfast, and afterwards, nothing.'

'Has he been in the shop?'

'He goes downstairs. He sits. He does nothing, Bella says. And always so rude, I'm ashamed for my customers. If only I knew where he got them. If only . . . '

'Rabbi Zweck,' the doctor said gently, 'even if you found where he was getting them, it would be of no use. He'd find another source. They're all the same, these addicts. They're so cunning. Come what may, they'll find somewhere to get it. It's expensive of course. Does he have so much money?'

Rabbi Zweck was silent. Then without looking at Doctor Levy, he stretched his hand towards him over the table. 'Doctor,' he said, 'I'm ashamed, but you're a doctor, and is confidence what I tell you.' Dr Levy patted the Rabbi's hand.

'He's stealing it?' he said.

Rabbi Zweck hung his head. 'My own son,' he whispered, 'a *ganuf*, and from his father's money. The till,' he said, 'last week, my Bella is missing fifteen pounds. What can I do? Every minute I can't be with him.' Dr Levy opened his black case. 'We must get him better, at least over this bout, then we must try again to persuade him to go to hospital. It's the only way. Six months, a year, away from the drug. He might get over it.'

'I've tried,' the Rabbi said, 'Bella's tried. Each time he gets over it, he says he'll stop it. Then he starts again. What will become of him?'

'Let's get him over this lot first,' the doctor said businesslike.

Rabbi Zweck squeezed the doctor's hand. 'I am thinking,' he said, 'perhaps *takka* is silver-fish in his room. Perhaps when they come from the cleaning people, they don't look so thoroughly. Like Norman said, a real spring-clean we should have. So we should find them and take them away.' He looked at Dr Levy pleadingly.

'You will drive yourself mad,' Dr Levy whispered. 'You are trying to defend him at the risk of your own sanity. There is nothing in his room. You know it as well as I. Listen Rabbi, it's very simple.' Dr Levy leaned forward and spoke very slowly with the patience of one who has explained the same situation over and over again. 'When he started to take the drugs, they gave him what they call, a kick. You understand?'

'What should I know from a kick,' Rabbi Zweck said wearily. At each of Norman's breakdowns, and at each explanation, he refused to acknowledge that the diagnosis had anything to do with his son. 'Doctors' talk,' he muttered to himself. 'A real spring-clean Bella will give,' he said.

'When Norman started,' Dr Levy went on, ignoring the interruption, 'it took just one tablet to make him feel good. Then as time went on, in order to get the same effect, he had to take more, and more and more. Until, like now, he's taking them by the handful. Now these drugs are dangerous. If you take enough of them, you begin to see things, things that other people don't see. Snakes, elephants, pins, or like Norman, silver-fish. He sees them all right, but he's hallucinating. They're not there, Rabbi Zweck,' Dr Levy said firmly, 'no matter how much he convinces you. You know they're not there, don't you.'

Rabbi Zweck sighed. Sometimes he hated Dr Levy. 'How are *you* so sure they're not there?' he mumbled.

Dr Levy took a small tablet out of the box. 'I won't go in and see him,' he said. 'It will only make him worse. Persuade him to join you and Bella for some coffee during the morning, and crush this into the sugar. Let Bella do it. It will dissolve and with luck he won't taste it. If he drinks the whole cup, he'll sleep for a few hours and I'll come over later and give him an injection. Same as before. We'll give him deep sedation for a fortnight. Like last time.'

'And the time before that,' the Rabbi put in. 'And the next time.'

'Let's cross this hurdle, shall we, and afterwards we'll try to talk to him. All of us. It's you I'm worried about, Rabbi. More than Norman,' Dr Levy said. 'You're letting it kill you.'

'You want I should dance?' Rabbi Zweck muttered.

'Remember the times when he's all right. In between the bouts. These times are time to live for and look forward to. The times when he's a good son to you.'

'They're not so often, these times. Not any more,' Rabbi Zweck said. He banged his fist on the table in sudden anger. 'I should only find the murderer who sells them to him.'

'Walk me downstairs to the shop,' the doctor said gently. 'You can sell me some cigarettes.'

Rabbi Zweck stopped at his son's door. 'Norman,' he called.

'You can tell Dr Levy from me,' Norman shouted, 'he's a psychiatrist like the cat's psychiatrist, and he can take his injections to hell. There's nothing the matter with me,' he yelled, half-sobbing. 'It's you and your lot. You're mad, the lot of you. Just leave me alone.'

'I'm going downstairs to the shop,' his father said evenly. 'Soon I'll come back. We'll have a tea together, huh. You, me and Bella.'

'I don't want any family conferences,' Norman said. 'Just leave me alone.'

Dr Levy put his arm round Rabbi Zweck's shoulder and led him downstairs to the shop.

An hour later Bella and her father left the shop in charge of the assistant and returned to the flat. They whispered together in the kitchen as Bella ground the white pill into the sugar at the bottom of the glass. Then she covered the mixture with a piece of lemon.

'It'll be better once he's sleeping, Poppa. We'll have to ask Auntie Sadie to come over again and look after him. Shall I phone her?'

'This is already the sixth time.'

'She loves it. You know she does. I'll phone her from downstairs.'

'Wait. Wait till he sleeps,' her father said. 'Then we'll see.'

The tea was ready and they stared at each other, neither of them willing to call Norman.

'You should tell him his tea's ready,' Rabbi Zweck said.

'You tell him. He won't listen to me. All right,' she said, seeing him hesitate, 'I'll tell him.'

She shouted through the passage, 'Norman, your tea's ready.'

'Norman, your tea's ready,' he mimicked her.

'You want your tea or don't you?' she said angrily.

'You want your tea or don't you,' came from behind the door.

Bella went back to the kitchen. 'I can't get anywhere with him,' she said. Rabbi Zweck got up wearily and went down the corridor. 'Norman,' he called gently. 'You want tea?'

'I told you. I don't want a family conference. You'll have Auntie Sadie here next in a white coat pulling a Florence Nightingale on me.'

'You want it in your room?' his father said timidly.

'Put it outside the door.'

'Please,' Bella prompted from the kitchen. She found it hard to treat him as an invalid. She wanted to punish him for what he was doing to her father. To her too, for he had already done enough to her. She looked down at her feet. Of course, she didn't have to go on wearing those white ankle-socks. But it was habit by now. She would have to start being another person if she wore anything else. That was all his fault too. She resented the feeling of obligation she felt for him. They had nothing in common; all they shared were the same parents, the same miserable childhood, and the same mutual embarrassment. She tried not to wish him dead.

Rabbi Zweck picked up Norman's cup from the table. 'This one?' he said. He gave it an extra stir and carried it to his son's door. 'It's outside, Norman,' he said. 'Careful, is hot.'

He returned to the kitchen where they both sat and waited. They heard Norman's door open and close again. Rabbi Zweck peeped out and saw that the cup had gone. 'Thank God,' he said, 'at least he'll drink it.' But hardly had Rabbi Zweck sat down again than they heard Norman open his door. 'What d'you think I am?' he was yelling. 'D'you think I can't taste it?' He stormed into the kitchen, and put the cup on the table. 'What are you trying to do? Murder me?'

'What, what?' Rabbi Zweck mumbled, 'what's the matter?'

'You've put something in my tea,' Norman said. 'Go on, taste it.'

'There's nothing in your tea,' Bella said coldly. 'We've all got the same. It all came out of the same pot.'

'Is the lemon perhaps too bitter?' Rabbi Zweck tried. Deception was not his forte.

'Lemon, my arse,' Norman said. 'Go on then, if you're so sure there's nothing in it, *you* drink it.' He pushed the cup towards his father.

Rabbi Zweck had not envisaged this eventuality. But he had no alternative. He picked up the cup gingerly and took as small a sip as was possible without raising his son's suspicions. 'Is all right,' he said. 'Perhaps more sugar you need.'

'Drink some more,' Norman ordered, 'you'll taste it.'

The Rabbi raised his cup again to his lips, while Norman stood over him measuring his dose. 'More, more,' he kept saying, until his father had drained half the cup.

'Is all right,' he said again.

'You taste it then,' Norman pushed the cup over to Bella.

Bella was horrified to discover how much her father had drunk.

'Go on,' Norman said, as he saw her hesitate. 'Poison yourself a little.'

She took a mouthful. It had an undeniably bitter taste. Dr Levy must have been crazy to think that Norman, with his gourmet taste in drugs, would not have noticed it. She hated Dr Levy. She hated everybody for all they'd done to her. She hated her sister Esther for marrying and opting out of the responsibility. She hated Norman for what he was doing to all of them, and even her father because of the love she could not deny him. 'There's nothing wrong with it,' she said, 'it's your imagination. Like your silver-fish.'

She hated herself for saying it. Why couldn't she pretend her brother had jaundice, or measles, or rheumatism, or any other respectable talkable-of malady. She looked at the black stubble that shadowed his jaw and the sallow shadings on his cheeks. He looked ill, terribly ill. Wasn't that enough for her?

Norman pushed the cup back to his father. 'Go on, taste it,' he said petulantly, 'you know there's something in it.'

Rabbi Zweck took another dutiful mouthful, and pronounced his verdict. 'Nothing,' he said. He already felt drowsy and he put his hand to his forehead.

'Leave him alone, can't you,' Bella said.

'Well, you taste it again then,' he sulked. 'If anyone's going to croak in this house, it's not going to be me.' He stood over her while she drank. After a mouthful, Bella managed to put the cup down.

'Well,' he said, standing at the door, 'I wish you long life, both of you.' Bella heard him stamp back into his room and lock the door behind him.

'What now?' she said helplessly. Her father slipped his head over the table. She shook him gently, but he was fast asleep. She sat beside him wondering how to shoulder the responsibility alone. She couldn't forget the look on her brother's face as he stood over her watching her drink. If only she had not been his sister, she could have put her arm round him and believed in him for his sake. She could even have loved him. But blood was a buffer to that kind of loving, the unselfish kind. She had loved him once and he, her, when they were both children and she legitimately in those white socks. Neither had mentioned it since, no-one had ever shared their secret, 'though God knows, the thought occurred to her, Dr Levy must have got it out of him by now. She got up to clear the table, but felt her knees give way beneath her. She didn't try to fight it, she wanted to opt out of it all for a while. She even hoped she'd sleep for ever. She slumped back onto her chair and surrendered to the stupor that gradually overcame her.

Norman pushed the sideboard against the door and squatted on the floor. Even though he had drawn his curtains, the light that insisted through the thin material, had driven his companions away. He decided he would buy some thick velvet curtains, lined with heavy black, so that it would be night in his room always with his crawling proof around him. It was in the daylight and in his undeniable lack of company, that the terrifying question of his sanity nagged at him. Even to ask it of himself was an admission that his father and sister had a case to argue. No, he must not on any account allow that question, but with what force, in the naked daylight, could he oust it from him? He sat there, unarmed, the question surrounding him. It was only a matter of time before it would gently invade his privacy. Am I mad? Are there really silver-fish? If there are, where are they now? It's Bella fault that she's given me these curtains. They scurry away from the light. Why did she not believe him? Nor his father? What particular madness did they have that they were so blind to his sanity? And if they couldn't see them, why should it then outrage him? Now the questions had had their fill and were satisfied, and they left him wounded and alone, waiting through the long day for the night to come and gather his forces.

He heard the door bell ring. They were coming to fetch him. It was that clot Levy with his needle coming to put him to sleep, like last time. He leapt up and moved the chest of drawers against the door. He only wanted to hold out till nightfall when more evidence would be available. Then he would let them in, all of them. 'Then we'll see who's mad,' he said to himself. He listened, but no-one seemed to be answering the door. He hadn't heard anyone go out, so his father and sister must still be in the flat. He hoped that the caller, whoever it was, would go away, but the bell rang again, longer this time, and repeatedly. He waited. In between rings, he heard the silence in the flat. They had slipped out without his hearing. Where had they gone? Had they gone to fetch someone to take him away? And was that someone already at the door? He heard the letter-box flap. 'Miss Zweck?' a high-pitched voice hissed through the hall. It was Terry, the assistant in the shop. He was safe, little too, and frail. Norman moved the sideboard away and opened his door. 'What d'you want?' he called through the hall. 'Miss Zweck,' Terry said. 'She hasn't come back to the shop. It's my lunch hour.'

'She's not here,' Norman said. 'You'll have to go downstairs and wait for her. Sorry,' he added. He felt very tender towards the boy, as the only person in his orbit who did not think he was mad. Terry had seen them. One night after the shop had closed, and his father and sister were out, Terry had come to his room and seen them. He had stood riveted to the carpet, terrified, his hand clutching the door to run away from them. 'I can't stand it,' he said eventually. Norman let him go, grateful for his understanding.

'Can't *you* come down?' Terry said timidly.

'I can't. I'm trying to get rid of the things in my room.'

He heard Terry's steps down the stone stairway, taking them two by two, and landing on the stone floor at the foot of the stairs.

Norman stood in the empty hall. He wondered where they had gone. He heard a faint breathing noise, and with overwhelming joy, he knew they had come back to his room. But the noise grew faint as he entered. Then he heard it behind him, echoing through the hall. He leaned against his door, taking in the full meaning of this new development. Without doubt they were in there, in complete and total invasion of the whole flat. He was satisfied. Now they would *have* to listen to him, because they were everywhere. He was vindicated. But he wouldn't revenge himself on them. He would be gentle and tolerant, and forgive them their accusations. He longed for his father and sister to come back. He opened his bedroom door wide, and drew his curtains. He no longer needed his privacy. He walked through the hall towards the kitchen. He noticed how the noise increased, but it did not trouble him. The kitchen was the obvious place for them to congregate in a mass. He himself had seen them there before; in fact, there were few places he didn't see them, if he wished to look. But now they had grown tired of being ignored, and they had come to the kitchen in armies, for recognition. He reached the kitchen door. It was ajar and the noise by now was thunderous. He hesitated with joy, postponing the final confirmation of what he knew would be his salvation. Then he threw the door open wide.

His father sat there, slumped over the table. Snoring. His father was snoring. That was all. Even Norman, to whom sounds of life and death and the imagination had become so confused, even he had to equate the noise with his sleeping father. Bella, at his side, contributed a humble descant to her father's theme. What an ugly pair they are, he thought. He looked at Bella's white-socked feet under the table, and the coarse tufts of black hair that the elastic had bunched around the rim. Everyone blamed him for those socks, but Christ, she didn't have to go on wearing them. He avoided looking at her face. He had loved her once, because it was forbidden. Really, he reflected, the only time in his life he had loved. He looked quickly at his father. His skull cap had slipped over onto one ear, and the visible half of his head was veined like an old woman's hand. This was the man who had told him that the sea had parted for the Jews, the man who believed in miracles, the man who believed in all good men except his own son. Norman felt pity for him, but he stood his ground. He would not allow himself to be moved, neither by his father's old head nor his sister's white socks. He had to go on hating them, until they would begin to understand. He took his stand between the two of them, and opening his mouth, he let out a long piercing scream. They moved simultaneously, the one towards the other, as if in half-sleep, sensing disaster, and seeking protection. Bella was the first to open her eyes, but she quickly closed them again, as if to obliterate the split-second reality she had faced. Rabbi Zweck opened his eyes slowly, moaned, and kept them open. His sleep had been profound, but it had embraced all the while the picture of his son's tragedy. So he looked at Norman and adjusted quickly, because not for a second in his sleep had he dismissed him. Bella opened her eyes again and was compelled to come to terms with the awakening. 'The tea,' she said to herself, that he had survived, her mad brother, with his silver-fish. And his sister Esther, married and out of it all, and their mother dead, and him killing their father with his madness. She stood up and put her arm on her father's shoulder. 'What shall we do?' she said helplessly.

'What time is it?' Rabbi Zweck asked.

'It's just two.'

'Then what about Terry's lunch?' he said. He grasped at the problem as something concrete. At least it was a problem that could be solved, and quickly. 'Go, look after the shop,' he said to Bella.

'What about *him*?' Bella said. She gave him the anonymity of a lunatic. 'What are we going to do about him?' Her anger and hatred were consuming her.

'Don't worry about me,' Norman said, 'I'm going to burn up my carpet and get rid of them.' He smiled at her innocently.

'Oh God,' she said, collapsing onto a chair, 'how much more must we take? You're wrong,' she screamed at him suddenly, 'there are no insects in this flat. You're wrong, you're wrong,' she shouted. 'Madmen are always wrong.'

Norman went back to his room. He leaned against the keyhole and listened for the next move. After a while, he heard Bella walking across the hall and out of the door, and the ring on the telephone as his father began to dial. He moved away from the door. His father was calling Dr Levy; they would go through it all again. He became suddenly weary of the whole situation. 'It would be so much easier if I were really mad,' he said to himself. 'Then they would make me better and I wouldn't see them any more.' He toyed with the idea of pretending he was mad, so that they could 'cure' him, and then after the 'cure', he would still see them, and maybe then they would believe him. But he couldn't pretend he was mad. 'Only fringe mad-men can fake lunacy,' he said to himself. 'I could never take them in. Why, even that clot Levy would see through me. Straight away. He thinks I'm mad, but only as long as I'm sane. He's got to think that. It's his living. If old Levy ever thought I was sane, I'd really get worried.' He smiled to himself. They were all mad, all of them, and with this supreme conviction, he locked his door.

His father was still on the telephone, but he did not want to listen. He didn't want to be forced into making plans. Deep inside him, he felt the terrible pre-pain of surrender, that he had felt a few months ago, when Dr Levy's needle had jabbed his arm. 'This time,' he said aloud, 'I must resist them. I'm right, I'm right,' he screeched into himself, and he heard the echo of his sister's contrary accusation.

He squatted on the floor and tried not to think of what they would do to him. After a time, he heard the letter-box rattle and he waited for his father to open the door.

'Does Norman Zweck live here?' he heard a man's voice say, and somehow or other he knew that the man was carrying documents in his hand.

There were two of them, clad in black and bureaucracy, with identical brown briefcases, and Rabbi Zweck let them in. Like two undertakers, they could well have carried a tape-measure.

'Could we go somewhere and talk,' one of the doctors enquired, looking around the hall for a convenient corner.

'In the kitchen,' Rabbi Zweck said tonelessly, and the two men followed him. They sat down at the table and came to the point straight away. 'Dr Levy has told us the position,' one of them said. 'You understand of course, that it is necessary for us to see your son. We have to recommend that he is suitable for hospital treatment. It's the law, you know,' he added gently.

'Yes, it's the law,' Rabbi Zweck repeated. He could not understand why he had let these two men into the flat. He had invited them in to certify his son. He was helping them to put his boy away. He was agreeing with them that his son was mad. 'But,' he started to protest, realising the magnitude of the situation, 'is absolute necessary he should go to the hospital? Is only a little mad, my son,' he pleaded. 'I'll tell him he shouldn't take the pills any more, and he'll get better. I promise you,' he was pleading with them. 'I promise you, on my poor wife's memory, *olav hasholem.*' (What did these *goyim* know of such things?) 'He's not mad,' he protested, 'my son. Is tired he is a little. Not much sleep he's had, is confused in his mind a little. I also, when I'm tired, a little bit *zemischt* I am.' He heard the utter feebleness of his argument, and he resented that he should have to beg anybody for his son's sanity. He got up quickly from his chair. 'Please go,' he said to them. 'Thank you for coming. I'm sorry to put you to inconvenience. Is raining outside,' he added, with painful irrelevancy.

The doorbell rang again, and one of the men made to go to the door, while the other restrained Rabbi Zweck from moving. Rabbi Zweck brushed his arm away. 'In my own house,' he said quietly, 'I can answer my own door.' But he did not try to leave the room. Instinctively he felt that there would be a battle in the hall, as losing a battle as the one he was trying to ignore in the kitchen. He waited for the doctor to return. With him came another man, Mr Angus, as he was introduced, with the terrifying appendage of Mental Health Officer. Mr Angus put out his hand to Rabbi Zweck, and squeezed it with obscene professional understanding. Rabbi Zweck backed away and slumped weakly on his chair. 'Is raining outside,' he said again.

The two doctors left the room. Mr Angus shut the door after them, and drew his chair to Rabbi Zweck's side. He put his arm on his shoulder, and knew that he could say nothing. It was never easy, his job, but dealing with the next-of-kin was the worst part of it.

Some of his colleagues, he knew, revelled in the *Schadenfreude* of their work, but he was different. And he promised himself, once again, as he had done so often in the last ten years, that he would find himself some other kind of work. They sat together and there was nothing to do but listen to the noises outside Norman's door, and as they grew louder, Mr Angus moved his chair closer to the old man's, and gently stroked his arm.

'Get out,' Norman was yelling. 'What right have you to come into my room?'

'Open the door,' the doctor said gently. 'We just want to talk to you. You don't want us to force the door, do you? Now be a good boy.'

It was the word 'boy' that triggered off Rabbi Zweck's tears. He was a grown man, his son, and you called a grown man 'boy' only if you had contempt for him. 'He's not mad, is he, my son?' he whispered to Mr Angus. Mr Angus squeezed his arm. 'This is what's best for him. I promise you. It'll only be a few weeks, and he'll be out again. It'll all be over,' he said. He refrained from adding, 'until the next time'. He had dealt with lots of similar patients. He had comforted the stunned parents, or the weeping wives and children. By standing in front of doors, and wooing them with gentle lies, he had sincerely tried to camouflage the hideous paraphernalia of putting people away. It wasn't so bad when they went voluntarily. It was when they resisted, like this one was doing. That was the hell of it, not for the patient himself, but for those who were watching and could not bear it. 'When the doctors have seen him,' he said, 'I'll talk to him. I'll do what I can.'

There were so many things that Rabbi Zweck wanted to know. How would they force him to go? Would they use a strait-jacket? Would there be policemen at the door? Would he go in a white ambulance? And what kind of place was he going to? And was it full of madmen, of real *meshu-goyim*, not like his son who was going to be better soon? But he daren't ask any of these questions. He did not want to acknowledge the situation. But it screamed at him from outside the door. A large resounding kick and 'We'll have to get the police if you don't let us in'.

'Tell them to go away,' Rabbi Zweck pleaded. 'Or let me talk to him.' He half rose to go to Norman's door. Norman would never forgive him. He sat down again and put his hands over his face, and rocking gently to and fro, with praying and weeping, he stilled himself into a semblance of calm. He heard Norman's door suddenly open, and again he started weeping at his son's surrender. He heard the doctors go inside, and shut the door behind them.

'He's better now—he'll be all right now,' he said to Mr Angus. 'They've given him a shock and he's better. It's just he needed someone to teach him a lesson. Go home now, all of you.' He was offering a last-minute alibi, but his son had already confessed. Rabbi Zweck felt Mr Angus' hand leave his arm, and he knew he was alone in the kitchen.

He didn't want to think of what was happening in Norman's room. He couldn't even understand that it had anything to do with him. He was only conscious that it was raining outside, with a thin endless drizzle. He heard two men walk through the hall and out of the front door. He was glad they hadn't come to say goodbye to him. He just hoped they'd brought their umbrellas. He heard murmurings from Norman's room, and he recalled the same quality of murmuring from the dying-bed of his wife, and he sensed that a similar catastrophe awaited him.

'Papa,' Norman called from his room. His voice was desperate and imploring like a little boy's. It was a cry for immediate help and protection. It was a cry of physical pain, and Rabbi Zweck responded. Whatever had happened to his son, he would kiss it better, and tell him a story to keep his mind off the pain. He hurried to Norman's room. Mr Angus was sitting on the bed, looking at Norman helplessly.

'Papa,' Norman pleaded as his father came in. 'Tell this man to go away. People come here, strangers, and they come into my room, and they want to take me away. I haven't done anything Papa, tell them I'm all right. Don't let them take me away.'

The doorbell rang, and Mr Angus went out quickly to open the door.

'They've come for me,' Norman said. 'Papa, Papa,' he beseeched him, 'don't let them take me.'

Rabbi Zweck held him in his arms. 'It's only for you to get better,' he said gently. 'I'll come with you,' he said, 'we'll go together.'

'No, no,' Norman screamed. He tore himself away from his

father and looked at him in utter bewilderment. 'Papa?' he said again, as if to question his father's right to a son. 'You . . . you can't.' He opened his eyes wide in sheer incredulity. He stared at his father without hate, without bitterness, only with complete and innocent refusal to believe what his father had said. It was a look that Rabbi Zweck would shoulder to his grave.

'Come along now.' A new figure, another stranger, this time in uniform, came into Norman's room. 'Let's go quietly, shall we,' it said. 'We don't want any fuss.'

'Look at them,' Norman was saying, 'they're taking me away, and you just stand there and don't say a word. Papa,' he said tenderly, 'what's the matter with you? Aren't you well? D'you want to go to bed? Shall I look after you?'

As he was talking, the uniformed stranger came up behind him and motioned Mr Angus to stand by his side. But Norman didn't feel their movement. 'He's not well,' he said to them without looking up. 'I must put him to bed and call the doctor.'

Rabbi Zweck looked into Norman's face and shuddered at the unwitting blackmail of his son's love and concern. Then, flinging his frail arms around him, he clutched him with a strength that Norman remembered from his mother's dying embrace. 'My father must be dying,' he said to the stranger.

'Come along now,' the man said, taking his arm.

'You'll need your mackintosh,' Rabbi Zweck sobbed. 'Is raining.'

Mr Angus and the stranger took Norman on either side, urging him to go along.

'Leave me alone,' Norman shouted. 'I've got to stay home and look after my father.'

The men were losing patience and they grabbed him and dragged him barefoot to the door. Rabbi Zweck saw his son's empty shoes on the floor. 'Put your shoes on, put your shoes on,' he sobbed. He couldn't bear to see them there, empty. The stranger picked up the shoes and kicked them towards Norman's feet. Norman slid into them helplessly, his bare shiny heels sitting on the turned-down leather.

Rabbi Zweck followed them downstairs. From the back his son looked suddenly very old, his black thinning hair sticking out on each side, his dressing-gown hitched up by the men's grips, his pyjama-legs creased up to his knee. He was astonished to notice the amount of hair on his son's legs. And possibly for the first time in his life, he acknowledged his son as a grown man, an old man even, old enough, he thought, to die from natural causes.

There were two flights of stairs to the ground floor and into the back entrance of Rabbi Zweck's little grocer's shop and general store, which was the only way out into the street. Norman was struggling between the one man's grasp and the other's, but he said nothing, sickened by the injustice of it all. They reached the narrow entrance to the shop. Norman's dressing-gown cord trailed on the floor. Rabbi Zweck bent down and picked it up tenderly, as if he were carrying a bride's train. Folding the end in front of him, he followed the group into the shop.

Bella was serving a customer, while a group of women waited at the counter. Bella stared at the little procession. She knew she would have to raise part of the counter for them to get through, but she too wanted no part in his going, and dared not let Norman see her contribution. But the customer who stood by the counter division, an unaccusable bystander, lifted the wood partition, and Bella inwardly blessed her for it. 'Must you go too?' she said to her father. Neither of them were concerned about the customers in the shop.

'Is much harder to stay,' Rabbi Zweck said.

The three of them had reached the door, and Norman, until now silent, swung round suddenly and faced the customers in the shop. 'I've got witnesses,' he shouted triumphantly, 'all of you, you're witnesses they're taking me away. They're putting me in a loony bin,' he screamed, horrified as the full meaning of his words struck him. 'You'll be sorry,' he shouted to no-one in particular. 'I'll sue you, all of you. There'll be damages.'

Mr Angus and the stranger pulled him into the street, and Rabbi Zweck followed, still holding the cord of his son's dressing-gown. At the door of his shop, he turned to his customers. 'I'm sorry you should be embarrassed,' he whispered.

Bella stared after them. She saw the men handle her brother into the back of a black car, and then the stooped black back of her father as he stumbled in after them. She watched the car out of sight, then she turned back to her customers. 'It's raining outside,' she said.

Emanuel Litvinoff

was born in London in 1915 and from a
young age worked in tailoring, cabinet
making, and the fur trade. He served in the
British army during the Second World
War and became known as a war poet. Litvinoff is the author of six novels and
three collections of poetry and the editor
of the *Penguin Book of Jewish Short Stories*
(1979) and the journal *Jews in Eastern Europe;*
he also has had fifteen television plays
performed. He is best known for his fictionalized memoir *Journey through a Small
Planet* (1972), which has remained in print
since publication. The excerpt here is a
self-contained chapter from his memoir
which illustrates, with poetic economy,
Litvinoff's folkish storytelling. 'Fanya'
encompasses the history of Yiddish theater, the growth of an adolescent East End
boy, and the differential fate of men and
women in London's poorest districts in the
1920s and 1930s.

Emanuel Litvinoff

Fanya

When I was growing up you could spend three hours in the gallery of a picture palace for fourpence and see two terrific all-star features. The living theatre couldn't compete: no wonder everyone said it was dying. Then Herschel Rosenheim broke Fanya Ziegelbaum's heart when the New York Yiddish troupe played a season at the Whitechapel Pavilion, and because I tasted a drop of that bitterness Rosenheim's Hamlet remained with me long after I'd forgotten *The Four Horsemen of the Apocalypse* or who played Al Jolson's sonny boy in *The Jazz Singer*.

Fanya first came to work for us when she was fourteen, a scraggy brown-faced orphan whose stockings wrinkled on her matchstick legs. She smelled of dirty knickers and aroused all my nine-year-old mistrust of girls. My mother took her as an apprentice because it was a *mitzvah*. She lived with a stingy aunt in a tall barrack-like building in one of the worst streets off Commercial Road. The aunt economised on Fanya's food to stuff the mouths of her own four fat children. She and her husband made a living out of watching corpses, a ritual requirement, augmenting their income by selling the deceaseds' clothes to a second-hand dealer with whom they had an arrangement. Such an environment could have a dreadful effect on a young girl, but Fanya had the remedy in her own hands. Quick to pick up the essentials of dressmaking, after a year or so she went up West with my mother's blessing to earn good money in the high-class trade. Still, she was always ready to help out with a big wedding order or in other emergencies, and so never became a stranger.

Every time she returned skinny Fanya seemed to grow plumper, particularly in the tender region of the chest and behind, where the flesh curved like twin full moons. She'd left her aunt to lodge with a young widow, a saleslady in the cosmetics trade who knew a lot

about being smart. As a result, the change in Fanya became startling.
She walked around in West End dresses copied from ladies maga-
zines and stitched by her own hand. Her mouth pouted kissprufe
lipstick the colour of raspberry jam. She scented her breath with
cachous and did something to her eyes to make them large and
brilliant. In short, she'd suddenly turned into a beauty, and although
not everybody approved—some of the women said she'd made
herself look common—most people agreed that such a picture as
Fanya was sure to find a marvellous boy, maybe even with his own
business. I hoped so too because she was one of the first girls I
really loved.

The summer my mother was pregnant with David, Uncle Solly's
third child, Fanya came over to help out most evenings. She was a
stimulating influence. Abie, nearly fifteen and rather cocky because
his wages were a pound a week, hung around her speaking in a
gruff voice and blowing smoke from Player's Weights through his
nostrils. Uncle Solly practically stopped going to boxing or the dog-
track. He talked restlessly of old times in South Africa before he
was married, or even further back in the trenches, pulling up his
trouser-leg to show us his shrapnel wounds and letting Fanya feel
the metal under the skin. As for my mother, for whom things were
going well at the time, she sang as she treadled the sewing machine,
remembered Odessa, spoke seriously with Fanya about love, and
occasionally turned towards Solly with the eyes of a young girl.

Late one night, about eleven o'clock, I was detailed to walk Fanya
home. Her route led under the railway arch where goyim were supposed to lurk maddened with drink and lust. My mother wouldn't
let her go alone, nor with my stepfather, nor with Abie, for that
matter. Not that she didn't trust them exactly, but she was inclined
to believe the dybbuk of temptation haunted certain dark and evil
places and I suppose it seemed less likely that the fiend would seize
a sexually unready boy of thirteen. For my part I was flattered to
play the protector of so lovely a girl and felt older every minute as
we walked side-by-side.

There were no unusual signs of debauchery when we came to
the railway arch although couples grappled against the dripping
walls and tramps lay around parcelled in old newspaper. The evil
of the place was in its gloom, its putrid stench, in the industrial

grime of half a century with which it was impregnated. The sinister possibilities excited me: I was not immune to the dybbuk, after all.

'We're walking past the scene of Jack the Ripper's most famous murder,' I announced. 'It was a foggy night. The woman came out of a pub when she saw this figure in a black coat. He dragged her under the railway arch and slashed her so much, the blood ran down the gutter.'

'You're trying to frighten me.' Her eyes were black and enormous. 'I'll tell your mum.'

I hadn't realised that scaring girls was so thrilling. 'God's honour, Fanya. He was a famous doctor who got a disease and became a sex maniac. That's why he cut up women. You can read all about it in the library.'

'They haven't got things like that in the library,' Fanya said, beginning to go faster. 'It wouldn't be allowed.'

'But, Fanya———'

'I don't want to hear any more!' She spoke in a severe, grown-up voice, so I shrugged and let her walk on alone. She'd only gone a few yards, glancing back at me nervously, when two men lurched round the corner, roaring drunk.

They staggered along the narrow pavement towards us singing a dirty song. We clung together for mutual protection, pressing close to the wall. The softness of her was a shock of illicit delight: my pressure became urgent. As our bellies touched my boy's cock strained towards a premature maturity and even when the men had gone, we did not immediately separate. We were about the same height. She had a rich dark smell like a pungent animal. Our mouths came together clumsily and I tasted the sophistication of cachous on her breath. A sinful corrupt, oriental flavour.

She wrenched herself away. The night throbbed with darkness and shame. We walked along in silence, interminably. At last we reached the lights of Whitechapel and exchanged a sideways glance. Electric music came out of pin-table saloons. Young men with heavily padded shoulders swaggered by whistling aimlessly. Fanya was obviously anxious to get rid of me as quickly as possible. I understood her embarrassment. She didn't want to be seen promenading with a boy in short trousers, especially after what had happened.

As she hurried away a youth with brilliantined hair called out in an American drawl: 'Hey, sugar, what's your hurry?'

I went home very slowly, remembering the shape of that softness and confused by it. Undressing for bed, I looked at the hair that had started to grow below my thin belly. It reminded me that I must inevitably inherit the hairiness of men, their grotesque, depressing lusts. And all night long I burned with a shameful fever.

The New York Yiddish Theater opened its London season that autumn with what the drama critic of our building, a watchmaker named Shmulik, described as a daring translation of Gotthold Ephraim Lessing's *Nathan the Wise*. I heard him discussing it with old Mrs. Rosen, the grocer, while she was at her daily task of weighing sugar into blue paper bags. Lessing was an assimilationist of the worst kind, according to Shmulik, and consequently he made his heroine, Recha, fall in love with a goy of exceptional vulgarity, a *sheigetz*. Mrs. Rosen shook her head with disapproving vigour, her ritual wig almost slipping into the sugar. Even at the best of times *Nathan the Wise* wasn't Shmulik's favourite play, but on top of every thing he had the bad luck to sit next to a woman who didn't stop eating fried fish the whole performance. She must also have been a critic, he remarked sourly.

The failure of *Nathan the Wise* was redressed by the next production, a Goldfaden comedy, the title of which I have forgotten. It succeeded because it made people laugh and cry and remember the past, all at the same time. And even though one always heard how bitter everything was in the past, the old people were still crazy to relive it. After the triumphant first night, there was a stampede for the box-office by every class of Jew from master tailor to underpresser. The moneyed rolled up in taxis all the way from Park Lane and Stamford Hill but mingled on equal terms with class-conscious proletarians. Toothless crones who could barely hobble to the market place, raced along Whitechapel as if rejuvenated and used their stick-like elbows to reach the front of the uproarious queue. Trampled peanut shells and discarded sweet papers made the pavement look like Victoria Park on a Bank Holiday. There were vendors selling hot beigels, baked potatoes, fruit, chestnuts, fizzy drinks. Down-at-heel rabbinical types with matted beards solicited alms for *yeshivot* in Vilna or Jerusalem. Street musicians who hadn't played the fiddle for years scratched out their rusty tunes. Everybody said it was like the old days at the Pavilion and elderly intellectuals in Goide's restaurant, squeezing the last drop of lemon juice into their tea, predicted a miraculous revival of Yiddish culture.

All this, of course, hardly affected the younger generation and Fanya Ziegelbaum might never even have met Rosenheim if the American troupe's costumes had not needed constant running repairs. She was introduced to the wardrobe mistress by a mutual friend. On her very first evening Rosenheim strode off-stage wearing buckskin breeches and cavalry boots. He was full of fire and tenderness, still under the influence of his romantic role. Fanya went down on her knees to stitch up the split seam and as she did so, she was later to tell my mother, the actor put out his hand to stroke the back of her neck. He must have been pleasantly surprised by her youth and freshness for even *ingenues* in the Yiddish theatre were performed by actresses who'd already married off their own daughters. As for Fanya, she must have been parched for the touch of such a hand, and from then on there was nothing in life she wanted more than to stand under the *chuppah* and become Mrs. Rosenheim. The second Mrs. Rosenheim, in fact, the actor soon confessed, but certainly, he promised, the last. When the season in London was over, he'd take her back to America and there make her his own little angel bride.

Afterwards, when the damage was done, everybody said they'd known it would end badly, but if so they were careful not to say it to the girl's face. Whenever she came round to us, the neighbours were never short of an excuse to drop in. Suddenly they ran out of sugar, or were in need of change for the gas meter, or just looked in as they were passing. The springs of the sofa sagged as one by one they settled down comfortably to stay for a cup of tea.

Fanya was excited and talkative. 'Such a cold audience last night,' she would say, 'you wouldn't believe!' Or, with evident satisfaction: 'Six curtain calls yesterday.' All of a sudden she was an expert. The future of the Yiddish theatre worried her. People would rather go to see any rubbish at the movies nowadays. And where were the playwrights, the new Sholem Aleichems? The public no longer had respect for a Jewish actor. They spat in his face. Harry—that was what she called Herschel Rosenheim—had turned down offers to play the biggest roles on Broadway, but how long could he go on making such sacrifices?

The women would surely have preferred to hear less of Rosenheim the actor and more of Rosenheim the lover. It was hard for us to believe actors were real people. Did they bleed real blood, experience real suffering, go to the lavatory? Musicians, yes. Prizefighters also. But actors? Fanya was young, foolish, she had romantic notions. Maybe it wasn't even true about Rosenheim: it could be an exaggeration. And even if it was, an ordinary working girl, what did she want with an actor? About such people one thing was sure, morals they didn't have.

My mother said: 'An orphan like you, without even a mother or a father, you have to be careful somebody doesn't take an advantage.' Everybody knew what that meant. Two minutes pleasure, nine months pain, and unspeakable ruin. 'After all, how long do you know him? Practically from yesterday! Sometimes a man pays a compliment. He makes a flirtation. Marriage,' my mother said heavily, 'is for a whole lifetime.'

Fanya was a serious girl. She thought for a while before replying, then looked into my mother's face with the solemn eyes of one who had seen her destiny. 'Sometimes you can be sure in a single minute,' she said with sombre conviction and added humbly: 'I don't know why I should be so lucky. Once Harry danced with Gloria Swanson. At a charity ball. I don't know what he can see in me.'

One Sunday morning I was standing in a crowd in Middlesex Street market absorbed in watching a small Irishman working the three card trick. 'All you got to do is keep your eye on me hands,' he confided out of the corner of his wide rubbery mouth. 'Now watch it, sports!' He showed us the lady and dexterously shuffled the cards on a folding green baize table.

At that moment Fanya came out of Strongwater's delicatessen holding a brown paper bag. She was with a man in a curly-brimmed hat worn well back on a thatch of red hair. I could tell he was an actor by the elegant way he smoked his cigarette. Otherwise he looked no different from a tailor. Excited, I was just about to follow when the Irishman grabbed hold of me. 'There's some o' you wouldn't trust an Irish feller wid the price of a drink,' he said gloomily. 'Now look at this young laddie, a face of innocence like a holy choir boy. Put your finger on that card, lad. Now, listen! If I was to say this boy's digit is on the lovely Queen of Hearts, would any of you sports venture to believe me for ten bob?' No one ventured. Disconsolately the Irishman turned up the card. It was the Queen and I hurried away.

Fanya leaned against Rosenheim and kept turning her head with quick nervous movements as if she wanted to catch people looking at them. She was wearing a yellow sleeveless dress and her long hair gleamed like rich mahogany. Men stared at her, as they always did, but no one gave Rosenheim more than a glance. He was probably only acting the part of an ordinary person and I admired this modesty, although his lack of height disappointed me. I'd imagined him a tall, commanding figure, but without his hat he'd have been shorter than Fanya.

In Fieldgate Street I slipped over to the opposite pavement to get a good view of the actor's profile and they saw me. I gazed intensely into a watchmaker's window at a man fishing for tiny cogwheels with a magnifying glass screwed into his eye and pretended to be there accidentally. They came over.

'Well, stranger! What are you doing in this district?' Fanya said, in a modulated voice, as if we were as far afield as Oxford Street at least. I looked round and gave a simulated start of surprise. Rosenheim's hand rested on the soft inside of Fanya's upper arm and he stroked the skin musingly with his forefinger. She told him who I was. They'd obviously discussed her connection with our family because he looked at me with interest.

'I hoid a lot about your mudder and fader,' he said. The accent was just like a Chicago gangster's. 'What Fanya tells me, dey is marvellous pipple.' His pale grey eyes blinked with sincerity. 'Especially your mudder. She look after dis young goil like her own dotter.' He squeezed Fanya's plump arm and she gazed back adoringly. 'Nu, ve gotta go. Give my best to your pipple, Sonny,' he said and, as they were about to leave, remarked as an afterthought: 'Liebchen, bring the boy vun efening. Maybe he's interested to see the backstage. Vy not?'

Frankly, I didn't expect much from the Pavilion—a Jewish theatre was not the London Palladium, after all—but it was a shock to discover that the stage-door led into a building as filthy, neglected and unromantic as the corridors of our tenement. Fanya took me into the costume room. There was a treadle machine and a bench for pressing clothes. A yellowed Ministry of Labour poster on the whitewashed wall was prosaically concerned with fire regulations and you could smell the toilet next door. Mrs. Myers, the wardrobe mistress, was a heavy-breasted woman whose square face disappeared into the folds of her neck. But she was nice and gave me a mug of syrupy coffee. A remote drone of voices reached us from the direction of the stage, a sound that resembled the kind of argument one heard at home through the walls of a neighbouring apartment.

They were doing Hamlet. Mrs. Myers told me the plot, although she'd never actually found time to see the play right through. It was about a Prince who had a mother, a monster. Together with his uncle, the King's brother, she poisoned his father, her own husband, then married with the murderer. From this the Prince had such aggravation, he turned against the whole world. Even to his fiancée, a beautiful girl, he behaved so badly that she drowned herself.

Mrs. Myers described it all so vividly, I could hardly wait to see the drama for myself.

In semi-darkness, Fanya led me to the wings. Her hand was hot and I could feel it trembling. In a sunken well that made him look like a trapped grey mouse, an elderly man peered along his pointed nose at a copy of the play-text. Battlements rose to the rusty grinding of pulleys and were replaced by gloomy palace chambers. A man in baggy trousers picked his teeth with a matchstick held in one hand and moved a spotlight with the other. I couldn't quite follow the Shakespearian Yiddish. It wasn't in the slightest like the iambic pentameters spoken in our classroom through the pinched Gentile nostrils of Mr. Parker, my schoolmaster, and it didn't sound like anything my mother said. Only when Rosenheim, gravely pacing the stage and plucking at his chin, began the famous soliloquy, did I start to get the gist of things.

Tzu sein, odder nisht tzu sein,
Dos is der frage,

said Rosenheim in a slow, perplexed but remarkably resonant voice.
Fanya gazed at him with petrified eyes as if afraid he might make
the wrong decision. Her lips were parted like a listening child's and
she responded to Rosenheim's voice as the strings of a piano vibrate
to pressure on its keyboard. As he declaimed to the half-empty
auditorium, she clenched her small hands and breathed faster. Her
bosom was palpitating like a small, agitated animal and I had to
restrain the temptation to stroke it into calmness. Nothing that
happened on the stage, not even Hamlet's grief over Ophelia's
drowning, moved me so much as the madness of Fanya's love.

But soon I became terribly bored. It was more diverting to eavesdrop on the actors who stood around smoking between scenes,
scratching their itching faces to avoid smearing the greasepaint and
grumbling about the audience. Hamlet's mother, the famous Esther
Friedenthal, nibbled a chopped-liver sandwich, talking to another
actress about her son in New York who had sensibly decided to
study business administration.

One by one the actors stubbed out their cigarettes and went on
stage to be murdered. When it was Rosenheim's turn to die, he
jerked and quivered for a long time. The final curtain descended to
scattered applause and the cast bowed and smiled a couple of times,
exchanging supercilious glances when Rosenheim stepped forward
to receive solitary homage. Patches of sweat showed on his tunic as
he spread out his arms and drooped his flaming head in a crucified
gesture. The sound of crunching peanut shells could be heard all
over the theatre as the audience stampeded towards the exits. He
stood motionless until the curtains swished together.

Fanya hurried to him. 'Harry,' she said, 'darling . . . that was so
. . . marvellous! I can't tell you.' Rosenheim squeezed her hands
without a word, too moved to speak, then left the stage. As he
brushed past me I got a close-up of his face. It was pale, wrung-
out, ecstatic. 'He really suffers,' Fanya said tearfully. 'When he plays,
he gives his heart and soul.' She ran after him and disappeared into
the dressing room.

There was nobody around. I advanced stealthily into the centre
of the empty stage. 'Ladies and gentlemen, people of the world,' I
said quietly in deep tones, gesturing towards the auditorium. Then,
louder, 'Tzu sein odder nisht tzu sein?' My voice went squeaky in the

middle of a word. From pit to gallery empty rows of seats gave me their attentive silence. I felt as if at any moment a terrible eloquence would burst from my mouth and fill the whole city with resonance.

'I . . . am . . . ' my voice began. 'I . . . am . . . am?' What? I would soon be fourteen. I wore glasses and had failed the scholarship. There was nothing to say.

Rosenheim's door stood slightly ajar. It was very quiet in there. A corner of the room, tilted at a crazy angle, was reflected in the dressing-table mirror and Fanya was drowning in the kisses of her red-haired Hamlet.

At home, the King, my father, was also dead, and his usurper was in a bad mood. 'Where you been till twelve o'clock, eh? Eh?' he demanded. I pierced him with the glitter of my sword-sharp eyes.

The New York Yiddish Theater ended its season and departed. I never saw Rosenheim again. The reason he couldn't take Fanya with him right away was because as soon as the actors returned to New York they would have to go on a tour of all the places in America where Jews lived. She begged him to take her along. After all, it was useful to have someone who was handy with the needle. But, no. Such a dog's life of travel, cheap boarding houses, draughty public halls, she should never experience, God forbid. Rosenheim wanted her to come to him like a princess. For this everything had to be made ready—a nice apartment, wall-to-wall carpets, a good air-conditioning so summer and winter would be always the same. Maybe, even, a coloured maid in a frilly apron. For his angel bride-to-be, nothing but the best. The whole of New York, America, the world, he would give to her—but it would take a little time, a little patience.

Fanya was disappointed for she only wanted Rosenheim, not the world, but love gave her strength to wait. She brought round a postcard he sent from New York. Over the towers of Manhattan he had written in Yiddish: 'My love is bigger than the Empire State, tallest building in the whole earth, Your Harry.' From Chicago, at the back of a picture of Lake Shore Drive, were the words: 'I miss you, sweet angel, and my tears fill the lake.' The message from Pittsburgh was shorter. 'Thinking of you always.' There was a gap of some weeks, then a card from San Francisco. 'The "Examiner"

writes "Rosenheim's Hamlet a triumph". Wish you were here to
see.'

Next time Fanya came to tea she was wearing an old dress and
her face without make-up looked as thin and hungry as when she
first came to be an apprentice. My mother gazed at her keenly and
led her into the bedroom. They talked in low voices, then Fanya
rushed out and left, drowning in tears.

'Of course she's pregnant,' my mother muttered to Mrs. Benjamin next door. 'Anybody can see.' She leaned back in the chair,
hands clasped over her own big belly.

Mrs. Benjamin stared in horrified delight. 'Pregnant? From him?
From the actor?'

'How else? From a wind in the stomach?'

Mrs. Benjamin slapped herself on the cheek and rocked from
side to side. 'Aie, aie, aie! Such a bandit, that Rosenheim. You should
never trust a ginger, Rosa. In a ginger the blood boils like in a kettle.
And when,' she added eagerly, 'is she expecting?'

'Tomorrow I'm taking her to see Fat Yetta.' Tears dripped from
my mother's nose. She'd unsuccessfully visited Fat Yetta on a couple
of occasions herself. 'Please God, it should work. That poor child
is like my own daughter.'

Fat Yetta was at first reluctant to take the case, my mother told
Mrs. Benjamin the following day, when it was all over. She'd agreed
to do so only out of pity for the plight of such a young girl. My
mother got up heavily and closed the living-room door so that none
of us should hear the shocking details. So, of course, we eaves-
dropped.

'It was terrible,' she said in an agonised whisper that penetrated
the wall. 'A living child was torn from her body. Each fingernail was
perfect. And the neshumah, the soul, was struggling to breathe. If I
live to a hundred, I'll remember it all my life . . . ' There was a
prolonged silence before she resumed speaking. 'It should be put
in a coffin and sent to . . . that murderer!' my mother declared in a
terrible voice. She opened the door. 'Go out, children. Go out and
play!'

When I came back in, Mrs. Benjamin had left and the whole place
was filled with the spicy aroma of boiling chicken. My mother filled

a jar with soup and sealed the lid with wax paper. She told me to take it to Fanya.

It was one of those leaden Sunday afternoons in January. I carried the soup under my jacket against my breast and its warmth was the only comforting thing in a bleak walk along Brick Lane. Shreds of a poster advertising New York's brilliant Yiddish players still adhered to a board outside the Pavilion. The poster was still there months later when Fanya Ziegelbaum moved up to Manchester where no one knew of her disgrace. Night times, passing under the railway arch, I thought how different it might have been had I been older, uncommonplace, enhanced by the glamour of strangeness.

Eva Figes

was born in Berlin in 1932 and emigrated
to London in 1939. She was educated at
Kingsbury Grammar School and Queen
Mary College, University of London, and
has worked as an editor at Longman,
Weidenfeld & Nicholson, and Blackie.
Figes has translated work by Martin Walser
and Renate Rasp and has written one of
the defining texts of the women's movement, *Patriarchal Attitudes* (1970). Her
nonfiction also includes *Tragedy and Social
Evolution* (1976) and *Sex and Subterfuge:
Women Writers to 1850* (1982). The author
of thirteen novels, Figes suffuses her
modernist fiction with a poignant sense of
dislocation. Her memoir *Little Eden: A
Child at War* (1978), excerpted here,
recounts her arrival in England as a
seven-year-old just before the outbreak of
the Second World War.

Eva Figes

EXCERPT FROM Little Eden: A Child at
War

I

I do not know why I never went back before. I saw it marked up on
a signpost at odd times over the years, unexpectedly, and each time
I was tempted to change my plans for the day and go there instead.
But I do not drive a car, and as a passenger I was always whisked
off in the wrong direction, unable to explain adequately, or in time,
why I wanted to go somewhere else on impulse. Once, crammed in
a minibus full of youngish authors and poets, on our way to a lunch
date from Cheltenham, I suddenly recognised the curve of the lane
along which we were speeding. I had not been taking much notice
of our route when I glanced out of the window and exclaimed 'I
know this place' before I could even put a name to it, the high trees
and the old iron gate followed by open fields on the left, the low
stone wall enclosing the wooded grounds to the right. Like driving
into a dream, and even while you dream saying, I have dreamed this
place before, I found myself knowing each tree and blade of grass:
the massive old beech tree in the middle of the field to my left, an
island of shade or shelter, the fringe of woodland on the horizon,
the slope of the land and the way the lane would curve, following
the old stone wall, until we came to the junction with the London
road. I knew one had to turn left for London, and right to reach
the centre of the town. But we drove straight on for our lunch
appointment, already late, whilst I craned my head to catch a
glimpse of my childhood, buried by years but not forgotten, lost,
and now suddenly found.

That was ten years ago, but since then the image of myself speeding along that stretch of unchanged road has recurred like a
haunting snatch of melody. Having, by a minor miracle, found

myself suddenly back in the past, in a landscape unchanged, frozen
in time nearly thirty years later, I travelled down it often now,
between sleeping and waking, or in daydreaming intervals, walked
down the muddy avenue of high trees shedding their leaves under-
foot, heard the creak of the iron gate as we came into Grove Lane.
My brother and I had once taken a delight in shuffling through a
pile of autumn leaves which the roadsweeper had only just swept
to one side, scattering them anew, while my mother protested at
our antisocial high spirits. I was lucky to have found it just in time.
When I finally did go back the narrow lane had become a dual
carriageway and the old iron gate had gone.

My sense of continuity was strengthened by another small coincidence which stuck in my mind. That the subject should have come
up at all during such a necessarily brief conversation was odd, and
should have told me something. But what struck me, and what I
remembered afterwards, long after the organiser had dropped me
at Oxford station and thanked me for my lecture, was the fact that
he had taught at the local grammar school, knew the family on the
farm and had taught Jack, the farmer's son. What was more, he
thought the family still ran the farm. I stored that bit of information
in my head and, after another few years, acted on it. The ex-teacher
from the Department of Education and Science was right: Jack
answered my letter.

But long before I acted on it, I kept remembering his words as
he dropped me at the station: 'To think of you walking up and down
the Whiteway as a small child all those years ago—from now on I
shall think of you like that.' I saw myself trailing the long weary
length of that road without a turning as dusk was falling, stopping
with aching legs to search for small diversions in hedgerow or
ditch—berries, rosehips, a feather caught in the tangle of thorn. It
was late in the year and there were few wild flowers left to find. A
long road, a boring road for small children trudging home with the
mists of winter closing in, and the fact that it had cut through the
countryside into the mists of prehistory long before the Romans
came and left, that carts had trundled and men had stumbled
through puddles and ruts which froze in winter long before, taking
the same direction across this stretch of flat land, was unknown to
us. We began to cheer up only when we saw the gateway to the farm,

the outline of barn and outhouses through the avenue of trees, because it meant we were nearly home.

The long hedgerow and the flat field beyond it have gone, swallowed up by a new housing estate. The town has grown since the war. Windows of neat suburban postwar prosperity look across the old orchard wall to where, through the trees, the old Cotswold stone farmhouse with its high chimneys is still visible through the trees.

Jack had answered my letter. Yes, he had taken over from his father many years ago. Why did I not pay them a call? I walked through the gateway and under the quiet old trees almost on tiptoe, holding my breath in the hushed excitement of a moment I wanted to savour for as long as possible, as I recognised each branch, tree, puddle, gate, shadows and smells, walls and outhouses. On this peaceful afternoon of early summer I could not believe my luck. I had walked into a sanctuary of the past as though into a church, and I responded to the atmosphere of what was for me, just then, a holy place. . . .

13

We came back to London, briefly, during the summer holidays. It was odd to come back to the small flat as a visitor. My tiny room overlooking the concrete yard and the row of garages had been let to a schoolteacher, but since she had gone home to her native Wales I could sleep in my own bed. This wartime lodger decided my future: there was no question that when I passed my eleven-plus I would go on to the school where she taught geography.

Even after she moved on to larger lodgings she kept in touch, sent me birthday cards, came for tea in fluffy pastel jumpers and chiffon scarves which looked odd on her stout figure. There was never any doubt in my mother's mind that her recommendation of the grammar school in which she worked was more than enough in choosing a school for me. And, being a child, I was proud, as a first-former, to have a family friend on the staff.

My first glimpse of her was unforbidding. She was indulgently kind to small children, smiled a lot, and sniffed through her nose when she laughed. Pretty features in a middle-aged face, a heavy woman with a taste for feminine frippery.

London was much quieter now. We played on the grass verge, thick with wild peppermint, of our jerry-built medieval castle, finished just before the outbreak of war. It was genuine enough in some ways: odd-shaped rooms, no flat with the same layout, not a single window with a normal vista. They all looked either on to the concrete courtyard with its line of garages or on to a piece of embattled wall. And the plumbing was in tune with the spirit of the age: each winter the pipes froze, then burst, and the flat was laid out with buckets and bowls placed at strategic points to catch the drips. My brother slept in the dining room with an umbrella above his pillow.

After a couple of winters my mother had had enough. Her terror of mice was probably the decisive factor. One could hear them scuttling in the ceiling overhead, and we were warned of the dire consequences of allowing crumbs of food to fall on the floor: a mouse invasion. I puzzled my head about how mice could get down through the apparently impenetrable ceilings, but I was assured that mice had ways and means of getting in anywhere. In 1942 we moved down the road to a more solid block of flats. It was noisier, with much more traffic, including buses, passing outside. Once the onslaught of flying bombs and rockets began it was even less quiet, but the building was solid enough to withstand both blast and heavy vibration.

'Reinforced concrete', our night visitors would reassure each other, murmuring the words like some magic spell of protection as the guns thundered, the night shook, and explosions followed in rapid succession. But flying bombs came by day as well as night, and without warning. By 1944 the reinforced concrete block had become little more than a ghost town, with most of the flats empty. It was the time when nerves began to fray, visibly. Even mine. Once I had sneaked off to school after an air raid warning when my mother's back was turned. I liked my new grammar school. In the first form we had taken end-of-term examinations with a prefect keeping watch on the school roof. When the whistle blew we got under the desks and took the opportunity to compare answers. But since I had mistaken the sound of a VI for a 52 bus, scoffed at my mother's warning and been caught, seconds later, in a terrifying blast which shattered every shop window across the road and sucked out my guts together with our net curtains through closed windows, I had become a nervous child who took shelter before she was told, who retired to the hallway with a book under one arm and a cushion under the other at the least ominous sound.

But that was still to come. In the summer holiday of 1941 we played peacefully enough on the top of our suburban hill crowned with its three fake castles where four roads met. We played cowboys and Indians at the foot of turrets with slit windows, ran along walls and up crazy-stone stairways chasing each other, and somehow as a girl I was always an Indian being shot at by boys who had the guns, trying to find a place to hide. And we sat in my dolls' cot and rolled down the hill on it. At the bottom of the hill we met other kids on what had once been the village green. Now it housed a bus shelter backed by a public lavatory. Main roads made up two sides of the old triangle, with bus stops on both of them. At the north end was the blue police box and the high mast of the air-raid siren. When you saw the bobby on duty move from the telephone to the siren we knew it was time to break up the game and go home.

Other things were still to come. The identity that Isolde had planted on me so bewilderingly one night in the dormitory, that strange word 'Jewish', was to acquire less mystery and a terrible reality. Unnamed tensions attached themselves to this state of being, of things unsaid, hinted at, a dark horror at the heart of the family which could not be spoken about but brooded over the dining table, turned small disputes about everyday trifles into momentous schisms, minor scratches into gaping, gangrenous wounds that required a sort of amputation. But the dark mystery which Isolde had first invoked remained, because I still did not know just how much was involved in the words that I did hear. I knew that my grandparents had been 'deported', for instance, by the time I had passed my eleven-plus and become a first-former at the local grammar school, but I did not know all that the word implied, and it was not something one could ask questions about at home. And I felt that adults were themselves groping at a dark heart of half-understood horrors, where reluctance to come to terms with the probable was overshadowed by anxiety about the possible. There was also a wish to spare the children, not to become too explicit. But children cannot be spared. Instead of sharing the burden, they become its ignorant victims. When tension became too much and the storm finally broke, I found myself like a lightning conductor, suddenly charged with what for me became a guilt of horrendous proportions.

Now that I have been a mother myself, coping alone, I know how easily unhappiness and anxiety which you are trying to keep to yourself can build up inside until one small annoyance, the irritating obstinacy of a child who dawdles, argues, or refuses to obey a simple request can be the last straw and unwittingly cause an outburst quite disproportionate to the offence. I also know that during those six years my mother was coping alone with stresses which my generation has not had to face. But I did not know it then; I only knew that I was a child living with a mother who often seemed harassed and preoccupied, so that I felt excluded, shut out, or unjustly persecuted.

And then the abnormalities of war seemed normal to me. I had grown up with them, they formed the daily background of my growing up, with its self-centred daydreams and ambitions. But one day there was yet another minor argument which flared up between us and my mother blurted out the truth: how could I be so difficult when she was worried out of her mind because her father and stepmother had been deported?

I was crushed. Appalled. I sat by myself in shame and misery, thinking: *why hadn't she told me?* I told myself it was unfair, how was I supposed to know, and at the same time I felt it was all my fault, her unhappiness, my unreasonableness, even the death of those I loved. From now on there was no escape from the burden of guilt.

My father's infrequent home leaves were spoiled for me in advance because, hardly had he come through the door and deposited his kitbag in the passage, taken off his heavy boots, hugged me in his rough, scratchy battledress and found some chocolate in his breast pocket, than he would be shut up in the bedroom with my mother and given a long account of my bad behaviour. I would listen to their voices through the wall, miserably certain that it was all about me. By now my brother had proved so unruly without a man in the house that he had been packed off to another boarding school and, frankly, I envied him. Considering that his own existence at that time was no picnic, my father would be remarkably understanding and patient. When he finally came out of the bedroom and into the living room, where I sat waiting for my turn, he was very gentle: 'Now try to understand. Your mother is having a very difficult time just now. You must try and help.' I protested that I did . . . but . . . but. But it was all too much for me.

The time came when I understood completely, and the last shadows of secrecy were torn away. One bright afternoon in early spring my mother gave me ninepence and sent me to the local cinema. 'Go and see,' she said. 'Go and see for yourself.' I sat alone in the dark cinema and watched the newsreel of Belsen: mounds of corpses, dazed survivors with huge haunted eyes staring out of skulls which had become too heavy for the frail emaciated bodies, mute evidence for the prosecution posing for the camera. At last I knew what it meant to be a Jew, the shameful secret which had been hinted at but kept from me for so many years, the mark on my head which I did not recognise but which Isolde had known about four years before, in the dormitory, when I was a small child, innocent as Eve in the Garden of Eden, and as ignorant.

In those days, in Cirencester, I did not know what it meant to belong to the human race. Now I knew. I was not a child any longer. I came out into the cold suburban sunshine, where the trees in the front gardens were just beginning to break into blossom, blinking in the sharp light after the cavernous dark of the cinema, mute, tearful, and stupefied. I walked down the road in my cotton socks and the child's gingham frock with the white collar. Underneath the straight gingham front my nipples had begun to swell painfully, like small hard boils.

We did not talk much at home. The subject was avoided. But I began to have a recurring dream, in which I regularly relived the moment of departure, the point of no return. The dream was faithful to reality: the plane waiting for take off on the tarmac of Berlin airport. And a row of abandoned loved ones standing outside the airport building, waving wistfully at survivors whom they could no longer see.

The dream recurred with great regularity all through my adolescence and into my early twenties. Having shrugged off my guilt as irrational, I thought nothing of it until one day, on a psychoanalyst's couch, I mentioned it in one of those awkward silences when one talks about last night's dream simply to get a sticky session moving. For something to say. I described the grey overcast day, sitting in the plane, watching my relatives through the window, tiny remote figures on the edge of the airfield. And instead of going on to discuss it I found myself, for the first and last time, crying uncontrollably and beyond words.

My other grandmother, a wealthy widow who, before the war, had lived in a vast apartment of gloomy splendour on the Kurfürstendamm, managed to outwit the Germans. We heard that she was still alive from an elderly woman who managed to get herself 'exchanged' very late in the war: she was Jewish, but had British nationality because she was the widow of a man, dead for decades, who had left England at the age of two. Frau Landsberg had become a friend of my grandmother, who was living in hiding and was, it seemed, planning to buy her way out of Germany together with a number of other wealthy Jews. We heard the story, and my parents were sceptical, the plan seemed so far-fetched and unlikely. A Swiss bank was involved, and the deal was for the group of Jews to buy a shoe factory in Guatemala from a Nazi who wanted to return to the fatherland in its hour of need, in return for safe conduct to a neutral country. Months went by. We had never even started to hope. The summer of 1944 arrived, my father came home on leave, embarkation leave before being shipped to Normandy, though he kept that little detail to himself. He was shaving in the bathroom, stripped to the waist, when the telegram arrived. His mother was in Stockholm. We gathered in the bathroom, hugged and kissed my father's soapy, half-shaved face as he sat on the edge of the bath, smiling but half dazed.

That was June 1944. By September, prematurely aged from the years in hiding, her heart worn out, she was dead. My father was away in France. We had exchanged a few letters. I looked forward to having a grandmother of my very own once the war was over. I felt cheated by her death, but I also felt a guilt which I carefully kept to myself. In one of my letters I had told her of my outrageous and daring plan: I intended to go on the stage. Actresses were not respectable: I felt guiltily convinced that the shock of having a granddaughter on the stage had been too much for her.

I never really knew her. I had an image of a grand old lady, imperious as a dowager duchess, with a chauffeur-driven limousine and an apparent immunity to the charms of small children, whose whims were strictly subordinated to her personal routine. She was capable of ignoring me altogether while she ate pineapple and a boiled egg for breakfast, and I fidgeted in a chair opposite her, licking salt. And when I told her that she snored as she took her afternoon nap in the room next to mine I was quite disgraced for a while.

I never really knew her, except through the eyes of a very small child, and the image I had was not very favourable. One of the rewards of this book has been to find something of her more than thirty years after her death, a touch of the real human being. Checking on dates, my mother told me that she still had those few letters she wrote between her escape and death. They are heart-rending in their longing, gratitude, and humility. She hoped my father had forgiven her for making life more difficult for him through her own shortsightedness, for not seeing things as they were until it was too late. She wrote of her dreadful fears for her daughter Margot, who had moved with her husband and children to Paris in 1933 and gone underground in the Dordogne after the German invasion. By the time my father had managed to reach Paris in his British army uniform and learnt from a suspicious concierge that his sister and her family were safe, my grandmother had died of heart failure. There was a letter to me and my brother. She longed to know how much we had grown, whether we had changed out of all recognition. Each time she wrote she begged for photographs of us, and never got them, because of wartime censorship.

The war, and our situation, would unfold and grow in dimension as I grew older in understanding and left the best years of my childhood behind. I spent the latter years of the war looking forward to that unimaginable time of bliss, known as Peacetime, or When the War is Over. None of us kids were old enough to have any clear conception of what such a time could be like, and we looked forward to it as something remote, not understood, but blissful, like faithful

Christians thinking about the rewards of an afterlife in heaven. Sweet rationing would stop.

I was old enough to share in the excitement of D-Day, which at long last signified the beginning of the end. A first-former now, at the local grammar school, I walked home one sunny June afternoon: every window was open, and from every window came the sound of the wireless giving the latest news from the front. Next day at school we all drew a map of Europe in our exercise books and, starting with a tiny red blotch at Caen, copied the line of the Allied advance from the blackboard each day. It was slow at first, but then our crayons took in broader and broader sweeps, until the speed of events made our exercise books look a mess and we gave up the project and waited for the inevitable end.

We had two days' school holiday. I stayed up half the night to watch the fireworks, the bonfires, and to join in the dancing with total strangers to music relayed on to the front lawn of the block of flats. My mother did not celebrate. She went to bed and smiled sadly when I came back indoors to tell her what was going on outside. I tried to persuade her to come out, but she was in no mood to celebrate.

And so the time that, as kids, we had tried so hard to imagine, had finally arrived. It was not much different from before, except in little ways. The heavens did not open, the skies were as grey as before, in spite of Vera Lynn. And sweets were still strictly rationed.

But in the summer of 1941 all this was still in the future. I was aged nine, I was going back to Cirencester after the holiday, and a vestige of magic, of a childhood paradise, still clung to my existence.

14

All I remember about coming back was my mother taking us for lunch on the first floor of Viner's which then, as now, occupied two floors in Castle Street near the Market Place. 'You'd better eat as much as you can', she said in a matter-of-fact tone, like a general preparing his troops for a long winter campaign. I stared out of the window and thought about going back, looking down at houses and streets and stonework which had become so familiar, with the inevitability of the everyday. Round the corner in Lewis Lane the spare old house with its many echoing rooms, bare floors, rather cold, would be waiting for me. Zoë, brisk of manner but loving, beaked nose and humour lines etched round her eyes, and her no-nonsense-you're-not-babies way of talking, would be expecting us. If I wanted to go back, this reminder of daily gnawing hunger had a dampening effect. We had been eating as much as we could, my brother and I, throughout the holidays. We found it an odd experience: now and again we would look at each other and exchange rather sheepish grins, compounded of disbelief not unmixed with a touch of guilt, as we made pigs of ourselves, thus Zoë would have put it, by eating until we had had enough. My mother only had to utter a simple 'Would you like some more?' for our eyes to widen in amazement. We would exchange glances, giggle in nervous incredulity before we learned to relax and make the most of our chance. The tiny larder was like an Aladdin's cave capable of satisfying our most unreasonable wishes. But now we were back on the verge of reality.

So we fortified ourselves with a final lunch at Viner's, which seemed to me then the last word in sophisticated high living for some reason. Perhaps because the rooms were light and airy, and downstairs fancy cakes were displayed on glass shelves. It must have been the modernity: most of the inns and tea-rooms in the town were darkish places, with little parchment-shaded lamps, tables and chairs of stained wood in Windsor style, and low ceilings with oak beams. The floors and walls were often uneven, tapering off to dark corners where you sat hidden from the rest of the room. But here we sat in light and airy splendour, with the town spread out below. I felt that my mother had somehow staked everything on this last lunch together. I tried to do justice to the occasion, but after several weeks in London I had stopped being ravenous. Alas, human beings cannot store up food in advance. I knew that a week from now I would think back to this meal with regret. But even so, I could not manage a second helping.

The images of that last term are of winter closing in, days grow-ing shorter. The mournful smell of mist and damp leaves turning to rot, it hung in the garden, in the park, it seeped into the stonework of the house and clung to the damp basement, so we shivered if we had to go to the lavatory first thing in the morning when thick white air curled in through the black iron railings of the area gate. The lime tree turned yellow and dropped dead leaves on to the damp lawn. Soon it became too cold to spend our break between lessons outside. Occasionally we took a quick look at the rabbits huddled in their hutches, then abandoned them to the cold, quivering with pink eyes and rheumy noses in their fur coats. Somebody would be sent out with a bucket to feed the chickens. In the abandoned kitchen garden the beehive had stopped humming.

On our free afternoons we went to the park and shuffled through the fallen leaves under the ancient trees, searching for beechnuts which complemented our meagre diet, picking up chestnuts and pine cones to take back. The shadows would be closing in now, quite fast, as we passed through the high iron gates beside the Armoury and walked down Cecily Hill and through the narrow winding streets. Bats wheeled and screeched like wild black leaves high above the giant yew hedge at the main gate to Cirencester House, barely visible against the faintly luminous dark night sky. We stopped to watch them, and told each other, in some awe, about how bats could get caught in your hair, which meant having it all cut off. Wide-eyed, shuddering with not unpleasurable horror, we filed on past the museum and walked towards the Market Place, through the winding narrow streets, back home.

Tea in the long room overlooking the garden now already swallowed up by the night. A coal fire burning in the grate. Perhaps Miss Betts, her ostrich features and long legs relaxed now, mellowed by lamplight and fireglow, would read us a story before it was time to go up to bed. Or we would stand round the fireplace until fingers and toes thawed out and tingled, making chilblains a certainty. Occasionally we roasted chestnuts, waiting for them to pop and explode on the grate. And on hairwash nights I squatted alone in front of the fire, the room empty and in shadow, until it was dry. My hair was considered something of a problem, too thin and silky, pigtails which were mere wisps. Zoë and Hillie's remedy was probably Victorian, and consisted of regularly singeing the ends. The potent smell of burning hair clung to that schoolroom and fireside for all time. As a reward for being brave during this nerve-racking ordeal Hillie heated a pair of curling tongs in the fire and produced locks and ringlets on my head as if by magic.

The winter closed in. My brother's face looked miserable and sickly. He did not whine, but looked at me reproachfully. Zoë marched him off to see a doctor, but in spite of the prescribed ultra-violet treatment, the spoonfuls of cod liver oil and malt from the big jar in the scullery, he stayed whey-faced and listless.

My mother came to take him home. I had been stitching a traycloth, the first of many, for her birthday: Miss Betts taught me lazy daisy, stem stitch and an edging of blanket stitches. I apologised for not having it ready on time, and found out that I had muddled her birthday in November with her wedding anniversary which had come and gone in September. So I went back and filled in all the lazy daisies on the transfer and sent if off in good time for the first of many Novembers. Each year the cloths got bigger, the stitches finer and more ambitious. Neat daughterly duty, carefully stitched, from blue transfer patterns.

My brother gone, I was left behind in the old house with its large echoing rooms, winter air seeping in from attic schoolroom to basement scullery. The mornings were dark now, it was hard to get out of the narrow iron bed with its rough grey blankets, army style, now that the air was shivering cold. The room, like the long schoolroom below, had a fireplace, but this one was never lit. We were provided with stone hot-water bottles and took to slipping into bed in our underclothes, vests, liberty bodices, and navy blue knickers. Lying in bed, I rubbed at my itching swollen fingers and feet until the chilblains broke and Zoë came with ointment and bandages. My sufferings were rewarded by being excused piano practice, since nobody could be expected to play properly with a bunch of swollen reddish purple sausages. For me it was a relief not to be expected to play properly, since the tension and anxiety associated with my piano lessons from Zoë had never entirely subsided, and I was dreadfully conscious of my own inadequacy.

But even the hardships of school life had by now become so familiar that I took them in my stride as something normal. Bare floorboards, shared baths, the damp lavatory in the basement with squares of old newspaper in the lavatory paper holder, these were simply aspects of a way of life which had become mine: the normal everyday flavour of a cosmos infinitely rich and strange, a household ruled by two spinster sisters who were constantly opening doors behind which lay untold riches; songs, stories, books, legends, walking, memories caught in a sepia photograph, hedgerows filled with history, the flotsam of a world as miraculous as dandelion clocks blown into the wind. Even the door to my remote childhood had been unlocked when, in a singing session round the piano, Zoë asked me to sing a song because it was in German, and by Schubert, and a childhood dream of a youth in fancy dress who picked a wild rose and put it in a box suddenly found its source.

Food continued to be an obsession, but it had been going on so long that my body had adjusted. The raw, desperate edge went out of the gnawing hunger. I found comfort in the lumps of sugar or cheese which Zoë sometimes handed round just before bedtime, the burnt toast from the teacher's table, and any other scraps which came my way by whim or chance. And by now I knew myself to be a survivor: it was my brother who had succumbed and gone home. I knew, my mother knew, that all he needed to get well was more food. I felt sorry for him, but no envy. I was too busy opening doors: reading books, looking and listening, dreaming, fumbling for words and arranging them on a page, and finding me, a person in my own right, with eyes that could see, ears listen, mind master and think and put words together and respond to the kindness and expectation of people who did not claim ownership over me but saw me as me, someone unique and individual of whom much could be expected. A child whose needs were amply catered for, including wintergreen for chilblains, and hair singed in front of a glowing coal fire.

One dark winter morning in December I was woken at five o'clock to catch the train for London. I was going home for Christmas. Miss Betts accompanied me and my small suitcase. I remember shivering on a bleak railway platform in the half-light, waiting for the train to come in. We got out at Swindon, where I was put in the charge of a nun I had never seen before. She was escorting several school-girls back to London, and I made one more. Nobody said much on the journey in the overcrowded carriage, which had the bizarre quality of a dream in my tired fuddled state. I felt an outsider, a parcel unceremoniously dumped on people I did not know, but the nun was kind enough, and seemed quite like a normal human being, in spite of her odd clothes.

I was going home just for the Christmas holiday. Woken in the early hours of the morning, when it was dark and cold and I was dazed with lack of sleep, I had hardly spoken to anyone. A few brief words with Zoë, but no goodbye. It would only be for a few days anyhow. My mother waited until we were back in the flat and I had taken my outdoor clothes off. 'I've got a surprise for you,' she said. I waited. Christmas was the time of year for surprises, good things. 'I've got a surprise for you. You're not going back after Christmas.'

The shock left me speechless. A trick had been played on me. 'I didn't want to tell you before but . . . ' So Zoë had also been tricked: she did not know, any more than I did. 'The bombing is not so bad now so . . . ' My misery was boundless, it welled up like a sea and threatened to engulf me, trickle out of my eyes, gush out of my mouth. But I knew there was nothing I could say. She was waiting for me to look pleased. She was pleased. I managed to hold in the tears, hold in my misery, but not much more. I do not think she noticed, since she took it for granted that I would want to be home for good. It was only natural where a child was concerned. I tried hard to behave naturally, as though nothing had happened to me. But the gates of my happy childhood had clanged shut behind me; I had become adult enough to recognise the need to conceal unbearable emotions for the sake of others. In their own way the two sisters had prepared me for life after the inevitable expulsion.

Ruth Fainlight

was born in New York in 1931 and has lived in England since the age of fifteen. She was educated in both the United States and England and studied at Birmingham and Brighton Colleges of Arts and Crafts. In 1985 Fainlight was made poet-in-residence at Vanderbilt University, Tennessee, and in 1994 she won the Cholmondeley Prize for Poetry. She has published twelve books of poems, has written opera libretti, and has translated the work of Lope de Vega and Sophia de Mello Breyner. Her short stories are collected in *Daylife and Nightlife* (1971) and *Dr. Clock's Last Case and Other Stories* (1994). 'Another Survivor' (1978) and 'A Wizard's Robe Patterned with Stars and Moons' (1994), from her later collection, demonstrate Fainlight's ability to endow everyday objects with a wider historic and symbolic resonance. Her characters are typically cosmopolitan, viewing a supposedly comfortable world from a range of competing perspectives.

Ruth Fainlight

Another Survivor

He's fifty now, but the day his mother and father took him to the railway station with the one permitted suitcase, clutching a satchel crammed with entomological collecting equipment he refused to leave behind—that chilly, too harshly bright day of a windy reluctant spring—was in 1938, and he was twelve years old. With the other children lucky enough to be part of this refugee group on its way to England, and their agitated and mournful parents, they moved to the far end of the platform in an attempt to make themselves less conspicuous. Rudi recognised two of the boys from last year at school. Since the holidays he had been kept at home.

A few children had begun to cry, unable not to respond to the tears their parents tried so hard to repress. The entire group emanated a collective desolation, unaffected by any individual attempt to put a good face on matters, or hopeful talk of future reunion. For all of them, as the adults already suspected, it was to be their last sight of each other. Sharing a stridently upholstered couch with three men as withdrawn into their separate worlds as he is, staring unseeingly at other patients moving restlessly around the crowded day-ward, Rudi's face is still marked by the same appalled expression which had settled on it that morning.

His parents belonged to families that had lived in the city for generations. Though Rudi was an only child, there had been many houses and apartments where he was at home, many celebrations to attend and cousins to play with. The family ramified through the professions: doctors, lawyers, architects, academics—part of that cultivated, free-thinking flowering of Jewish emancipation whose crucial importance to the European spirit only became apparent after its destruction. His father had been a biologist, his mother a talented amateur pianist. At night, in the dormitory of the school he was sent to by the same kindly people who sponsored his rescue, he tried to fall asleep by reconstructing themes from the music she had played. He remembered creeping up behind her, steps deadened by soft Persian rugs whose silk nap glinted in the mote-laden beams of afternoon sunlight filtered through creamy lace curtains, hoping to reach the piano and put his hands over her eyes before she even realised he was home from school.

That was the most precious image on the iconostasis of memory during the years when there was no news of them at all. That, and another one, from a Sunday country walk with his father. Even now, through the distractions of hospital life, he can relive the surge of pride and intellectual excitement that came when he finally understood his father's explanation why the hills had their particular structure and composition: a lesson in geography and geology; remember also how he had called upon that memory to sustain him through every boyhood crisis.

Though he mastered English quickly and did his schoolwork well, the prospect of taking part in the war and adding his energy to the fight against Nazism was what obsessed him. But he had not even crossed the Channel before it ended. And then, after seven years of suspense, of great swoops between hope and an absolute conviction that his parents had vanished, the camps were opened up and the first reports and pictures began to appear. The effort he makes, even now, is to shut off parts of his mind, to push all that information away. Nightmares, day-mares—black, white, bleeding, disembowelled, flayed: Goya-esque mares with staring, maddened eyes had been galloping across the wincing terrain of his brain ever since. Yet he was unable to stop accumulating the facts; nor stop imagining that every atrocity heard or read about had been suffered by his parents.

Then he calmed down, came through: another survivor. So much time passed that he could even acknowledge how privileged and fortunate he was, weighed in the balance of the global misery. Every morning he could read in the newspapers stories of war, famine, torture and injustice, and recognise that he was no more affected than the newspaper-readers of that past time had been by reports of the catastrophe which engulfed his family. He was healthy, prosperous, successful. His wife had not left him. His children were growing up. His work presented no real problems. It was just that now, after more than thirty years, he was overcome with the most intense yearning for his mother. He still felt like a boy of twelve, gone away from home for the first time: the adoring son of a proud, doting mother who cannot be diverted by promises of even the most fabulous pleasures if they will keep him away from his mother one moment longer. And the strength of this need made him aware of how much grief had been repressed when they parted.

For the first time, he could remember his mother before the war began. Since their separation, he had only been able to imagine her as a victim, not a woman at the height of her vigour and self-confidence. During the intervening years, memory had been blotted out by imagination, always the stronger.

Twenty years ago when Rudi and Barbara bought their house, the streets between Camden Town and Primrose Hill were neither fashionable nor expensive. They had lived there ever since, while houses around them changed hands for ten and twenty times what they had paid. It had been redecorated periodically, but retained the style of the era when they moved in: austere and utilitarian, with white-walled, charcoal-grey and neutral-coloured rooms intended as a background for rational living. He had been attracted to Barbara because she seemed so rational. Nothing about their house reminded him of where he had lived until the age of twelve. The two interiors were entirely different.

Barbara had never shown any interest in how the house looked. As soon as the youngest of their three children started school she had trained and qualified as a social worker, and was out of the house all day and most evenings. Rudi, who had become an accountant after the war, found he was bringing more work home, and often spent whole days at his desk in the big open-plan all-purpose room on the ground floor.

There was nothing wrong with his corner—it had been especially planned so that everything necessary was within reach; but looking up from his desk one early winter afternoon he wondered at the many years spent in this bleak and characterless environment. At home, he thought—and became aware that home did not mean this house—everything had been so much prettier and more comfortable, more comforting, too; gratifying to the eye and the spirit in a way this room gave no indication of understanding or allowing for. He had a strong, momentary hallucination of his mother as she must have been in 1933 or '34, perfumed and elegantly dressed for the theatre, taking a few steps through the door and glancing around. He had become inured to and then unaware of the frayed, stained upholstery they had never bothered to replace after the children outgrew their destructive phase. Through her slightly slanted pale blue eyes he saw the muddy, formless paintings friends had given them years ago which remained the only decoration, and watched them narrow with distaste and incomprehension before she disappeared without having noticed him.

Walking home from the tube station next day, Rudi was surprised by the number of antique shops that had opened recently. A lamp on display was like one in the dining room of his childhood home. It had stood on the right-hand side of a large ornately carved sideboard, and he had loved those winter evenings when its opalescent glass shade glowed like a magic flower. Antique shops had always made him feel ignorant and gullible, but he forced himself to go inside. The lamp was more expensive than any comparable purchase and, writing a cheque, he sweated as heavily as if committing a shameful and dangerous act. Standing on his desk, the lamp's soft light made everything else in the room seem even more nondescript.

'That's new, isn't it?' Barbara remarked, tying a headscarf over her short blonde hair. 'I forgot my papers for a case conference, or I wouldn't have come back. I've left something in the oven for you and the children.'

'That's really beautiful. I'd like to do a drawing of it.' Faith was the elder of the two girls, and had just become an art student. Circumstances had made him an accountant, but Rudi often wondered if he had betrayed his potential. Faith was the only one of the children who took after him. It would be hard to guess that Mavis and Tony had a Jewish father. They favoured Barbara's side of the family.

Most men would be more likely to spend time at the weekend with a son rather than a daughter, but Tony had never given him an opportunity to develop that sort of relationship. When not at school the boy was out with friends: an eminently social being. Mavis, the baby, had been her mother's girl from the start, and so Rudi and Faith were left to make their own Saturday entertainment. Visiting museums and art galleries with her produced a combination of pleasure and anguish. He was grateful for an opportunity to revisit paintings and statues not seen for years. It was wonderful to watch Faith's knowledge and appreciation increase, to witness the development of this lovely, perceptive being. The anguish came when he remembered visiting museums with his mother and recognised the inherent quality of Faith's responses, so similar to hers; when he realised that his mother must have felt the same parental joy he did now.

Often they had set out with no particular destination or purpose, but now Rudi had an aim—the search for pictures, rugs, china, bits of furniture, anything that evoked his childhood home. Faith thought it perfectly natural to buy so much, and he found it easier to spend money in the company of his pretty, auburn-haired seventeen-year-old daughter than when alone. He had loved her from the first sight of her newborn face, with its unmistakable and strongly marked resemblance to his mother. The echoes and parallels and actual duplications between daughter and mother incremented like compound interest once he began to look for them. He vowed to do whatever possible to help her, as though the years torn from his mother's life could be made good if Faith were happy and fulfilled.

The difference in style between his recent acquisitions and the other furnishings gave the house a hybrid and disturbing appearance. Rudi was irritable and dissatisfied, suspecting he would never achieve a convincing reproduction of his parental home. It became harder to summon up his mother's image. The lamps and rugs and little tables were useless magic. Yet even the memory of that first, vivid return as the person she had been, rather than the dehumanised victim he imagined, was enough to change his relationship to everything.

Each day it was more difficult to believe that he and Barbara were actually husband and wife. She was so calm, so busy and mature—

like a kindly, abstracted nurse. He'd had a nursemaid rather like Barbara when he was about six years old. Apart from commenting on the amount of money he must be spending, she was benignly indifferent to the transformation of the house. In bed, when the light was out and her warm, silent, acquiescent body lay nearby, he could not stop himself from thinking that she was his mother. But rather than inhibiting him, this image increased his sexual desires. Frequently, he felt about to burst into tears. The sight of his glaring eyes and pale, tense, puffy face in the bathroom mirror repelled him.

Rudi had avoided talking to the children about the war, the camps, or how he came to England and his parents died. He had never even attempted to explain their connection to Judaism. It was far too late now to begin, and he was bitterly ashamed of such cowardice. Of course his mother would have wanted her grandchildren to be told everything. Perhaps that was why she had come back and, because the action had not prompted fulfilment of his duty, the reason for her withdrawal. This thought put him into a deep depression for several days. The next Saturday afternoon, on the Portobello Road with Faith, he saw a dress very like one his mother used to wear, dangling from the rail of an old-clothes stall. It gave him an idea. If his mother would not appear of her own free will, dressing Faith in similar clothes might force a return.

Faith was delighted with the garment and hurried back to the empty house to try it on. When she came down the stairs Rudi was astounded by the resemblance. This was not a revenant or hallucination but a solid, breathing figure of flesh: his mother even before he had known her, before his birth, when she had been a young girl. Unaware that she was being used for conjuration, his daughter had innocently assumed the identity of the dead woman.

This was success beyond his imaginings. No doubt that his mother was in the room—but which and how many of her? There was the young girl incarnated by the natural laws of genetic inheritance in his once-more-recognisable daughter; the beloved being for whose appropriate setting every object had been purchased; and the one he never wanted to meet again, the victim who had haunted his adult life.

Perhaps the lamps and rugs were not meant to lure back the girl and untroubled woman, after all—but to ward off this one. Gaunt, dirty, cowed, huddled defensively near the foot of the staircase and wearing the threadbare clothes of a camp inmate, she glared with sick, unrecognising eyes. It made him want to die. He could see her and Faith at the same time, they were only a few feet apart, though inhabiting separate universes.

'Take off that dress,' he commanded. 'Go upstairs and take it off right now.'

'I don't want to take it off.' The concentration camp woman vanished at the sound of her voice. 'I love it. I want to wear it all the time.'

'You look stupid in that dress,' he said desperately. 'You look ridiculous.'

'I don't think I do.' Her expression was defiant and challenging.

The only way to control the fear of breakdown was to stiffen his spirit with anger. Faith could not understand what was happening. 'Take off that dress immediately or I'll tear it off.' Though he had never threatened violence before, she knew he would, yet she refused to obey and stood her ground.

It took less than a moment to cross the empty space between them. The cloth was soft and old and gave easily. She screamed with shock and fear. The turmoil of his emotions was sickening. He thought he would lose consciousness. She was in his power and he could not resist exercising that power; he was tormenting her as though she were his specially chosen victim. There must have been someone who singled out his mother in the same way.

She clutched the pieces of torn fabric across her small breasts and ran up the stairs shouting 'Fascist!', voice thick with tears. He opened the front door and walked out of the house.

It's dark and cold, but he walks rapidly ahead, with no plan or choice of direction, completely indifferent to where he is going, his mind empty. After a time, the emptiness on all sides makes him realise that he must have crossed the road on to Primrose Hill. He tries sitting down on a bench, but the moment he stops moving he is swamped by such self-contempt and self-loathing that he cannot bear it, and starts to walk again. He fears that if he goes back to the house he will break into Faith's room and beat her to death. His stride lengthens. He is walking down Park Road now, down Baker Street, crossing Piccadilly, crossing the river; a tall, thick-bodied man unable to stop walking. He is going to keep walking until a car knocks him down or someone fells him with a blow, until he reaches the end of his endurance and drops in his tracks.

Ruth Fainlight

A Wizard's Robe
Patterned with Stars and Moons

The playground was surrounded by tall, stained brick buildings, and the young of the neighbourhood's nations and races ran and shouted on its concrete. Ellen imagined Martians hovering above, wondering what those darting small creatures in the deep pit below might be. She was the only one to notice them, and her upturned face would be their first sight of a human being. Being almost ten and a half, she felt too grownup to play with the little ones, but the older children made her painfully aware of her small size and immature appearance.

That summer, Ellen thought about Martians a lot. She would like to see some. One night she dreamed of a pale, white-bearded giant in a tall hat and a wizard's robe patterned with stars and moons, who floated over the city and loosed a rain of pinky-white stuff like sticky popcorn or small dead shrimps that clung to her clothes and skin. She could remember a hollow reverberating voice, perhaps the wizard's, louder than any siren, warning to take cover—but not whether she had ignored it out of bravado and curiosity, or had just left it too late. Though she hammered on door after door along the wide empty streets, pleading for shelter, no one would let her in. She screamed as the burning corrosive flakes settled as soft as snow and bit into her bare arms and legs, then woke in a cold sweat, quite different from the usual hot discomfort of New York summer nights. The dream seemed to be connected to those half-comprehended reports of battles and bombing raids she heard on the radio, and the fact that she and her mother and younger brother were here while her father was on the other side of the world.

Recess ended and they went inside. One wall of the classroom was window, banks of glass so dirty it was hard to tell the difference between the frosted lower panes and the higher ones that only gave a view of bricks. A complicated network of manila rope to open and shut them hung like the rigging of a pirate ship. Ellen imagined scrambling to the crow's nest and scanning the horizon for rescue. She wasn't making up for work missed last year because she hadn't been here then, and in any case, always got good grades. The library had been locked for the summer, so she couldn't borrow a book. It was a relief when one of the young women helpers handed out sheets of cardboard and glass and said they were going to make pretty pictures to take home to their mothers.

The oblongs of glass were crudely stamped with the silhouette of a boat (nothing as grand as her pirate-schooner), with thick black wavy lines for the sea, and a shoreline and clouds. Sheets of shiny metallic paper were passed around, then the teacher showed them how to put it between the painted glass and cardboard backing. Ellen persuaded two of the others at her table to exchange some of their paper for bits of hers, and ended up with a blue sea, silver clouds, and crumpled golden sand. She could imagine her father joking about how awful it looked, but the realisation that her mother would praise the picture with exactly the same uncritical intonation and expression she would use if shown a masterpiece, for a moment made it seem almost as magical and beautiful as the teacher said.

They must have been invited to the party because of some gallant, secret and dangerous exploit of her father's, she decided, studying the embossed square of thick white card that arrived with the morning's mail. Her mother laughed when Ellen explained this theory to Hugo, and told them not to be so silly. New York was full of children whose fathers were on war service, and they couldn't all be heroes. But Ellen and Hugo exchanged looks of faith and resignation, like true believers faced with an apostate.

There was still the fresh damp smell of water sluiced through the gutters by the early morning street cleaners, and the sun had not yet mounted high enough to reach the sidewalk as they hurried between the tall apartment blocks.

'What can I wear to the party?' Ellen asked anxiously, running ahead to look into her mother's face without either of them having to slow down.

'One of your dresses will do very well.'

'Can I make myself one? You won't need to buy anything for it. I've got it all worked out.'

'What on earth are you talking about?' Her mother's voice was distracted and irritable. They had reached the entrance to the school. 'Now don't forget to find Hugo and give him his sandwiches. And the two of you go straight to Aunt Lena's this afternoon. No hanging around on the street, understand?' A neighbour had agreed, for a price, to supervise the children during those difficult hours between the end of school and her return from the mid-town office where she worked. With so many women in a similar position—rusty from years of being housewives, and not able to manage on what the authorities regarded as an adequate allowance—she had been lucky to find a job.

A jumble of images from the movies was all that Ellen had to draw on, when she tried to imagine the elegant hall where the party was being held. A movie star was guest of honour, the invitation revealed, so she knew there would be lots of photographers. If only she could get her picture in the papers . . . Then it wouldn't be merely a matter of Hollywood directors fighting each other for a chance to work with her. The whole family would be able to move from their one-and-a-half-room apartment into a mansion, and her mother have nothing else to do except advise and admire her triumphant daughter. And that was just the start. The President would certainly want to have a private fireside chat with such an extraordinary girl, and doubtless arrange for Ellen's father to fly back from wherever he was to deliver a front-line report. Whether she would actually be able to stop the war . . . Here, the unreeling film must have snapped. There were no images at all for a moment.

Everything depended on the marvellous garment she was going to make from the large ecru-coloured lace curtain which Lena had given to her after noticing how much Ellen admired its deep fringed border of birds and flowers, when they had been straightening her closet one afternoon. 'You take the old thing if you like it so much,' she said, putting it into a brown paper bag. 'It's the only one left out of six I got when I was married. I haven't used it for years.'

Her mother's attempts to dissuade her from wearing a curtain to the party were unsuccessful. Ellen pondered every detail, lying awake in the stuffy room where the three of them lived and slept. It would be a shame to cut the piece of fabric—better to let it hang from her shoulders like one of the Greek or Roman togas in her history book. She'd always made clothes for her dolls, and a few weeks before a dirndl skirt for herself had turned out all right. Imagining the grand transformation, she eased as far away as possible from the body of her mother, who moaned now and then in her sleep and became hotter and hotter as the night progressed.

It didn't matter that none of the neatly suited men and smiling women in the reception line paid any attention to her. There was so much to notice that it was better not to be distracted. Ellen stared at the shining parquet floor, elaborate chandeliers and gilt pilasters with tall mirrors between, the waiters and waitresses in sober uniforms and the tables covered with plates and glasses ranged along one side of the vast room. The ceiling was so high that voices sounded lost and faint across the empty central space into which no one had yet ventured.

The noise level rose as speakers of different languages among the families of Allied servicemen competed for audibility. Then, by some mysterious process of communication, they all became aware that the guest of honour had arrived. Children quietened and moved closer to their mothers, and those who had been circulating with trays of food and drink stopped and stared in the same direction towards a small dark-haired woman with a pretty, heavily painted and bad-complexioned face, who slowly turned her head in a wide arc and made each person feel that she had looked directly at him or her alone. Ellen understood at once that this was the essential quality of stardom. A touch on the elbow brought her back to the present. A man standing in front of her said, 'Come over here, into the picture.' It was all beginning to happen, she thought.

Like representative beneficiaries of a charity, a group of guests was being formed to commemorate the occasion. 'Stand here,' he directed. Ellen heard a woman mutter, 'Don't you think she looks a bit odd?' but no one objected when she pulled from her mother's grasp and squeezed into the front row. There was a fusillade of flashbulbs, then it was all finished. The actress and her entourage moved briskly away, and the rest of the group drifted off like parts of an organism that no longer have any function. One of the men nearby called, 'Milly, for heaven's sake!' in a delighted tone of voice, and clasped her mother's hands. 'I didn't know you were in New York.'

Ellen hadn't seen her mother smile like that for ages. 'Yes, these are my two babies.' She gestured them closer. 'You wouldn't recognise her after so much time,' she laughed, and added, 'She loves to dress up.'

'Charming.' His glance passed rapidly over Ellen and then back to her mother's face. 'Come over and meet the others.'

Ellen turned to where Hugo had stood a moment before, but she was surrounded by strangers, all of whom seemed to have a great deal to say, though not to her. She might as well have been on another planet.

'Have you had anything to eat yet, dear?' an elderly English woman in a fussy brown hat enquired. 'I expect you must be feeling a bit lost.' Ellen followed towards the refreshment tables, and munched her way through several slices of cake, darting hostile stares at anyone who looked as if they might begin a conversation.

She was released by Hugo's voice in her ear. 'We're going home,' he said, grinning happily. 'Terrific ice-cream. Come on, Mum's by the door.'

'Who was that?' Ellen demanded.

Her mother responded with a shrewd and critical look. 'An old friend of your father's. He's over here doing some war work.'

'I'm glad my Dad's a soldier, anyway,' Hugo commented as they waited for the elevator.

Next day at school Ellen insisted that she didn't want to take the glass and silver-paper picture home but refused to say why. Later when the teacher told the class how Uncle Sam was helping all the people in Europe and described the falling houses and storms of flame menacing London children at that very moment, then played the record of a fulsome contralto singing 'Land of Hope and Glory', Ellen couldn't hold back any longer. As they all watched the tears run down her face and heard her sob, 'Daddy, Daddy', that little demon, chin on fist and faunish legs crossed, who always perched somewhere up in the top corner of the scene observing her performance, chuckled with admiration. Even though she moaned louder and squeezed her eyes tight shut to wipe out sight and sound of him, she knew he was there in his robe of moons and stars, her most reliable ally and familiar.

Clive Sinclair

was born in London in 1948 and was educated at the University of East Anglia and
the University of California, Santa Cruz.
He is the author of four novels and two
collections of short stories, including
Hearts of Gold (1979), which won the
Somerset Maugham Award. In 1983 he was
named one of the twenty Best of Young
British Novelists along with Martin Amis
and Ian McEwan. Sinclair has published
The Brothers Singer (1983), a critical account
of Isaac Bashevis Singer, Israel Joshua
Singer, and their sister, Esther Kreitman,
and also a memoir, *Diaspora Blues: A View
of Israel* (1987). 'Wingate Football Club'
(1979), his most explicitly British-Jewish
story, is in *Hearts of Gold* and is a good
example of his early work. 'Bedbugs'
(1982) is the title story of his second volume of short stories and remains one of
his most characteristic and disturbing
pieces of fiction. He has recently
returned to shorter fiction, his true métier,
in the prizewinning *The Lady with the Laptop* (1996).

Clive Sinclair

Wingate Football Club

There are some dilemmas it is better not even to think about. I'll give you a for-instance. Suppose England were to play Israel in the World Cup. Who should I support? Ah, you will say, such a thing is very unlikely. England's football is stale, Israel's half-baked. But I'll tell you, stranger things have happened, like when Wingate won the London League Cup.

When I was a boy I used to go with my father to watch Wingate play on Saturday afternoons. Wingate were the only Jewish team in the entire football league; named in honour of our version of Lawrence, crazy Orde, a *goyisher* Zionist. Wingate were never a great team, and though they always had a couple of good players they usually spent the season near the bottom. So imagine our astonishment when we won a hard tie away from home and found ourselves in the London League Cup Final.

Our opponents were a dockland team, notorious for their anti-semitic supporters. They came to our ground like a wolf on the fold. But that year we had a brilliant outside-right, in real life a ladies' hairdresser. To me his dizzy runs down the wing were a thing of infinite beauty; left-backs tumbled to the ground when he passed, felled as if by magic. Pursued by these humbled clods he sprinted for the corner flag and unleashed acute crosses that sent their goalkeeper flailing in the air. Our centre-forward leapt and dived fearlessly to meet the winger's passes, but each time he missed by a hair's breadth.

'Only connect!' we yelled in encouragement.

The supporters of our opponents were prepared to tolerate our precocious start; content in the knowledge that Jews lacked spunk they waited for the crunching tackles to crush the life out of our challenge. And then our centre-forward did connect; his head met the pass fifteen yards out. The ball had 'goal' written all over it as it shot like a bullet towards the net. The goalkeeper was frozen, as helpless as a rabbit, but—would you believe it?—even as we were celebrating the ball hit the post and rebounded back into the centre of the field. We cheered, nevertheless. But my father said sadly, 'A miss is as good as a mile.' And in my disappointment I felt the full force of the simile; all that marvellous approach-work had been for nothing because finally the ball had missed, the nearness of the miss didn't enter into it, a miss is as good as a mile.

A minute later I learnt another lesson. The rebound initiated an enemy attack which petered out harmlessly in the midfield mud, but then our centre-half made a disastrous error; although unchallenged he passed back to the goalkeeper, and to our horror the ball again stuck in the mud. It was a race for the ball between our goalie and their centre-forward, an ox. The goalie was first to the ball but before he could fully grasp it the centre-forward had crashed into him, not illegally, but carried by the momentum of his run. The ball spun from our goalkeeper's hands and bounced into the back of the net. We protested, hurled abuse at the referee, but the goal stood.

'Take note of that, young man,' said the Prince of Shmattes who sported a velvet-collared camel-hair overcoat. 'It is an important lesson to learn: that the end justifies the means. We Jews have always been too fussy. When did pussyfooting around ever get us anywhere? Why can't our forwards barge into goalkeepers like that? Look at me. Did I make a success by tapping on doors? Not on your life. No, I barged straight in. Believe me, that's the only way to get on in this life.'

Now that we were losing, the other side's supporters even cheered our outside-right and mocked their own left-back for being made to look foolish by the quicksilver Jewboy.

The second half started with a sensation. Straight from the kick-off the ball went to our outside-right who rounded his man with arrogant ease and set off on one of his runs. At the last possible moment he crossed the ball and our centre-forward rose like there were springs in his heels to meet that perfect pass. He seemed to be floating while the ball rested on his instep before he smacked it into the back of the net. The equalizer! We went delirious with joy, we felt the exultation that perfection excites; make no mistake, that goal was a work of art!

We breathed the ultimate in praise, 'The goalie never stood a chance.'

But try as they might Wingate just could not get that second all-important goal. Then ten minutes from time our right-half, laughingly overweight but astute with it, split their defence with a through ball which left our centre-forward alone with only the goalkeeper to beat.

'Shoot!' we pleaded.

He ran on, seemed to stumble, but kept his footing.

'Shoot!' we screamed.

But he hesitated. What was in his mind? Was he planning to dribble round the goalkeeper? However, before he had a chance to do a thing the goalkeeper suddenly rushed from his line and knocked him flat. The referee pointed to the spot. A penalty! Grown men, including my father, hid their faces as the centre-forward prepared to take the kick. This time there was no hesitation, before the tension had time to sink in the ball was in the goal. We could hardly believe it; less than ten minutes to go and we were ahead; we began to scent victory.

'WIN-GATE! WIN-GATE!' we chanted.

'How much longer?' I kept asking my father as the final minutes ticked away and the tension became unbearable. The attacks of our opponents grew increasingly desperate; their centre-forward charged again and again into our defence like a battering-ram. But our defence held. What a relief when the referee looked at his watch and put the whistle to his lips!

As the whistle blew a woman in a fake leopard-skin coat said out loud, 'Hitler was right! Send the Jews to the showers!'

The boy standing next to her was one of our supporters (he looked big to me, but I don't suppose he was older than fourteen). 'Keep quiet, you bitch!' he said.

Whereupon she slapped him round the face. He hit her back.

'You dirty Jew!' she cried.

Her companion moved in on the boy, but he never hit him more than once before Al Pinsky interceded. Now Al wasn't tall, so that golem just laughed, which was daft, because Al Pinsky was once

the lightweight champion of Great Britain. The golem dropped the
boy and took a swing at Pinsky. His fists were the size of hams.
Pinsky ducked, like he was taking a bow, then straightened up and
calmly knocked the fellow cold. When the police came and listened
to the various versions of the incident we tingled with the pleasure
of righteous indignation. That evening as I walked home with my
father toward the awaiting glass of milk and toasted chola I felt
elated; we had not only won the cup but also a great moral victory
over the yoks. They had called us dirty Jews and we had stood up to
them and got away scot free; on the contrary, it was they who left
with bloody noses.

Now I realize that part of the fun of going to Wingate was the
possibility of encountering just such anti-semitism. Among our
supporters it was axiomatic that if you scratch a goy you'll find an
anti-semite; our world-weary version of Shylock's great lament.
Perhaps we had the mentality of people who go to the zoo to tease
a caged lion and complain when it tries to bite them; but I think we
welcomed the anti-semitism because it proved that we were morally
superior; it may have confirmed our status as outcasts but it also
reaffirmed our role as the chosen people. Although our daily existence gave us no evidence to support the fact there obviously was
something different about us. And on Saturday afternoons we could
flaunt this difference with pride, knowing that it would be recognized; we were the Wingate Supporters Club; our badge was the
Mogen David. On the field our boys gave as good as they got, and
on the sidelines if the yoks wanted trouble they could have it from
us wholesale.

A couple of weeks after we won the cup, as if to rub in our moral
superiority, the Daily Mirror ran an exposé on the horse-doping
racket, and it turned out that most of the opposing team and many
of their supporters were involved, including their centre-forward
and the shiksa in the leopard-skin coat. That Saturday we were full
of the news; it was too good to be true, not only were they anti-
semites, they were criminals as well!

'What else can you expect from yoks like that?' said the Prince of
Shmattes.

My father, a wittier man, said, 'Goys will be goys.'

Of course my ambition was to play for Wingate. Every evening after school I would go into our backgarden and chase a football around. I divided myself into two imaginary teams: the first mounted dazzling attacks down the flank which were finished off by a deadly striker, and if a goal was not perfect they would not count it; the other was made up of plodders, grateful for any rebound or accidental goal, they were without grace and had no time for the brilliant individual. The first team did not necessarily win, but they were always a pleasure to watch. As I ran I daydreamed of being the prince of outside-rights; the outsider who hovers on the periphery of the match but whose brilliant interventions win the day. What better ambition for a Jewish boy?

Our games master at school had flaming red hair and a beak of a nose, though he wasn't Jewish. Since my natural expression was one of discomfort I was his constant butt.

'Stop looking like you are suffering,' he would say. 'Boys are supposed to enjoy games.'

My passion for football came as a surprise to him; in fact I was fleet-footed enough to be a good outside-right.

'Not bad,' he said, 'I didn't think your people liked physical activity.' He took a look at my expensive football boots and said, 'I bet your father earns a lot of money, eh?'

'I don't know,' I said. I hadn't been going to watch Wingate for nothing; I knew an anti-semite when I saw one. Because I enjoyed football I was spared actual physical torment. However, my friend Solomon was a different kettle of fish. Solomon hated all games, especially football.

Poor Solomon was a coward, and Beaky sensed this at once. He picked out the six biggest louts in our class and told them to stand in a line. Then he threw the ball to Solomon and ordered him to run at them. Solomon didn't move. He was too scared even to argue.

'Get going you milksop, or else,' said Beaky. Still no action from Solomon. So Beaky hit him, hard round the head. 'You have no choice, you greasy tub of chopped liver,' said Beaky.

Milchik or *flayshig*, it made no difference to him. Solomon ran at the boys in the line, kicking the ball far ahead of him, but not one of the boys bothered to go for the ball, taking their cue from their master they took Solomon instead. While Beaky watched they beat him up; not badly, but enough to make him cry. I make no excuses for my inactivity, I was only glad it wasn't happening to me; besides it was a part of our games lesson.

About the time I went away to university things began to go wrong for Wingate; lacking enough Jewish boys to make a *minyan* they had to co-opt non-Jewish players. It was true that Wingate was supposed to foster good-fellowship between Jewish and non-Jewish football-ers, but most of our supporters felt this was going too far; this was—bite your tongue—assimilation. Gradually they stopped com-ing to watch Wingate and sure enough, as they had prophesied, the club lost its identity. The last time I saw them play the team was made up of strangers, men with names like Smith and Williams. The old atmosphere was gone. Wingate had become just another football team. At university I would continue to listen to the football results on the radio, but I could never feel for any other team what I had felt for Wingate; that sense of personal involvement was gone for ever. But by then I knew that there was more to life than football.

My parents assumed I had gone to university to get a degree, but I really went to lose my virginity. I became educated as a by-product. I discovered that the seminars were the great showplaces. So I made myself shine. Society functions were another good place to meet girls. I picked up Linda at the Jewish and Israel Society. Linda called herself the most experienced virgin in the western hemisphere; she would allow any physical intimacy short of intercourse. We slept together frequently, and sometimes I would get such a belly-ache from frustration that I could hardly stand up straight. In public we acted like lovers, but we were just going through the motions, like footballers without a ball. Still, thanks to Linda, I learned all about the role of the kibbutz in Israeli life. Not to mention the role of the Arab, the artist, the woman, the socialist and the *frum* Jew. One night a real Israeli came to speak. I had never seen a sabra before. He was swarthier than I expected. His subject was the role of peace in Israeli life. He was optimistic. He pointed out that it was now over a decade since Suez, and while there was no *de jure* peace there was clearly a *de facto modus vivendi*. A policy of live and let live. He believed that the Arabs had come to accept the presence of Israel, and that given time a normal relationship would develop between the former enemies. Had he got the wrong number!

When the Six Day War began we didn't know that it was only

going to last six days, of course. What trauma there was in the
Diaspora! No one gave Israel a chance. Every night we saw a different
Arab army on the news. Their leaders promised to drive the Jews
into the sea. Then Abba Eban would appear, sounding like a Cam-
bridge don. The words of the Prince of Shmattes came back to me.
'We Jews have always been too fussy. When did pussyfooting around
ever get us anywhere?' Even Solomon's mother knew better than
Abba Eban what was what.

'The Israelis should give the Arabs a bomb already,' she said,
'they should only suffer one hundredth of what we Jews have been
through.' She looked about ready to *plotz*.

No wonder, her son was in the Israeli army. After school, instead
of going to university, Solomon had emigrated. We still kept in
touch. He had a room in Jerusalem. Till the war-fever got me this
had been my only real contact with Israel. But now it was time to
separate the Jews from the *goys*. Of course I couldn't enlist in the
Israeli army but I volunteered to go out as a driver of tractors or—
God forbid—ambulances. I was warned that I might come under
fire, but I brushed aside the possibility. However, my services were
never required. The war ended too quickly.

It made for excellent television. Don't forget, it was my first war; I
was too young to remember Suez. Every night I went to the television
room next to the library to watch the late news. It was marvellous,
our side were winning victory after victory. Films showed tanks
scooting over the Sinai desert; the enemy was nowhere in sight.
Soldiers hugged and kissed beneath the Western Wall of liberated
Jerusalem, looking like they had just scored the winning goal.
Experts explained with the aid of mobile diagrams the brilliance of
the Israeli strategy; the daring raids, the lightning strikes. I had not
felt such exultation since Wingate took the London League Cup; but
I was older and I savoured my triumph in silence. Linda, beside me,
was less circumspect. She screamed, she cried. I told her to shush,
because we were not alone. Sitting by himself, the only other person
in the room, was an Arab. Night by night his expression became
progressively gloomier. When, on the seventh day, news came in
of the Syrian atrocities, the captured Israeli pilot decapitated in
front of the cameras and worse, he got up and walked out. 'What
do you expect from Arabs?' said Linda.

Solomon's mother telephoned, *shepping naches;* her song was my son the hero. His next letter was modest enough, but it made me envious. Of all people, Solomon had become glamorous! An outside-right, as it were. Such madness, to feel deprived because I had missed a war! But both Linda and I were engulfed in the exuberant aftermath. We discussed the possibility of marriage. We planned to become Israeli citizens. My Jewish destiny was about to be fulfilled.

Or so I thought. But chance took control; I was offered a post at the university, too good an opportunity to be missed. My destiny was postponed. Many other things also happened; governments fell, El Fatah became fashionable, Germany were revenged upon England in the Mexico World Cup, my parents celebrated their silver wedding, Linda and I were married. We went to Israel for our honeymoon. Naturally we visited Solomon in Jerusalem. He was no longer the weedy Yid of our school-days; instead he moved through the city with self-confident ease. A man among men, a real Yiddisher *mensh.* One night after a street-corner supper of felafel we all went to the cinema in Zion Square. The first feature was a film about the Six Day War, made up cheaply from bits of old newsreel. It was received with wild enthusiasm. Though it is difficult to credit today the audience cheered every time Moshe Dayan or Itzak Rabin appeared on the screen. Unfortunately the main feature was less to their liking; the story of a man destroyed by Stalinism, fiction based on fact. The audience quickly lost interest, and only perked up when the unlucky victim was accused of being a Zionist. Finally, as the man looked through his prison bars towards the sky, someone shouted.

'He's expecting the Israeli airforce to come and rescue him!'

Everybody laughed. As we were leaving Linda, unable to restrain herself, started yelling at a bunch of the yahoos.

'What is the matter with you,' she cried, 'don't you have any respect for suffering?'

'*Ma zeh?*' they said, tapping their foreheads. Then Linda, out of control, spat in their faces. This caused them to forget their good humour; they swore at Linda, they called her a whore. They gathered their empty Coca-Cola bottles and flung them at us; and as the glass shattered on the concrete floor they began to close in. Four Esaus, looking for a fight. What sort of joke is this, I thought, to be beaten up in Israel by fellow Jews? With a single movement Solomon grabbed the leader, clutched him and positioned him; then with a graceful gesture cast him over his shoulder. The unsuspecting partner of this *pas de deux* performed a somersault in the air and crashed on to the floor. His hairy brethren rushed Solomon, but it was a halfhearted attack, and Solomon danced amongst them till they all fell dizzily to the ground, like the walls of Jericho.

'Where did you learn to fight like that?' I asked.

'In the army,' said Solomon, 'I was the lightweight wrestling champion.'

He invited us to feel his biceps. 'You know what,' he said, 'whenever I fight someone I still imagine I'm hitting Beaky, that anti-semitic bastard.'

'But they were Jews you beat up tonight, Solomon,' I said.

'Only Yemenite Jews,' he said, 'it's all they understand.'

So even in a nation of Jews there were still *yoks*.

Next thing we heard about Solomon was that he'd been chosen to represent Israel at the Munich Olympics. Quite an achievement for Solomon, the boy who hated games. We watched the opening ceremony on Solomon's mother's coloured television; you should have seen her *kvell* as her only son marched past behind the Israeli flag. I'll swear her chest swelled out a good six inches. Poor woman, it was her last bit of pleasure.

Solomon did moderately well in his competition, though he did not win a medal; but he had his day of fame, none the less. He was probably sleeping when the Black September terrorists burst into the Israeli athletes' quarters. All through that day we sat in front of the television set seeing nothing but those white walls and the gunmen on the balcony in the balaclava helmets, hearing nothing but banalities from sports commentators unaccustomed to dealing with such events. We knew that Solomon was inside. What could he be thinking? Deeper than the politics of the Middle East was he tormented by a single thought? That Beaky was having the last laugh. Solomon could not wrestle with men holding machine-guns; his skills were trumped, he was as helpless as a schoolboy again. When darkness fell we saw the coaches fill, ready to take the terrorists and their hostages to the airfield outside Munich. Linda swore that she could make out the features of Solomon, but all their faces

looked the same to me. Written on them all was the awful realization
that whatever they did the Jews were doomed to lose out; you learn
to fight to defend yourself against the yoks and—what happens?—
they get guns and shoot you instead. One of the athletes looked
back on the steps of the coach—perhaps that was Solomon—and
held out his hands as if to say, what more can we do? Then at
midnight came the surprise news. There had been a shoot-out at
the airfield. All the hostages were safe. The terrorists were dead.

'Thank God for that,' said Linda.

The Daily Mirror was sticking through our letter-box next morning, like a dagger in a corpse. The headline screamed: THE TRAGIC
BLUNDER. It seemed that the German police had made a 'tragic
blunder' in announcing the results of the shoot-out; they got it the
wrong way round; it was the athletes who were wiped out, not the
terrorists.

I began to shiver as the information sank in. Solomon was dead!
I recalled with what pride he showed us his biceps that night in
Jerusalem; but all the training was gone for nothing now. Solomon
was dead. Linda cried all day, she cursed the Palestinians. But I
could not see it like that, to me the Palestinians were instruments
of fate. Solomon's inevitable nemesis; it was merely a cruel irony
that this particular death struggle should be between two semitic
peoples. Out of habit I turned to the sports section of the newspaper. But what I saw turned me cold. 'Queens Park Rangers went
hurtling out of the League Cup,' I read, 'following two tragic blunders by Rangers defender Ian Evans.' It had been quite a night for
tragic blunders! The carelessness of some sub-editor had equated
the two events, the terrible with the trivial; or perhaps it did really
reflect how others saw the Munich Massacre. As a good away win
for the Palestinians. It was, indeed, confirmation of Beaky's final
triumph.

All this happened a few years ago, already. Since then the news
has not been too good; nothing seems to have gone right since the
Yom Kippur War. They have even built a mosque in Regent's Park.
Last week I met the Prince of Shmattes in the street. Only he isn't
so clever any more, these days he has to wear his own shmattes.
People stopped buying his suits and the economic crisis finished
him off. He was on his way to the post office to collect his pension.

Solomon's mother never recovered from the shock, and was senile before she was sixty. Now every young man who visits she thinks is her son, me included. And I go along with the pretence. What harm in that? My parents keep nagging me to give them a grand-child. But I want any child of mine to be born in Israel. *L'shanah haba-ah birushalayim.* Next year in Jerusalem.

Clive Sinclair

Bedbugs

During the night I have a vision of bedbugs in congress. A concres-
cence of male and female. The polluted mass pulsates, masculine
organs pullulate, grow into dangerous spikes that, blinded by passion, miss the proffered orifices and stab deep into the soft bellies
of their consorts. While I thus dream, my blood is sucked and the
satiated bugs, too bloated to return to their hiding places, excrete
their waste upon the sheets and make their getaway. When I awake
I observe the tell-tale black stains and become conscious of new
islands of itchiness erupting upon my body. Life has taken a turn
for the better for the dispossessed bedbugs, homeless since the
demolition of the ancient slums, with the construction of the concrete college. Here at last the flat-bodied bugs have found sanctuary
in the snug crevices, and plenty of food in the beds, even during
the long summer vacation when the abandoned beds are filled by
foreign students and their teachers—the former having come to
Cambridge to improve their English, the latter to improve their
finances. I am among the latter.

Some weeks previously I had been telephoned by a director of
Literature & Linguistics Ltd, hitherto unknown, and been offered a
job as a tutor at their Cambridge Summer School, held annually in
the vacated university. He was frank. He said that they had been let
down at the last minute and that someone had given him my name;
he apologized for the short notice and inquired if I knew anything
about the poets of the Great War, the course set by the deserter,
for which books had already been purchased and despatched to the
students; he added that these students tended to be young, German,
intelligent, fluent and—with a chuckle—female; he said by way of
conclusion that Literature & Linguistics Ltd was a reputable com-

pany and that the salary was equally respectable. I promised to let him know the following day.

Here was irony! Teaching First World War poetry to Germans, who had cut short the careers of most of the poets. Being Jewish I also felt a more personal thin-skinned irony. But was such irony justified? Neither I nor the students were even born in the days of the Third Reich, so could I blame them for the fact that had their parents proved victorious I would never have been born at all? Easily. Then what made me take the position? Money? Of course. But even more persuasive was Isaac Rosenberg. On account of a little-known biographical detail: his affair with my grandmother. He was ten and she was seven. They kissed one fine afternoon outside the Rosenbergs' house in Stepney, a few doors down from my great-grandfather's greengrocery. Furthermore, when Rosenberg decided to enlist he ran away from home and joined a bantam battalion in Bury St Edmunds. You can see his barracks from our bedroom window. The grotesque red-brick pastiche of a castle looms over me as I call the director to announce my acceptance. I do not mention that I have renamed the course Rosenberg's Revenge.

However, the German girls completely disarm me. They are charming, receptive and funny. Above all they seem so innocent. Our first class began in a tentative way, polite, giggly, until one of the girls demanded to know why we were studying such poetry.

'The concerns of the poets are out of date, they do not mean anything to us,' she said, 'especially since we are mostly girls here and not interested in war one bit. So why do you make us read about these horrible things?'

Other girls snorted, to be interpreted as derisive. In that parallel course running in my head, Rosenberg's Revenge, I rubbed the cow's nose in Nazi atrocities, but in our Cambridge classroom I was patient, persuasive. I did not mention the pink stain on her neck which I took to be a love bite, sign of her preoccupations.

'Why? Because the poetry transcends its environment,' I said. 'War becomes the inspiration. A source of destruction, but also creation. A paradox to contemplate. The proximity of death added to the intensity of the poet. Their minds were concentrated wonderfully.'

My allies moved in to attack. Women not interested in war? What nonsense! War involves everybody. My enemy was routed, isolated, leaving the rest of us clear to commence the course. In that introductory meeting, relationships were established, and I was pleased to note that foremost among my supporters was the most attractive girl in the room. Vanity also is an inspiration.

There are two tutors for the twenty students: myself for literature, the other for linguistics, with composition shared. Although Bury St Edmunds is only thirty miles from Cambridge I am expected to sleep in the college, since my duties include evening entertainment. Tonight my colleague is giving a lecture on phonemes, freeing me to telephone my wife. As I listen to the ringing tone I consider the fact that while each peal is identical, subsequent conversation gives it a retrospective value; from phoney, wrong number, to euphony for a lover.

'Hello, love,' says my wife, 'miss me?'

'Lots,' I say.

So our catechism continues, a pleasant exchange of self-confidences, until I realize with alarm that my answers are counterfeit. I am not thinking about her. I do not miss her. I am a liar. Second sight suddenly reveals this peccadillo as prophetic and I foresee the wreck of our marriage. Doubtless this is a romantic fallacy to be dismissed as easily as the psychosomatic cramp that has gripped my stomach. What harm can there be in euphemism if it makes her happy?

'Sleep well,' says my wife, 'sweet dreams.'

But the belly-ache won't go away. Back in my room I stretch upon the bed. My room is modernistic, without extraneous matter; for example there are no handles on the drawers, just holes for fingers to pull them open. Being double the room is a duplex, and in the steps that connect the levels the style reaches its apotheosis. Granted that only fifty per cent of a regular staircase is used, since just one foot presses on each step, what does the architect do? Lop off the redundant half, of course. Leaving steps that alternate, right, left, right, left, etcetera. True, the residents have tried to impress their personalities upon this chamber by decorating the walls with posters, but in their absence, devoid of their possessions, these emphasize the emptiness. Nor are there any books on the shelves, save my war poems, and a book marked with a single yellow star. The ghetto journal of a Warsaw Jew. The diary was discovered after the war, his body never was. Actually, I did not bring the book along to read, rather as a reminder of an evil that cannot be exorcized. Nevertheless, flat out with colic I read it from cover to cover. What can I say? In class we talk of literature but this is not art. The writer chronicles everything as dispassionately as possible, a record for future historians, until in the end he can restrain himself no longer. 'Daughter of Germany!' he curses. 'Blessed is he who will seize your babes and smash them against the rock!'

Sweet dreams! I dream of flesh in torment and awaken to find my body in a rash. No stranger to hives, I blame my brain, never suspecting the true culprits. But instead of fading, the hives swell so that by mid-morning, my class in full swing, they are throbbing in sympathy with the soldiers in the trenches. Fighting the temptation to scratch I ask my enemy to read Rosenberg's 'Louse Hunting'. Blushing she begins.

> Nudes, stark and glistening,
> Yelling in lurid glee. Grinning faces
> And raging limbs
> Whirl over the floor on fire;
> For a shirt verminously busy
> Yon soldier tore from his throat
> With oaths
> Godhead might shrink at, but not the lice . . .

And gets no further. Bursting into tears she cries. 'You mock me! You see the bites on my neck and you think I am dirty! But only here have I got them! There are bugs in my bed!'

'She means Franz,' says someone, referring to my only male student, likewise bitten.

'My dictionary tells me that a bug is a ghost, a bogeyman, a night prowler,' says another, 'so Franz could be defined as a bedbug.'

'But they are not the only ones who have been bitten,' I say, 'look at my arms.' Whereupon my enemy regards me with something like gratitude. 'You see,' I say, 'the poems are relevant to our condition after all.'

Tonight it is my turn to amuse the students. So I have arranged a visit to the Cambridge Arts Theatre. Since the play is Ionesco's

The Lesson, which ends with the pedagogue stabbing his pupil and donning Nazi uniform, we have made attendance voluntary. In the event I am accompanied only by my erstwhile enemy, Franz, and my most attractive acolyte. Naturally I am curious to see how my charges will react to the drama. Franz and Monika fidget as the dead girl drops immodestly into a chair and her professor pulls on his swastika armband. On the other hand Inge is impressed.

'Such a play explains much about fascism,' she says, 'and about Germany.'

'Perhaps Germany as it was,' says Franz, 'but today things are different.'

'Nonsense,' says Inge, 'we remain a nation of *Hausfrauen* who thrive on order. We didn't like the Jews so we make them disappear. Just like dust. We were frightened by the Baader-Meinhof gang so we killed them. Pouf! No more terrorism. We adore neatness. That is why Monika is horrified by her bedbugs. They leave marks. So she cannot forget them. She cannot sweep them under the carpet— is that what you say?'

'Suicide,' says Franz, 'they killed themselves.'

'That is what we are told,' says Inge, 'what you are pleased to believe.'

Monika looks at Franz.

'We must go,' he says, 'we are tired.'

'Not me,' says Inge, 'the play has given me an appetite.'

The Castle, an unexceptional pub on the road back to college. We request drinks and curries. The landlord motions us to a table. It is midweek and the pub is deserted save for a couple sitting in a darkened corner. The man is not in his right mind.

'Tell me, George,' he says to the landlord, 'now the season is a fortnight old what do you think of our esteemed football team?'

'My name is not George,' says the landlord.

'No spunk, that's their problem,' he says, 'not enough aggression.'

'They've only lost two games,' says the landlord.

'But how many more?' says the man. 'Listen, George, you know everyone in Cambridge. You tell the manager I've got some advice for him. A bastard I may be, pardon my French—father was killed in the war before he had time to do the honourable thing—but I'm related to lords, the highest in the land. Therefore the manager will listen to me. Did you hear about that Aussie coach who showed his team newsreels of Nazi war crimes before a big match? That got their blood up! Went straight out and thrashed the opposition. I've plenty of ideas as good as that. I'm counting on you, George. Tell the manager the bastard wants to see him.'

'Wash your mouth out,' shouts the landlord, 'I won't have bad language in this pub. Not when there's ladies present. If you won't behave you can clear off.'

But Inge is not embarrassed. 'That was a fine play we saw tonight,' she says, 'perhaps we could produce something like that in our composition class?'

'Good idea,' I say, 'but it will be difficult with so many people. You and Monika will never agree about anything. You'll argue over every word and nothing will get written.'

'You are right, of course,' says Inge.

'Maybe we could do something with a smaller group,' I say, 'you, me and one or two others.'

'But then those who are left out might become envious,' says Inge. 'They will accuse us of élitism.'

'Then we must arrange a cabaret for the last night,' I say. 'Everyone will be invited to help. I'll advertise for poets, singers, even stripteasers. Our contribution will be the play.'

Inge laughs. Her shoulders tremble. Not for the first time I observe the body beneath the shirt.

Two plates of curry stand in the serving-hatch growing cold. We watch them while the landlord sulks. Finally I deliver them myself. But before we can begin our meal the loony snatches Inge's plate and scurries to his table.

'You've taken our dinner,' he yells, 'we were here before you!' His companion looks miserable, but remains silent.

As if awaiting this opportunity the landlord reappears. 'You have gone too far,' he bellows, 'apologize to these people at once!'

The man is outraged. He puckers his lips as if about to blow a kiss. 'Sir,' he says, 'it is they who should apologize to us for stealing our food.'

The landlord's wrath descends upon the lunatic who flees for his life.

'I might be illegitimate,' he cries into the night, 'but I do not copulate with Germans.'

Now I am angry. But I am a hypocrite, the half-wit is a prophet.

Brushing my teeth in preparation for bed there is a knock on the door. Foaming at the mouth I admit Inge.

'This afternoon I purchased equipment to purge your bedbugs,' she says. 'I planned to tell you after the theatre but the events in the pub drove it from my mind.'

I rinse out the toothpaste. Inge meanwhile is crumbling a fire-lighter into a large metal fruit-bowl and mixing the fragments with charcoal chips. The result is ignited. Flames leap from the bowl like tongues ravenous for bedbugs.

'Now we must wait,' says Inge, 'until the charcoal becomes red hot.'

We sit looking at one another.

'You are married?' says Inge.

'Yes,' I say.

'I am not married, though I have a man in Germany,' she says. 'Here I am free, there I am a prisoner. You understand? Always we must do what he wants. Do you know the word "eudemonism"? It means you act for another's happiness. It is your moral duty. That is always the role of women, don't you think? Your wife, does she work?'

'No,' I say.

'Why not?' says Inge.

'She was pregnant,' I say, 'but she lost the baby. She is going back to work soon.'

'Is she—how do you say?—in a depression?' asks Inge.

'She is over it now,' I say, 'we don't talk about it any more.'

We feel the heat from the glowing coals.

'Let us hope the bowl does not crack,' says Inge, 'it isn't mine, it comes from my room.'

As if casting a spell she pours yellow powder on to the embers. Asphyxiating fumes immediately fill the room.

'Sulphur,' she says. 'The gas it makes will kill all the bugs.'

Coughing I lead her upstairs.

We stare into the underworld.

'Look,' says Inge, 'as I said.'

Sure enough, bugs are dropping lifelessly from crannies in the ceiling. Suddenly an unexpected twang! The bowl has split.

'Oh, no,' cries Inge.

Brilliant as the steps are in conception it is dangerous to descend them at speed, as Inge learns. She tumbles, hits the floor with a thump, and remains utterly inert. Spreadeagled, supine. There is no blood, but I do not know if this is a good or a bad sign. Her hand is limp. I feel for the pulse, but it is either stopped or I have my thumb in the wrong spot. Her heart. Situated, of all places, beneath her left breast. I place my hand upon the breast. It is warm certainly. But I can feel no heartbeat, though the nipple tantalizingly hardens. However, for all I know this may be a posthumous reflex action or even the beginnings of rigor mortis. I am no doctor. At a loss I rock forward upon my knees and part her lips with my tongue, intending to administer the kiss of life. But as I begin to blow into her mouth I feel Inge's right arm curl around my neck. And as she presses me closer I realize that my hand is still upon her breast.

Bugs continue to fall as Inge glides out of her pants. Possessed now, I turn out the lights so that Inge's naked body is illuminated only by the smouldering charcoal, a serpentine shape, splashed with red, an undulant stream of lava into which I fling myself.

'Take me,' hisses Inge, 'here, as I am, on the floor.'

While the madness lasts I pump my body into her, aware only of our sweat and the uncontrollable pleasure, dimly conscious of the mocking parody the dying embers cast upon the wall. Spent, prone upon Inge's salty body, I gasp for breath in the sulphurous air.

'Please,' whispers Inge, 'I am not finished.' She directs my hand down her belly to a damper place. Slowly my senses settle as I watch Inge's spectre writhe, and listen to her ecstatic groans, which dissolve as a deeper voice fills my ear:

> Soon like a demons' pantomime
> This plunge was raging.
> See the silhouettes agape,
> See the gibbering shadows
> Mix with the baffled arms on the wall.

A man emerges from the shadows. He is dressed in khaki and put-tees, but looks too delicate to be a soldier. 'Do you like my poem?' he says.

'Yes,' I say, 'you were a genius.'

'Tell that to the Germans,' he says.

I nod. I am. 'Do you hate them?' I ask.

'You cannot hate the dead,' he says, 'and you lose touch with the living.'

Inge, oblivious, cavorts on the end of my finger.

'I'm doing this for you,' I say.

He shrugs. 'Why bother with humbug when you've got bedbugs?' he says. 'Jews, Germans, we're all the same to them. They have cosmopolitan sympathies. We destroy one another and the bedbugs take revenge.'

'Not here,' I say, 'they're all dead.'

'So am I,' he says.

'Do you remember my grandmother?' I ask. 'Eva Zelinsky, she lived near you in Oxford Street.'

'What does she look like?' he asks.

'An old lady, white hair, in her eighties,' I say.

He smiles. 'Everything changes,' he says, 'except the dead.'

'Aaaaaaah!' cries Inge. She comes, he goes. There is quiet in the room. Inge is drowsy with delight. The charcoal has burned itself out.

'Come,' I say, 'let's go to bed.' During the night I have a vision of bedbugs in congress.

Throughout the day Inge wears a silk scarf to conceal the bites upon her neck. Likewise, when I telephone my wife, I hide the truth from her. Better keep quiet and skip the consequences. In two weeks Inge will be back in Germany with her jailer. At the moment, however, she is in my room again. We are awaiting another girl, selected to complete our playwriting team.

'When you took off your clothes,' says Inge, 'I saw something. That you are a Jew. Please, you must tell me. When you fucked me, was it for revenge?'

I shake my head. 'No,' I say, 'I did it because I wanted you. I forgot you were a German.'

'I am glad,' says Inge. 'You know, I have always admired the Jewish people. You have read Martin Buber?'

'Buber? Sure,' I say. 'I know my melancholy fate is to turn every *thou* into an *it*, every person into a thing. Last night you were a *thou*, this afternoon already you are an *it*, last night we had intercourse, a real spiritual dialogue, this afternoon we must write dialogue.'

Inge grins, 'And do you have any ideas?' she says.

'No,' I say, 'I am the producer. Ideas are not my responsibility. Do you?'

'Only simple ones,' she says 'like a husband and wife, eating dinner, watching television, talking but not communicating. Just one twist, a girl will be the husband and you must play the wife.'

The other girl arrives and accepts the idea with enthusiasm. We work on the play through the evening and into the night. The other girl goes. Inge stays. Martin Buber? A *boobe-myseh!*

On the last Saturday I escort all the students to Bury St Edmunds. A coach has been hired and I sit up beside the driver holding a microphone. As we approach the town along the Newmarket Road I indicate, to the left, the barracks where Rosenberg trained, on the right, my house. The coach halts in the large square at the top of Angel Hill.

'Okay,' I say, 'I'll tell you what there is to see in Bury St Edmunds. Opposite are the walls of the abbey, behind are the ruins and a park. There is a cathedral. Go up Abbeygate Street and you'll come to the market. Fruit. Vegetables. Junk. Beyond the market is Moyses Hall. Built by a Jew in 1180. Unfortunately for him all the Jews were expelled from Bury in 1190. Now off you go. Back here at three o'clock.'

Gradually the others slip away until I am left with only Inge for company. It is a hot day, dusty with heat. The locals look white and sweaty, like creatures unused to the light. The women wear drab moth-proofed frocks that show off the freckles on their breasts; the men roll up their shirt-sleeves to reveal the tattoos upon their arms. It is a mystery, this abundance of sample-book tattooing, all of course applied by choice. By contrast Inge's spectacular sexuality stops people in their tracks: her black scarf, her red tee-shirt, clinging like a second skin, her denim shorts and—this I know—no underwear.

'I feel so good today,' says Inge, 'I should like a souvenir. Is there perhaps a booth where we can have our photograph taken together?'

'There's one in Woolworth's,' I say. A photograph! Thus far the affair has been vague, nothing to do with my real life, as insubstantial as a dream. It will be a simple trick to persuade myself that it never happened. But a photograph! Our faces fixed, cheek by cheek, our relationship projected into the foreseeable future. Proof snatched from the lethal fingers of time.

The booth is already occupied by three small boys. We can see their legs, and hear their excited giggling. Then as the first flash fades we hear, above their laughter, the screech of a creature in terror. Inge tears back the curtain and exposes the boys, including one who is dangling a kitten by its tail in front of the camera. The kitten flails about uselessly, tensing and squealing in horror at each flash, only to redouble its efforts in the lacuna.

'You monsters,' cries Inge, 'stop torturing that poor animal!'

The boys grin. The kitten swings. Faster and faster. Until the boy lets go. The kitten lands on Inge's shoulders. Seeking to steady itself it raises its paw and sinks its claw into her ear. Inge gently lifts the kitten so her ear is not torn although the lobe is pierced and bleeding profusely, staining her tee-shirt a deeper red. I give her my handkerchief to press against the wound.

'It looks worse than it is,' says Inge, 'it does not hurt.'

'Nevertheless, you must come back to our house,' I say, 'you must wash and change. You can't go around covered in blood.' Once again a curious accident has left me with no choice. Inge will meet my wife.

We surprise my wife sunbathing naked in the garden.

'Hello, love,' she says, 'I didn't know you were bringing somebody back with you.'

'Only one of my students,' I say, 'she's been wounded.'

My wife, wrapping a towel around herself, approaches Inge and leads her off to the bathroom. They reappear in identical cotton shirts, bargains from the market. A stranger might take them for sisters. I cook omelettes for lunch, with a few beans from my garden, and serve them on the lawn where my wife had been alone less than an hour before. I am astonished how relaxed we all are. Inge rattles off examples of her lover's male chauvinism. We all laugh. I feel no guilt, my wife feels no pain. She suspects nothing. She waves the flies from our food and throws breadcrumbs down for the sparrows.

'Are you enjoying the course?' she asks.

'Very much,' says Inge, 'especially our little playwriting group. Has Joshua told you about our play? Yes? Of course. You must come to our cabaret and see it performed.'

'I shall look forward to that,' says my wife. She removes the plates and returns with a bowl of peaches. They are sweet and juicy and attract many wasps. Our fingers become sticky.

'I am glad everything is going so well,' says my wife, 'without any problems.'

'Only the bedbugs,' I say, 'look what they've done to my arms.'

'Poor thing,' says my wife, 'can't you move into a different room?'

'No need,' I say, 'they've been exterminated.'

My wife smiles. What contentment! I realize now why I feel so untroubled; I do not really believe that I have made love to Inge. She is what she seems, just a visitor. My wife is my wife. We belong. Cambridge is a foreign city. To which I must return, however.

I kiss my wife. 'See you on Wednesday,' I say.

'What a nuisance,' says Inge as the coach passes our house, 'I have left my scarf behind.'

'Never mind,' I say, 'I'll pick it up on Wednesday. Besides, you can hardly see the bites now.'

On Tuesday we complete the play. In the evening the heatwave breaks with a tremendous storm. Knowing how much my wife dreads thunder I telephone her. She does not answer. Later, when the rain has stopped, Inge and I stroll to the Castle to toast our success. Afterwards we return to my room where Inge now sleeps as a matter of course. In the morning I telephone my wife again. No reply. Probably shopping. Lunch over, teaching being at an end, I drive home to collect her. There are three milk bottles on the doorstep, the first already sour. Its top is off, filling the stagnant air with a nauseous odour. Within is a different smell, naggingly familiar. I shout my wife's name. But there is no response. The house seems deserted. Bedrooms, bathroom, dining room, all empty. On the table is Inge's black scarf, neatly folded, and a note:

Don't forget this, Love Rachel.
PS. Hope the bedbugs have stopped biting Inge.

Then in the kitchen I realize what the smell reminds me of. A butcher's shop. Naked, legs splayed, my wife sits up on the kitchen floor with the wooden handle of our carving knife protruding from her belly. Her back rests against the wall, her arms hang stiffly down, her eyes are open wide. The blood is dry. It flowed down from her wound, between her thighs, and formed puddles on the floor. The only sound is the buzzing of flies. They walk upon her breasts, mass around her vagina where the hair is matted with blood. This horror is too shocking to be true! It is a phantasmagoria produced by my conscience. Art, not life.

'Your face is very white,' says Inge, 'is everything all right?'

'I'm just nervous about this evening,' I say.

We have gathered all the props we require: cutlery, crockery, sauce bottles, and a starting pistol loaded with blanks. And while Monika—of all people!—strips down to her underwear in front of the directors of Literature & Linguistics Ltd, Inge and I exchange clothes. A suit and tie for her, a dress for me. 'This is Cambridge,' I think, 'this is my life. There is nothing else.'

We hear Franz sing his folk songs. Then applause. We are joined by the third member of the cast. We walk out to cheers and laughter.

'Your wife is in the audience?' asks Inge.

'I hope so,' I say, 'she is coming by train.'

The play begins.

Inge—my husband—is a bank clerk. I am a housewife. The other girl is a television set. Inge orders me to switch her on. We hear the news. I serve dinner to my husband and our two children who are invisible. An argument develops between us over the boy's long curls.

'You'll turn your son into a pansy with your ways of bringing him up,' yells Inge.

'They're always my children when there is something the matter,' I shout. 'I don't think you really wanted them. I won't forget how you treated me when I was pregnant. You didn't even try to hide your disgust. But you're the one who's disgusting!'

What am I talking about? Why am I pretending to be my wife? Wife? I have no wife. How these silly words have confused me! What next? Oh, yes, I am supposed to take the gun from my handbag. I point the gun at Inge. Why? Because I hate her. But why? Because she seduced me? Because she murdered my wife? Wife? I can't even remember her name. With her shirt and tie and pencil moustache, Inge looks like a creature from pre-war Berlin. I hate her because she is German. A Nazi! I fire the gun. The blast fills my head.

'Daughter of Germany!' I scream. 'Daughter of Germany!'

I shoot at her until the gun is empty.

Elaine Feinstein

was born in Bootle in 1930 and educated at
Cambridge University. She is the author
of ten collections of poetry and twelve
novels. In 1980 she was made a Fellow
of the Royal Society of Literature and in
1990 was awarded the Cholmondeley Prize
for Poetry. Feinstein has also translated the
poetry of Marina Tsvetayeva, Margarita
Aliger, Yunna Moritz, and Bella Akhmadul-
ina and has written a biography of Bettie
Smith and a sequel to D. H. Lawrence's
Lady Chatterley's Lover entitled *Lady Chatterley's Confession* (1995). Set in Vienna
before the *Anschluss*, *The Border* (1984),
Feinstein's eighth novel, is written in diary
and epistolary form. This work is made
up of three passionate accounts of an
erotic triangle, Inge Wendler, Hans
Wendler, and Hilde Dorf. The excerpt here
is the whole of Inge Wendler's diary.
Inge is a scientist who is forced to decide
whether to leave Europe just before the
war, and she has just discovered that her
husband, the poet Hans Wendler, is having an affair with his student, Hilde Dorf.

Elaine Feinstein

EXCERPT FROM The Border

Inge Wendler's Diary

*Natural guilt . . . befalls man not on account of action and decision
but through idleness and hesitation.*—Walter Benjamin

PARIS: 1938

3 September
Hans has been so elated by the success of his play, that he walks
like another man. He strides about our rooms, whistling, as if he
owned the whole world; as if our friends still in Austria were not
being horribly abused and tormented. I don't grudge him the happiness, but I resent the frivolity. When I say so, he laughs and says:
Write more letters, Inge. Perhaps you will find a job, after all.

I write letters every day. It has not been easy. We are thought of as
aliens, here in Paris; there were too many physicists from Germany
already. To be German, and a woman, and now to be counted as
Jewish: these are handicaps.

And whatever rewards Hans' play may have brought him, the
money was no fortune; and I am told the piece will be taken off any
day now. Our savings, which I was lucky to get out of the country,
cannot last forever. When I say as much, Hans nods, and seems to
know; but his thoughts are elsewhere. He is living in a dream.

We arrived in Paris only days before the *Anschluss.* Chance, Hans
calls it. It is possible. He has no idea what it would mean to apply
that principle to the universe I once investigated daily. When I try
to explain, he falls into bored preoccupation. He has never under-

stood the relevance of magnetic fields to the God in his poems, never seen any relevance to the human heart in the laws by which the atoms move. And yet he asks himself whether we are creatures with whom God is amusing himself, as if at dice.

I have spoken to enough refugees from Germany now to understand what horrors we escaped. People who left Germany six years ago still speak of their experience with fear.

And then, from the personal point of view, I am happy whenever I think we have left behind whatever entanglement my poor Hans had found himself so caught in before we came away.

6 September

Hans' friend, Hilde, has found us a cheap room in the Marais with some Jewish friends of hers. Convenient as it is for the moment, I gather she herself is living in some splendour near Les Invalides. Not for the first time, I wonder why she has chosen to run away from the Nazis. I have satisfied myself she is not even partly Jewish.

Someone, certainly, is supporting her. I observe it is the latter suggestion which produces spasms of indignation in him.

These days I do not even dare to cry.

10 September

I am grateful that I brought the letters from our son Frederick with us. It was an impulse rather than foresight. They were so painful to me, those first bewildered letters from his twelve-year-old pen: resentful, fearful, unexpectedly bossed by my cousins in their Los Angeles suburban home. How strange he found American schooling. How he was unused to being at the bottom of the class. To hear music ridiculed by quite intelligent children; to be so lonely, so terribly in need of love.

It used to squeeze my heart every time I looked at them. Only this year did he begin to write coolly, and often in English.

Hans used to blame me for sending him away; but even if I never live to see him again (and these last few days I have been choking with some bronchitic infection, I cannot imagine how I will get through the winter) even then I rejoice to think he has been released from this European dungeon. Because, for all the pleasure Hans takes in it, and for all the splendours of its gay heart, Paris as we live in it is a dungeon.

I have sent Frederick our new address, but so far there has been no word.

10 September
I like the district: cobbles, narrow streets, continuous bustle, unfamiliar smells. A butcher's shop round the corner sells goods, cheap offal, even spleen; I wish I had room enough in the gas stove to cook it as it should be prepared.

The attic room is small, with room for only one desk. Yesterday rain brought down the plaster over the bed. I wash clothes in the sink downstairs; it's not such a hardship. The other lodgers are friendly; many of them refugees as bewildered by their situation as we are.

12 September
Last night, we went to see a group of German students in *Faust*. A marvellous play. Hans has often explained all its ambiguities to me. Tonight he seemed fascinated. Particularly by the girl who plays Margarita. Certainly she is a particularly beautiful actress. They are all students, none of them more than twenty-two or twenty-three. Afterwards, we went to the theatre backstage, which we can do as members of the University. It was Hans' idea; I wanted to please him, but I was tired. I said so.

—When are you *not* tired? When were you *ever* young? he demanded: I want to have a drink at the bar and see if that girl is as sensitive to speak with as she seems on the stage. You can go home if you like.

As I sit shuddering, at the wall, I watch the ease with which he picks her up. No stammering in these situations I thought bitterly. No fear, even as he looks at her first shyly, then slyly; soon he buys them both a drink. For twenty minutes or so, he turns all the benevolence of his face upon her. That night, as we were dropping off to sleep, he said: 'I have never loved you enough, and that is what I am being punished for.'

—Punished? I asked, puzzled. But he is asleep and doesn't answer.

16 *September*

I do not know what to do about Hans' *affaire*, which continues, he maintains, only as friendship. The pain of it puzzles my head.

—Why didn't you tell me? I asked.

—I didn't want it to spoil our love, he said. I could only gaze at him with incredulity.

—It's over, he said: I promise you.

—Really? I wanted to believe him. There was enough in the newspaper to frighten us into closeness again.

—Look at what has been happening in Vienna! They have old women mopping up streets. And such delight in looting and rape. Always rape.

He sighed. But I could tell the shadow that crossed his face was from another threat.

—Have you arranged to see her again? I asked him, evenly.

—See who?

I knew he understood, and shrugged. So that he was forced to reply.

—Yes. Listen. Trust me. Will you trust me?

I didn't see what sense it made but I nodded.

—Surely you can trust me for one night?

My heart ran cold again.

—To be out all night?

I hated to be alone in the flat, and of all times now.

—Not alone of course, he reassured me: Look, I'll arrange for my brother to call round, he has sent his wife to England. Such a graceful woman you know. A mistake . . .

I murmured something: *Why* all night?

—Trust me. Believe me.

Almost I did believe him.

—She can do us terrible damage.

—Politically?

—Perhaps.

—How? Is she *mad*? Or what?

—A little mad, he said: Please. Think of this as some little lie you might tell me about the butcher's bill to keep me happy. When you do that it is to protect me, isn't it?

—You are going to *her*, tonight, to protect *me*? *How*?

—Trust me.

Suddenly I didn't believe him at all. I said: What worse can she do? You don't deny she is your mistress.

—Worse. Much worse. Darling.

Reluctantly I let him go, and with him the whole peace of my mind.

His brother came late and hungry, and expecting more than the cold supper I had provided. I could hardly bear to talk to him. In dim lights, the resemblance to Hans was close enough to disturb me; but I did not see what else there was in the world to talk about.

He on the contrary was filled with gossip. Did I know that? And that? And had Hans and I yet taken the necessary steps for?

We have done none of these things; poor improvident creatures and I was glad to see him go.

Hell. I am in Hell. I suppose he is with her now. And I don't know and can't know, what is really going on, or what is the nature of this terrifying power which he so fears, and which he will not even put into words. To protect me? How many more grey nights, sleepless and waiting must I bear with the question that he will never answer.

Dear Lord, what is to become of us? Does he know how frightened I am? He says that I am real, and I haven't lost him, and yet. What does he tell *her*? What has he promised *her*? She has summoned him to her and he obeys. What are they doing? Does he not, frankly, find it more entertaining with her? Will she bind him to her with sex, and youth, and lively conversation?

—I'm slowly disentangling, he says.

Why slowly?

When at last he returned, it was morning again and I had begun to cry with a wild abandon I knew must be close to madness.

—Must you do that? he asked.

There are women who can look enticing when they weep, but my own animal abandon frightened me as well as repelling him. What if I lost my senses altogether? How could such a situation be coped with?

—There, there, he said awkwardly. And I heard the falsity in his voice: We'll work out something, you'll see. Some compromise.

—Never, I shrieked. Never. I won't be condemned to that.

And then I began to moan: What's to become of me? What's to become of me?

Hans appears to me now to have been the centre of my life all the time. Not my work, as I had imagined. How could he not know the difference in me?

When I tried to explain as much, he looked sardonically upon me, and inquired whether my work was now going as badly as his own once had.

I am too cowed to provoke further cruelty.

16 September

Things can't go on like this.
And yet the remedy is worse.
Worse than this torment of fear and waiting?
Yes, since loss is what I fear, and loneliness.
How can I leave without him?
Such sweetness to remember his arms around me.
His comforting whisper.
Even if I don't believe the comfort.
Do people recover from such pain, or are
they damaged forever?

17 September

A hot night. Impossible to sleep. Hans is not usually out so late without phoning.

The rehearsal must have ended long ago. Even if he went on talking with the keener actors. Why do I go on sitting here? It is because I am afraid to go to sleep, and wake alone. . . .

18 September

Today I lectured at the Sorbonne on Niels Bohr. I have barely slept, and must look like a gargoyle. I was not sure I could even face so many unfamiliar faces; to move from a chair takes more energy and will than I can muster. And yet, the lecture was an amazing success. The taste of the applause lifted me for a moment, like alcohol; and yet, stupid and pointless as I know it to be, I could not linger. I dashed away from my friends to catch the Metro back to Hans. So he should not feel alone?

He has no such worries about me.

Or is it, as his eyebrows suggest, to make sure he is at home? I am ashamed of my own obsession.

21 September

I have lab space now, following a letter from Brandt (who is in New York). It does not much hearten me. Hans and I are moved further apart as soon as I begin to work.

It is strange how our situations have changed. Once, he seemed only to be interested in squeezing some *pleasure* out of life: in consuming theatres, galleries, books, lively people. And now, suddenly, all that has become frippery, and all that counts for him is his writing.

And I, who once grudged the time to accompany him into the cafés he loved, and the galleries he enjoyed so much more than I did; I, who thought all these years that the true centre of my life was work, can barely face the task of lifting a pencil. I force myself to go into the laboratory; but I am only pretending. No one is deceived except Hans. I know now that, all the time, I was in some sense working for him. To impress him? Not precisely, though perhaps I had once hoped for that. But yes, in some sense to have him admire me. It was *his* admiration I craved; and I do not know if I can bear life without it.

27 September

He will not let me question him. He will not let me react naturally in any way. I have to swallow my fear and my rage or else he will not come home at all. I know that in some womanly piece of myself from my adolescence. I made one attempt to explain the severity of that demand.

But as soon as he began to feel the blackness and bitterness rise in me, he moved towards the door. Hans, what am I to do with my rage if you won't let me speak it out? It will kill me. I shall be the one that dies, not you, you old hypochondriac. He paused only to ask whether I had made any further inquiries about visas.

—How many visas?

—Three. Naturally.

I had indeed begun to make inquiries, but the impudence of using me to find a visa for Hilde choked me.

—It is still possible, of course, in theory, but we should not count on it. In any case, it will be too late for me, I could not help adding bitterly.

—So you mean—if I can't love you enough, then you won't help me? he asked directly.

I hesitated: It's hard.

—Then I won't leave, he said simply.

—It is the crudest form of blackmail, I sobbed: I have tried to trust you.

1 *October*

Last night I behaved shamefully. Without dignity. I deliberately came home early, and waited for Hans to leave. To see where he went. He had claimed to have met some marvelous new friend, a man called Walter Benjamin, whose ideas inspire him with a new sense of purpose. He said he was to meet him at a café. Little as I know we can afford it, I took a cab to follow his. And watched him sit down at a table (with Hilde, certainly, but also with another man). I was almost disappointed, as I dismissed the cab. Why? Did I want fresh evidence to convict him?

I watched the three of them. They were so animated and full of joy as they talked, I sat and watched them from my corner across the street, with tears pouring down my face.

When they all rose to shake hands in farewell, Hans and Hilde left together.

Thank God I had the self-restraint to go straight home, since, absolutely contrary to all my expectations, Hans returned only minutes after I did.

He was full of the talk he had been enjoying.

—Magical. A Marxist who is not a materialist. He has come to grips with all the horrors of our time. Even the horrors of Nazism. And he has a whole library of which I know nothing to help him. Imagine. He uses the Kabbalah. The work of an old theologian like Abulafia. He laughed at me when I drew back from my own Jewishness. I didn't even know there was a Jewish mystical tradition.

—And even if there is? I responded sharply.

—I understand you, he replied, mercifully: It was what I said myself. But the point is that this man knows Brecht. Writes about him knowledgeably. He has read everything. And yet. He has this other face, which makes me read my own differently.

—And your face, too. He kissed me.

I can only take in, that, for some reason, our lives are entwined closely as a result of that meeting. It is almost as if, a book-list, and a few holy names, and sacred texts, have led him to forgive me for my Jewish grandparents. Perhaps it will even lead him to forgive his own father, as one rotten apple fallen from a fine tree?

I can only thank God I followed him no further.

4 October
Hans loves me.

His lips are warm, and his tongue is in my mouth, and I am not dreaming. He calls me lovely, blesses me. I am radiant with happiness. Fearless.

5 October
In my relief, I spent this morning walking about the Marais. It was as if, only now, with the warmth of Hans' love once again around me, I could spare the attention to observe, among the bustle on the Rue des Rosiers, the stalls of fruit and shoes, the piles of fish, the pedlars from Kovno or Kiev who filled the pavements with a babble of energy. Even the shops in the walls seemed to bulge out into the streets. I must have been blind or asleep; today I woke to find myself in the heart of Asia.

And that is not all I have missed. There are strange archways, too, through which I stare at secret gardens and statues moulded with a baroque loveliness that reminds me of Vienna. I can see as much without pain. The tight clamps in which I have been living for so long seem to have released me. I flow out into the world about me now with avid curiosity. Museums do not usually excite me. (It was something which long came between Hans and I.) This morning, almost as if in celebration of our new-found closeness, I took a few tentative steps into the Musée Carnavalet, which had once been the house of Madame Sevigné. Hans must have once given me some account of her life, since I could not remember reading any of her books; and it was for a time an unexplained pang that pursued me among the splendours of her carved chairs and glittering clocks. Then I recalled the unthinking, monstrous passion she had felt for her daughter; and with that memory, a flicker of my own early morning dream. There had been some childhood glimpse of Frederick, with his arms out, calling for me, as I drove off resolutely to the laboratory. Did I cry then? I am crying now, as I think of it.

Frederick. My only son. Though I must remember, when I asked him about it, only six months later, he claimed to have no memory of my desertion. His impudent face opened into an uneven grin; the charm of it mocked me. His mockery and his confidence were alike precocious, and I loved them equally. Even now, I only have to close my eyes and his whole childish presence is there. Black eyes, solemn in their concentration upon some piece of balsa wood sculpture. Or black hair flowing in the wind as he climbed some dangerous peak to pose, his thin, precisely balanced body, as if defying us to fear for him. He was always an artist. An artist, or a pianist, or perhaps a chess player of genius. The school could not be sure.

As the memories crowd back upon me, I marvel again at the insanity of sending him so far away. Only my crazy terrors of these last months have kept out the longing for him; with the first release from that pain, another knowledge rushed in to take its place. Not exactly anxiety.

I think of him at six, at the piano, his feet too short to reach the pedals, playing Mozart, Beethoven, Chopin. How much I hoped from him, how much I took from his gaiety. His spirit was the gaiety of our house. And his courage. At six, he outfaced bullies with his nimble wits. My own cowardice made me plead with him to placate rather than tease. But it is not his nature. He reminds me of my own father, who never bent his head to anyone in his life. Yet Frederick is so much more frail. My father was built like an ox; and Frederick is delicate boned. His wrists are thin. When he came back bruised from fighting, my heart was squeezed with a sense of his fragility. It is part of his beauty, which seems to spring neither from Hans nor myself. And yet there is nothing feminine in his carriage. He holds himself bravely. Like a matador, I often thought; prepared to take on the whole world with a sweep of his cloak. And by the same token, he was much the most fastidious of any of his class in his choice of clothes. Taking him to a tailor was an ordeal; where Hans could not have been more casual in his choice of clothing.

Was our closeness unhealthy? At least, Hans was never excluded. How could he be, when so many of Frederick's chief joys were those he had given the boy? Hans could play the violin and sing; it was he who had taught Frederick to sight read. They spent hours in the music room together. And their affection for one another gave me pleasure.

And yet it is true I was more dependent on the boy than Hans was. Hans had another kind of magic in his life, the pleasure in his own creation which my own work in a laboratory could not give me. In any case, gaiety was his element; he lived in it. Perhaps his example gave Frederick the secret of inner joy. He understood how much I was dependent on other people always: colleagues in the laboratory, recognition, awareness of what contributions I had made. Both of my men seemed free of such obsessions. Just as neither of them seemed to need, as I did, to belong to a team.

If there were quarrels over the child, they were always on questions of order which concerned Hans. I suspect he saw discipline as a way of freeing the child from the inheritance of his own family. He meant so well; yet I could not help interposing myself between him and the boy; could not help trying to protect him, as I felt it. And yet Frederick himself made no objection. I know it enraged Hans; because it was an echo of the way his father had punished his mother. The worst he could imagine for himself was to become like that. And by my resistance I could tell I was in danger of putting him into that role. How long ago it seems. And my fatal mistake was my attempt to placate Hans by suborning Frederick's charm to offer him. Soon he became impatient with it, saw through it, and began to look for duplicity. Some mistake I must have made; for their love for one another soured on absurd arguments.

Hans began to worry that the child would waste his talents, for all his wonderful perkiness; always, and in everything else an optimist, this he was not prepared to leave to chance. And so we quarrelled. How it hurts me now to think that we could ever have quarrelled!

When we had the chance, the one chance, in the one and only life I have ever believed in, *why* did I deny Hans the decent ordinary home he demanded for his son?

For there is a sense in which I felt we were a little above such concerns. Our ambitions put us above them. And Hans, in particular, since I always saw him, as it were, in the vanguard of our family fame, even if my stubborn muscles provided the bedrock of our fortunes.

How is he now, our Frederick? I think of him. Tenderly at ease with all animals. The appointed caretaker of all the potted plants that abounded in our house. Green-fingered, so that an avocado pip would sprout for him into a tree. Where is he now, and how does he remember our old voices over his childish head?

It is a long while since I have wept for anyone but myself. Now I weep to think of him, imagining him as an orphan, imagining his loneliness. Or perhaps even these tears are selfish, and what I dread most is his forgetfulness.

When Hans came in that evening I burst out: we have lost him. Frederick. We have given him away to strangers. And he watched me oddly.

—It was wisdom to send him away.

—You opposed it.

—You were right to persist.

And he took me warmly in his arms, and soothed away the fears in my heart.

6 *October*

The morning was so brilliantly blue and sunny that we decided to breakfast expensively at a small café at the corner of our street. I have never tasted such delicious coffee; never relished the melting of butter into croissant in the same way. And the trees astonished both of us simultaneously. I do not usually observe the changing of nature, except as Hans once teased me, through a microscope. Now it seems to me that Parisian trees are actually a different green from our old familiar Viennese varieties. Even their approaching autumn has only increased their loveliness.

—I always said you should read the poets, he smiled.

—But the books you put in my hands never spoke of trees, I protested: Verlaine, Mallarmé, Apollinaire, René Char. I only remember the names.

—But Char writes of vegetation. He is a lush poet.

—Well, my French is not good enough I suppose, I confessed, without anxiety.

—What hours such a confession would once have taken to force from you, he exclaimed.

I perceived myself on dangerous ground.

—Perhaps.

—Don't answer mechanically like that. It is a way of dismissing what I say.

My heart began to stir and beat heavily, and I bit my lip. When he saw as much, a recognition of what he was risking seemed to touch him also, and he leant forward to recover my hand with one of his.

—Frederick loved poetry, I continued bravely: You taught him to do so.

—Yes, he replied.

But I could see that the thought of Frederick no longer had the same power over him as it had yesterday.

Whereas I was much troubled by a nightmare I recognize now I have had before. Frederick has been caught stealing a musical box. It is one of those so charmingly made in Czechoslovakia or Hungary, where it is possible to watch the moving parts going around. It is familiar in some other way too; inlaid with mahogany or rosewood. I think it is perhaps something from my parents' home.

Why should Frederick steal such an object? For I can see that he is indeed responsible for the theft. There he is, in some American desert town, with the box behind his back, being threatened and still outfacing his questioners. His stance is belligerent and a little sulky. He is being threatened by unknown adults; police, not relations. Adults who keep asking my own question:

—Why? again and again.

He never admits the crime, and, at last, a man brings out a leather thonged whip with which he proposes to punish him.

My cry of horror wakes me, as I think it may have done before.

As I try to explain the horror of the dream, and at the same time make sense of it (for after all it was to escape whipping, or worse, that we sent him far from the barbarities of Europe) I am not at first soothed as I expected. Instead, Hans reminds me of how often he had called my attention to the boy's dishonesty. Appalled at his insensitivity, I realize I am still inside the dream, that I have *not* woken up! Or *cannot* wake up. And when at last I do, I am bathed in a villainous sweat as though in the grip of a fever. Hans is still deep in his own sleep; and I snuggle gratefully against him, waiting for the full morning light to come round to our window, and wondering what my mind intends me to understand by such a vision.

8 October

This morning I woke feverish. Sweat pours down every limb, gathers in the hollow between my breasts and runs down my face. My breathing also is alarmingly shallow and fast; Hans says I must have an infection, but the sweating may have more to do with a lack of oxygen in my blood. In times of tension, my mother often presented the same symptoms. Hans teased me. He hoped I was not going to become like my mother, for whom he had no great liking.

For the first time it comes through to me clearly that I may easily die without ever seeing Frederick again. The thought is so overwhelmingly painful, that, even though I know it is the very worst thing for my condition, I abandon myself to great sobs of grief.

Self-pity. Self-indulgence. I know. And yet it is as if my body will not obey my will. Tears choke me. And my mind presents febrile visions of my son in different guises. He is nine. One foot up on a footstool, playing a lute and singing. Mischievous eyes denying the angelic perfection of his voice. Then he is running home through the snow, a bundle no larger than a small piece of hand luggage, muffled to his eyes. I watch him fall down in front of me, unable to catch him. I look into his clear eyes. He refuses to cry. His courage hurts me.

—What will become of Frederick if I die, I call out to Hans.

Hans says: Don't be silly. Lie calmly. I will call a doctor.

He is frowning. But I cannot tell why he is worried for me. I know my face is red and puffy with grief. But, usually, he takes my toughness for granted. Finds my hypochondria faintly irritating.

Today, he seems to be taking my illness very seriously, and another little clutch of fear touches my heart.

I'm finished. I'm finished. I have been destroyed by everything that has happened.

As the terror rises, I can hardly breathe. My chest hurts too much even to speak. Only hot tears continue to trickle down my cheeks.

I shall never see Frederick again.

I know it.

About half an hour later, Hans returned with a doctor from the flat below, who is also a refugee from Vienna. He will take no money; and insists on giving me sulphonamides nevertheless, which must be very expensive. Then he sent Hans away so he could talk to me.

I burst into tears as I tried to tell him my fears.

He listened seriously. Then he began to talk about his own son. He and his wife know very little about what happened to him, since he was first dragged out of his class at the University of Heidelberg two years earlier.

They try to hope he may only be suffering privations in prison; and that his health is not altogether ruined. His eyes tell the true terror. He no longer believes his own son is alive.

Hans brought me up hot milk with some tang of alcohol in it. He is protective. Calming. He reassures me: the decision to send Frederick away was the only sensible choice we could have made. I let him say 'we', because it reduces my own sense of lonely guilt, even though we both remember well how the decision had been taken after many battles.

—My brave Inge, he says: you will recover. You must recover. I need you. Don't you know how much I need you?

The warmth of his words, the milk, and the pleasantly aniseed-flavoured liquor send me into a luxuriant, pleasant doze such as I cannot remember enjoying for months. Perhaps years. Whenever I wake, with a start, Hans is still there at my side. He has a small bedside lamp on, and he is reading.

Sleepily, I ask him: what is the book?

—A typescript. Of Walter Benjamin's.

So we pass the night.

By the morning, I was in normal health; though still bothered with phlegm in my lungs.

—How strong you are, Hans greets me.

I wanted to get out of bed, and help him make our rudimentary breakfast. But he would not hear of it. He is as tender to me as if I were a child myself. I wonder if he, too, is thinking of Frederick. When he brings me my pills and another hot drink, I study myself carefully in the glass. Lying against the pillows, and still a little weak, my face has lost some of its tension, and I can just catch the old fleeting resemblance. The same ambiguously flecked eyes, roughly curling hair. I once became used to the ease with which other parents recognized me as his mother. And though I had never particularly rejoiced in my face, the strength in my features was excellent in a boy. Without vanity I could see that what might be ponderous in me would be handsome in him.

Hans has gone out this afternoon. The pills have made me dozy, and I slept without anxiety. Before he had returned home, I was out of bed (for all his protests). My throat was free, my cough gone.

—You are trying to impress me, he accused, but I could tell he was only teasing.

We are happy, I discover, wonderingly.

9 October

As for my brief joy! This evening we went to an early party in the sunlight of Erlichman's patio. Iced champagne. Hans looks so young, so triumphant. Leaving, I say as much proudly; and he smiles, with just a touch of complacence 'So. Would you let me have an adventurous life?' Dryly I reply: 'I wouldn't have any choice.'

He finds that a grudging response, and our mood of friendliness vanishes as if it had never been.

Tonight Hans dreamed that a man had damaged his penis, and he was afraid that it would not heal.

10 October

There is only one thing for it. We must meet. All of us. I cannot go on with this unexplained threat hanging over us. I asked Hans if the girl would come round to supper.

—I have a right to meet her.

—I cannot see what good can come of that, he replied.

—I want to understand her, I said.

And my real motives? I think I wanted to put Hans in a position where he could not say one set of things to me and another to her.

—You are precipitating a crisis, he groaned, as if guessing as much.

—No.

—How can it go well?

—She is the girl who found us this room, I know that much. And I think I met her once at Mass before we left Vienna: Won't you arrange it?

Reluctantly, he agreed.

12 October

I felt very confident I could handle the girl, and whatever threat she presented. It was only a matter of facing her with our true situation surely? All day Hans tried to dissuade me.

—I'm not sure this is a good idea. I don't *feel* it's going to go well.

—Why not?

There was a long pause.

—Are you afraid I'll get hysterical? I won't. I promise to be perfectly calm.

—Not exactly hysterical.

—What then?

—I don't fancy it. I think we should call it off.

I don't know why, but his reluctance made me all the more determined. I should be on my home territory. I could handle everything, I thought.

—What time is she coming?

—Please, he said: I want you to think about this. I can't see what good it can do.

A little bead of sweat began to form on my upper lip, and I wiped it away. I longed for a strong drink, to steady my hands. There are important things I don't know, I thought. Hans is saying as much.

—Don't say anything about me, will you? he asked: That will make her see me as feeble. Or finished.

—Of course not.

He too was pale and wet-skinned.

—You look very nervous, I said brightly.

—Well, darling, you must realize. At the beginning of a relationship. You say things. You don't always know where it is going. You won't talk *coarsely* about her? I should have to defend her then, wouldn't I?

14 *October*

She sat in my room, radiant with confidence.

—We have to rid ourselves of all these bourgeois ideas of property, she said: No one belongs to anyone, as if he were a thing.

Her face was broad, and flat-nosed; not exactly pretty, perhaps, but healthy-looking, and young.

—Here you are foreigners, refugees. Can you not smell the stink of defeat in France? It will need a Revolution to save her. A war might help. Might at least temper her energies. She might emerge from any nightmare strengthened.

—War means dying. Many people die. A whole generation, sometimes. How can you want war? Still less Civil War? Are you a Communist? I asked stupidly.

—I am proud to be so. That is how I know, the terrible, possessive love you feel for Hans will only stifle him. You must let him go free. Let him do what he likes. Relinquish your hold over him. His soul is dying in your hands.

—What about *my* soul? I demanded energetically: Why do I have to connive at anything that breaks *my* human spirit?

—If you loved him, you would want him to have anything that makes him happy.

—You are suggesting I accept you as a kind of official mistress? But isn't that exactly the self-indulgence the old France you mention stinks of?

—There *is* an altogether more important struggle, said Hans.

—We are only a part of it, the girl insisted. Of course, I don't know if I can make Hans any happier than he has been with you.

—Have you known one another long enough, even to wonder *that?* I asked crisply.

—A year.

—You were away, surely. Much of that year.

—There was hardly a day when we didn't speak. On the phone, at least.

My heart cringed with the pain.

—I see.

—Darling, you aren't saying enough? Hilde turned to Hans.

And Hans was smiling all the time, always that familiar sweet smile I loved so much, but given to her, the stranger: You see, there is more pain here than you imagine, Hilde. You must be gentle.

And even then, I did not really doubt his love, until I heard the soft voice he used to say goodbye to her. It was a family voice. They were close. I could no longer pretend.

15 *October*

Hans has begun work on a new play. He says it concerns the historical dimensions of Nature. I do not understand a word of it. He is taking it round to his typist tonight with a great deal of excitement.

—What excites you?

—The whole phantasmagoria of the nineteenth century.

Yes, I thought, the ghosts and the voices, those I can hear. The myths and the lies: I can put my roots down into that holy mud any time I want. Those who are dead and those who will die and those who will smell long after the New Europe is built over them.

—How can I look to you for strength? he muttered before leaving.

Strange how he loves the modern; as if this whole century has not delighted in exhuming prehistory. It is almost a deliberate regression, isn't it. To childhood.

20 *October*

A letter today from Frederick. It is cheerful, and I should have been made happier by it. But I could hear the distance in his voice. He is forgetting us, I thought. He is making his own life, and adjusting; soon he will not only behave like a little American boy he will feel like one, and even if we meet again soon he will look strangely at me, as if I were a peculiar foreigner.

The thought made me fall to the floor and weep. Hans found me there, but I didn't care. I didn't care about anything else but the distance between myself and my only son.

He watched me with surprise as well as horror.

—Inge. What is it?

—It is Frederick. I have made a mistake. I have made a mistake. I did not know it would break my heart, I wept.

—You? You are like steel, was all he said, turning on his heel.

From this, I gather something new has happened, but cannot guess what.

21 October

Hans has been telling me the news from Germany. He is nearly distraught. Why? The news is bad (looting and baiting, and extraordinary sadism) but his misery looks as if something closer to home is disturbing him. All Jews of Polish extraction have been deported over the Eastern border; and, as the Poles refuse them, they have to inhabit a no-man's land in sickening conditions. Perhaps this hurts him.

And yet. It is a terrible thing to say, but I have only ever seen him look so wild-eyed about disasters which involve himself. His stammer, which we had almost forgotten, returns as I try to question him.

29 October

Hans has just told me that Hilde has been asked to return to Moscow. She is uneasy about it, as well she might be. Both Hans and I know of loyal Communists who returned in 1937 and then disappeared without trace. Hans is afraid to suggest she stay on in Paris, however, since the arm of the NKVD is long enough to reach her, even there; and her disobedience would certainly provoke some disciplinary action.

My one fear is that Hans might decide to go with her. I suspect she has been pressing him to join her.

Much may be forgiven to those who bring converts.

5 November

7:00 A.M. Hilde has left for Moscow. Hans accompanied her as far as Le Havre, where she is taking the boat across the Baltic. Every minute today I have been afraid I should hear he has decided to leave with her. He has taken all our money. What will I do if he decides to throw his lot in with her completely?

1:00 A.M. Not so. Praise God. Hans has returned to Paris. But he looks at me with pink eyes filled with hatred, as if their separation in some measure is my fault.

I have a sense that I will be punished for being a factor in his decision to stay.

7 November

Something terrifying has happened. A seventeen-year-old boy, Herschel Grynszpan, who is at present living in Paris, has been driven out of his mind by the fate of his parents herded into a camp near Zbonszyn. He has shot and fatally wounded one of the Secretaries of the German Embassy, Ernst von Rath. The indignation in Paris has swelled to the most terrifying proportions. And it isn't only the French that are behaving disgracefully. The leaders of the Jewish Community here are themselves among the first to insist on his foreign origin.

10 November

The news has begun to come through of reprisals taken against Jews still living in Germany. I can hardly believe what is happening. It is like an apocalypse. Synagogues razed to the ground. Shops burnt. Thousands arrested. Hundreds killed.

We listen to the news together, alongside the sycophantic mouthings of our Western leaders.

—You see? I should have gone with her, says Hans.

I renew my attempts to contact my old friend Brandt to beg his help for a visa to the United States. But the pressure on that haven is by now so strong that they have put up barriers against us. It is very difficult to imagine them listening, even to Brandt, when one imagines how many important men in their midst have the direct ear of the President. And even people with the strongest protectors in the States are failing to get visas.

—I was a coward. I should have gone with her, said Hans before we went to sleep.

England should be easier, I think. But the walls are there too.

11 November

Hans said this evening: I had a drink at a café with that Walter Benjamin again. He spoke of Palestine. He has never done so before, with Hilde present. Zionism! It's pretty alien to me. And the Arabs are probably as dangerous as Europeans.

—Whatever makes you consider it? I asked the man.

—I can hardly stay alive on what I earn here, he said.

He is in such dire financial straits that I lent him a little of our money. In return, he offered me one of his death capsules, from which I turned in horror.

I listened to all this with attention. Perhaps Palestine is not such a bad idea? In Hans' dream there is no threat to France. Not even to Czechoslovakia. I remember the plebiscite we were promised in Austria that was called off at the last moment.

There are worse things than dying; we knew that too. And if, in Paris, you cannot hear the shouts of *Juda Verreck*; thousands of voices are waiting, as in Germany. The whole of Europe is contaminated with the same hatred.

Yesterday we had another letter from our son. It is difficult, but not yet impossible for us to join him. I long to do so. If I were close to him, I could even bear the terrible gap that is growing between Hans and myself.

22 November

Hans no longer believes Hilde is alive. Many loyal Communists who returned with her have been shot. I laughed at him.

—Who would go back to be shot? Clearly, she did not believe anything like that herself, or she would scarcely have returned.

—Those who don't obey orders can be shot here, he repeated quietly.

I was still incredulous.

—Is this what you had been protecting me from?

—In a way. She has been working with several intelligence services.

25 November

He has received his first letter from Moscow. His joy is open and unashamed.

Nothing has separated us more.

Howard Jacobson

was born in Manchester in 1942 and educated at Cambridge University. He is the
author of five novels and three works of
nonfiction, *In the Land of Oz* (1988), *Roots
Shmoots: Journeys among Jews* (1993), and
Seriously Funny: An Argument for Comedy
(1997). The last two were also television
series, and Jacobson is well known in
Britain as a critic and journalist. He has
taught English literature at Cambridge
University; Sydney University, Australia;
and Wolverhampton Polytechnic. The
excerpt that follows is the Prologue to *Peeping Tom* (1984), Jacobson's second novel,
which was runner-up for the Guardian Fiction Prize. This comic novel is a study in
cultural masochism, as Jacobson's Jewish
persona, Barney Fugleman, is defined in
terms of what he thinks are his opposites.
These opposites include Thomas Hardy
(the 'peeping tom' of the novel), the Cornish countryside, and rural English literature in general. As the novel progresses,
Barney Fugleman discovers, to his horror, that he is Thomas Hardy's reincarnation.

Howard Jacobson

EXCERPT FROM ## Peeping Tom

Prologue

Remember to keep faith with those three great sources of your strength: Earth, Sea and Air. Walk barefoot on the Earth whenever you can. Learn to swim, and return to the Sea from which all life originally came. And always wear as few clothes as possible. It is important to allow the Air to circulate freely around those parts of the body which are not usually exposed to it.

And don't forget: it is no good working on your body if your mind is drugged with cigarettes and television.—Lance Tourney, Lad of Destiny: A Boy's Guide to Health and Confidence

Signs are, even to my drugged eye, that the village is finally coming out of winter. I am not witnessing a return to robustness and sanity exactly—that's too much to expect down here, so far from the soundness of cities, so deep into the obsessional neurosis of Nature— but there is an atmosphere of fragile convalescence abroad, as if the patients have been allowed their first unaccompanied turn around the walled gardens of the institution.

The wind has dropped. The water in the harbour rocks itself, brooding on its delusions. The squinting sea birds look as if they believe they might just eat again. Those hoteliers who changed wives or husbands at the start of the off-season—hoteliers are always the most romantic and expectant inhabitants of any remote place— have changed back again and are freshening up their Vacancy notices. Autographed copies of this year's print run of Lionel Turn- bull's pamphlet (Lance Tourney is, of course, a pen-name) have started to appear in the post office and the village stores, and Lionel himself has begun those naked ritualistic swims which will con- tinue every morning now until the Atlantic freezes over again. And already the first serious walkers of the season have arrived in their fetishistic boots and with their Ordnance Survey maps in protective plastic packets tied around their necks like bibs.

I meet them in the early morning during my penitential walks along the harbour walls or out on the cliff paths, and although they all nod me a bracing greeting or wave their blackthorn sticks, I can see that I am an extraneity and a blemish for them. In my long sleek-piled fur coat (resembling ocelot and bought on an Austin Reed charge account) and my Bally slip-on snakeskin shoes decorated, rather tastefully I've always thought, with a delicate gold chain and having the added advantage of slightly built-up heels, I am not what they have taken a week off work and kissed goodbye to their children and strapped methane stoves to their backs to find. At a stroke I domesticate the cliffs for them. Many of them, I fancy, will spend the rest of the day in a pet, not even noticing the wild sea below; fearing that at the next precipitous turn of the path, beneath the overhanging crags, above the foaming waterfall, they will come upon more like me, wearing jewels and stoles, contradicting one another in broken accents, and picnicking on smoked salmon sandwiches from the boot of a white Daimler. That's the extent to which I have blotted their landscape.

But if my being here is a disagreeable shock to them, imagine what it is to me!

I have just been sitting on the rocks watching a group of schoolgirls watching Lionel Turnbull preparing for a swim. Whether Lionel saw the schoolgirls or whether the schoolgirls saw me it is impossible to say. We were all, in our own ways, separately engrossed. With the exception of a neat square rug of hair on his chest and back Lionel is a smooth man. Bobbing about in the water he is indistinguishable from the brown seals he has befriended. Anyone familiar with rustic persiflage will be able to imagine the sorts of jokes that circulate about Lionel and his relations with those seals. For all the influx of summer tourists this is still essentially a farming community—there isn't anything that farmers find improbable.

Once he had peeled off his posing pouch which he wears under his exercise briefs which he wears under his swimming trunks which he wears under his perambulating shorts, Lionel stood for a while with his legs apart and his arms raised, for the purpose, I guessed, of letting the air circulate around those parts which had been stored away all winter. Then, with slow rhythmic movements, he began the sort of examination of himself that is recommended to women for the location of unfamiliar lumps in the breasts; except that he didn't confine himself to one area, but examined his neck and his armpits also, and the region of his lumbar ganglion and his prostate, his rib cage, his kidneys, his liver, and, with lingering deliberation, his testicles. This was too much for the schoolgirls who, being visitors to the village, had never before seen an adult male standing on argillaceous rock and rolling his balls minutely around the outstretched palm of his hand.

It puzzled me also, I must confess, although I didn't almost fall into the sea with laughter, because if those were cancer lumps Lionel Turnbull was searching for then he must have let himself go quite badly over the winter. Chapter V of *Lad of Destiny* states categorically that cancer is merely a consequence of lifestyle, being ascribable entirely to smoking, television, and bad bodily habits. From the confident manner in which he plunged finally into the water I deduced that he had found nothing in his body that shouldn't have been there, but it has not gone without my noticing it that he thought he might.

There is something about this part of the world—it might be the light or the towering cliffs or the perpendicular fields and meadows—all offering incomparable opportunities for high profile—that attracts exhibitionists. A year and a half ago a whole family of them took a winter let on a small holiday cottage in the harbour. Grandmother, mother, two sons, and a daughter-in-law. That's only approximate—domestic confusion as to who is related to whom and how is not uncommon in this neck of the woods. The rule of thumb seems to be that if a person sharing your house looks twice your age then there is a good chance it is your parent and oughtn't, therefore, to make a habit of sharing your bed—at least not until you're married; otherwise it's fairly open slather. Anyway, in the case of the family of exhibitionists, I can say for sure that there were three women and two men, and that the National Trust didn't take at all kindly to the manner in which they disported themselves both within the cottage and without it. Just in case that sounds unreasonable, let me make it clear that the cottage stood inside the area designated as the harbour, and that the harbour is the property of the National Trust. Gossip had it that they received an official typed complaint on Trust notepaper, in response to which the grandmother (if that *was* who she was) sent back a signed group photograph of them all lined up against the harbour wall in a state of Nature, the women concealing their ultimate immodesty behind their National Trust membership cards and the two men more flagrant in their National Trust ties. Was it the colour of their skins, she sent a covering note to enquire, that the Trust found out of keeping? This was a sly allusion to an argument which was occupying the attention of the village at the time, on the issue of the colour of the motor cars the Trust preferred the villagers to own. For that jibe alone their emmet foreignness and impudicity might have been forgiven, but the youngest son, the ostensibly unmarried one, went and blew it.

As long as he merely roamed the cliffs, in his earrings and his bright orange wig, with his ornithologist's binoculars strapped around his neck and his cock hanging out of his trousers, nobody gave him any trouble. If you came upon him unexpectedly he would immediately put his glasses to his eye. Whether this was exquisite tact or complete confusion as to his role—an inability to make up his mind whether he was a shower-off or a looker-on—who could say? For my part I was never very interested in him. But Camilla— there! I've named her at last, my beloved and much-missed Camilla, whose spirit fills and frets this place for me—Camilla was, in that perverse way of hers, entirely sympathetic to him. Unforgiving of just about everybody, enraged by the smallest omissions of her friends, she was massively tolerant of aberrations. And according to her, this was an aberration every bit as massive as her tolerance. He had shown it to her in a queue at the post office once, and she had understood immediately how tragically limited were his options. 'You've no idea what an enormous size it is,' she tried to explain to me. 'I can see why he has to show it, the poor bugger. There's absolutely nothing else he could possibly do with it.'

Well, she was wrong there. One thing he could do with it was to trundle it up the hill to the village school, poke it through the protective railings, and get the children—girls or boys, he didn't much care which—to measure it. And that was how, one afternoon, the village parents found him: standing on the old slate wall, one arm hooked around a cast iron railing, his binoculars pointing out to sea, his trousers open, and all their pretty ones gathered round him with their tiny rulers and protractors.

Camilla was a Parish Councillor again that year, but although she liked to make matters of public morality her own there was nothing she could do, even in her official capacity, to soothe parental wrath. This was not the sort of subject, either, that she was likely to be at her most understanding about. She didn't throb parentally herself. She didn't much care for children. And she certainly didn't believe they were in possession of any innocence worth troubling oneself to protect.

'The only thing you've got to worry about,' she told the near murderous mother of one little girl, 'is what this has done to her expectations. I myself don't see how men can be anything but one big disappointment to her after this.'

'I very much doubt that the experience will turn Colin into a homosexual,' she assured the harbour master's wife. 'But if it does, look on the bright side—one more homosexual in the world means one less compliant wife and mother.'

It took the police though, not Camilla's reassurances, to forestall the terrible vengeance demanded by outraged decency and to escort the five frightened flashers safely from the village.

It seems to be doing me some good, forcing myself to remember actual words that Camilla spoke. Her presence has been getting unhealthily generalized and diffused of late, particularly when I'm not walking the cliffs or following the course of rambles that we used to take together deep into the Valency Valley. There has been a touch of Heathcliffe about me recently, I fear, that is if someone who is called Barney Fugleman and what's more looks as if he is called Barney Fugleman can approximate to such a gentile, such a Christian, such an English, such an essentially Cornish spinster's fantasy. But then why not? Might it not be possible to show, without going so far as to claim Jewish parentage for her Liverpuddlian gypsy foundling, that it was precisely someone such as me, swarthy and saturnine and inhospitable and liable to vent my spleen on other

people's pets, that the poor girl dreamed about, my fur coat and
Bally shoes notwithstanding, in the back room of that draughty
rectory? It's not out of the question. I've stirred the imagination of
more than one lonely bookish vicar's daughter in my time. Either
way, it's a surprise to me how morbid I've become. I listen to voices
in the wind for God's sake! I trudge moors. I haunt country graveyards. Dogs I have always wanted to kick and I might myself, at any
time, have hung up Isabella Linton's—the more the worms writhe,
and all that—but now, I swear, and this is absolutely uncharacteris-
tic of me, if I knew what an ash tree looked like or where one was
to be found I could very easily fall to dashing my head against it.

To convey the extremity of my condition let me tell you that I
toyed, for longer than I care to admit, with the notion of having all
Camilla's words printed in a different type-face—in something
thin and spectral and wraith-like, in tribute to her rarity and other-
worldliness and ventriloquial genius. The only thing that changed
my mind was the realization that Camilla herself would have hated
it. She didn't see herself as a wraith. And she loathed every kind of
tricksiness. Her preference, in all things, was always for simplicity
and directness. As indeed, when I am myself, is mine. This was one
of the many fastidiousnesses that united us. Together we were very
choosy in our ideas of what constituted good art. We couldn't stand,
in just about equal measure, novels that took an interminable time
telling you who was telling the story and how he came by it, both
of us being perfectly at home with the convention of invisible omni-
scient narrators, no matter what people said about the breakdown
of social certainty and the consequent necessary fictiveness of fabu-
lists. We had no patience for films that could in any way be described
as experimental, enigmatic, or surreal; and we could not abide plays
that were about tramps, lunatics, savages without language, the
terminally infirm, or the problem of writing plays. When I think
of the number of theatres we stormed out of together and the
quantity of paperbacks we tossed into the fire to keep us warm in
winter, or into the sea to keep us young in spring, my heart aches.

Stuck out here, so far from the civilizing amenities, all efforts to
keep in touch with written or spoken English were labours of love.
We had to drive for an hour to find an even moderately well-stocked
bookshop. If we wanted to see a play in the West End we had to set

out early in the morning, leaving food for the cats, messages for the milkman, and the telephone number of the hotel we were staying at in case anyone important to us died while we were away. And yet before ten minutes of the first scene had elapsed we were up out of our seats—often on the front row, sometimes in a box—and into the nearest bar. We weren't particularly interested in drinking; we just wanted somewhere quiet to sit where we could talk over the insult that had just been delivered to our intelligence. We didn't just sneer; we discussed and analysed conscientiously. Our conversations on these occasions were almost certainly the best things on anywhere in London.

In the second of our summers together (the really good one) I think we must have seen as many as twenty-five plays without getting to the final act of any of them. One—I suppose it must have been a Pinter—we walked out of before a single character had even said anything. On top of that we consigned to the flames or the waves one Gunter Grass, two John Fowles, a Nabokov, a John Berger, three Doris Lessings, a Gore Vidal, two John Barths, and the whole of Jorge Luis Borges. I remember that I even tossed in a Norman Mailer but Camilla dived in—she was a stupendous diver—and rescued him. I think she detected my unclean unliterary motive. I knew that she had a soft spot for Norman Mailer and that for him she might leave me. We were very much in love that summer. We had a ball.

I didn't worry too much about Norman Mailer. There didn't seem any realistic danger of his turning up here with a rucksack, so far from the jazz and the booze and the hot bitches and the hellish stench of home. It was already stretching probability that I should be here, and I was not, more's the pity, Norman Mailer, I did not have his rival distractions, and I had come for a purpose.

Of course the village has had its share of literary celebrity. Even leaving aside Lance Tourney, Camilla and myself, and the dozens who are at this very moment scribbling down their dreams in low-rent fishermen's cottages all around the harbour, this spot is consecrated by one who came and courted here, and roamed and wrote awhile, and returned famously, full of remorse and rhyme. Many of those who visit today, whose mornings I interrupt and spoil up on the cliffs, are on a sort of pilgrimage and have come to inspect

the church and walk the valley, to see the stiff escarpments, to stride
the purple strand, to lose themselves in the flounce flinging mists.
Don't think that you detect any irony; you won't hear a word against
such pilgrims from me. After all, Camilla made her living out of
them. And I welcome tourists for the very reason that the National
Trust fears them: there is a good chance they will eventually wear
away the countryside.

Let them come in their thousands. It's not their fault, individually,
that they cannot read a word of the melancholy poems and novels
they have journeyed here in order to topographically reconstruct.
The whole culture conspires to blind them. Camilla was always very
wary of my conspiracy theories; she believed she could smell in
them the airless odour of ghetto fears. But we differed not a jot
about this one: some rural plot it is, hatched over the centuries in
countless village halls and parlours, that convinces the English there
is an indissoluble connection between literature and lakes, between
meaning and mountains, between poets and peasants, between
honesty and haylofts. I remember one long hot afternoon, sitting
with Camilla on the little wooden bridge halfway up the valley, dangling our bare feet in the water, discussing this and related topics.
It must have been a very hot day because I do not take willingly to
uncovering my feet. I always like to feel that I am fully dressed and
ready for flight. Another ghetto fear. I think the pretext—for our
discussion, not my barefootedness—was the news we'd received
that morning that Lilian Stinsford, a woman who occasionally
worked for Camilla at the school, had been taken into hospital and
was not expected to return from it. Lilian Stinsford had been a
blooming energetic townswoman brought down here, kicking and
screaming every inch of the way, by a husband in retreat from the
modern world. He put her in a white thatched cottage in sight of
the sea, gave her advice, babies, and more advice, and scratched
together a pittance himself painting birds on local slate and selling
them to the tourists he abhorred. They became a familiar sight
around the village, Ken and Lilian Stinsford, once their children
grew up and got the hell out, he stooping to croon over some marvel
of growth or colour in the hedgerows, his face contorted into a
horrible simulacrum of simple pleasure, she always a foot or two
behind and to leeward of him, tossing pebbles into the fields or

swiping at flowers with the stick he'd carved and insisted that she carried, her hair a pure white, her eyes puffed out with the poison of unused life. 'And not once has that man paused to consider the wrong he's done her,' I recall Camilla saying. 'Not once in the thirty years he lived here. But then why should he? Who or what in this place could ever plant the idea of erroneousness in his mind? He goes out into his garden in the morning, feels the pulse of God beating evenly in the soil, detects the same unhurried rhythm in his own breast and in that of his goats and chickens, and therefore knows that his poor frenzied wife is the anomaly, not him. Women don't have a chance in Nature, Barney. The heat and the tempo are against them. Nature belongs to men. Look at a ploughed field— have you ever seen anything more brutal or tyrannical in your life? All farmers are fascists, Barney. By instinct. The only future for women is in the cities. Not that there's any future for poor Lilian.'

I can still see Camilla swinging her legs as she spoke, absently kicking the surface of the stream, her toes painted a deep Clytemnestra purple, frightening away the summer flies that had paused to feed and cool off.

'Admit I'm right,' she said, after I'd failed to respond. 'Admit that there isn't a single person in the village that isn't sorry for Ken for being stuck with a neurotic wife. Decent old Ken who just wanted to paint birds and collect worms in peace. Admit that the assertion of the male will begins, like everything else, in the country.'

What could I say? I wouldn't have argued with her if I'd wanted to. She looked brown and strong and immovable. And I was sitting on the very edge of the bridge. True, the stream was shallow, but I couldn't swim an inch and was quite capable of drowning in a hip bath. And anyway, I didn't wish to quarrel with her. I didn't think anything good came out of Nature either. Even food had nothing to recommend it to my taste until all trace of the earth had been grilled or sautéed out of it. I was the last person to argue that it wasn't the same with human beings.

I nodded and smiled, but before I could get around to shaping a fuller answer we were disturbed by a couple of wonder-struck students from Camilla's summer school. Camilla had founded the school three or four years earlier—before my time, that is—on the shrewd hunch that there would be some amongst the annual literary

pilgrims who would welcome serious organization, the provision
of expert lectures, properly researched and conducted rambles, and
above all the opportunity to meet like-minded enthusiasts in an
atmosphere conducive to devotional exchanges of findings and
opinions. On perfect days like this Camilla sent everybody off in
different directions, with copies of the poems, in order to find the
field where and the bridle path from whence and the high cliff
whither. Well, wasn't this the little bridge on which? Yes, yes, it
was. How clever of them to have recognised it! And had they also
noticed on the way the selfsame small weir and the very stepping-
stone? Camilla was marvellously encouraging and informative. To
an untrained eye she even appeared to have a passion for her subject.
But then he was her living.

Long after the ecstatic intruders had left us—Camilla had sent
them next in search of the stony stile—we remained quiet, brooding separately. It really must have been a marvellous day, because I
can distinctly remember taking off my tie and rolling up my shirt
sleeves and commenting on how nice it was out here. Such avid
naturism was not called out of me without good reason. But my
words served only to remind Camilla of her theme. Her anger
against mankind in general had been aggravated, it seemed, by
her being forced to recall the one man in particular, that presiding
genius who had grieved upon this little bridge. 'And when the
woman has been bullied and harried unto death,' she said, assuming
that I had been following all her silent thoughts or that I was smart
enough to fill in the gaps myself, 'when she has attained to the only
peace and independence she is likely ever to have known, then along
he comes again with his bent back and his remorse and his generous
gift of guilt, making her death yet one more triumph for him, mus-
cling in once more on whatever dignity or sympathy or attention
happens to be going. Another Hamlet taking on all-comers in Ophelia's grave. Fucking men with their obtrusive fucking guilt!'

I didn't take it personally at the time—I seemed a long way from
country graveyards then—but there is no possibility of my not
noticing now that some of the flak from Camilla's firing was meant
to come my way. Guilt was one of my words. It helped me to understand myself. I believed I carried it in every pocket and that the

weight of it was the reason I bent slightly at the knees. It's certainly the reason I'm not entirely upright now.

Don't mistake me, though. The guilt I've always been interested in is not the usual variety of cosmic unworthiness. I'm not a self-hater. I don't wonder what such a creature as I is doing crawling across the face of the earth. I don't feel that I'm largely to blame for starving Africans or camps of futureless refugees. What I'm referring to is a very particular sense of having let women down, not just the odd woman and not merely at random, but as it were the whole sex, systematically.

Perhaps a fragment of family history will help me to explain more exactly what I mean.

On the night he was married my father turned in his sleep, slipped both his hands inside the pure white nightdress of his softly slumbering wife—this is my mother I'm talking about: I have the right to heightened language—and murmured, 'Lucetta, ah Lucetta, comme tu est douce! Que je t'aime!'

This was a surprise to both of them, for not only could my father speak no French, my mother's name was Rachel.

To this day my father swears that he was as innocent as Adam of knowledge of any other woman, had never even heard of anyone called Lucetta, and that his whispering for her in his first sleep as a husband was just another example of that atrocious luck that has dogged him all his life when it comes to remembering my mother's name. God knows whether he is telling the truth. Certainly my mother did her best to understand the sorts of associative confusions that might have been behind her receiving anniversary flowers accompanied by a card 'To my darling Rose', and gifts of jewellery on her birthday 'For Golda'. But I know for a fact that she had never been happy about the letters my father sent her all those years ago from Germany—he had entered Hamburg with the British 2nd Army, just a month before my fifth birthday—addressed to 'Liebe Helga'.

In fairness to him it must be said that he has made no better a job of remembering the names of my wives. The only time he got my first one's right was on the day I was marrying my second. 'Here's to Barney and Sharon,' he proposed, raising a tumbler of champagne, for all the world the proudest and the happiest of fathers-in-law; only Sharon had not, for reasons to do with good taste, been invited. Camilla—how vividly I recollect it!—roared with amusement. But she was capable of doing something like that while having her own thoughts.

The odd thing about this idiosyncrasy of my father's is that names are in a sense his living. I've never known what precisely he does in that comfortable room of his in Somerset House, directly above a Tuscan column and with wide views over the Thames, except that he is involved in some way with births and birth certificates. In earlier times, when his job was new to him and he had a young family to entertain, he would come home, take off his coat, and without further preliminary explanations rattle off the latest batch of cruel and comic christenings, the day's dirty tricks that parents had played upon their children. 'Ivor Soredick,' he would say, as we all fussed around him, bringing him tea and helping him off with his shoes. 'Greta Warmley, Eva Brick, Nelson McCollum, Noah Arkwright, Ava Crisp, Russell Spring, Albert Bridge, Clyde Banks, Treta Wright, Atossa Day.' And after supper, if we were lucky, he might remember some more. 'Mavis Sphincter, Nola Blower, Rosina Hattrick, Yule Grocock, Rosy Titball, Neil Downs, Melvyn Bragg, Carrie Waters, Ellen Evans, Willie Wanklyn, Montague Gaylord, Butch Walker, Patricia Plaything.'

On some nights he would go on for hours. There is no possibility that he could have made these names up. There were too many of them. And we never caught him out repeating any. He simply remembered them. He saw them once and he never again forgot them. From which it must follow that there was nothing organically wrong with his memory. Some other explanation must therefore be found for why he so often suffered amnesia when he came to address or give something to his wife, and why he so frequently confused her with other women, real or imaginary, who might or might not have enjoyed some separate and individual existence in his life.

Guilt, of course, is where I'm heading, guilt husbandly and filial, guilt personal and atavistic, but I've no objection to pausing briefly, on the way, at guilt's greatest ally, love. 'Twice or thrice had I loved thee,' I tried to convince Camilla on countless cliff walks or valley rambles, 'Before I knew thy face or name.' But I was never successful. 'You'd say that to anyone,' she told me, 'you've said it to I'll never know how many others.' Which showed how far she was from grasping what I was telling her. It wasn't her fault. No member of her sex can ever understand how, for a man, love is a continuum. They cannot bear the idea that all previous women are but a dream of them, because that must mean that they themselves are but a dream of someone else. It's no coincidence that Plato was a man.

'I don't want to be a part of your continuum, thanks very much,' Camilla told me, as though this was an area where either of us could exercise any choice. Lucetta might just as well have protested against popping up in my father's wedding-night dreams. My poor father—he is only a man like the rest of us; no wonder he could never be absolutely certain who his wife was: sometimes I have woken up next to Camilla and not known whether she was herself or my mother or my cousins or Sharon or the little girl whose head I split open on bonfire night, 1947, because her fireworks rose higher in the sky than mine.

And so, although Camilla happened to be the last and best, and although these are exclusively her haunts I try each day to track her down through, strictly speaking I walk this wild western shore, attired as if I'm on the way to a wine bar, for all of them.

That is not, of course, and I am the first to admit it, any kind of adequate explanation of how I came to have wound up here, washed up like that bit of exotic wreckage that was found on the rocks this morning—a splinter of a roulette table, the fishermen reckoned, from some capsized pleasure boat. And if I am ever to get away with a clear conscience and a clearer head—yes, that is my intention, despite the liquid looks I am getting from the local bean-eaters and other assorted fantasists I meet in the pubs and who want to tell me that they can see I have fallen fatally for the place as they have done—if I *am* going to escape, then I must follow Camilla's old advice to me and come clean. I don't expect it to be easy. It is not in the grain of my nature to be candid and confessional. 'I'm an embroiderer,' I told Camilla, I don't know how many times. 'I'm interested in the filigree around the edges of the truth.' 'You mean you haven't got a straight bone in your body,' she used to reply.

Ours was, as I think I have already made plain, a very verbal, argumentative connection.

Well, I can't argue with you now, Camilla. But wherever you are, prepare to admit that you were wrong. Turn your fine stern eyes in this direction. Look at me. See how straight I'm growing. Watch how clean I'm coming.

Cleanish, anyway.

Simon Louvish

was born in Glasgow in 1947 and taken to Israel at the age of two. His Israeli army service from 1965 to 1967 included the Six Day War, in which he served as a military cameraman. In 1968 he attended the London School of Film Technique and began a series of political documentaries on the Middle East, southern Africa, and Greece. Louvish is the author of ten novels, a biography of W. C. Fields, and *Moments of Silence* (1979), a memoir of his time in Israel. He has lived in London since 1968 and teaches at the London International Film School. The excerpts here are taken from *The Therapy of Avram Blok* (1985) and *Days of Miracles and Wonders* (1997), which are, respectively, the first and last novels in his *Blok* quartet. In the first selection Avram Blok is caught up in the mobilization of reserve soldiers for the Yom Kippur War of 1973. The second piece revolves around the failed author Danny Hohenlohe (aka Pick), previously a patient of the therapist Avram Blok. He is here developing his plot to assassinate his publisher, Gordon McTeague, amid the preparations for the start of the 1991 Gulf War.

Simon Louvish

EXCERPT FROM The Therapy
of Avram Blok

Meanwhile, back on the battlefield: 16th October, 1973, while the
forces of General Arik Sharon were sneaking across the Canal north
of the Great Bitter Lake (by what was known as the 'Chinese farm'),
Blok and Sa'id were pinned down by Egyptian artillery ten kilome-
tres east of Suez. Another counter-attack had bitten the dust and a
large number of Israeli soldiers were stuck on a makeshift Bar Lev
line not far from the Mitleh Pass. If the enemy could capture the Pass
all Sinai would open up to them and they could roll on, presumably,
towards the heartland of Israel. The measly piece of dry beach that
the two armies were deadlocked on was therefore of vital importance, although the only people who could bear to linger there in
normal times were the bedouins who lived off the kif trade, and
even they were just passers-by, blowing their minds on their mer-
chandise and leaving behind nothing but exhausted roaches mingled with camels' turds.

In the bunker, with Blok and Sa'id, were about two dozen soldiers
from an Ordnance Corps rearguard who had somehow found themselves at the front. They were bone weary and shell-shattered and
loudly bemoaning their fate. The war had lasted a full ten days now
and there appeared little chance of anyone here attending the victory
parade. If indeed it did not end up being cancelled, one wag suggested, due to a lack of wheelchairs.

In a rare lull, a discussion developed over the best way to cash in
one's chips. Each person took it in turn to soliloquize upon their
preference. One man said: 'A direct hit, in the torso, by a 105 shell.
You don't feel a thing, and since you're blown to atoms, your family's spared the expense of a funeral.' Another man countered him
with morose logic: 'The army buries you free anyway, so where's
the saving in that? The best way,' he said, 'is to have your head

sheared off by shrapnel, since your brain is separated from your heart you can't possibly feel any pain.' A recruit with an eccentrically religious bent said: 'The best thing would be for my penis to be shot off, because then I could devote my life to meditation and study, without the fear of temptation.' They all leaped on him furiously. 'What d'you mean by that? How could you say that? How did they let someone like you in the army?' So incensed were they, they nearly tore him limb from limb on the spot. 'The best way is to be killed in your sleep,' muttered a fourth man. 'You just wake up and presto! you're no longer there.' 'How d'you wake up if you're dead?' everyone asked him. They had entered a frenzy of pedantry. 'Poison gas,' one fool said. 'LSD,' said another. 'You laugh your way into the grave.' And yet another said: 'Nuclear Holocaust, then you won't be alone in the Next World.' An atheist scoffed, 'Listen, brother,' he said, 'when you're dead you're dead, that's the end of the whole shtik.' The devout protested, 'Why don't you go back to Russia?' they demanded, though the man was from Uruguay. 'I'll go anywhere,' he responded reasonably, 'if you postpone this bloody bordello.'

Blok was taking all this down on his Nagra tape recorder. With grim relish he was committing every blasphemy, every obscenity, to a magnetic posterity. Sa'id contributed a number of condoms as containers in case the tapes had to be left on the spot due to death or similar misfortune. ('Is that what you brought to the war, daddy?' Blok asked him. 'A man should never be caught short,' Sa'id answered, with supreme sangfroid.) He had also recorded a selection of rigorous, harsh, unremitting commentaries, for a dream issue of *BABASIS*. They went something like this:

Dawn, over the Suez Front. The flies settle once again for their breakfast on the eyes of a dead infantryman. Desert ants carry off to their lair the intestines of a youth from Afula. Over a spared transistor radio come the sweet grandmotherly tones of Golda Meir, telling us everything is under control. The hevreh spit in the sand at the sound of her hated drivel. The old bat, whose corrupt and greedy policies led to this disaster, will not escape the wrath of the soldiers who, if they survive, can think of nothing more satisfying than fitting their hands round the rump of her scraggy neck. . . .

Or:

Why are we killing each other, the soldiers, in their waking delirium, ask. What have I got against some poor Ahmed who's been torn from the bosom of his sheep somewhere in Upper Egypt and marched down to this hell hole and told to shoot down the Jews? I know he would much rather be fucking his girlfriend or wife, just as I would, or play shesh-besh on the banks of the river until the cows come home. I mean, if we have to shoot somebody, just to satisfy the bloodlust They tell us is the Lot of Mankind, why don't we shoot the people who got us into this mess? If we have to commit brutalities, and obscene atrocities, why don't we find a way to do it which would, somehow, benefit our fellow oppressed? For example: roasting the war criminal Dayan on a spit, till his stomach splits open and his other eye pops out, squelching into the fire? Why don't we put a grenade up the arse of Sadat and scatter his foul carcase, not ours, over the desert sands? Why don't we napalm the Presidential Palace in Cairo, or the Knesset in Jerusalem, instead of Stronghold Number Forty-five? Why can't the politicians, in their immaculate suits and ties, their shampoo, manicure, pedicure, become blazing, shrieking torches, rather than the men of Ordnance Company Eighty? Why shouldn't They get a phosphorous bomb in the eyes for the sake of the Security Effort? There is no doubt, Company Eighty determine, that a parachute drop of parliamentarians into the battle zone would do no end of good for morale.

And so on.

After a time, as is their wont, the tapes finally ran out. There were no more reels to record on and Blok was loath to wipe previous material to make way for new revelations. Outside, the shells were still keeping up their fearful barrage. Some said the bombardment seemed to be slackening, but the sceptics said No, we are merely all going slowly but steadily deaf. Once this latter idea gained credence it became, inevitably, imbued with a certain mad attraction. One could see, from people's faces, that they were giving serious thought to the proposition of poking out their own eardrums in order to end the incessant clamour. A bizarre telepathy spread: if anyone produced so much as a toothpick he would be instantly pounced upon, wrestled to the ground and divested of the dread weapon of potential self-mutilation. A man who merely wanted to sew his socks up during a brief lull was beaten almost black and blue when he took out his needle. It was a madhouse without a doubt. The elements of mutual protection and bare aggression had become completely confused. And the whole thing might go on for days. The food might run out, and people might eye each other with sinister new desires . . .

But a miracle happened. Suddenly it was over. What had occurred was this: the forces of Arik Sharon, having bridged the Canal above the Great Bitter Lake, had begun pouring across in strength. The Egyptians, waking up to their oversight in downgrading the Canal crossing, hastily diverted their forces to deal with this unforeseen body blow. The tanks and artillery, earmarked to blow Blok and his colleagues apart so as to proceed to the Mitleh, were now rushing north to kill some other poor bastards. Thus Sharon, whom Blok and many others regarded as the most dangerous right-wing fanatic in the entire Fertile Crescent, had actually saved Blok's life, at the expense of others' . . . Blok and Co. emerged, brains mushed and ears ringing, into a moonscape of smoking craters. But at the rim of the bunker he and Sa'id stopped short, stunned by a further miracle: the *BABASIS* jeep, from which they had scrambled pell mell into the hole thirty-six hours before, was standing there serene and untouched except for a few shrapnel scratches. A centurion tank, thrown by a blast on its side, had shielded the jeep in its shadow throughout the entire bombardment.

'If it'd been us out there,' Blok scoffed, kicking the vehicle, 'and not this dumb asshole machine, you can be sure we'd have bought it proper.'

They loaded the tapes, secure in their condoms, on to the jeep's back seat. Sa'id brought from the bunker the dusty but undamaged Nagra. 'Where should I put this?' he innocently inquired.

'Give me that thing!' cried Blok, wresting it from him savagely. It had 'Property of *BABASIS* magazine' taped over its battery hatch. 'I'll show 'em *BABASIS* magazine!' he said. 'Fuck 'em all! I'm not going to carry this deadweight with no tapes to record on.' He turned to the soldiers, who were hesitantly taking the air, 'Hey, hevreh— has anyone got a grenade?'

He was handed one and, with a surge of confidence such as he had never felt before in his life, taped it round the recorder with the last of the sellotape spool. Then, while Sa'id wagged his head, scratched his chin and mumbled incoherently behind him, he strode forward, ten, twenty, thirty metres out into the open desert and, facing north-east—Tel Avivwards—he set the thing down in a crater and, pulling the pin out, ran hell-in-his-pants back to cover.

'Grenade!!' he bellowed, throwing himself on his face. Sa'id, and everyone else in earshot, dived, hugging the ground, thinking the whole shtik was resuming.

CRASH-BANG!!!!****!!!—One Nagra tape recorder, State Property, left this sad vale of tears. Cogs, screwlets and levers, cams, pinwheels and sockets, leads, wires, transistors, all assembled with loving care in Switzerland, land of the Alp and yodel, the slalom and Toblerone, sprayed, twisted, burnt, splintered all over the Sinai dunes.

Blok, in mock ceremony, made the sign of the cross over the smoking remains. 'Pax vobiscum,' he intoned, dredging, from his addled memory, the words of an old school howler.

(But after all, doesn't everyone mean well, in their own funny way? Take Napoleon, for example: he wanted to unite Europe. Or take Hitler: he wanted to unite the Germans. He wanted them to walk proud, and the hang with anyone else. Was he so different from you and me, in some of our darkest hours? Genghis Khan, Tamerlane, Attila—they just couldn't stop moving, sweeping stick-in-the-muds out of the way. Yes, they meant well. And Jesus, the most well meaning of all, they say, but look at the consequences. Look at Buddha, and at the Samurai. Mohammed—and the sweeping sickle . . . Karl Marx, for example, wanted to free the whole world. Bakunin, Lenin, Trotsky-Bronstein (steeped in the blood of Kronstadt). Stalin-Djugashvili was more modest, he wanted Socialism in One Country. No doubt he meant well. As did the good parliamentarians of Europe, circa 1914, who sent their young men to die in the trenches. And ditto those of today . . . and the sellers of arms, to blacks, browns and yellows, to balance white national budgets. And Nobel, of gunpowder and the Peace Prize? Einstein, with e=mc² . . . ? Or the social utopians, Owenists, Fourierists, et al. . . . Zionists, who wanted their people to walk proud and ended up grinding another people's face in the dust for the sake of the highest ideals . . . ? They were no different from anyone else. They just wanted to do their own version of Good, but ain't we the ones who get done, meine kinder?)

★   ★   ★

At the moment of blowing up the *BABASIS* Nagra between the
Mitleh and Port Tewfiq, Blok declared his own private, unilateral
cease-fire. He took to the road with Sa'id, proclaiming absolute
neutrality. They became the Phantom Scribblers' Command Car,
and were able to vanish for five days between the gaps in the jurisdic-
tion of different brigades and battalions. Technically, was this
desertion in time of war, carrying, according to GHQ law, a possible
sentence of life imprisonment? Certainly there were still serious
opportunities for sudden and heroic death in the Land of Goshen,
which was what army mapmakers were already calling the cross-
Canal territories conquered by Arik Sharon's venture. Journalists
and photographers were streaming over with the troops, all agog
to set foot on Africa. But Blok said: 'I do not wish to go there. Our
forefathers kicked up such a shry about being let out I don't see
what's the rush to get back.' 'Let my people go home, to Safad,'
said Sa'id, being in complete agreement.

'The two of us,' pronounced Blok, 'shall be the reverse of Don
Quixote and his Sancho Panza. Don Quiblok and Sa'adiah, an
unbeatable combination! We shall do everything the other way
round: when we see giants and ogres we shall say—pschtt! these
are just innocent windmills, and get the hell out of harm's way.
When we see damsels in distress, apparently threatened by Brig-
ands, we shall know they are merely the secretaries of Brigade
Thirty-five pursued by lecherous Field Security Officers. When we
appear to see prisoners, led in shackles to the gallows, we shall
know it is nought but the Nation, en route for the front, clutching
their call-up papers. Wherever and whenever we see an opportunity
to do something noble, courageous and chivalrous, we shall turn it
down and, taking to our heels, nip to the nearest shelter. Where the
sounds of battle be, there shall we not. We know with absolute
certainty now that nobility, magnanimity and heroism are trash,
that there is no princely castle in the mist at the end of the road,
and that our Dulcinea Del Toboso, Golda Meir, is truly a whore and
a witch.'

'Anything you say,' said Sa'id, 'as long as we can get at the mun-
chies.'

They had left the main routes, of which there were only a handful, and were following classified concealed army trails marked on a map they had found in the bunker. They had traded it from an Ordnance Corps Sergeant for their last bar of Lieber chocolate. Sa'id had a compass, which they thought was in order, though of course they could not be sure: heading, apparently, into the depths of the peninsula in the direction of Mount Sinai, they might crest a dune and find themselves on the Gulf, facing the Egyptian Fourth Army. This reverse Don Quixote gambit was not without its metaphysical pitfalls . . .

The sky was blue, the ground was red, ochre and grey, wrinkled and scuffed by the pitiless hammer of Time. It might well have been here, along these labyrinthine secret IDF paths, that the Tribes of Israel under Moses got hopelessly lost and wandered for forty years. No wonder they turned out such a cantankerous lot, and their God such a crusty old bugger. They had both mislaid their steel helmets and army berets. Sa'id was wearing a triangular blue and white tembel hat with 'Club Méditerranée' upon it, and Blok a knotted handkerchief, faded and tattered, a left-over Bar Mitzvah present.

As they drove, Blok repeated derivatives and anagrams of the name Don Quixote, first under his breath, then loudly, rolling them against the bare hills:

'DONKEY SHOT!' he cried, conjuring a nine type headline. 'Darn key's short . . . dankish sort . . . dun key sought . . . dun quiche sought . . . dank ee, sot . . . dunk Ishot!' et cetera. Or: 'Ned Toxique! Quotid Oxen! Quex Doonit! Quoted Onix! Untide Xooq! Oot Denquix!' And so on. The hills did not answer, but they approached, perhaps to hear what the fuss was about. Pretty soon the shadows were lengthening, the landscape reddening, and an appalling loneliness could no longer be bellowed away. It was nearly teatime and they had not eaten since elevenses, when they had met a 105 battery whose commanding officer, shell-shocked gaga, had been carted off to the rear. ('Are we on the right way to Suez?' they asked, after opening their K-rations. 'No,' Blok told them. 'Very good,' they said, continuing upon their course.) They had not even reached, at this stage, the Jebel Musa range. 'Damn it!' said Blok, breaking off his literary musings. 'The map says there's an Ordnance supply camp, right punkt at the foot of that mesa.'

'Maybe they pulled up and went west,' said Sa'id, ever ready with the mallet of logic.

'Why on earth should they do that?' Blok fumed. 'Don't they know there's a war on there?'

They drove on, low in spirits, food and, naturally enough, petrol. But eventually they were succoured by roving bedouin, who, appearing like Apache Indians on jagged crags above, offered them a kip for the night. They ate freshly baked pittas with goats'-butter, Sa'id regaling the nomads with the tale of the Rubber Woman From Beersheba, and, in lieu of pudding, they smoked a brand of hashish which almost took the top of Blok's head off. ('A head without kif, strike it off with a knife,' say the bedou.) They also discussed the movies of Joan Crawford, on which their sheikh was a devout authority. ('Have you seen *A Woman's Face?*' asked the old fox. 'I could hardly keep from wetting my seat.') In the night Blok imagined he could hear, in the distance, the sounds of the unceasing battle. But it was merely the pounding of the cells in his totally roasted brains. In the morning they thanked their hosts profusely and continued south, upon their Quiblokian destiny.

Simon Louvish

EXCERPT FROM The Days of
Miracles and Wonders

Guilty as Charged

There is no doubt. McTeague is evil, he must be destroyed. This is
Danny Hohenlohe sprachen to you here. Do you receive me? No
matter. The guiding principle grows ever clearer as the summer
drags on. Prospects of war east of Suez making the consummation
even more poignant. Was it not Chaplin, in *Monsieur Verdoux*, who
commented, at his trial for murder, on the hypocrisy of holding
one man to account for a few measly homicides when governments
were prepared, at the drop of a hat, to incinerate hundreds of
thousands? Selah. Peter Lorre, also, I recall, directed his only film,
Die Verloren, on a similar theme. Ah, those old frayed prints projected
dimly across the cavern of the old Electric Cinema . . . Memory
lane, memory lane. The vast dark theatre, the icy cold, the tattered
seats whose springs sprung straight up your anal cavity, the jingle-
jangle warm-ups by the worst rock groups in town, but the joint,
wafting down the rows, towards you, in the middle of Godard's
Breathless . . . But these are sterner times. Peter Lorre's murderer, an
M for the Nazi era, was shunted aside because no one in the age of
mass murder had time for an amateur. Monsieur Verdoux, on the
other hand, was guillotined. It is a far, far better thing that I do, et
cetera. The world will be a better place. There is no doubt the planet
is teeming with people, one less should be a boon, should it not,
to an overloaded ecology?

Nevertheless, I still feel motive is crucial. Monsieur Verdoux killed
his wives for their money, but I don't believe one should kill the
innocent, no matter how grotesque they might be. McTeague's
crime, on the other hand, cries out for vengeance. Though there
might be pangs of reason. Why blame the lackey for his master's

voice? The rude factory-horn blast of McTeague's boss, media mogul Brent Browbeat, with his worldwide empire of crud: Shipping, communications, newspapers, terrestrial and extraterrestrial television stations (I picked up this jargon from a copy of *Variety* I found on a bench at the South Bank whence I hied to examine the techniques of the cardboard-city homeless in panhandling the National Film Theatre's patrons. One should always be on the look out for tips, if all else fails. Grabbing by the lapel and swearing undying gratitude for the few pence to be tendered turns out unexpectedly fruitful, while sitting sprawled at either end of the Hungerford Bridge looking woebegone under a blanket with a flea-bitten dog and a sign proclaiming HOMELESS AND HUNGRY, PLEASE HELP is no bloody use at all). An evocative vision of antennaed Martians gawping at, or more likely transmitting, Brent Browbeat's crap across the ethereal spheres, but referring in fact merely to the hunks of orbitting metal bouncing the uncouth North American's junk down to selected homes. 'Invasion of the Soul Snatchers.' That was a short story I sent once to *Jake Akimbo's Science Fiction Magazine*, but as expected it boomeranged back with a condemnation of a familiar redundancy. So why not eliminate the master, not the slave, Lucifer, not Mephistopheles? But no. Targeting Brent Browbeat would be too popular. An act that would presuppose an ideology. Innumerable cranks would queue up to adopt me, environmentalists, print workers, animal-rightists, moralists and humanists of every shade and hue, not to speak of the dispossessed of the third world, whose countries Browbeat International despoils with gusto, deforesting their forests, demineraling their minerals, sweating their labour into sweatshirts . . . A solid case against Lucifer, but it would be a pyrrhic victory. Cut off one head of the hydra, it sprouts ten more. I remember this from ancient Bolshevik tracts. The octopus's tentacles spread, from the central blob, the beady eyes, the ceegar and top hat, on one scaly arm the star-spangled banner, on another the union jack, the tricolour, the double-headed eagle. One cannot vanquish Capital. That much at least Elena and Nicolae Ceausescu found out. One can only accumulate a fair wack of it, for a time, till people get wise. But the Ceausescus made the mistake of conspicuous consumption. You got to have some finesse in this field. Caress 'em first, kill 'em afterwards, not the other way around.

On the other hand, it works for Saddam Hussein. So who am I to complain?

But I have not set out to save the world, merely to exact a personal revenge. I want McTeague to know there can be no defence of I vos chust obeyink orders. When Brent Browbeat orders a cut in the list to dump unprofitable authors, he-who's-hand-wieldeth-the-hatchet cannot deny the blood on the palm. Remember the hours of innocent hope? The first advance, the cheque borne proudly to the disbelieving bank clerk, the joy of proofs, the cups of tea in messy offices, the piles of volumes of those who have made it and the manuscripts of those who have not, about to be poleaxed by the familiar riposte: Dear Author: Fuck off, The Publisher. Slipped through the net, one basks, wallows, in the adoring glances of those willowy nymphs in literary arcadia, the little apples of desire balanced on their blonde heads. Go for it, Willum! Can one fail to split the core? The shining finished tome in your hands. 'Whatdayasay, Danny boy? A virgin birth!' He was the virgin, you see. Robed in white, above the toiling masses, the burning halo of patronage, the quiver of his Cupid arrows ready for the next clown.

So much for classical metaphors. Ah, the dregs of an English education. Well, at least they can spell 'homeless' and 'hungry.' One shouldn't chuck it all out of hand. As I sit, on the outside benches of the film buffs' Mecca, under the Waterloo Bridge, watching young Lochinvar tightening his grip on the lapels of his two trapped marks. 'You don't know what it's like mate, having somebody 'o knows what it's like. Kno'-amean?' An older colleague approaches me with a proferred torn handkerchief. 'I already gave.' He passes on to greener pastures. Ah, to see McTeague reduced to this . . . But one needs a more permanent outcome . . .

There must be more in life than thoughts of murder, though you might not know it, scanning the daily press: WASHINGTON'S JIHAD. BUSH PREPARES U.S. FOR WAR. VICTORY IN THE AIR IN ONE DAY. SADDAM SOLDIERS WILLING TO FIGHT AND DIE. Rather you than me, brothers. MORE BRITISH HOSTAGES ROUNDED UP. There's an idea there, somewhere. But who would ransom Gordon McTeague, or even Brent Browbeat for that matter? One would have to feed the blighters, even if only canned beans and spaghetti loops. Caveat emptor. Allahu akbar. Alas. I too, like Peter

Lorre, am becoming a faded *Verloren* in the dim space of the Electric Theatre. In the shadow of mass slaughter, what price Hohenlohe's skimmed schemes?

In 'Invasion of the Soul Snatchers,' an evil scientist, Doctor Xkalibur, discovers a method to leech souls from the bodies of innocent passers-by with a giant syringe pointed out the window of his house. The souls are then emptied into large glass vessels kept in his basement laboratory. As the de-souled inhabitants of the city continue about their daily business as automatons, the doctor proceeds to inject himself, little by little, with the stolen ectoplasmic essence. The memories, experiences and emotions of the city's populace flood into his veins and bloodstream. But the knowledge and secrets he hoped to appropriate become a hopeless, tangled knot. In desperation, he turns the syringe on himself, to suck his own soul out with the others before he loses control of his mind. But his machines cannot cope with the multitude and explode, burning the house down. Filled with thousands of souls, he staggers out into a city of mindless, passionless robots, making their way from home to work and back, performing sex and procreating without purpose, functioning without hope or desire. Only he feels love, rage, joy and anguish, pleasure and unhappiness, exultation and frustration. He wanders about, despite his manifold personalities, in a state of desperate solitude, until suddenly, one day, from a nearby building, he feels the tug of a giant syringe . . .

No, but seriously . . . Make an attempt, Danny, to throw an anchor to reality. I tried to conjure up a sensual tickle or two. Telephoned an old flame, who I had arranged to meet on the wings of my publishing success, but ferries passing in the blight . . . 'Martha?' Miraculously at the same number, although an automation from the Telephone Company interrupted, claiming: 'You have dialled an 081 number. Please redial using the prefix 0–8–1. British Telecom is not charging you for this call.' Oh yeah? Up your ass, sister! 'Danny? I was just thinking about you.' 'Are you all right? Are you ill?' 'No, I'm feeling fine, Danny. Are you okay?'

'I've been at a madhouse, in Scotland.'

'Was it interesting?'

'Dull to moderate. A visiting friend was kidnapped by terrorists.'

'I'm sorry I missed it.'

That's my girl. Trotskyist Martha, who wanted us both to seek employment at a Dagenham car plant and feel the oppression of the proletariat in the aching of our bones. Halcyon days. Instead I rode the charter winds to Manhattan and began squeezing out those old redundant ideas bought for a dollar from the wizened old Chinese in Orchard Street. Two years of painting lofts, sans La Passionaria of the International Revolutionary Communist Front (membership fifteen and falling). She burnt my Erle Stanley Gardner collection, as it was propaganda for Imperialist justice.

'I'm sorry,' she told me now in the Patisserie Valerie. 'That was a dumb thing to do.'

So long ago. 1973. The oil embargo, another Middle East War, Tricky Dicky, Watergatey, Veet-Nam. But she looked no different. Still a wild thing in sweaters, though now with *pischifkes* in her earlobes. I am lying, the skin is drier, crow's feet, stretch marks. But from my papyrus face, who am I to speak. An American couple at our elbow are arguing about Dante. Rather, he is lecturing her. 'Of course, Dante was the first structuralist. His deconstruction of reality is way ahead of his time.' Like Woody Allen, I wish I could say: 'I have Signor Alighieri right here with me, and . . .' A flamethrower would also be handy.

'So what's new, now that communism is kaput?'

'Oh Danny, you're so naïve.'

Guilty as charged. I take everything so seriously, such as the evidence of my own eyes and ears. But she had left the Party, which she accused of patriarchy and sexism. All her energies are now charged with opposing war in the Gulf: 'Saddam Hussein is a scapegoat for the West's bankrupt ideas. He's the bastard we put in place, now he challenges us where it hurts, we get all high and mighty. It's a setup for the oil companies. Everybody knows that.'

I try to tell her about my betrayal by McTeague, but her mind is in Arabia Deserta. All agog with her plans to join a group of peace activists who were going to fly to Baghdad and then bus south to form a peace camp on the Kuwaiti border, to interpose themselves between the belligerent forces, so that when the dogs of war are finally unleashed, the peace militants will cry 'Down, Fido!'

'That doesn't sound very healthy.'

'Sometimes you have to stick your neck out. In the Party we

marched and chanted slogans. Now here's a chance to do something.'

Pouring petrol over oneself and lighting a match at the gates of the palace. That too has been tried. 'You should take a lot of suntan lotion. And woolly sweaters. The sands are cold at night. And scorpion repellent.'

'You're not fooling me, Danny. You know you really care, under that spiky armour. But you deflect all that anger against the wrong targets. Against yourself. It's such a waste, Danny.'

'I intend to use it all in good faith.' I riposted. 'I'm going to kill my ex-editor, and rid the world of his scourge.'

'You're not going to kill anybody, Danny,' she said, wearily. 'It's just another fantasy of yours. Here, sign this petition.' She plunked a wrinkled document down on the table. It was headed: IMPERIALISM, OUT OF THE GULF.

'Where else should Imperialism be?'

'You're a wanker, Danny!' she exclaimed.

'I always like to approach that question through the mediation of a text,' the idiot at our elbow drawled. I too like to read a book sometimes. But this was getting me nowhere, and certainly not into the lady's pants. We parted curtly, she to her battlefields, me to mine. The humid night of Oseney Crescent. Just e-shout if you need. Aaaaaaaaaaaaaa! No dice. The peeling walls still stand. Filled with the city's pilfered souls, I swell and suffocate. Or perhaps it's just the dust mites after all. Their tiny damned ghosts. We are surrounded by anguish. If it's not the living, it's the dead beating their wings against the panes. The morphic resonance of trillions. How are we supposed to cope with it all?

Somewhere in this vast metropolis my enemies are enjoying their repast of blood and fresh entrails. Penguin suits under the chandeliers. Or has the wife popped the Tesco's Chicken Supreme into the microwave? Domestic bliss, or corporate relish? Exeunt, for a Kentucky Fried Chicken, to Eat Here, rubbing elbows with the lumpenproletariat. Yobs Without Necks. Fat ladies with their squawling brats. Hold on to that pram, chile! You'll never get another chance! Junior Macnuggets. Eat your fish, Danny! I know it's cold, it's your own fault! Against one's will, one's bones elongate, one's flesh stretches, skin folds. Growth and entropy entwined. The passing blob of protoplasm. The gravedigger's forceps. There is so very little time.

Should I forgo revenge? The milk of human kindness curdles like everything else. But, nevertheless, beatifically, I float, over the rainbow, exuding absolution, for McTeague, for Brent Browbeat, for George Bush, for my mother, for Andrew Mackenzie and the fake therapist Avram Blok, for International Peacenik Martha, for Karl Marx, Margaret Thatcher. (Among the excluded: Adolf Hitler, Stalin, Genghis Khan, Saddam Hussein, Lyndon Johnson, Harold Wilson. One has to draw the line somewhere.) The moving automatons, sucked dry by Xkalibur's syringe . . .

There is a bad habit, in the Kentucky Fried Chickens, of servers picking out your two pieces, one from the newer, one from the older batch. Usually the leg from the former, the breast from the latter. One is so helpless, before fate. Four black youths have taken an adjacent booth, launching into an incomprehensible multilogue loud enough to raise Colonel Sanders himself from the tomb. I am a martyr to this booming London patois, which is like a wooden corkscrew driven into the skull. Not, I hasten to add, a racial comment, but one of class alone. Oh, for conscription to dispatch them all to struggle in the Saudi sands! All glottal stops and chicken bones.

I am, despite what peacenik Martha believes about my inner drives, drawn by all this talk of combat and death. To sit, comfortably in one's armchair, watching the electronic fog of battle on one's Sony twelve-inch. The telephoto explosions, the burnt-out chassis of tanks and zapped aircraft. Nowadays, unfortunately, we can't escape from the concomitant images of what the Americans in Vietnam quite properly designated 'ambulant non-combatant personnel.' The civilians caught in the carnage, their remoteness annulled by close-ups, guilt bored into our hearts. Even extraterrestrial television, I suspect, will not protect us from this. Conscience. Compassion. Empathy.

Bad news for the anti-McTeague axis. Should feed the demon better vittles. Short rations for the cherub. You gotta take the longer view. Harden your heart, as the Lord did unto Pharaoh. Just hang tough in thar, baby! The world is not made for sissies . . .

Return from the old Kentucky karma. My homestead, with bilious-green wallpaper. The battering neighbours have battered each other into silence, and I am left with the ghosts of old gas meters, the coin-swallowing ghouls of yesteryear. Open a window for air. This is where the good fairy enters to save me from my elongating nose. But no nose-job dame from outer space tonight. Instead a scrabbling at the window-sill, and Nick and Elena Ceausescu heave themselves into the room. Dishevelled and grimy from their sojourn in the mountains, they make a beeline for the mini-fridge, grabbing a hunk of cheddar cheese and a festering Milano salami, which they begin to tear with their cracked and filth-encrusted talons. They insist on staying the night. It's a tight fit, lying between the two. They are blanket stealers, pulling and tugging all night long. Eventually, I fall asleep, and dream. I am in the old Electric Cinema, watching a movie of my childhood in Wembley Park. It's one of those drab old English black-and-white affairs, with dingy curtains and absymal wallpaper. My father, Pick the Elder, is slouched dead in his arm-chair with a paperweight through his heart. My mother, on the sofa, is turning the pages of the *Jewish Chronicle*'s Brides & Homes Supplement. I, a small, weedy child, look upon this scene dispas-sionately, then turn away, stepping into the closet in the hall, among my father's musty jackets, the brooms and mops and battered shoes. A strange muffled wailing comes from beyond the wall. I push against a side panel, which slides open, leading to a dark descending flight of stairs. The wailing, accompanied by a mechanical sound, increases. I step out of the dark passage into a vast laundromat, lit by buzzing neon lights, with hundreds of machines churning their dirty linen round and round. On a raised dais, at the further end of the hall, I approach a man dressed in army fatigues, whom I recog-nise clearly from press photographs and television as the President of the Republic of Iraq, Saddam Hussein.

'Do you do a service wash?' I ask him.

'We are alone here,' he replies.

I look around and we were indeed the only persons visible along-side the machines. But as I look closer I can make out, inside each appliance, an agonised face revolving in the froth and bubbles, mouth open in a silent scream.

'What about them?' I ask him.

'They are of no consequence,' he answers, with a dismissive flick of his hand. 'Self-service riff-raff, Mensheviks.' I walk down the lines and peer inside. Many faces appear familiar, childhood friends, neighbours, relatives. In one window McTeague revolves, his face contorted in a faded plea: 'Help me, Daniel!' A far-off, miniature squeak. I see my parents, turning, my father's dead-fish eyes, my mother clinging to clipped-out coupons. And poor Martha, tangled in a tattered red flag.

'But this is inhuman!' I protest to the dictator. His face takes on a frightening grimace, a malicious grin. He points towards another chamber I had not noticed, hewn out of the rock. It glows, with a multitude of roaring fires, licking in the maws of giant engines——

'AFTER THE WASH—THE DRY!'

This cannot go on much longer. Something has got to give. Either my mind, or the universe. There's no room for both of us in town. Nevertheless, I face the morning with a renewed confidence. Nicolae and Elena have departed, taking the remains of the salami and a rancid tub of my landlord's taramasalata. I hie to the local store, to replenish the losses and buy a thick string of garlic. That should keep the dead dictators from my door. The live ones, on the other hand . . .

Save the world! There must be a more deserving cause. Somewhere in space, a better species. Open that third eye, you hidden Martians! You thirty-six wise men, speak up! I'll accept women too, or intermediates. Anyone who has a reasonably good idea. Perhaps it's time to return to my little Chinese chap in Orchard Street, to buy another couple of phials of cheap inspiration. The soup to turn Jekyll into Hyde. Or vice versa, one may never decide which is best. The bottle imp. The elixir of life. Transmuting base metals into gold. The incompetent and the inconsequential flourish, while . . .

Is there anything dumber than hubris without cause? I walk the streets, with my fizzing ego concealed in a brown paper bag. Taking every now and then a surreptitious sip through a straw. Hair of the God that bit me. Everyday life continues. Couples ogle cakes in windows. Tourists gape at Indonesian restaurant menus, punk girls float down the street with translucent skin, satellite-television salesmen pile out of a Volkswagen van with striped shirts and peaked red caps, grabbing unwary passers-by and forcing them, by painful judo holds, to accept free subscriptions to extraterrestrial broadcasts, by a newsstand poster which proclaims: SADDAM GIVEN LAST CHANCE . . .

What will they do? Ring his doorbell and run? The gangrene of imperial dreams. Is Trotsky Martha already lying down a barrage of Pete Seeger ditties between the kennels of war? 'We'll call on the soldiers on both sides to lay down their weapons and embrace each other,' she told me, in the Patisserie Valerie. And they shall beat their swords into British Gas shares, at 120 pence. The beardless youth from Chippewa, Minnesota, will brush the bristles of the fellah from Wadi el Brouj. Soon they will all be humping in the dunes, like in Antonioni's *Zabriskie Point*. Come back, Monsieur Verdoux, all is forgiven. A little spot of personal violence, for cash or pleasure, would do us all a world of good. The private, rather than the public vengeance. Do it for old time's sake, and don't spare the mustard! Anything but self-delusion and false hopes. . . .

And so we hang about, waiting for the Apocalypse, again. Picking our nose on the street-corners of history, flicking the snot into the road. Will the police arrive, in their Black Maria? Or is it open season, out there?

IS ANYBODY LISTENING? IS ANYBODY AWAKE? WILL ANYONE PLEASE START THE BIDDING? DO I HEAR A VOICE IN THE BACK?

Michelene Wandor

was born in London in 1940 and was educated at Cambridge University and the
University of Essex. She has worked as a
poetry editor and theater reviewer, and
her nonfiction work includes the influential *Look Back in Gender* (1987). Wandor
has written extensively for theater and
radio, and two of her best-known dramatizations are *The Wandering Jew* (1987) for
the National Theatre and *The Brothers Kar-
amazov* for BBC Radio Four. She is the
author of three books of poetry and one
collection of short stories, *Guests in the Body*
(1986). 'Return to Sender' (1986) is taken
from this volume and, along with 'Song of
the Jewish Princess' (1989), demonstrates Wandor's ability to rewrite literary
texts and biblical and classical mythology in new and radical ways.

Michelene Wandor

Return to Sender

(Adapted from a section of *Daniel Deronda* by George Eliot)

Come in.

I do apologise for arriving here two days later than I said I would, in my letter to you. But no doubt you have had ample time to see round Genoa, perhaps even take a boat, so that you might enjoy the magnificent view of the city and the harbour from the sea.

Do sit down.

Whenever I see the grand harbour, I imagine the multitudinous Spanish Jews, centuries ago, driven destitute from their Spanish homes, suffered to land from the crowded ships only for a brief rest on this grand quay of Genoa, overspreading it with a pall of famine and plague—dying mothers with dying children at their breasts; fathers and sons agaze at each other's haggardness, like starving prisoners turned out beneath the midday sun.

I imagine that the colourless wording of my letter gave you no clue as to what might be in store for you. I imagine also, that Sir Hugo has been correctly reticent and not anticipated any of my disclosures. Yes. I thought so.

It is hot here at noon. The oleanders in the tubs along the wayside gardens look more and more like fatigued holiday-makers, and the roads get deeper with dry, white dust. I love the evenings, the scattering abroad of all those whom the midday sun has sent under shelter, the tinkling of mule bells, light footsteps and voices; the buildings, forts and castles, seem to come forth and gaze in fullness of beauty after their long siesta, till all strong colour melts in the stream of moonlight, which makes the streets a new spectacle, with shadows, both still and moving; and then the moon descends slowly into deep night and silence, and nothing shines but the port lights of the great Lanterna in the blackness below, and the glimmering stars in the blackness above.

I have told the servants that you are a doctor whom I am consulting. They are not surprised to know that you have met me here, in the library, in the cool of the evening. They may be a little surprised, however, to see someone so young, so vibrant. An eminent physician, whom I have come to Genoa to consult. So vibrant.

'To my son, Daniel Deronda: I shall be in Genoa on the fourteenth of this month. My health is shaken and I desire there should be no time lost before I deliver to you what I have long withheld. Bring with you the diamond ring Sir Hugo gave you. I shall like to see it again. Your unknown mother, Leonora Halm-Eberstein.'

You may rest assured that the love Sir Hugo bears you will not be altered by anything.

You are a beautiful creature. I knew you would be. You are blushing. Yet you are not overcome with emotion. You must have lived through so many ideal meetings with me. No doubt they all seemed more real than this. Perhaps you can see some likeness to your own face in mine? You have a painful sense of aloofness about you.

I suppose you must have begun to wonder about the mysteries of your parentage. Well. I am your mother. But you can have no love for me. I have not the foolish notion that you can love me merely because I am your mother. I thought I chose something better for you than being with me. I did not think I deprived you of anything worth having. I don't mean to speak ill of myself, but I had not much affection to give you. I did not want affection. I had been stifled with it. I wanted to live out the life that was in me, and not to be hampered with other lives. I was a great singer, and I acted as well as I sang. All the rest were poor beside me. Men followed me from one country to another. I was living a myriad lives in one. I did not want a child.

I have cast all precedent out of my mind in telling you this. Precedence has no excuse for me. I can only seek a justification in the words I can find for my experience. I did not want to marry. I was forced to marry your father—forced, I mean, by my father's wishes and commands. And besides, it was my best way of getting some freedom. I could rule my husband but not my father. I had a right to be free. I had a right to seek my freedom from a bondage that I hated. And the bondage that I hated for myself, I wanted to keep you from. What better could the most loving mother have done? I relieved you from the bondage of having been born a Jew. I chose for you what I would have chosen for myself. You are an English gentleman. I secured you that.

Why did I do it? When you are as old as I am, then it will not seem so simple a question. People talk of their motives in a cut and dried way. Every woman is supposed to have the same set of motives, or else to be a monster. I am not a monster, but I have not felt exactly what other women feel—or say they feel, for fear of being thought unlike others. When you reproach me in your heart for sending you away from me, you mean I ought to say I felt about you as other women feel about their children. I did not feel that. I was glad to be freed from you.

Do I seem now to be revoking everything? Well, there are reasons. I feel many things I can't understand. A fatal illness has been growing in me for a year. I will not deny anything I have done. I will not pretend to love where I have no love. But shadows are rising round me. If I have wronged the dead—I have but little time to do what I have left undone.

Your grandfather never comprehended me, or if he did, he only thought of fettering me into obedience. I was to be what he called 'the Jewish woman' under pain of his curse. I was to feel everything I did not feel, and believe everything I did not believe. I was to feel awe for the bit of parchment in the *mezzuza* over the door; to dread lest a bit of butter should touch a bit of meat, to think it beautiful that men should bind *tephillin* on them and women not—to adore the wisdom of such laws, however silly they might seem to me. I was to love the long prayers in the ugly synagogue, and the howling and the gabbling and the dreadful fasts and the tiresome feasts, and my father's endless discoursing about Our People, which was a thunder without meaning in my ears. But I did not care at all. I cared for the wide world, and all that I could represent in it. I hated living under the shadow of my father's strictness. Teaching, teaching, 'this you must be', 'that you must not be', pressed on me like a frame that got tighter and tighter as I grew. I wanted to live a large life, with freedom to do what everyone else did, and be carried along in a great current. You are glad to have been born a Jew? That is because you have not been brought up as a Jew. That separateness seems sweet to you because I saved you from it.

I am still the same Leonore; within me is the same desire, the same will, the same choice. But there are new events—feelings, apparitions in the darkness. We only consent to what we love. I am obeying something tyrannic. I am forced to be withered, to feel pain, to be dying slowly. Do I love that?

I have been forced to obey my dead father. I have been forced to tell you that you are a Jew.

You can never imagine what it is to have a man's force of genius in you, and yet to suffer the slavery of being a girl. To have a pattern cut out—this is the Jewish woman, this is what you must be. A woman's heart must be of such a size, else it must be pressed small, like Chinese feet. Her happiness is to be made, as cakes are, by a fixed receipt. My father wished me to have been a son; he cared for me as a makeshift link. He hated the idea that Jewish women should be thought of by the Christian world as some sort of material to make public singers and actresses of. As if we were not the more enviable for that. That is a chance of escaping from bondage.

I don't deny that your grandfather was a good man, and a clever physician. A man to be admired in a play—grand, with an iron will. But such men turn their wives and daughters into slaves. They would rule the world if they could, but not ruling the world, they throw the weight of their will on the necks and souls of women. But nature sometimes thwarts them. My father had no other child than his daughter, and she was like himself.

Your father was different. Unlike me—he was all lovingness and affection. I knew I could rule him; and I made him secretly promise me, before I married him, that he would put no hindrance in the way of my being an artist. My father was on his deathbed when we were married; from the first he had fixed his mind on my marrying my cousin Ephraim. And when a woman's will is as strong as the man's who wants to govern her, half her strength must be conceal-ment. I meant to have my will in the end, but I could only have it by seeming to obey. I had an awe of my father. I hated to feel awed. I wished I could defy him openly, but I never could. It was what I could not imagine: I could not act it to myself that I should begin to defy my father openly and succeed. And I never would risk failure.

My mother was English—a Jewess of Portuguese descent. My father married her in England; through that marriage my father thwarted his own plans. My mother died when I was eight years old, and then my father allowed me to be continually with my aunt Leonora, here in Genoa, and be taught under her eyes. My father did not hinder it; but I saw it again and again in my father, that he did not guard against consequences because he felt sure he could hinder them if he liked. That I was taught music and singing meant nothing to him. He meant that I should obey his will and marry my cousin. My father died three weeks after we were married and then I had my way. It has not lasted, though. My father is getting his way now.

I think perhaps there is something of your own father in you. He was devoted to me. As I loved the life of my art, so he loved me. Let me look at the ring on your hand. It was your father's ring.

Look how like mine your hand is.

Do not look so distressed. I am suffering, but with a suffering that you cannot comfort. I did not send for you to comfort me. I do not expect anything from you.

Sir Hugo tells me that you have a wonderful mind; you are wiser than he is, with all his sixty years. I think you are glad to know that you were born a Jew. Well. Your feelings are against mine. You cannot thank me for what I did. You owe me no duties. It is better so.

When your father died, I resolved that I would have no more ties. Sir Hugo Mallinger was one who courted me, who wished to marry me. He was madly in love with me. One day I asked him, 'Is there a man capable of doing something for love and expecting nothing in return?' He said, 'What is it you want done?' I said, 'Take my boy and bring him up as an Englishman, and let him never know anything about his parents.' You were little more than two years old. I had not meditated much on the plan beforehand, but as soon as I spoke of it, it took possession of me as something I could not rest without doing. At first he thought I was not serious, but I convinced him. He agreed that it would be for your good. A great singer and actress is a queen, but she gives no royalty to her son. Afterwards, I made Sir Hugo a trustee of your fortune. And I had a joy in doing it. You were my son and it was for me to say what you should be. I said you should not know you were a Jew.

It was no shame to me. I have rid myself of the Jewish tatters and gibberish that make people nudge each other at the sight of us as if we were tattooed under our clothes, though our faces are as whole as theirs. I delivered you from the pelting contempt that pursues Jewish separateness. I am not ashamed of what I did.

Before I married the second time I was baptised. I made myself like the people I lived among. I had a right to do it. I was not like a brute, obliged to go with my own herd.

I have not repented. But yet—it is illness. I don't doubt that it has been illness. My mind has gone back. It has all come fast. Sometimes I am in an agony of pain—I daresay I shall be tonight. Then it is as if all the life I have chosen to live, all thoughts, all will, forsook me and left me alone with my memories, and I can't get away; the pain seems to keep me there. My childhood—my girl-hood—the day of my marriage—the day of my father's death— there seems to be nothing since. Then a great horror comes over me. What do I know of life or death? And what my father called 'right' may be a power that is laying hold of me—that is clutching me now. Well, I will satisfy him. I cannot go into the darkness without satisfying him. I have hidden what was his.

Often, when I am at ease, it sinks away, my whole self comes back. But I know that the other will come back—the poor, solitary, forsaken remains of self that can resist nothing. And now you have made it worse for me—but I shall have told you everything. And what reproach is there against me, since I have made you glad to be a Jew? I hoped you would have become a proud Englishman, who resented being touched by a Jew. I wish you had been.

I meant never to marry again. I meant to be free and to live for my art. I had parted with you. I had no bonds. For nine years I was a queen. I enjoyed the life I had longed for. But something strange befell me. I began to sing out of tune. It was like a fit of forgetful-ness. People told me of it. It was horrible to me. I could not bear the prospect of failure and decline. Another woman was thrusting herself in my place. The world of art and beauty is also a place of cruelty and ruthlessness. I was driven to marry. I made believe that I preferred being the wife of a Russian noble to being the greatest lyric actress of Europe. I made believe—I acted the part. It was because I felt my greatness sinking away from me. I would not wait till people said, 'She had better go'. My husband and other children do not know of your existence.

I can bear no more now. You see, I had no life left to love you with. That singing out of tune passed—it was like an illness—but it was too late. I could not go back. I need nothing that the skill of man can give me. But perhaps now that I have satisfied my father's will, your face will come to me in my dreams, instead of his—your young, loving face.

I have told you everything that could be demanded of me, I think. And now, we must part. You could not love me. Don't deny it. You don't like what I did. You are angry with me. You think I have robbed you of something. You are, perhaps, on your grandfather's side and may condemn me in your heart. But you would be wrong to be angry with me. You are the better for what I did. And yet—and yet . . .

My father never thought of me except as an instrument. Because I had wants outside his purpose, I was to be put in a frame and tortured. If that is the right law for the world, I will not say I love it. If my acts were wrong—if it is God who is exacting from me that I should deliver up what I withheld—who is punishing me because I deceived my father—well, I have told everything. I have done what I could. And your soul consents. That is enough. I have, after all, been the instrument of my father's desires. 'I desire a grandson who shall have a true Jewish heart.'

I wanted to thwart my father. And you would have me love what I have hated from the time I was so high. That can never be. We must part and not see one another again. You are angry that I banished you. You reproached me that I parted with you when you were small, and now you are come back to me and I cannot make you a joy. Have you the cursing spirit of the Jew in you? Are you not able to forgive me? Shall you be glad to think that I am punished because I was not a Jewish mother to you?

You shall give up nothing. You will be happy. You shall let me think of you as happy. I shall have done you no harm. You have no reason to curse me. You shall feel for me as they feel for the dead whom they say prayers for—you shall long that I may be freed from all suffering—from all punishment. If you think Kaddish will help me, then say it. And I shall see you instead of always seeing your grandfather. You will come between me and the dead. When I am in your mind, you will look as you do now—always, as if you were a tender son—always—as if I had been a tender mother.

Take this portrait—this miniature of me, as I was in my youth, full of fire and promise. There. When I was young, I looked for the blending of a complete personal love in one current with a larger duty. Perhaps you will do the same.

Goodbye, my son. We shall hear no more of each other. Kiss me.

Michelene Wandor

Song of the Jewish Princess

My thunderer blew in through the door, autumn leaves swirling behind him, green and brown scraps of the fading year barbed on the frayed strands of his wild woollen cloak, dry twigs pinned on his shoulders under the wide strap that held his bag, one lone leaf poised like a dancer on the brim of his hat.

Today, he who was always on time, he who always closed doors behind him, he who held himself carefully in his own space, today he was tousled, windswept, his cheeks red, his nose glowing and bulbous, his eyes wrinkled against the winter wind, his mouth taut with hurry and cold against the grin that I knew could warm his face. Well, he said, what are you waiting for?

I hushed my body's desire to rush to him, and began to play.

I am the original Jewish princess. The authentic article. The instrument on which the real music, according to the text, can be played. Play me. I shall sound true to you.

It was a long day, stopping only for wine and bread, and the bitter goats' cheese Carlos had brought with him. He worked himself and us hard and did not talk to me, except to make points about the music. By early evening, I was shivering with tiredness and expectation. As we all walked through the cold stone halls to the Hall of Mirrors, I huddled into my own deep blue woollen cloak, the colour of the evening summer sky. Coming in from the cold, the wave of heat in the Hall hit me full in the face. The guests hardly noticed our arrival, and scarcely nodded an ear in our direction as we began to play. As usual, Ferdinand and Isabella talked throughout, though I knew that any flaw in the performance would invoke sarcasm the following day.

Halfway through the evening, some late guests arrived, and as the huge wooden doors were opened to admit them, the gusting wind blew out all the candles—except for two; one behind me and one behind Carlos. Momentarily the Hall was in silence, and without any sense of pre-planning, Carlos and I began playing our star piece of the evening; strings, wind and voices flashed into the dark, and between verses Carlos and I improvised. For the first time that day he and I looked full at each other, our eyes, so alike, green flecked with brown, flashing across the Hall, each lured by the pool of light behind the other's head. I swear that we invented fire that night. Flame spiralled and pirouetted between our notes, and for those few moments, the chatterers were silenced.

At the end, the ripples of music bowed their way into the corners of the Hall, and we were applauded. Carlos nodded his head at me, in approval and desire.

I can pick up any instrument and bow or pluck or blow and it will speak. My mother was the same. The bow cuts deep and springy into the string and I curve my body in reply.

When Carlos came into my room, he shut the door quietly and carefully. We still did not speak. Under my blue woollen cloak, his body felt as familiar to me as my own. His green eyes held mine and as we deepened into each other, our movements fitted easily, as they always had.

Play me. I shall sound true to you.

Later we lay, my face nuzzled into Carlos's armpit, smelling cloves and camomile mixed with the acrid savour of satisfaction. There is something I must tell you, he said. I caught my breath. You're going back to her, I said, I knew it. It was only a matter of time. He flipped himself over on top of me so that he could look at me. It isn't that, Isabella, he said. I began to cry. Every time I see you, I said, I feel it's for the last time. She won't let go. You can't leave the children. I hate goats' cheese.

He put his hand over my mouth. I bit his fingers. Isabella, he said, you must listen. And then he whispered. He was late this morning because he had heard that before very long all infidels would be banished from Spain. I am Jewish, Isabella, he said softly, and you know what that means. I must leave before I am killed.

I stroked him. I knew you were Jewish, I said. Not just because of this—many men are circumcised in this world of mixed races. I just knew. You couldn't know, he said. Not in the way the Inquisition will know, not in the way—I interrupted: I'm coming with you, I said. No—he began. This time I put my hand over his mouth. Then I told him about my mother.

Never have an affair with a musician, she said. A scribe, a soldier, a goat farmer if you must, but not a musician. When I was tiny, she let me pluck the strings on her fiddle, showed me how she tightened the tension, let me hold the bow in my fat hand and promised that one day I would be able to play as she did.

She was right about that, although she did not live to hear it. She also didn't live to see me disregard her advice about musicians. No doubt she would have smiled. My father, you see, was an itinerant musician, a man from North Africa, a Jew, a wandering minstrel who probably left behind him as many children as musical memories. He came to our village one night, in the height of summer. My mother's husband was away in the mountains, with the goats. It was late, no-one saw him arrive. My mother gave him shelter. He played to her. The next morning he wrapped his Ud, the instrument which is so like the courtly lute that every amateur plays here, and he disappeared. My mother described his fingers like spider's webs, trailing and caressing the strings, no frets to hurdle the fingers, allowing him to bend their tunes to his will. He was dark skinned. With green eyes.

My mother told me all this the night before she died. The soldiers came, looking for infidels. My mother was Jewish, but she thought no-one knew. She told me the story about my father, gave me her blue woollen cloak, and made me go and hide with the goats. Her charred body was flung on the ground some days later. I think about her often. I wonder how long it took for the thick earth to rot her flesh. I prefer to think about that than to wonder what the Inquisition did to her. I also worry, because I cannot remember the colour of her eyes.

*   *   *

When a string is ready to snap, it plays sharper and sharper. It cries
for the attention that can do it no good. My life is fraying at the
edges. I begin not to sound true to myself.

The following afternoon, two musicians, carrying instruments,
strolled towards the town walls. Carlos and I also each carried a
small phial of poison. His alchemist friend assured him that anyone
who took it would fall asleep long before the poison began to eat
them away. We promised each other through our tears that we
would die rather than be subjected to torture.

The soldiers on guard by the town walls laughed and applauded
as we cavorted with our fiddles, mad court musicians aping their
wandering minstrel brethren, a lower caste, vulgar and uncertain
and despicable. So harmless and silly were we, that they allowed us
to wander through the gates and serenade a flock of goats herded
on a hill opposite.

I have left my texts behind me.

We slept in a field. Next day, lulled by the quiet of the countryside,
we were reckless. A small town, sleepy in the early afternoon haze,
suddenly came alive with shouts and screams. Soldiers and locals
chased a small group of people, men, women and children. An old
man tripped and fell, just beyond the entrance to the alley in which
we hid. The crowd kicked him bloody and limp. Then they hurtled
past us, knocking us aside and when they had passed, Carlos was
no longer with me. I waited, huddled in an abandoned house, hoping he would come back. When it was dark I searched a little. The
streets were strewn with dead and wounded. No-one dared to touch
them. I dared not stay.

I have had to learn how to improvise all over again.

Memory can be kind. I remember endless roads and fields, green
streaked with brown, brown with green. I could not eat. I felt sick
all the time. My fiddle opened doors to me, gave me beds and food.
I took it all, and more often than not gave it to the next beggar I
met on my way. I searched every face for the familiar mouth, for the

green eyes. I learned that northern Italy, Mantova, Ferrara, Venezia even, were the places to go. I hardly noticed that my periods seemed to have stopped. The road changed everything. In any case, the real me was somewhere else, with a man whose hair curled over his collar, whose crooked nose could wrinkle in glee, whose eyes were like mine.

When I finally cried, my imagination flooded out of me. I bled for four days as I had never bled before. Now I knew that Carlos and his child were gone from me for ever. To the rest of the world, he had never been. To me, he could never be again; neither cloaked in rage, nor clear in love. Just misty in my music as I played.

My text comes from the heart. Nothing can be more authentic.

Giovanni has brown eyes. He is kind. He is good. He is my rock. He is calm and decisive, and he waits for me to love him. I should love him. I am grateful to him. After all, he picked me out, a grubby, weary, wandering minstrel, travelling round Italy, playing anywhere, and he made me into the highest in the land—in the region, anyway. I am the Duchess. Of course, no-one knows that I am Jewish. Merely that I am Spanish. I speak Italian impeccably, but with a soft, sibilant accent. When I am asked when I left Spain, I say 1490; if I told them the true year, 1492, they might associate it with the expulsion of the Jews and wonder.

Giovanni is much older than I am. His first wife died in childbirth. The son, a wayward child, was sent to fight with Giovanni's mercenary army against the Turk. Make a man of him, they said. When he returns, he will be Giovanni's heir. So it does not matter that I do not seem able to conceive. I can make love when Giovanni desires, except that for me there is no love in it, just gratitude.

I ached so much from wandering. I had to stop. This seemed the only way. Here I continue to play as I please. My musicians are the finest in the region, envied by the whole of northern Italy. I even pay them on time.

When my strings have settled, you can play me. Then I shall sound true to you.

⋆　⋆　⋆

And then, on a rough, blustery winter day, Carlo came home. Here in the north, in the vast flat plain, on the river that flows to the sea, it rains and rains. Nothing is ever free of mud.

The concert was almost over. I played in the last piece. Just as we were about to begin, the door burst open and a young man thundered in, bringing gusting rain and leaves with him, cloak flung over one shoulder, rough boots, a crooked nose, hair curling down over his shoulders.

I played just for him, my heart pounding, my arm quivering, my sound small and sweet. His eyes were on me the whole time, burning me in tune.

Every text contains within it the music of a thousand others.

The next day Carlo came to see me. A young man, weathered, with no sign of the previous night's thunderer. Teach me to play, he said. Teach me to play like you. He looked at me, and in his eyes I saw Carlos again, and the baby I had never known, and something else, someone new, whose body was as familiar as my own, and whom I could not touch except strictly in the line of duty, to show how to balance the instrument, to show how to hold the bow, how to flex the wrist, how to find the notes.

He was an exemplary pupil. He rewarded my efforts by working hard and throwing himself into the music like a child. He hated being a soldier, he told me. He was not going to be a ruler. He wanted to be a wandering minstrel, to go on the road, to live free of all ties and responsibilities. I teased him. You're too spoiled, I said. And I gave him the most fiendish musical exercise I could conjure up, as if that would keep him with me for longer.

Let us play our texts to each other. Perhaps we shall sound true.

There was nothing I can think of that precipitated the crisis. One day he blundered through everything, careless, discordant, sullen. When he finished I exploded. Why? He flung his bow on the ground. You, he said. I cannot play to you. You create the conditions of performance. Who do you think you are? You make me nervous.

I am your audience, I said. If you can play to me, you can play to anyone. I can't play to you, he said. Then you'll never make it on the road, I taunted. Music happens because of you, not because of the road. But you're such a natural, he said. Who taught you? No-one, I said. I taught myself. I learned as I travelled. I learned as I played in fields and I learned as I played in courts. You're the real thing, he said, the authentic article.

He said it with sadness, his shoulders dropped, his back bowed, his legs apart, his elbows on his knees, his fingers clamped together in a double fist. A lock of hair fell forward over his face. I lifted it and one finger brushed his cheek. He looked up, his eyes green, just like mine.

I am newly strung, with fine gut, translucent, springy. Play me. I dare you.

What can I tell you. That in the moonlight, in the haven of my tower room, the room of my music, his body felt more familiar than my own. That his skin was warm where mine was cool, and mine warm where his was cool. That we fitted easily until we were the same temperature and could not tell who was who, and he was not Carlos, and he was not a baby, and he was not my stepson and I did not know who he was.

You have everything you want, he said, his cheek against my breast. You have a husband who adores you. You are gifted. You are beautiful. Guilty, my young lord, I said. Don't call me young, he said sharply. I am sorry, I said, my hand on his belly, where the pulses fluttered. I stroked him calm. You know nothing about me, I said. I have heard you play, he said. That is enough.

I am not what I seem, I said. I don't care, he said, I should have married you. I cried and he kissed my face. He smelled of cloves and rosemary and permanence.

And then the door was kicked down.

It takes only a split second to snap. Much longer to be tuned.

Tonight I shall take poison. I shall go out into the dark. I shall cross the river by the small stone bridge that curves over the water at an angle. I shall turn right on the opposite bank and walk along by the river for a few paces until I am opposite the tower in which Carlo and I made love.

I am taut.

The guards let me have my fiddle this evening. They think my husband is wrong to have his adulterous wife beheaded. I think he is wrong too; but he knows that he has no alternative at his own court. If he let me live, he would have to face me every day, and see his son in my eyes.

The guards have brought me my cloak and the cushion on which Carlo and I lay. I shall put the cushion between me and the cold, damp stone. I shall wrap myself in my deep blue cloak. I shall drink the poison. I shall fall asleep before it begins to tear me apart.

I am the real thing. The first Jewish princess. The authentic instrument on which the musical text can be played. Play me. I shall sound true to you.

In sunlight the river is green. My mother's eyes were green.

Anita Brookner

was born in London in 1938 and was educated at King's College, London, and the
Courtauld Institute. She was a lecturer in
Fine Art at the University of Reading
from 1959 to 1964 and the first female Slade
Professor of Fine Arts at Cambridge
University. A fellow of New Hall, Cambridge, she taught at the Courtauld Institute, where she specialized in eighteenth-
and nineteenth-century French art.
Brookner has published seventeen novels
and five works of nonfiction. Her fourth
novel, *Hotel du Lac* (1984), won the Booker
Prize. *Family and Friends* (1985), set in the
1930s and 1940s, was the first to allude to
Brookner's Polish-Jewish antecedents. It
was followed by *The Latecomers* (1988), her
eighth novel, the first chapter of which
is excerpted here. Brookner defines 'latecomers' as the influx of German-Jewish
refugees into England in the 1930s. The
novel charts the friendship of two such
'latecomers,' Thomas Hartmann and
Thomas Fibich, who arrived in England
from Germany as schoolchildren and
became firm friends and business
partners.

Anita Brookner

EXCERPT FROM The Latecomers

Hartmann, a voluptuary, lowered a spoonful of brown sugar crystals into his coffee cup, then placed a square of bitter chocolate on his tongue, and, while it was dissolving, lit his first cigarette. The ensuing mélange of tastes and aromas pleased him profoundly, as did the blue tracery of smoke above the white linen tablecloth, the spray of yellow carnations in the silver vase, and his manicured hand on which the wedding ring fitted loosely, without those deep indentations that afflict the man who has gained weight or age, a man to whom in any case his wedding might be presumed to be an affair of the irrelevant past. Hartmann gazed around the hotel dining-room, coming to rest benevolently on the youngish men with briefcases at the adjoining tables—middle management, he believed they were called—for whom lunch was inextricably bound up with discussions of a business nature. My dears, you do not look well, thought Hartmann: your complexions are not clear, your haircuts unbecoming. You give your time and attention to business and save too little for yourselves. There is not a lot of point in talking about a zero-growth scenario, as you are apparently prepared to do, if you are going to dispatch a lobster cocktail followed by steak and kidney pie: mineral water will not save you. He himself ate sparingly, grilled fish with a vegetable, followed by coffee. He had long ago learned the pleasures of sobriety, of extracting the essence from the example, of attaining and completing rather than striving and collapsing. He would not even allow himself a second cigarette. That would come much later, after his frugal dinner. Since his wife had started going to evening classes, he preferred to prepare something for himself. Before going back to the office he would select and buy cheese: another treat, another exercise in worth.

Hartmann aspired to the sublime. If, as Hegel says, in the true

sublime a sharp consciousness of inadequacy is required, Hartmann resided somewhere in the more comfortable territory of the
false sublime, for inadequacy rarely troubled him. He considered
his life's work to lie in the perfecting of simple pleasures, mainly
of a physical or domestic nature, far from the strife and pain of
more ambitious purposes. The idea of God, for example, he rejected
as derogating from his own serene existence. To the proposition,
'I am that I am', Hartmann, if he ever thought about it, would have
replied, 'Et moi?', not meaning any disrespect, but rather acknowledging a simple division of activities in which paths would never
cross. On the other hand, a mundane task supremely devised and
carried out, however small—the buying of cheese, for example—
filled him with a sense of completion for which many more meta-
physically inclined men might envy him. Hartmann's joy was apparent in his beautifully cut hair, his expensive suit, his manicured
hands, the faint aura of cologne that heralded his approach; in his
mild and habitually smiling face, too, his expressive walk, in which
the body, leaning slightly forward, seemed to indicate amiability, a
desire to please. He was now middle-aged, in the closing stages of
middle age, even old, he daringly thought. He had an impressionistic
attitude towards his age, as he did towards his daughter's marriage,
sometimes resigned to it, sometimes deciding to ignore it entirely.
Thus it occasionally pleased him to take up the benign posture of
an elderly man while safe in the secret knowledge that he had plenty
of time in hand. Now in his sixties, he felt himself to be unchanged
from his earlier self, but noticeably improved on the miserable boy
whom he tried not to remember. There were in fact certain memories that Hartmann had consigned to the dust, or to that repository
that can only be approached in dreams. For this reason Hartmann
took a sedative every night and ensured untroubled sleep. He
defended this practice, as he defended all his habits, as sensible:
his own glossy head was his best justification. 'I eat well. I sleep
well', he was in the habit of saying, when asked how he did. 'What
else is there?' He knew there was more, but thought that wisdom
consisted in reducing the purchase of such nebulous matters or
indeed of any imponderables that might darken his own impeccable
consciousness.

However, no man is free of his own history. Hartmann was no

exception. But in the interests of damage limitation he had struck a bargain with the fates: he would, in so far as he could, employ the maximum good will at his disposal in an effort to screen out the undesirable, the inadvertent, those shocks against which the mere mortal is powerless. He would, he had long ago decided, be deliberately euphoric. It was a technique which he could practise and perfect, although sometimes it nearly eluded him. Thus, from his earliest days, he remembered scenes that might have been devised by Proust. He remembered his father, in a magnificently odorous and gleaming emporium, pointing with his cane to a pineapple, a box of peaches, and asking for them to be taken out to the car. Or himself, when tiny, walking with his nurse in the Englische Garten. Or first love, at the age of ten, and a game of hide-and-seek with the beloved at Nymphenburg, beside the long paths rustling with fallen leaves and the commotion of birds. He did not remember, because he had never witnessed the event, his elegant parents, dressed for some *fête-champêtre*, being hoisted, slightly puzzled, on to farm carts, but behaving with good grace, thinking this part of the entertainment. They were driven off, never to be seen again, but how could he know that? How could one remember absence? Was it not one's duty to fill the void, when there were so many agreeable ways of doing so? He had a sense of his own life progressing to its conclusion and was therefore ruthless in dispensing with the past, since every minute of the present must be valued. And, after all, he had survived: that was all that mattered in any life. And he was here, in this hotel dining-room, waiting for his bill, replete, contented, even lively. What mattered was to intensify the pleasure, to ensure that it might be repeated. On such satisfactions Hartmann constructed his happiness.

He cast a long lingering glance at the middle management, now flushed and talkative, and reflected how even his business life managed to avoid such infelicities. It may have pleased his gloomy partner, Fibich, to behave like a harassed salesman, to eat a sandwich at his desk or to stir his tea furiously with an HB pencil, but that was not his way. Fibich felt guilty about having made so much money so easily: that was his way. Hartmann mentally shrugged his shoulders at the folly of such a reaction. He had never been ambitious, driven, ruthless, as so many men seemed to be. Even

Fibich thought such behaviour ridiculous. There was even, to Hartmann, something reassuring about the absurdity of their trade:
greetings cards, of a cruel and tasteless nature, which had paid
their way very nicely for about twenty years, until Hartmann, who
did little work but was valued for his *Fingerspitzengefühl*, his flair, his
sixth sense, suggested that the market in this commodity was self-
limiting, and that there were fortunes to be made in photocopying
machines. They had both been printers by trade in the years that
Hartmann had forgotten about, and it was easy for them to diversify
from their original specialization. Of course the work was anathema to them both, but the money was charming, delightful. Fibich,
clutching his neuralgic head, might groan at every suggestion that
Hartmann put to him, but it was understood between them that
they would agree on everything, as they did, and always had done,
the ebullient Hartmann literally dragging Fibich along with him,
into sheds, warehouses, shops, wherever their greetings cards had
led them. And now they sat in splendour in Spanish Place, in an
office got up to look like a flat, for domesticity was important to
them both. Each had a room or salon, in which decisions were
taken; coffee was served morning and afternoon. Their accountant,
Roger Myers, and their company secretary, John Goodman, shared
the apartment, though slightly less expansively; their typists were
encouraged to take time off for shopping. Thus a family atmosphere
was maintained, for which neither Hartmann nor Fibich thought to
take any particular credit. It was simply that they preferred to feel
themselves at home, for the idea of home was central to their lives.

In that unexamined area that informed their first beginnings
Hartmann was aware of much that he had decided to forget or to
overlook: those years at the print works which had been the final
discomfort of their anxiety-ridden adolescence. Indeed, with his
customary fleetness, Hartmann was able to turn even this memory
to good account. I have come through, he said to himself. What he
meant by this was that he was no longer an apprentice, nor would
he ever be one again. And even the print shop had been a welcome
release after the horrors of school: if Hartmann ever thought to
congratulate himself, and he did frequently, it was because he was
no longer at school. Sent to London as a frightened boy to live with
his father's sister, Marie, who had providently married an English-

man named Jessop, and staring from the window of the taxi at the huge red-brick cottage in Compayne Gardens which he did not recognize as an apartment house, he struggled with his tears and the incomprehensible language until the ultimate betrayal took place, and he was sent away to school. Here, unfortunately, the memories were vivid and would not always go away. Doubly, even trebly an outsider, he knew, even on his first day, that he was doomed. Had it not been for the accident of being paired with Fibich—but both were forbidden to speak German—he would have died or killed himself. Only the knowledge that someone else's experience reflected his own reality saved him, although Fibich was arguably worse off even than Hartmann, for he knew no one. Aunt Marie, visiting one weekend and arousing much ribald attention from the other boys with her tweed cape and the pheasant feathers in the band of her brown felt hat, immediately said that Hartmann must bring Fibich home with him, meaning to her gloomy flat in Compayne Gardens, and the winding hilly streets so unlike home. And so they had been together since childhood and could no more think of living apart than they could of divorcing their wives, although their temperaments were diametrically opposed and they rarely thought alike on any matter. It was even natural to them to live separated by no more than a single storey: two apartments in Ashley Gardens, near Victoria, had attracted them, not because they particularly liked the district, but because each would feel the other near at hand. They had retained the habit of closeness, of being allies: everything was called in to reinforce their bond. They were both called Thomas, and turned as one whenever the name was spoken. For this reason their wives addressed them as Hartmann and Fibich, as they addressed each other, and always had.

Hartmann, waiting for the bill, frowned. He felt discomfort at the insistence of such memories, which were no longer relevant to anything that crossed his amiable mind in the sunshine of his deliverance. This ritual of lunch, which he enacted so often and so regularly, bore somewhere in its train the memory of meals unspeakable, eaten in fear, never properly digested. Those school meals were, in effect, the source of all the loving little luxuries with which he surrounded his present life, just as the aromatic dormitories proclaimed his future need for sybaritic comfort. The bleak wet

Surrey countryside in winter, and the incomprehensible hours spent running up and down a muddy field, ensured his devotion to London, its soft mornings, its stony heart, the inexorable streets in which the doctors and the dentists plied their trades, and the suburbs with their flowering trees and the motor bicycles on the pavements. Everything amused him now, all prospects were viewed with indulgence. He was a sophisticated man, sophisticated enough to know that fond recollection of the past was mere sentimentality; this, as it were, intellectual attitude reinforced his active physical discomfort whenever schooldays were discussed. He was apt to turn away questions about his early life, which, now that he was middle-aged, or old, depending how he felt, and successful, were often forthcoming. It was Fibich, who, with a groan, alluded to past ordeals, until silenced by a nod from Hartmann. The past still worked actively in Fibich, seemed from time to time almost to take him over. Hartmann acted as his censor, bringing him forcibly back to the present. 'It is over', he would say, simply. On his face, when he spoke these words, there would pass, unknown to himself, an air of great weariness that was at odds with his dismissal of times long gone. Of course, he remembered them perfectly, or would have done had he allowed himself to dwell on them. He even remembered them better than Fibich, whose obsessional examination of these memories had led him for a short time to a psychoanalyst. When he read Oliver Twist Hartmann marvelled that Dickens had had such an acute understanding of the misery of boys. Girls, he thought, did not, could not, suffer so much. He thanked Heaven that his only child was a daughter.

He sat back with a sigh. Since, in this context, reminiscence was safe, permitted, he cast a selective look back to his beginnings. Schooldays still loomed large: he took this to be a sign of his assimilation, since schooldays figured so impressively in the accounts that Englishmen gave of themselves. His school, their school, in fact, had been one of those decrepit but expensive establishments created and run by an ex-army officer and his harassed wife that proliferated in England in the years before the Second World War. The masters were incompetent, irascible, lacking all faith in what they were doing, lurching from one expedient to another, aware that what little luck they possessed was running out. Hartmann and

Fibich, metaphorically and almost physically twin souls, marvelled at the bad but fattening food, the indifferent hygiene, the rudeness of the servants, all of whom were emboldened by the increasing haplessness of the headmaster and his wife to indulge in forms of self-expression that both Hartmann and Fibich found to be unacceptable. The Matron, in particular, caused them acute discomfort. She was a youngish woman called Joy, thick-legged, red-cheeked, apparently quite at home in this community of half-grown men. Hartmann, even at the age of fifteen, found something retarded in her make-up. Fibich, the younger and more agonized of the two, winced at her jovial enquiries into the state of his bowels, information that he could not bear to disclose to another living soul, particularly when it was required of him in a loud and cheerful voice which, he felt, demanded his collusion in urgent and unwelcome terms. His frightened modesty often spurred her to excessive attention. She had a way of cross-questioning him while rolling up pairs of socks with swift thick fingers, pretending to be not very interested in his answers but studying his long lowered eyelashes in repeated sidelong glances. There was something menacing as well as flirtatious about these interviews. Fibich heroically fought back the symptoms of genuine maladies in order not to be ministered to by her, and carried on with a fearful toothache, which he hoped to have the courage to endure until he could take it back with him to Compayne Gardens and there ask for help.

The man who looked after the boiler and was supposed to be responsible for maintenance—the lukewarm water, the damp slimy towels in the downstairs cloakrooms, the windows that were never quite open enough to dispel the smell of boys—lived in the basement surrounded by tins of dried-up paint, his radio permanently turned to a foreign station playing nostalgic tea-time music. Although it was said of this man, Henderson by name, that he had a taste for small boys, inducing them into his malodorous quarters with offers of tea and biscuits, Hartmann and Fibich found themselves lingering in the passage outside his rooms just in order to listen to the music. The announcer's voice, which they strained to hear, would be abruptly eclipsed, as if Henderson were angry at such alien intrusion into his domain. Seconds later the music would be resurrected, all too faint echo of the life they had left behind, too careless of its existence to have studied it more closely. Some genetic trace kept them yearning for its sweetness, its suavity, even its falseness, while their stomachs suffered from the weight of potatoes, sausages and custard they were forced to ingest.

Since he had come to this country at the age of twelve, this ordeal had lasted a long time. Then came apprenticeship to the printer, until the order of release came in the form of a letter from Switzerland informing them of the deaths of both their parents. Certain monies had been put aside for them, and these, together with reparations after the war, had enabled them to set up on their own. The day they had both installed themselves in their first little office in the Farringdon Road had been one of deep emotion for them both. Nothing, perhaps, would ever affect them so again, apart from the birth, health, and destiny of their children.

Since that time Hartmann had been blithe. He was modest about his good spirits, was not foolish enough to think that he had earned them. Luck, quite simply, had come his way, that was all. Throughout his adolescence he had been frightened. The first step towards emancipation had been his ability to master the language. This had come with a rush, as he was about to leave school; it was as if the prospect of freedom had released something in him, had suddenly induced ability where there was none before. The second step, oddly enough, had been his National Service, which had been an unexpected introduction to conviviality. Sent to mind stores in Wiltshire, there was little for him to do except check deliveries, and he was much in demand as a source of supplies. Fibich, whose stoicism in the face of toothache had left him with a legacy of migraines, was not accepted for the army. He remained in London, at the printing works, lodging with Aunt Marie, whom he now considered to be an authentic relation. It was the first time the two had been separated. Fibich sent his cigarette ration to Hartmann who was gradually discovering the delights of generosity. Open-handed among the boxes of dried bananas and the sacks of dried egg, Hartmann marvelled at the ease of friendships based on mutual interest. He found his fellow conscripts charming (his favourite adjective), and, as he listened to their plans for the future, he began to dwell on the possibility of making plans of his own. Fibich had been keen on the idea of publishing—he was the more learned, the more serious of the two of them—but Hartmann saw that they must attack from the flank. They would never know enough to be insiders, that was clear. The trick, therefore, was to find a trade which was in a sense superfluous but also gratifying. That was how the greetings cards had been conceived. In the beginning the cards had been sentimental. A Happy Birthday to my dear Wife, they proclaimed. Or, Baby is One Today! Gradually they allowed realism to creep in, and found that the more outrageous the message the more eagerly it was bought. Get Well cards soon topped their sales, particularly lugubrious or insensitively cheerful greetings for the post-operative patient. They had never looked back.

The odious feel of rough khaki on the backs of his knees and of his neck also inspired in Hartmann at this time his love of luxury. In this he was aided by the sight of his fellow conscripts sprucing themselves up for a night out. Such applications of grease and water, such furious polishing of boots! Hartmann had tried to emulate this activity when they kindly included him in their invitations to spend the evening in a pub, but such exercises were not for him, any more than the flat beer and the dark and aromatic room in which it was consumed were for him. Instead he took advantage of their absence to strip wash himself, writing to Fibich to send him bars of scented soap. And ever since those days he had been a devotee of his morning toilet, and his bathroom was filled with scented essences, with rose-flavoured mouth-wash, and with colognes which he would pat into the skin of his face, so that his wife, on kissing him goodbye, would say to him, 'You smell better than I do.'

Now he had reached the age when the odours of the body are more insistent and more difficult to dispel, when the day's work, minimal though it was, felt like a more serious operation than in the early days when there had been so much more to do, when waking from sleep was a more lengthy process. These days his wife enlivened her hitherto flawless complexion with a geranium flush. He had no feelings of resentment against the passing years, counting each day a triumph, particularly when the winter sun shone strongly, as it did today. Rather he welcomed old age, or what he supposed was old age, having done too well, spent his time too fruitfully, to wish it all back again. Certain attitudes of mind and body were no longer available to him, or if available no longer becoming. The young men at the adjoining tables (and he was forced to revise their status upwards, hearing one of them remark that he had passed the previous evening at Annabel's) aroused no feelings of envy, that mean-minded desire that he occasionally noted among his contemporaries to deplore young people's lack of style, or what was considered their lack of style. Silver-haired now, and with a slightly more prominent stomach, Hartmann was still recognizable to himself, as was Fibich, as gaunt as ever, but with expensively rearranged teeth. The skin of Hartmann's face was still dry and glossy, although the body was more capacious: dressed, he managed to mask from himself the sight of the unwieldy forked animal that had earlier emerged from the bed. Upright, bathed, burnished, he still evoked a smile from the face in the mirror; his wedding ring was still loose on his finger. And after his lunch, which he preferred to take alone, he could now afford to wander a little in the sun, a pleasure denied to him in those days when the sun had never seemed to shine at all, when the only refuge from the hard-packed dirty snow was the single bar of Aunt Marie's electric fire. Stoical, she had refused to 'give in', as she put it, to the cold, although her own early years had been warmed by district central heating. Now both Fibich and Hartmann insisted on almost tropical heat, and the air inside their homes was soothed by scents of cigars, lavender polish, and rich cooking that never entirely dispersed. He vaguely remembered such scents from the parental home, which he otherwise did not remember at all, or did not try to. It was Fibich, at the suggestion of his analyst, who longed to return, but was fearful of doing so, and thus existed on the horns of a dilemma that would never be resolved. Hartmann's solution to this problem had been breathtaking in its simplicity: get rid of the analyst. 'A meddler,' Hartmann had said. And, 'Psychiatrists! What do they know?' Hartmann understood that Fibich was still unhappy, and occasionally, but only occasionally, acknowledged the reason. But why dwell on the past, particularly when the past was so uncongenial? Better to eat a good lunch, rejoicing in prosperity, and then to select a piece of Brie, a piece of Cantal, perhaps to point to a fine pineapple, in preparation for his evening meal. Television was marvellous at keeping one in the present. He loved the American soap operas, rejoicing in the extravagance.

The head waiter came up to bid him good-day: Hartmann was a customer of long standing.

'The family well?' Hartmann asked, genuine in his enquiry.

'Very well, sir, thank you. We saw Mr Fibich the other day.'

'And the account for Mr Goodman and Mr Myers is up-to-date?'

'Yes, sir, all taken care of.'

'Good-day then, Monsieur Pierre. Thank you.'

'Thank you, sir.'

They appreciated each other wonderfully.

Out in the street the winter sun was at its zenith, soon to retire its light and its shadows. Hartmann waved his hand to the woman arranging a jacket in the window of the dress-shop—he had known her for thirty years—and strolled in the direction of Selfridges. A little shopping, the purchase of the evening paper, and he would be back at the office in time for a second cup of coffee. Very civilized, he thought. Well, he had earned it. And this evening his daughter was coming round, an occasion for great rejoicing. He would ask Fibich and his wife to join them, since they both loved her. And their boy doing so well: a miracle. It was an uncertain profession, of course, and nothing was guaranteed, but it seemed that he had the gift. This, he was aware, was an attitude of indulgence in him for this particular young man, for the idleness of which he approved in women was, generally speaking, anathema to him in men. (He ignored his own, which was in any case ornamented with much ceremony of a business-like nature.) But enough of that. Today was another blessed day, like so many. Had he been a praying man, but of course he wasn't, he would have given thanks. Instead he settled the collar of his coat more closely round his neck, and stepped devoutly towards Selfridges.

Ronit Lentin

was born in Haifa in 1944 and moved to
Ireland in 1969. She has worked as a journalist and radio broadcaster and teaches
sociology and women's studies at Trinity
College, University of Dublin. Her radio
plays include 'Friends' (1979), and she
has also published a collection of interviews, *Conversations with Palestinian
Women* (1981) and coauthored *Who Is Mind-
ing the Children?* (1980). She is the author of
two Hebrew-language novels, *Stone of
Claims* (1976) and *Like a Blind Man* (1978),
and three English-language novels, *Tea
with Mrs. Klein* (1985), *Night Train to
Mother* (1989), and *Songs on the Death of Children* (1996). Her autobiographical *Night
Train to Mother* traces four generations of
women from Bukovina in Romania to Israel.
Excerpted here is the prologue to the novel,
in which the Israeli Ruth, Lentin's alter
ego, contemplates her journey back into
her parents' past.

Ronit Lentin

EXCERPT FROM Night Train to Mother

Ruth 1984

When did the journey begin?

Did it begin when you asked grandfather Mendel to draw family trees? You were only eight or nine and he sat, patient, and put down Hirsches and Laxes, Hellers and Königs and your father's Goldmans on pieces of paper he tore out of his account ledgers.

Or did it begin when he took you by the hand and brought you to Zamenhof synagogue in Tel Aviv, a place where he was an important man, where people took notice of him and therefore of you?

Or when Oma Rosa made masses of food, urging you to eat, always more and more? Eat maminka, eat mein Kind, put some flesh on your skinny bones, get stronger, a real sabra, not a pale little girl from there. But Oma, you protested, it's too much, I am full already. But she stood over you, watching your every mouthful.

Did it begin on the slopes of Mount Carmel, in a field full of grey rocks and yellow thorns where you had escaped and sat holding your knees obstinately because you didn't like the woman from there who was visiting them? And later on, when they found you, white with worry, father slapped you across the face, a hard, angry slap.

Or when you sat on grandma Tattu's bony knee and had your photograph taken, she all white and stern-looking and you a squirming two-year-old, wriggling to get away from the musty smell and her arthritic hands holding you too tightly?

Did the journey begin when going to Tel Aviv was long and boring and when arriving was only when you reached Oma and grandfather's shady avenue where the sandy ground was hard on knees and elbows which scraped when you fell?

Or with the eternal arguments between mother and Oma? Why

do it this way, why not like this and let me wash up already, you never let anyone do anything and sit down now, I am doing it. Guilt was fostered like this. Two hard-working women, the men sitting while they worked. And as you grew up and they argued and worked, you were made to feel more guilty for not offering to help. They were good at fostering guilt, Oma and mother. They knew the tune from early childhood when your best was never enough.

Did the journey begin with being told by grandfather Mendel never, but never to think about God in the water closet and then, for years, thinking only of God when you peed and did the other thing? And being told off, softly but very sternly, that writing on Shabbat was forbidden, something good children never did because He saw everything. And then writing only at home, on the slopes of the mountain, so grandfather's beautiful features wouldn't crumple in anger. And the eternal guilt.

Did it begin on Saturday afternoons, when Oma and grandfather's families gathered in the two rooms which had a heavy glass door between them and where you slept behind the glass door, always hearing her moan and shout in her sleep, particularly in later years, when he was not there to listen?

They came, strange people, the women wearing dark lipstick, always kissing you, making red or purple marks on reluctant cheeks. And the men wearing dark suits when no one else did. And smelling of other places. Not musty like grandma Tattu but a there smell. And speaking no Hebrew or if they did, you couldn't understand it. It was heavy with thick accents, the Hebrew of people who came from there. There was Tante Hetti, limping, fat, her eyes small and unsmiling and Tante Hanna, already stooped, her serious face grimaced with pain. They all spoke German. You got to understand because father and mother spoke it to each other, but not to you. To you they spoke Hebrew. They wanted you to grow up here, not share a there language which many school mates said was a Nazi language.

It could have begun when great-grandmother Dora came to live with them. She scared you, sitting on the veranda where lizards climbed the pebbly wall, hiccupping endlessly and asking every hour is it already one? Is it already two? Her toothless mouth fixed in eternal expressionless pain in her wrinkled pale face framed by hair, even whiter than grandma Tattu's, pulled back in a tight bun, making her head look small, like the scalped heads you had read about in Karl May's cowboys and Indians books.

When did the journey begin? When did you first know that love was a word from novels and dictionaries, a word no one talked of? Only Oma said it from time to time when she hugged you too tight, pressing you to her big bosom, her sweat trickling down her body, arrested by sweat pads, carefully sewn on to the summer dresses Grosstante Hetti made for her? When did you learn that Oma and grandfather did not hug and that mother and father did not hug but that they never fought before you children? And when Oma said that word, you recoiled. Her attention overwhelming, you wanted her older, remoter, like other children's grandmothers who didn't interfere.

When did you learn that grandfather Mendel didn't do very much when he went to town, joking with you when you begged him not to go? He then brought back little chocolaty sweets covered in tiny coloured things and sugared almonds in brown paper bags. One for you and one for Avner and one for Yossi when he stayed. He allowed you to run your thin fingers along his large, veined hands, the softness of which you will never forget as he sat with his fat Polish partner in the third room, speaking fast in Yiddish which no one spoke at home.

When did you learn that Mendel Heller, the big businessman from Dorna and Czernowitz, broke his heart in the land of his dreams? That promises from political colleagues came to nothing and business was not business though he never said a word against this cruel land? When did you realise that Mendel and Rosa belonged to a lost generation? That they could never forgive themselves for escaping in time and leaving their families behind? That they couldn't live with the guilt?

Till her dying day, you heard Rosa cry in her sleep for the parents she had left behind. When her mother came, broken, old, there was not much left of beautiful, strong Dora. And Rosa continued to cry, shedding tears she couldn't shed while awake.

When did the journey begin?

When was the first time you remember being told about there? Was it Grossonkel Shmaya or Grosstante Hanna who first spoke about there and when they saw you listening, stopped talking and instead started eating Oma's cheese buchtels or spooning strawberry confiture they washed down with iced water?

The word Dorna rang golden on their lips but other words, Tate, Grossmutter, Transnistria, Tod, were only whispers. Lost and poor, until the reparation money started coming, they replayed a solitary board game in Oma's glass-panelled room, passing the code words cautiously, hoping their Israeli-born grandchildren wouldn't pick up their clues.

Hard to remember when you first realised the past was always bad. The goyim, the troubles, the endless moves, the camp, the sick stomachs. They all had sick stomachs. From the goose schmalz they had been fed as children so that they wouldn't catch TB like Dora's poor sister-in-law Rosa. And from the camp.

All the while when they talked opaquely of there, grandmother Dora sat alone, older than her seventy-odd years. Her mouth hollow when she smiled one of her rare smiles. She hiccupped continuously and never spoke to the children, scaring you, she and the lizards on the wall. Rosa spoke to her without gentleness and the others shook her hand when they came and before they left. When she died you stopped thinking about her, but your brother wept.

Oma Rosa ruled these gatherings, urging them to eat, talking a shade louder than the others. Grosstante Hanna sat quietly but from time to time said something which put Rosa in her place. You must always be right, you heard Rosa hiss, more than once. Grosstante Hetti, when she came from Haifa, was also quiet, looking at Rosa with what you thought was envy. Rosa's family was in the minority compared with Mendel's large family but with the years the balance changed as Mendel's family died off. You grew up and left home and then left the country and every so often mother would write and tell you who died.

When did the journey begin? Was there ever a time when you didn't journey, searching mother's hand, gasping for air, your asthmatic bronchials rasping to her reassuring voice? You were too thin, too ill, not eating enough, not sleeping enough, standing obstinately shaking your cot sides for nights on end, never secure in the knowledge.

You could have been a child from there, but they did all they could so you would be a child from here, a strong, earth-smelling sabra. The children at school mocked your skinny body and you developed an acid tongue in reply.

You could have been a child from there, but mother, golden-haired Carla, who had been too European for father's pioneering friends (she paints her lips, they whispered behind her back when he first introduced her to them), and father, for whom there had been nothing but a vague, distant childhood there, feared for your ability to withstand. Did they, secretly, think you wouldn't have survived had you been born there?

Father said, I want you to grow up not fearing the anti-semites. And he also said, when I was a child in Vienna, we often had to eat potato peels and chicken skins (you said yuk). You, my sabra, father said, must eat and be strong. He showed you the country, talked of art and of music and of queueing up to see Kaiser Franz-Josef in Vienna where grandma Tattu and grandpa went when they left Bucovina. And of his youth in Jerusalem, a new immigrant in a society of sabras, mocking his otherness already then. But he never spoke of there. Poor lost father. He wanted to give his children a gift of the free Jewish land, but your brother Avner and you ended leaving it. Replaying their fate. Your exile.

The others averted their gaze when you listened in while they talked of there. You listened avidly to their frail voices as if your life depended on the knowledge. You wanted to know but they wanted to forget. And couldn't.

And mother said I hated it there, this is where I belong. Oma was not quite so certain. When you made her talk, she embellished the past with small details. We weren't uneducated, you know, she would write in the long letters you made her write. We studied much more than just Torah and Yiddish. Or she would write about what she thought made picturesque reading. Mother was more ruthless but she too decorated her stories with tales of ice skating and coffee houses.

All the rest you had to fill in for yourself. The longings, the searching for true love, the perpetuation of women looking for acceptance and men yearning for power which eludes.

Then there were the empty pains of a generation which thought it was coming to a promised land and found itself in a harsh climate, struggling to make sense of the eternal rifts, the bureaucracy, the wars, the hopes for their children, the realisation that the children had to live their own pangs of separation, make their own journeys.

Where did the journey begin? Was there ever a time when you didn't feel Dora and Rosa, Hetti and Tattu and Carla were you? Was there ever a time you weren't journeying to connect the here and the there, the now and the then, love and other words?

You don't know when the journey began. But one day you are in Bucharest airport arguing with a fat official about visas and dollars. Something you wanted to do for years. Put pictures where only words had been.

It hadn't been easy. Whenever you mentioned it to mother, she shuddered. Why go there when there are so many places? I wouldn't go there for anything. And then one year she said she would come. The only way I'd go back is with you. But she didn't come and you had to go alone.

Romania? You must be going to the Black Sea, friends say.

Bucovina? The fat official laughs, calling a colleague to share the joke. There is no place of that name. Vatra Dornei? Yes, but it's in the county of Suceava. Suceava, he repeats, remember, not Bucovina. And you worry there will be nothing to find. Not even the name.

Contemporary Romania rears its head. Visas, foreign currency, transport to town for the price of a packet of Kent. Later you learn you can get everything here, from an appointment with the doctor to a kilo of meat the butcher would otherwise not sell, for a packet of Kent. 'Saint Kent' they call it here.

Poverty and deprivation hit as soon as daylight fades. Streets, hotel rooms, public buildings are all under-lit. Bucharest is ghost city, slave to the energy crisis. Jokes about Bucharest tough winters: close the window, the street will get cold. There is something chilling about it even in June.

Money exchange is constantly on offer. The greed for foreign currency incredible. The official exchange rate is nearly 20 lei per pound. Waiters offer 40 and later you will get 58 lei per pound ending up with too much money and little to spend it on.

Bucharest. Here mother, Herbert, Oma and grandfather waited for their Turkish transit visas in the cold winter of 1940–41. They lived not far from where you are now, off the Calea Victoriei, a broad street, its beautiful buildings ageing but still elegant. The Paris of the East they called Bucharest.

Your first night. Think of Carla here alone, nineteen years of age, waiting for her parents and brother in a small pension off the Calea in the middle of the war and stop being scared. There is an unshaven man slouching outside the room in Muntenia, a shabby city centre hotel. Is he a secret agent, a randy local preying on innocent female tourists or simply a tired Romanian, resting on the conveniently placed armchair? You'll never know. You turn the key to the room. You wouldn't have got very far if you had to flee the fascist Iron Guard, you think, your heart pounding.

In the morning you wake early. It's Sunday and the streets below are crowded with strollers, buying flowers, the only commodity never in short supply here. You leave the room carefully but the man is gone.

Bucharest in the morning is softer, less menacing. This is going to be a total journey, right to the centre. For years you had probed, questioning Carla, Rosa, Hanna, Hetti, about there. I am here now, mother, you want to scream. I am on my way.

Marshall is an elderly American Jew. Angry at a young official who is helping you to book a night train ticket to Vatra Dornei because he expects the same service you'd get in America. He agitates, gesticulating and in the commotion you meet.

He has been here for a while to find a wife. He takes you to see Jewish Bucharest, where Jews still live under the auspices of Rabbi Moshe Rosen, His Pestilence, as he is ironically called by the few Jews who still inhabit Bucovina, once a major Jewish centre, today a land without Jews.

The Jewish museum. Your first meeting with Transnistria. Yellow stars they had to make themselves and bars of rein jüdische Fett. Later Mimi will say that after years in the camp without soap, she washed herself in RJF soap. She had nightmares for years afterwards. Eighty per cent of the Jews exiled to Transnistria did not return—like Menashe and Anschel they died of hunger, cold, typhoid, depression. Death without annihilation.

You are starting to connect. Slowly. Jewish Romania has disappeared by and large. The remainder is kept alive only by U.S. dollars brought into this beleaguered state by Rabbi Rosen. Every Jew allowed to leave has his hard currency price.

The Coral Synagogue, a beautiful pink building in the centre of Bucharest, is full this Sunday morning. Talmud Torah, choir practice, lively debates about the rights and wrongs of immigration to Israel.

Yet Jewish Bucharest has the sadness of people living on borrowed time. You meet several who have already got a visa to Israel but cannot work until they leave and haven't enough funds to travel. For others Israel has never been a possibility which is why they didn't leave with the rest of Romanian Jewry of whom only fifteen-thousand remain in Bucharest and several thousands scattered throughout the country.

Marshall takes you to meet a former Lebanese minister. As you sit with him, his second wife, a shy, beautiful daughter and her moustachioed Falangist fiancé eating tabouleh on the second-floor landing of the sleazy Hotel Opera, changing sterling travellers' cheques into lei, you feel in the centre of a Balkan drama. Was this how Carla felt during those long 1940 winter months calling daily at the Turkish embassy?

Marshall envies your journey. You hate him talking about it in those sentimental, American-Jewish terms but allow him to see you to the dark Gara de Nord where your night train awaits.

You sit up all night with two couples just back from the Soviet Union, chattering about the gold they purchased. They will sell it at great profit. In Romania gold is at a premium. You will be constantly approached for your two wedding rings, one yours and the other Rosa's, inscribed, 'Mendel, 31.12.1919', her wedding day.

The dawn lights familiar place names, appearing through the wet green fields like pictures in a family album. Gura Humorlui, father's birthplace. Frasin, where Mendel and his brothers set up the family timber business. Cimpulung and finally, in the grey morning light, Vatra Dornei, mother's birthplace and your destination.

The railway station, a charming Bucovinian style white and yellow building, looks disappointing in the grey morning light. Your first encounter with this magical town, about which you have made Rosa and Carla talk for hours, is a fiasco. You lie on your hotel bed in a square sparse room, its large curtainless window looking onto the town hall clock tower, playing every hour on the hour a tune by Romania's national composer Ciprian Porumbescu, sobbing your heart out. What are you doing here, why have you come, two weeks alone on the eastern outskirts of the once flourishing Austro-Hungarian Empire in a hotel room with no hot water? Why this obsession with journeys into a past which doesn't seem to exist? Why the need to connect with the part of you which is Dora, Rosa, Hetti, Carla?

It takes a sleep, a short walk and a meeting with Helena, mother's school friend, and her husband Siegmund to fix the sights of Dorna in your head and get it into focus. Helena and Siegmund are two of forty-two Jews in a town which was once mostly Jewish.

They met in Mogilev, Transnistria, and married when he was discharged from the Red Army after the war. He then worked in the local timber company, once a Heller enterprise, today the nationalised Dorna Foresta, and during Stalin's time was tried for sabotage with a group of local Jews in a show trial. He was found not guilty but in a subsequent case, although nothing was proven, was sentenced to prison.

Helena, whose voice and tone remind you of Rosa, dead now almost five years, has harboured bitterness all her married life. Others received money from abroad to get themselves out of prison, we had no one, she says. To this day Siegmund has to pay a third of his meagre pension to cover his fine, 58 million lei in all, a sum no ordinary citizen can dream of repaying. They have no children. First there was the trial, then his imprisonment. Helena had several abortions and when he left prison, she could not conceive. They are still in love, two solitary, dignified figures, spending their days dreaming of food, always dreaming of food, bartering, dealing, concocting their next meal.

How lucky you were, Carla, to have left this place, where a mere rumour of lemons arriving in town sends shivers of delight down your school friend's spine. Costica, a young farmer from the mountains, works their vegetable patch which they have to cultivate, by governmental decree, in return for half the crops. Every morning Helena makes your breakfast and Siegmund brings fresh radishes and scallions to go with the hard cow's milk cheese Helena makes in hanging muslin bags, as they used to do since Dora's days.

A famous spa, frequented by many tourists, Vatra Dornei lacks
the greyness prevailing in Ceaucescu's Romania. It has all the charm
and natural beauty of Bucovina, always a frontier region and a symbol connected with the struggle for Romanian national freedom.
Its name was initially used to designate the beech (buk) forests
covering its mountain peaks. The traveller, journeying, like you,
through its picturesque villages and from hairpin curve to hairpin
curve on its wooded mountains, will, say the guide books, forever
cherish the image of the soft green hills, ivory citadel walls, the
natural elegance and the honey-coloured light which enwraps
Bucovina in a golden halo.

Dorna itself, situated between the mountains where the Dorna
stream flows into the Bistritsa river, is one of the most picturesque
towns in this otherwise grey country. Every day, after breakfast and
a bath Siegmund heats for you with precious timber, you walk into
the little town centre. Six Martie Street is a pedestrianised shopping
street with little to buy. A woman in a red jacket and white trousers
sticks out in the greyness. Down the road is Hellergasse, today
Dobreanu Gherea street, named after a Jewish writer. In consider-
ation?

Here is Carla's first home, named after her, Villa Carla. Today it's
a tenement, housing several families. You glimpse poverty, unmade
beds covered with grey blankets. In the yard, surrounded by the
glass veranda, an old woman. You manage to explain your mother
once lived here and she allows you to take photographs, declining,
in the generosity of the poor, an offer of a tip.

You love the street. You can see Onkels Faivel and Shmaya and
grandfather Mendel hurrying home from the family bank, the family
sawmill, the family hotel, to be greeted by the aromas of their wives'
cooking. The children, all of an age, studying together in the Heder
Mendel organised for them, sharing French and English tutors after
school, running up the mountain to pick blueberries late in summer.
You can see Carla and Helena coming home from school in their
thick black stockings, having to speak Romanian, their mother
tongue, German, forbidden by nationalist and anti-semitic school
mistresses.

You stroll with Helena up the mountain to the Jewish cemetery.
Here is a tombstone for the RJF soap and the desecrated Torah

books. Helena sighs at her parents' graves, looking down towards the beautiful valley. I love it here, she says, but in the years after Siegmund's trial I made myself ill. Now we try to forget. When we have, we eat, when we don't we don't. Life under a dictator is tough, she whispers, looking around at the wild flowers, to make sure nobody hears.

You were lucky, Carla, to have got out of this place, where your school friend is scared the militzia has seen her with your daughter, where people live in constant fear.

The old synagogue, once a formidable temple opposite the Lycee, lies empty, a store house for ritual vessels guarded by a gruff old Jew, embarrassed by your visit.

You walk to the banks of the Dorna stream, where Dorna Foresta, once Mendel's sawmill, still stacks timber as it did in his days. You walk in the park, by the casino, where Mendel took Rosa when they first met here after the first war.

Why do you feel so good here? Why does it feel like home? It is nothing like the Israel of your childhood, the Israel you have since left. But somehow it feels right, despite the harshness of the present. The journey is beginning to have a sense of destination.

Gura Humorlui, father's birthplace, is another story. Not a spa town, there are no tourists here, there is little charm. Father's cousin, an ageing piano teacher who spends his days in bed surrounded by photographs of days gone by, tells how ashamed grandma Tattu had been when she discovered, at 45, she was pregnant with father. They left for Vienna and later, having followed her scholarly but utterly unworldly husband to the dusty Jerusalem of the mid-twenties, she was to spend the later part of her life shunted from daughter-in-law to daughter-in-law, penniless, her only asset a carved silver candlestick which now stands in your living room, a million light years from her dreams.

Another cousin, Mimi, whose husband is regional doctor and therefore one of the favoured citizens in this corrupt society, lives in style in her parents' large glass-encased house. They too met in Mogilev, Transnistria, and live in its shadow, like all its survivors.

On the way back from visiting father's cousin, you meet three elderly Jews returning from Shabbat morning service. With twenty-four Jews, there isn't even a prayer quorum in Gura Humorlui. The local cemetery is overgrown and the synagogue is but a tiny room.

Bucovina is a land without Jews. Those who stayed had to because of sick parents, trials or illness. They are ageing fast. A year after your visit, Mimi and her husband would leave for Israel and father's cousin would die, leaving just twenty-one Jews in Gura Humorlui.

Then there is Friedrich Ausländer, the old advocate. Once an officer in the Kaiser's army and never a very religious Jew, he is an isolated relic of old times. About Jews like him Anschel said to Dora that only assimilated Jews who don't care for their Torah served in the goyim's army. Anschel died in Transnistria, his Gemarra books on his lap, and Fritz Ausländer survived to live in abject poverty, alone in a roomful of old, dusty lawbooks, dreaming of the last days of the Empire. Dear, dear, Onkel Fritz.

Another night train takes you to Czernowitz, today Chernovtsy in southern Ukraine. It takes a lot of bureaucracy and considerable bribing simply to buy a train ticket here. Romania is a most wonderfully corrupt society. The golden rule seems to be never buy anything without bribing if you can buy it with a bribe.

Mimi and her husband take you to the railway station in Suceava, a large county town at which the Sofia-Moscow train stops. The summer night is pitch black and they are worried about driving in the dark so they leave you to wait for your train which leaves at ten.

The station's waiting room is crowded with peasants, children, chickens, baggage. Was this how they waited for the trains to take them to Transnistria? Under-lit, with layers of dirt accumulated for years, the scene is that of a refugee transit camp. Half asleep, people jump up from their benches as trains pull into the station. Finally you are almost alone with an elderly Jew from Düsseldorf whose incredible name is Hitler.

Why should I change my father's name? His name is all I have after he died in the camp, he smiles toothlessly before he staggers to his train, dragging his suitcase, on his way to Tel Aviv, to see his Israeli grandchildren.

A young man approaches. The station is almost deserted now. His talk of exchanging lei for dollars sounds unreal here. His is the face of contemporary Romania. An engineer and part-time taxi driver, speculator and hustler. Though you politely reject his advances, he sees you, very courteously, to your approaching train, making sure you get on safely.

Did anyone make sure you got on safely, Hetti? Did anyone see you off, Dora? Trains carry a strong emotional association with death here and you are now on another one, journeying towards another unknown.

At three in the morning the train stops at Vadul Siret to change tracks. Alone on a stationary night train between Romania and the Soviet Union, with no one speaking a language you understand. Bureaucrats come and go, asking for papers, visas, money, each obliquely looking for his pound of flesh. You bribe no one, uncomfortable with this corruption. You would have given them a lei or two had you travelled here forty-odd years ago. And Helena's voice: give them something, don't be so moralistic, this is how this society works.

The bureaucratic nightmare ends, no bribes, no victims. Soviet officials find nothing among your papers, not even the one address you had hidden. Romanian officials succeed in confiscating all your Romanian money, promising to return it all when you come back. Two cultures, one greedy, the other suspicious, controlling. The train travels on towards another, greyer dawn.

Were you scared, Hetti, when you travelled alone with Yossi back from the camp southwards to Dorna, then Bucharest, then Israel? Were you all alone in the Displaced Persons camps, the transit camps, with a pale, thin child who refused to be comforted by his lame mother? Trains bring you in contact with Carla on her solitary journey to Bucharest. With Hetti and Hanna on their hopeful journey to the south. With Dora, beautiful Dora, on her last journey, old before her time, away from her devastated home, away from her Anschel's roughly dug grave.

It is on this train, between Suceava and Czernowitz that you, true sabra mother and father had worked so hard to nurture, start getting in touch with there. Why should Jews have a state? Germans have a state, as do Romanians and Poles. Jews have an eternal diaspora, you think as the train chugs on through the dawn.

Arriving at Czernowitz, that cosmopolitan centre where village girl Dora had come to buy her engagement outfits with her mother-in-law Helen Lax and her dear friend, ailing Rosa, is another anticlimax. The Austrian style station is painted white and yellow. Your guide, polite, modern, efficient Vladimir, picks you up.

It is here that mother stood watching over the family linen and crystal, you want to say to him. Here she and her parents took the last train to freedom.

But you don't. You exchange civilities and he takes you to Hotel Bucovina, the only tourist hotel in Chernovtsy, a large building on the broad Lenin avenue. An empty sensation of fear takes over from the old sabra arrogance of nobody is going to tell me what to do and where to do it.

What would you like to do in our city, Vladimir asks courteously, not really awaiting a reply. Just roam around, just walk, you say. My people came from here, you know. You smile and your jaws ache.

First you walk to the Ringplatz. Now a large statue of Vladimir Illich Lenin stands in the middle, surrounded by bright red wreaths. Flowers everywhere, beautifully tidy. Der Schwarze Adler at one end of the Platz, painted light green, now town hall. Which of Der Schwarze Adler's large rectangular windows did Dora look out of in her first bewildering visit to the big city? At what dining hall did Mendel treat Hetti and Menashe to their wedding drink?

You spend the next three days walking up and down Herrengasse, today Olga Koblianska street, pedestrianised, full of shoppers. Visualising young Carla with her student friends sipping eternal cups of coffee. You enter a coffee house but there are no cakes, only watery coffee and thick rolls. In the crowded streets you shut your eyes, trying to see Hetti and Menashe walking after a movement meeting in the deep snow. Which corner did you turn, Hetti? Where did you first lie with your Menashe?

The street is full of courtyards. You peep into several. Was this where Rosa and Mendel's apartment was? What grace this city must have had, what a glorious past. Even today, the stuccoed stones have the faded charm of an ageing beauty.

You are alone and the city envelops you. You will not find our type of Jew there, mother had warned. They were all taken away. The Jews of today are new arrivals, Russian Jews. You hear Yiddish in the street. Your people never spoke Yiddish. There is something Russian about the two men conversing in Yiddish in the middle of Herrengasse. Definitely not our people.

Our people? What are you? Where do you come from? They tried to make a sabra out of you, but here you are part of the story. This is my place, mother.

You visit the university where David Greifer wanted to study but could not because of the first war. It's a lovely red and gold brick building, busy with end of year students who don't look twice in your direction. Only the guard tells you not to walk on the grass. By order.

On your last day a young man approaches you in a book shop. Yevrei (Jew), he says. Me too, you say enthusiastically. His name is Boris and he invites you to walk with him. Life is not bad, he says, only it's hard to be a Jew. He takes you for a ride to his factory where he exchanges a large sum of money for some spare parts. You have the feeling you are witnessing an illicit deal but you ask no questions. He takes you to see the Jewish cemetery, vandalised the previous year. You can find no family graves, the cemetery is overgrown, its synagogue in ruins. Look there, across the road, Boris says, at the Russian cemetery. How tidy it is.

The synagogue is a tiny building in a small side street. The big temple had long since been turned into a cinema. Chernovtsy in southern Ukraine lives on. It may have many Jews, but your Czernowitz is dead. A deserted Jewish graveyard.

Boris drives you back into town. Later they will tell you he must have been sent by the KGB to check you out, hence the money deal. All this for you, you wonder, in this Jewish desert?

The night train back to Suceava is easier to take. When searched copiously, you can laugh in their faces. What do you take me for, a criminal? The searcher and the two men who oversee him smile back, very polite.

Coming back to Gura Humorlui and Dorna is like coming home. It feels like you have never left Dorna, like Carla had never left it. Yet every waking moment you bless her for not having stayed behind like Helena who, childless, wakes every morning dreaming of food.

Harold Pinter

was born in London in 1930 and was educated at Hackney Downs Grammar
School, the Royal Academy of Dramatic
Art, and the Central School of Speech
and Drama. He has worked as a professional actor and also as a waiter, a door-
man, a dishwasher, a snow shoveler, and
a door-to-door salesman. His screen-
plays include John Fowles's *The French Lieu-
tenant's Woman* (1980) and Margaret
Atwood's *The Handmaid's Tale* (1987), and
he has also written extensively for radio
and television. Pinter has received more
than fourteen major literary awards, and
since the 1960s his work has been
acclaimed both in the West End and on
Broadway. The author of twenty-nine plays
since the 1950s, Pinter is widely regarded
as the foremost postwar dramatist in Britain. His autobiographical novel, *The
Dwarfs* (1990), was written between 1952
and 1956, although it belies its East London origins. European literature and philosophy, as well as the fiction of James
Joyce, inform this youthful bildungsroman. This novel shows the extent that,
from the beginning, Pinter wished to transfigure his particular background and
place himself in the tradition of literary
modernism.

Harold Pinter

EXCERPT FROM ## The Dwarfs

Eleven

What are the dwarfs doing, in their journeys to the streetcorners? They stumble in the gutters and produce their pocketwatches. One with a face of chalk chucks the dregs of the day into a bin and seats himself on the lid. He is beginning to chew though he has not eaten. Now they collect at the backstep. One scrubs his veins at the lower sink, now he is gorged in the sud. Spruced and preened, in time for the tuck. Time is kept to the T.

Pete is in the cabin. He cannot hear the backchat of bone from the yard, the crosstalk of bristled skin. He is listening to himself. Now Mark, who combs his hair in mirrors. He holds six pocket-mirrors at related angles. He sings the song of Mark to the cocked glass. He does not see the market outside the window. He sees himself and smiles.

The floor is scrubbed to the grain, my own work.

It is to this fund I donate, and sublet the premises. I strike a shrewd bargain. I am the promoter, although neither Pete nor Mark is aware of the contract, nor of the contractor.

They are still there, the two of them. Or perhaps they have gone. We must wait. I am prepared to wait. I do not want to stop waiting. The end of this vigil is the beginning of nothing.

Twelve

—Come away, come away, death, and in sad cypress let me be laid, Pete sang.

The sun was setting. Lilac hung heavy on the arched tree. The garden flickered. In low deckchairs Len and Mark were lying. Pete gravely ended the dirge, standing at the garden door.

—I like this garden. It's tranquil.

In a lower garden a bonfire, burning, collapsed, in a gash, splintered. Smoke smarted thinly across the fences.

—My mind's a blank, Mark said.

—Say the first thing, Len said, that comes into it.

—Shaving in the asylum of Wednesday I saw a toadstool sitting on a blank rabbit, Mark said in one breath.

—Blimey!

—There you are.

—I'll tell you what, Pete said, thinking got me into this and thinking's got to get me out. You know what I want? An efficient idea. Do you know what I mean? An efficient idea. One that'll work. Something I can pin my money on. An eachway bet. Nothing's guaranteed, I know that. But I'm willing to gamble. I've never stopped gambling but I'm a bit cramped these days. That's what I need. Do you know what I mean? Of course, some people are efficient ideas in themselves. You might be an efficient idea yourself, Mark. You can never tell. I wouldn't like to pass judgement. But I'm not. I've got to sweat for one. And if I can get hold of one I've got to make it a going concern. No grafting and no fiddling. Some people can afford to take three or four days off a week. I can't afford the time. Do you know what I mean?

—I should think they're very few and far between, efficient ideas, Mark said.

—They may be. But I told you, thinking got me into this and thinking's got to get me out.

—I once knew a man who didn't think, Mark said. He rushed home as fast as he could every evening, turned the armchair round, sat in it and looked out of the window. After about two hours, when it was dark, he'd get up and turn on the light.

—Yes, Len said, but I know what you mean about an efficient idea. Like a nutcracker. You press the cracker and the cracker cracks the nut. There's no waste of energy. It's an exact process and an efficient one. The idea's efficient.

—No, Pete said, you're wrong. There is waste. When you press the cracker with the proper purchase the nut cracks, but at the same time the hinge of the cracker gives out a friction, a heat, which is incidental. It's unnecessary to the particular idea. It's nearly efficient but not quite. Because there's an escape and wastage of energy to no purpose. It's uneconomic. It's exactly the same, after all, with a work of art. Every particle of a work of art should crack a nut, or help form a pressure that'll crack the final nut. Do you know what I mean? Each idea must possess stringency and economy and the image, if you like, that expresses it must stand in exact correspondence and relation to the idea. Only then can you speak of utterance and only then can you speak of achievement. If there's any excess heat or friction, if there's any waste, you've failed and you have to start again. It's simple enough.

—But what about the sun and moon? Len said. Isn't there something ambiguous about the sun and moon?

—Then again, Pete went on, there's nothing against a geezer constructing his own efficient idea, but he's got to be quite sure, in the first place, what he means by the term efficient. And once he's understood it, he's got to determine to what the idea is relevant, or whether it's relevant at all. Some ideas that were adequate enough in the past wouldn't take you farther than the Edgware Road now. You've got to be able to distinguish between a workaday efficiency and a relative one, one that might have been relevant once, or might be relevant in different circumstances, but isn't now. It's a matter of considering what world you're relating it to.

—Well, we can't make any mistake about that, said Mark.

—I don't know, Pete said. I don't know that we quite agree on that point, Mark.

—You mean we may be talking about two different things?

—Yes. What it comes down to is what world, exactly, are you talking about?

—What world? The whole gamut as far as you can sniff. Backwards and forward and in and out.

—Yes, but I sometimes think you're omitting to sniff relevant

matters which are right under your nose. You know what I
mean?

—I think I sniff what you're getting at all right.

—Well, quite frankly, Mark, I suggest you don't pay enough
attention to what goes on around you.

—You mean the headlines.

—There's more to it than that. You're subject to what goes on
around you and you depend on it for your welfare and existence.
I don't see how you can fail to be involved. This is the society
you live in and I wouldn't say you're fulfilling your part of the
bargain.

—You refer to the busticket world.

—All right. You have tuppence in your pocket and you pay your
fare. But it seems to me you regard that tuppence, and more
to the point, the conveyance itself, as a divine right. The way
you pay your tuppence you don't really pay it at all. You're
getting a free ride. You don't fully realize that the tuppence is
sweat and the ride is sweat too.

—I'm a liability on the world's bank balance.

—You're not only a liability, Pete laughed, you're a bloody hallucination! Sometimes I can't believe you exist at all.

—But where you do believe I exist, Mark said, is as a parasite.

—Not entirely.

—A parasite, Mark said, standing up. But it's inaccurate. I don't
live on anyone's earnings. I don't pinch anything from the till.
I've nothing but contempt for the till. I'm not concerned with
the standards you're talking about. I follow my itch, that's all.
It's not going up your alley, it may not be going up anyone's
alley, so what? I don't aspire to the great standards. They don't
apply to me. I don't live with them.

—That's the point, Pete said. What I'm accusing you of is
operating on life and not in it.

—If I'm a ponce, Mark said, I'm my own ponce. I'm nobody
else's ponce. I live and I operate in my own life.

—You can't live safely tucked up in a test tube.

—You're off the beam.

—Your danger, Mark, is that you might become nothing but an
attitude.

—Not while I've still got balls, mate.

—They won't save you. They might drop off.

—I keep them well oiled.

—Look. What I'm objecting to is that you tend to take a bit of a holiday in between times.

—If I do, they're not with pay. I fork out. Anyway the term holiday isn't valid. You use the term holiday because I'm deviating from your course. I'm not deviating from my own.

—Ah, Pete said, there may be some truth in that. I told you, you might be an efficient idea.

He passed Mark a cigarette and struck a match.

—What you don't understand about me, Mark said, is this—I've got no ambition.

Pete looked at him.

—Oh, he said. I see.

—Listen, Mark snapped. It's about time I told you people something else—for your own good.

—What?

—Did you know I was born circumcised?

—What!

—The geezer came along with the carvingknife to do the necessary and nearly dropped down dead with the shock. They had to give him a doublebrandy on the house. He thought I was the Messiah.

—Well, Len asked, own up. Are you?

Later, they left the house and walked past the pond to the Swan café, to meet Virginia. She had arrived, and was sitting in the corner.

—Well, Pete said, as they sat down with tea, how's Marie?

—She's very well, said Virginia.

—Marie Saxon? said Mark. What's she doing now?

—She spends most of her time, Pete said, in Soho. Prancing about with all and sundry.

—Is she still in love with me?

—She didn't mention it, Virginia said.

—She was mad about me, Mark said, in the old days.

—She isn't the one, Pete asked, that you banged round the earhole once?

—No. That was Rita.

—Oh yes. Rita.

—What was that? Len asked.

—She was leading him up the garden, Pete laughed, or something, so he knocked her teeth in.

—Not quite, Mark said, but she asked for it, anyway. It was the biggest surprise of her life. I've got no regrets. Taught her respect. Listen Len. Don't look at me like that. You didn't know the girl. There was room for no other action, I assure you. So Marie's not in love with me, any more, eh?

—Love? Pete said. She's flogging her whatsit to bellboys and pisshounds.

From the inner room of the café came the sound of a guitar, strummed heavily.

—What have you all been doing? asked Virginia.

—Chatting, Pete said. A social evening.

—Right, said Mark.

—I was trying to explain to Len, Pete said, how he'd benefit under my health scheme, but he wouldn't listen.

—What's the book, Virginia? Mark asked.

—Hamlet.

—Hamlet? Pete said.

—What's it like?

—Do you know, Virginia said, it's odd, but I suddenly can't find any virtue in the man.

—Really? Mark said.

—No.

—Why?

—No, she said, no, I—after all, what is he? What is he but vicious, maudlin, spiteful, and sensitive to nothing but his own headaches? I find him completely unprepossessing.

She sat back, tapping her spoon on the table. A voice was raised, from the inner room, singing in Italian to the guitar.

—Well, Mark laughed, it's a point of view.

—You're quite wrong, Pete said, of course.

—I don't know, Virginia murmured. What does he do but talk and talk, and now and again stick a knife into someone. I mean a sword.

—I find this rather amusing, Pete said. But we won't go into it.

—I've got to go, Len said, standing up.

—Yes, Pete said, we'll adjourn.

—Allnight shift? Mark asked, as they walked to the door.

—Yes, Len said. There's my bus.

—Be seeing you, said Pete.

Len ran across the road.

—You can see yourself home, Ginny? Pete said. I think I'll go straight back.

—Of course.

—Shall I see you home? Mark said.

—No, no, it's quite all right.

—My bus, Pete said. See you. Ta-ta, Mark.

He walked across the road.

—Well, Virginia said, I'd better be off.

Mark watched her lips move.

—I can easily—

—No, it's all right, Mark. It's only five minutes.

—How are you? he asked.

—Fine.

—Uh-huh.

—Well, she said, I'd better be going. I'll be seeing you.

—Yes.

—Cheerio.

—Goodnight, Mark said.

—Goodnight.

Thirteen

Pete walked quickly out of the office and across the road. He found an empty telephone box and went into it. While the bell rang he looked into the street.

—Ginny?

—Yes.

—Are you in?

—In? Of course.

—All right. I'm coming round now.

—What's the hurry?

—I'll be there in half an hour.

—Is anything wrong?

—Don't go out.

He caught a bus to Dalston. At the trafficlights he jumped off and took a short cut behind the station. Virginia opened the door of her flat in her bathrobe.

—You were very quick. I've just had a bath.

—What for? Pete asked.

—What?

He went into the kitchen, took off his jacket and tie and washed his face at the sink.

—Did you have a bad day?

Seizing the towel, he turned.

—What do you mean, bad day?

—Bad day. Bad day.

—Why have you had a bath?

—It's hot.

He threw the towel aside, returned to the living room, sat down in an armchair, lit a cigarette, blew the match, and looked up to see Virginia, her bathrobe open, regarding her body.

—Look how pink my nipples are. Like a virgin, she said.

—Will you do that thing up?

—Why?

—Do you mind doing it up?

She tied the cord and sat at the table. From her handbag she took a cigarette and lit it.

—Who was round here this afternoon?

—How do you know anyone was here?

—The cups, the cups. Who was it?

—My friend Marie Saxon.

—What did she want?

—A cup of tea.

—What did she want?

—Christ. She didn't want anything.

—She's a prostitute.

—No she's not.

—She's a scrubber.

A breeze blew the curtains. Virginia smoothed her hair.

—Did you have your bath while she was here?

—Why?

—Did she soap your armpits?

Pete looked about the room.

—Where are the drawingpins I left here, and the drawingboard?

—Here. Somewhere.

—Where?

—They're not down the bloody drain.

—If you become involved with Marie Saxon, Virginia, that's where you'll end up.

—Christ.

—Will you stop saying that?

—No, I don't know what to say.

—Why say anything?

—Ah.

—And for God's sake, he shouted, keep that robe done up! I don't want to see the hair on your crutch. What do you think I am?

She stood up, closed her robe and sat again.

—I don't know what I think you are.

—I know you don't. I'm damn sure you don't. It's about time you stopped continually powdering your fanny and opened your eyes, mate. Why, for instance, don't you go and put some clothes on now? You've made your point. It only needs a little effort to get out of this masturbatory rut.

—What are you talking about?

—Don't you realize, he said, that someone might knock on that door and that you've no right to open it like that?

—You could open it.

—You're being very disappointing, Virginia. You know what you're doing, don't you? You're behaving like any other little tart who must show herself off or cease to exist.

—I've just had a bath.

—It's normal to dress after a bath.

—Oh for God's sake!

Pete threw his cigarette into the grate.

—So, he said, if there's a knock on the door, you'll go to it like that?

—I don't expect anyone.

—Don't be stupid. Anyone's liable to turn up. A man may come to examine the meters.

—He only comes in the mornings.

—How can you be sure?

—He's at home, Virginia said, mowing the garden.

She began to chew a crumb, and then rose and went to the sideboard, where she picked up a copy of Picture Post and flicked the pages.

—If you could start to think, Virginia, you might be a little more use to me. As it is, quite honestly, you're nothing but a dead weight. I know there are men who would be glad to accept you as you are, but I needn't enlarge upon them. We know their requirements. Of course, it may be that their requirements are yours too. It's quite possible that I've been suffering under a delusion about you. If that is the case, why don't you get Marie Saxon to introduce you to some motorcyclists, or all-in wrestlers?

—Yes, I'll think about that.

—What else do you think about, Virginia?

—Nothing else.

—I wonder, Pete said, what you and Marie Saxon discuss?

—Only one thing. Jockstraps.

—Yes of course, most women have minds like mouldy larders. It could hardly be otherwise, I suppose. I remember the last time I saw Marie Saxon. She was in a swimming costume. Her breasts were flopping about like washing on a line. She exists within that framework, such as it is, of course. Her life naturally resolves itself into a neverending bout of selftitillation. That's what she understands by life. But if you're falling into that error, I'm disappointed, to be quite frank. I've told you before where your beauty lies. If—

—Pete! What do you want? What do you want? What do you want? She ran across the room and fell at his knees.

—What do you want me to do? What have I done? Please! What have I done? Tell me. Tell me.

He looked down at her.

—Why did you say that thing about *Hamlet* last night?

—What thing?

—About *Hamlet*. Why did you say it? Why do you say these things? Do you know they're extremely stupid? It made me look very foolish. Did you realize that? You don't know anything about *Hamlet*, Ginny. Don't you understand that? And yet you come in with the book under your arm. Why did you do that, in the first place? Was it to make an impression? Are you mad? Did you think Mark would be impressed? If so, at what? Mark was amused. But I wasn't. It's up to you entirely—in point of fact it's a matter of distinct choice—a choice you'll have to make— but the point is, Ginny, that while we're together I can't have you making such ridiculous statements about something you know nothing about. It's out of all proportion. You made me look, in effect, a bloody fool. I thought I told you to leave Shakespeare for a while? Don't you think it was for your own good? I've told you you're nowhere near the point where you can begin to absorb his implications, and not only do you ignore what I say but you lug the book about with you like a pissy fifthformer, and parade these stupidities. It's quite absurd but it's more than absurd. It's pathetic. And not only is it pathetic but it's bloody niggling. I've told you to leave him alone, I've told you you're not capable of expressing an opinion about him, which isn't a reflection on you, because not two out of a hundred are capable, I've told you of the study you've got to do, I've surely given you an inkling as to the complexity of the whole question, I've even asked you to reach a position of being able to inform me, through study, so I must have had some respect for your powers, and this is how you act. Do you realize that that statement was an abortion? Where did you read it? Wherever you read it you didn't even digest the idea. Could you have argued upon that statement, with reference to the text? Of course not. Did you think such palpable emotionalism would pass as critical comment? In other less charitable company you would have had your balls chopped off. You were really very fortunate no word was said. I decided not to, then. You had showed both of us up enough, as it was. What must

Mark and Len think? I'm supposed to have some concern for
your literary development and suddenly, under my auspices,
as it were, you come out with that. But what, I want to know,
was your motive? What did you hope to prove? That you could
form your own opinions? To prove to Mark that you could
read? Do you think that if you carried a book on Advanced
Mathematics under your arm you would necessarily persuade
Len you could add two and two? You didn't seriously imagine
you were presenting a brand new idea? Don't you realize that
that idea, though not your crummy expression of it, has been
chewed over and gobbed up from start to finish, and mostly by
incompetents? Don't you realize that it is in itself incompetent,
superficial and gauche? But it's not worth talking about. What
I don't understand is your motive. Were you deliberately trying
to make me look a fool? No, it was probably just—here I am,
listen to me—but you forget you weren't in your school com-
monroom, Virginia. God knows what you say there that probably passes for God's word. It's lamentable. Now look here,
you're bound to think of what you say before you say it and
you're obliged, this is the point, to realize, once and for all,
your limitations. You're morally obliged. That was nothing but
an unforgivable error of judgement, as applied to time, place
and content. You seem to have no sense of fitness or context.
So far from doing any good you did positive harm. It was morally indefensible and morally objectionable. Because from what
did it spring? A desire to assert. It was pure bloody bombast,
illconsidered, faulty, inept, preposterous and shaming, and
what's more, entirely unpolitic. Did you think we were all going
to bow down at your altar? Did you think you would be excused
because you were a woman? Well, whatever you thought, Virginia, quite honestly it's not very satisfactory. I find it all very
dubious. I put a considerable degree of faith in you, I damnwell
do my best to educate you, and all you do is make a fool of
both of us. Now listen here, what I want you to understand is
this. In other societies you're entitled to do what you like, but
while we're together, I refuse to put up with this kind of behaviour. It's for your own good as well as mine. I'm willing to
help you all I can in such matters, but such an action on your

part almost amounts to a stab in the back. Now it's no use saying you won't repeat this sort of thing if you're still going to feel the inclination. What you must do is develop a sense of proportion, of judgement. You have the faculties but you seem reluctant to use them. Why are you crying? I tell you, you have the faculties. It's just a matter of bringing them into focus, of sharpening them. I've always admired them in you. You've no need to cry. I know you've understood me. All that happened was that your artistic sensibility, your sense of proportion, went astray. I'm quite sure, in fact, that you realize that, Ginny. I admire these qualities in you, I always have done, I merely felt bound to point out—

—I'm sorry, Virginia said, her head in her hands, I'm sorry. I won't do it again.

—No, Pete said, rising, sitting on the chairarm, and holding her to his chest, it's all right. It's all right.

—I'm sorry, Virginia said, I'm sorry.

—No, Pete said, it's all right. It's all right.

George Steiner

was born in Paris in 1929, emigrated to
the United States in 1940, and has mainly
lived in Britain since the 1950s. He was
educated at the Sorbonne, at the University
of Chicago, and at Harvard, where he
won the Bell Prize in American literature.
Steiner was also a Rhodes Scholar at
Oxford University and has worked as an
extraordinary fellow of Churchill College, Cambridge, and professor of com-
parative literature at Geneva University.
His nonfiction includes *Tolstoy or Dostoevsky*
(1959), *Language and Silence* (1967), and
After Babel (1975), and he edited the *Penguin
Book of Modern Verse Translation* (1966).
Steiner's many honors include an O. Henry
Short Story Award and the Morton Zabel
Prize by the American National Institute of
Arts and Letters. He is the author of four
books of fiction and one volume of poetry.
His novel *The Portage to San Cristobal of A.
H.* (1979) was awarded a PEN/Faulkner Fic-
tion Stipend and has been dramatized by
Christopher Hampton. 'A Conversation
Piece' (1991) was first collected in *Proofs
and Three Parables* (1992) and reflects his
current preoccupation with the Hebrew
Bible and religious thought in general.

George Steiner

A Conversation Piece

A humming as of bees, distant.

'But the Master, Eleazer son of Eleazer, in his commentary of 1611 said—'

'That Akibah, may his name shine in glory, had been mistaken—'

'When he wrote that Abraham was altogether free, a man at liberty, the father of freedoms, when God, blessed be His unspeakable Name, called upon him to take the boy, Isaac, to the place of burnt offering.'

'By which Akibah meant to signify that God's commandments are spoken to the spirit of man when that spirit is in a state of sovereignty over its own truth, that commandments to the enslaved and the maddened are empty.'

'To which Eleazer son of Eleazer, he of Cracow, retorted—'

' "What freedom has man in the face of the summons of the Almighty?" When He commands, our freedom is obedience. Only the servant of God, the absolute servant, is a free man.'

' "Not so," said Baruch to me, he of Vilna. "Not so. When God bade Abraham, our father, take Isaac, his only son, to Mount Moriah, He paused for an answer. Abraham could have said, 'No.' He could have said, 'Almighty God, hallowed be Thy Name. You are tempting me. You are putting in my path the supreme temptation, which is unthinking, blind obedience. Such is the obeisance demanded by the Dragon Baal, by the empty gods with dog-heads in Egypt's temples. You are not Moloch, eater of children. What you now await from me is loving denial.' " So Baruch, my teacher.'

'The journey to the mountain took three days. During which Abraham did not speak to Isaac—'

'Nor to God. Who listened closely. Hoping for the answer, "No." '

Whose patience was without end and who was saddened. So Baruch, in our *schul* at Vilna, where the almond tree—'

'That's crazy. God's foreknowing is total. What need had He to listen to Abraham. He knew that His commandment would be obeyed, that it was not for man to question. I knew Baruch, your teacher. He was so subtle that in his hands words turned to sand.'

'Yet God, blessed be the hem of His unsayable Name and the fire-garment of His glory, did not wholly trust Abraham.'

'Another madman.'

'No. Listen to me. God's confidence in Abraham was not total. Let me hammer out my meaning. Do not interrupt. If God had been utterly certain that Abraham would strike down the boy, He would have let the sacrifice come to pass. And brought Isaac back to life. For is it not said that God can waken the dead? By putting the ram in the thicket, by saving the child, He left uncertain the final obedience of Abraham. Did not Gamaliel the Cabbalist instruct us that there are moments, openings in the universe, during which God questions His own foreknowledge, during which the Angel of the Unknown, of the nameless, passes across the light of being?'

'Gamaliel the heretic. The witch and alchemist of Toledo—'

Many voices now, close-crowded.

'That accounts for the gloss—'

'Gloss? What gloss, chatterbox?'

'In the Talmud in the *yeshivah*. Written in by hand.'

'Which *yeshivah*?'

'Ours. At Bialik. Saying that Abraham was angry. That anger choked him all the way home. That he did not speak once from Mount Moriah back to Beersheba.'

'*Angry*? Our father, Abraham, to whom God had restored Isaac?'

'Because the Almighty had not kept faith in him. Because God had not been absolutely certain that Abraham would fulfil His commandment and strike the knife into the boy. In the night after he had heard God's voice, and during the unendurable march to the mountain, Abraham had died many deaths. His senses had frozen. His brain had become like black dust. The heart had stopped its song. There was no ground under his feet, no dawn under his eyelids. His steps were like those of a bullock when it has been stunned, when the blood is already out of its throat. Those who looked on

Abraham saw death walking. The faith in him had grown so mighty, the sinews of obedience so stretched, that there was no room for life. There was doubt in Moses, sanctified be his great name and remembrance. Mutiny in Jeremiah. But Abraham, he the father of our fathers, had been made faith. All else had been purged. He was faith in bone and nerve. No hair, no hair of a hair on him or in his unkempt beard but had become faith and obedience harder than steel. The knife was softer than his hand. The blade might snap. That was Abraham's last fear. But God did not know this. He did not choose to know it. His trust in Abraham, His servant, fell short. Now the Almighty would never have proof of Abraham's infinite faith. He would never know how tight was the knot of Abraham's obedience. As life came back into the old man, as pain came home to him, so did a towering anger. That, said the gloss, is why the silence on Abraham's return journey was more terrible than the silence on the road to Moriah.'

'Error. A false gloss. For has not Jehoshuah of Prague cleared up the matter of the silence? Has he not instructed us—'

'That Abraham's anger was the very opposite. He could not at first, and may he be forgiven, find it in his heart to praise, to thank God for the saving of Isaac. The terror had been too sharp. The temptation too severe for a man to bear. Unendurable because two-fold. The temptation to obey was murderous and beyond human understanding. How could God ask such a thing of Abraham, his most faithful servant? The temptation to disobey. But is there anything worse than to deny God's voice, to close one's ears against His calling? That the Almighty had saved the child did not take away even an atom, an atom's breath of terror from His commandment and the three days thereafter. And what if God *had* taken Isaac? What if Abraham's knife had struck? What then? How could the boy's resurrection make up for his sacrifice, for Abraham's act of slaughter? On the way back to Beersheba, Abraham could not speak to God. The hurt, the doubts gagged his soul. Had not the ram appeared too late in the thicket? How could Abraham live after that moment on the mountain, how could Abraham draw breath after he had carried inside him the slaying of his son? Hence the grey sweat on him during the return, hence the total silence. So Jehoshuah, whom they stoned in Prague.'

* * *

For an instant the voices dropped. But then, like a grape bursting—
    'Foolishness. Foolishness. Hair-splitting.'
    Almost in chorus.
    'God had promised Abraham, "I will make of thee a great nation." He had promised father Abraham that his seed would be as are the stars, numberless, inextinguishable even when scattered. he had renewed with Abraham the covenant of hope. That Israel would endure, that Abraham's seed would be sown across the earth. Indestructible as is the living wind.'
    'That it would endure despite—'
    'That the destruction of the temple and the loss of Zion—'
    'Despite massacre and dispersal—'
    'That we should not be consumed, not finally, in the fiery furnace, in the teeth of the mob, in the charnel house or the pogrom—'
    'That we shall endure even after they have torn the almond tree from its roots—'
    'Like hot ashes through the night. Alive even in death. Alive.'
    ' "A nation and a company of nations shall be of thee," said God to our fathers, despite—'
    'But how then could Abraham have believed, even for a minute, that the Almighty, sung be His Name of Names, would have him slay Isaac? For without Isaac there could be no lineage, no children of Israel? Answer me that.'
    'Was it all a game? Play-acting, as at Purim? When Haman roars through his black beard that all Jews, both young and old, little children and women, shall perish in one day, and the spoil shall be taken from them for a prey? O that black roaring. How it frightens us, how the children in the hall hold their breath and crowd close to their parents. Though we know that Esther is in the wings and that evil Haman will hang high. God and Abraham acting out the play of Isaac. To make our hearts breathless. To teach us by terror and by joy, as children must be taught. And Abraham was silent because he knew that all would be well, that he would, through Isaac, be a father to nations. Silent as was Joseph when he recognized his brethren and looked on Benjamin.'
    'But where then would be Abraham's merit? Play-acting? When the being of God is, as Maimonides taught, truth. A truth so pure

that there is no shadow, no shadow of a shadow where it prevails. Abraham was an old man, a very old man—'

'Who might have forgotten, in the numbness of that terrible calling, the terms of God's promise, so long ago, in the land of Ur—'

'Who might have thought, in the dizziness of his fear, that God would bring to Sarah another son, a child of late evening after Isaac—'

'Who could have believed that the Lord, blessed be His Name, had changed purpose, that some other people, and not Israel, would be sanctified among nations. Because even Abraham, father of our fathers, had known sin, being a man. Or so it is argued in the commentary of the learned Ephraim of Mainz. I remember the passage.'

'And for all these reasons, or others we are too blind, too unlettered to apprehend, Abraham might have taken for the voice of God that of a demon—'

'That of Satan himself.'

'Abraham in his numbness, in his dizziness, in his knowledge of perfection, mistaking the whisper of Satan for the voice of God. For was it not said by Soloviel the Cabbalist that these two voices, that of God whom we must not name and that of un-nameable evil, are so utterly alike. That the difference between them is only that of the sound of a rain-drop in the sea?'

'It *was* the voice of Satan. God is no play-actor. Neither is He a sadistic tempter. How do we best define God, how do we seek to imagine Him? Precisely as one who *cannot* ask of a man that he stick a knife in the throat of his child. There is no surer proof that God is than the incapacity of our souls, of our minds, to conceive of Him as tempting Abraham to murder his son, to conceive of Him as torturing Abraham our father during the journey to the mount. Even a gentile, albeit the wisest among them, understood that the definition, the being of God, is proved by the impossibility of the commandment to Abraham. That it was Satan who confounded Abraham and seduced him to his devilish purpose.'

'A gentile? What gentile?'

'He bore a name like ours: Immanuel. He lived in Koenigsberg.'

'In Koenigsberg? I have a cousin there. Menachem the draper.

Do you know him, the shop in the old town square? Do you know what has happened—'

'And having observed the confusion of Abraham, the Almighty betook Himself to Mount Moriah, set an angel to guard Isaac and wove the ram into the thorn-bush. Perhaps the selfsame bush that would burn for Moses.'

'Why then, *rebbi*, did God not intervene at once? Why did he not drive Satan from Abraham's door and take the old man out of his agony? The journey took three whole days. Three long nights Abraham lay awake with the face of Isaac before him, with that knife in his belt. An eternity. Why?'

'Our time is not His. Perhaps that ram was not yet born or the bush thick enough. Perhaps in His infinite mercy, the Almighty, praised be He, sought to give Satan a chance, to see whether the Fallen One would feel remorse seeing the sweat on Abraham, and undo his evil trick.'

'Though you are a learned man, you speak like a simpleton. You say that we know the being of God, the meaning of Him, just because He could not order Abraham to sacrifice Isaac the child, the only son. You would have us believe that so crazy, so obscene a commandment could come only from Satan. God's existence tells us that Abraham was mistaken when he took the voice of the devil for that of the Lord. You cite a wise man of the gentiles. Perhaps he was wise. But no true Christian. For is the God of the Christians not He who gives His only son in sacrifice, who let His son die in bestial pain on the Roman cross?'

A rush of voices.

'But that is not our God. Not ours. Not—'

'Our God is one. He does not beget. All men are His sons. The Nazarite was no Messiah. Only a man. Mad, perhaps.'

'Let me speak. I do not say that their God is ours, or that Christ was His child. I can attach no meaning to such words. But consider this: only Almighty God, only He who spoke to Job out of the whirlwind and slew the first-born of Egypt, could command Abraham to sacrifice Isaac. Abraham was not mistaken. His hearing was good. Listening to those terrible words, words which should never cross the lips of the living, Abraham *knew* that God was speaking. God is what He is because He alone can demand of His most faithful servant that he slit his child's throat. And it was this knowledge, this understanding beyond reason, which made father Abraham speechless on the journey to the mountain and mute on the road back to Beersheba. We who are fallen into the hand of the living God—'

Was the sound nearing? A sound slithering, like smoke across sand.

Next, a voice lime-green and acid.

'Who speaks for Isaac?'

Not yet a man's voice. Choked by the first starched collar and the bite of the collar-stud.

'Who speaks for Isaac? It was a hard march. His father Abraham walking too fast. Saying nothing, but pulling him by the hand. Black, impatient as Isaac had never seen his father before, but silent. Isaac saw the dry wood and the flint. He knew that his father was carrying a knife and a whetstone. But where was the lamb for the burnt offering? And when he asked, his father said that God would provide. But the words sounded strange, like the beads of sweat on Abraham's lips. Do you think Isaac believed him? I don't. He must have guessed. From the way in which they hurried from the house, from the way they camped in the night, hardly washing, all under one stinking tent-cloth. Oh, Isaac must have guessed and smelled the knife. And fouled himself in his fear. Marching three days with his bowels cold and loose, trying to sleep three short nights in the stench of his fear. Can you imagine their climb up the mountain? It may be that Abraham carried the wood, giving to Isaac the flint and shavings for the fire. But Isaac must have noticed the rope around the logs. Too thick, too freshly woven. A rope with which to tie a man's hands behind his back. Why did he not scream for help or run back to the young servants whom Abraham had left at the foot of the trail? Isaac's friends. The serving-men with whom he played in the courtyard of the house, who brought him the new grapes from the vine and cut arrows for him? Surely they would hide him and spirit him home. Why did Isaac not seize his father's hands and cry out for his life? Why did he not snatch at the knife and throw it over the side of the hill?'

'Because the spirit of God was upon him, because he was blessed in obedience.'

'Because Abraham's ass, the brindled she-ass whom Isaac fed, had whispered to him that he need not fear, that an Angel was beside him. There is a Midrash which says that the beast of burden spoke comfort to Isaac.'

'Fairy-tales. Lies. I will tell you why Isaac did not scream for help or run away or try to stop his father. It was because he was too frightened. It was because his voice had frozen inside him. It was because he was ashamed of the hot dirt and smell in his pants. The shame being even greater than his fear of death. But when Abraham bound him and laid him out on the altar, on that dry, sharp wood, when he heard the knife come out of his father's belt, he screamed. No one heard that scream. Because Isaac was vomiting, because the vomit was in his mouth, like a gag. But I know that he screamed.'

'Nowhere in the Torah, nowhere in the scrolls of truth—'

'But I hear the scream,' said the boy. 'All around me. And inside my head. Since we left for the station. It is Isaac's scream, which has never ceased.'

Refutation is made. But gently.

'You must be mistaken, boy. There was no scream. And even if there had been, it stopped at once. The Angel called out. And Isaac's heart leaped and sang at the great blessing: "I will multiply thy seed as the stars of the heaven, and as the sand which is upon the sea shore; and thy seed shall possess the gate of his enemies." And when they came home to Beersheba, they feasted and rejoiced in the Lord. The ass was put to pasture and Isaac the child was given the ram's horn, circled with gold, to blow on. It is that horn you hear, calling to the hills.'

'I don't believe you.' Even shriller. 'I don't believe you. I can't. It's like the sweets they cram in your mouth after you've had a tooth pulled. Do you know what those sweets taste like? You don't do you! Of blood and pus.'

'But Isaac loved Abraham. His love never wavered. It was Abraham his father who chose Rebekah for him. And when Abraham died at 165 years of age, his blessing was on Isaac and Isaac tore his hair in grief.'

'Bedtime stories. No man lives that long. Isaac never trusted Abraham again. Not for one instant. How could he? How could he forget the walk to Moriah, the faggots, the rope, the knife? The taste of his father's hand on his eyes and mouth, of Abraham's knee in his back, never left him. That is why Isaac was deceived by his sons, by Esau and Jacob. No Jewish father looks on his son without remembering that he may be commanded to take back his life. No Jewish son looks on his father without remembering that he may be sacrificed by his father's hand. How can there be trust or forgiveness between us? Blood and pus. Don't you smell it, you who call yourselves teachers, masters of the word?'

The young voice skidded, like a cracked pipe, soon inaudible. In the droning dark.

'And what of Sarah?'

A woman speaking. An angry chorus.

'Silence. Silence. Is it not ordained by the Law that no woman shall come to the Torah? That women, though blessed and honoured is their mystery, shall not comment on holy writ?'

'Then why are we here, behind the same closed door? You have never given us a sabbatical from pain. Never a leave of absence from massacre. Though you would have us be silent, we are branded like you. Sarah *knew*. How could she not have known? How can any mother not know when her child is taken from her to be slaughtered? Old Abraham told her to be silent, to stay out of God's unfathomable way. But she saw the wood, the rope, the knife. She smelled the cold fear in the old man's groin and the hot fear in the boy's hair. They stole away before sun-up, like foxes from the hen-house. But she was awake. She heard their lying steps on the threshold and the drowsy coughs of the serving-men. She lay awake, did Sarah, crazed with fear, her guts turning to stone. Six nights and six days, her eyes so hot with horror that she could no longer weep. And when they came back from the mountain, the men and the boy— her child, her only son—they told her to prepare a great feast, to deck the great table with fresh green, to send for flute-players and dancers from Ashod. When all she wanted was to hold the child, so close he would feel the fire in her bones, and cry out her pain. During those six days and nights, Sarah's whole life had passed before her. How Abraham had handed her over to Abimelech, king of Gerar, how he had handed her over for the king to whore with, lying to save his own precious hide, saying, "She is my sister." How other women had laughed at her, behind their fluttering hands, when she became pregnant with Isaac, how no one believed that the old frozen man was Isaac's father—did Abraham himself believe it? Sarah saw before her the years during which she had had to endure in her house, in her kitchen, in the vegetable garden, Hagar the Egyptian and the dark son she had borne Abraham, how she had had to endure the scent of burnt almonds from Hagar's skin, Abraham's scent. And even as she lay dying, Sarah heard, in Abraham's train, the chirping of women, of the concubines that came with him to Hebron. Do you really think she did not know, in her parched hollowness, that Abraham would, immediately after her death, take to wife Keturah, the girl with the good teeth? But what did it matter, what did anything matter after those days of Mount Moriah, after this boy's footsteps had been taken from the house? What could make up for that? The Holy Books report nothing of Sarah's torture. No learned commentator reports what she felt when she heard the lick of the ass's hoofs on the cobbles but dared not look whether Isaac was among the men coming home. No man, no one who has not borne a child, can imagine that. We women are not called up to read the Torah. A good thing for you. It is between the lines we would be reading, between every two lines. For in that space lies the silence of women. Who have had no say among you. It is the loudest silence in the world. Loud with the cries of labour and with the cries of all the mothers who have seen their children beaten to death in front of their eyes. But now you must hear it, you men. In this meeting-house we no longer sit and pray apart from you. Here we also are called, we daughters of silence.'

Another woman's voice, and a third: 'Dance, Miriam, dance. In this small house—'

Too small, really. Not a dancing-floor at all. Not that it terribly mattered. Men and women, oh, impropriety, young and old, were now welded so close that the merest motion, a raw breath out of a single mouth, quivered through the lot.

'A thousand years you men have argued, ravelled, spun words. You have read yourselves blind, crooked your backs, poring over the single letter or the missing vowel. A thousand years you have chanted and swayed as if truth could be caught in your fingers. You have burrowed for meaning like starved mice and pounded the

words so fine they have fallen to dust. Living men, their lips caked
with dust, as are the buried. You have hissed and croaked at one
another, owls at noontime. We have heard you when we passed the
closed shutters of the schools, we have heard you when you lay
beside us in the night, expostulators, litigants, cross-examiners,
word-peddlers even in your dreams. To what end? Have you found
those syllables which make up the secret name of God? What pun,
what game of hidden numbers has made us free? Was it all for this?'

'Thought is the dance of the mind. The spirit dances when it
seeks out meaning, and the meaning of that meaning. Perhaps
there is in the forty-ninth letter of the forty-ninth verse of the forty-
ninth chapter of the Book of Books, which lies hidden in the Torah
as the Torah rolls lie cloaked inside their shrine, a truth so mighty
that God Himself must pause when He remembers it. The dance-
steps of the soul are words, woman. The lords of the dance are we.
Are we not dancing now?'

Up steps of air.
    Which grew steeper and steeper.
    Mountainous. Higher than Moriah.
    'Dance, Miriam, dance,' said the spigot in the ceiling.
    'There is no ram now and the bush is burning.'
    Dancers, their mouths wide open. So that the hive swarmed into
their throats. And hummed to them the slurred slow song of gas.

Dan Jacobson

was born in Johannesburg, South Africa,
in 1929 and was educated at the University of Witwatersrand. In the mid-1950s he
traveled, via Israel, to England, where he
has remained ever since. Since 1976 he has
been teaching English literature at University College, London, where he is now
a professor of English. Jacobson is the
author of eleven novels and five collections
of essays, memoirs, and stories. His first
volume of short stories, *A Long Way from
London* (1958), won the Llewellyn Rhys
Memorial Prize, and his eighth novel, *The
Confessions of Josef Baisz* (1977), won the
H. H. Wingate Award. His nonfiction
includes *The Chosen People and Its God*
(1982), and he has also written a radio play,
The Caves of Abdullam (1972), based on
the biblical story of David and Saul. The
excerpt here is from the opening chapter
of *The God-Fearer* (1992), Jacobson's most
recent novel. In this work Jacobson
imagines an alternative history of Europe
in which Judaism is the dominant proselytizing religion and the 'Christer' people
are the oppressed minority. Kobus,
Jacobson's octogenarian protagonist, is
looking back on his life and is haunted
by the presence of two ghostly young
'Christer' children who force him to
question his own heartfelt assumptions
and his sense of chosenness.

Dan Jacobson

EXCERPT FROM The God-Fearer

As a man might dream of hurt he has received,
  And, dreaming, wish that it were a dream.
—Dante: *Inferno*, Canto XXX

His name was Kobus the Bookbinder. His whole life, aside from the period of his apprenticeship and early manhood, had been spent in a small town called Niedering. It lay in the most westerly region of the land of Ashkenaz.

When asked how old he was Kobus invariably replied: eighty-four. That was as good a guess as he could make. Dealing with numbers of any kind had long been difficult for him. It was impossible for him to recollect even the date attached to the current year, let alone the year of his birth. The one fact about both dates which was fixed in his mind was that each in its turn supposedly gave the sum of years that had passed since the very day on which God had created the universe.

What a story! Kobus did not believe it for a moment. It amazed him that anyone, the wisest or most self-confident of scholars included, should have had the impudence to imagine that he actually knew when the world had been created, or by whom, or for what purpose.

As with much else, Kobus kept his scepticism on this subject to himself.

By trade he had been what his cognomen suggested: a master printer and bookbinder. His achievements as a craftsman had at one time been known and respected all over his own part of the country and beyond. Together with a few journeymen and apprentices and some unskilled hands, he used to do jobbing printwork and binding of all kinds. He produced religious works in the sacred tongue, and tales of travel, poetry, medical books, and histories in our secular language. But the printshop and his stock had been sold a long time before. Neither of his sons nor his son-in-law had wished to follow him in the trade, and eventually he found it too burdensome to continue the business on his own.

His elder son had married the daughter of a landowner nearby and soon grew to look down on his father, the tradesman; the other son, the one whom Kobus had trained and favoured and nourished high hopes for, had left home to become a soldier under Manasse, the self-styled Sar of the Upperland, and nothing more had since been heard of him. Kobus's only daughter married a teacher in Niedering, a learned man in his own uninspired fashion, but quite impractical, useless as a potential successor in the printing business. His hands were plump and soft and pale, but in his father-in-law's eyes they had about as much adroitness as a pair of little trowels.

Enough of that. When he sold the house and workshop, which were on the outskirts of Niedering, Kobus and his wife Rahella moved into a smaller place: one big room downstairs, two rooms above, a yard at the back. They had thought it safer and more comfortable to be there, in a little street with neighbours nearby and the marketplace just a few minutes away. Naturally he missed (and especially at first) the space they had had before, and the orchard in front of the old house. Much to his surprise he found that he did not miss the work at all.

Rahella died about two years after they had made the move. She had been ailing and querulous for a long time before her death, which, Kobus had to confess inwardly, came as something of a relief to him. It may even have done the same for her, though he could not guess what she actually felt at the very end. By then she had fallen silent; her spells of apparent wakefulness had become as wordless as the ever-extending periods of unconsciousness into which she was constantly lapsing.

It would have been comforting for him to believe that she was resigned to her going. But for all he knew her silence may have been one of terror.

*   *   *

Even before the death of his wife, Kobus's own existence had seemed to him not much more than a kind of postscript to a life that was already concluded. Once Rahella had gone, that feeling inevitably became even stronger than before. As a man grows older—at any rate this had been his experience—it becomes more and more difficult for him to find good reasons for carrying on, quite simply. In earlier years, even when his children were quite adult, he had been able to tell himself that they still needed him, or to ask himself what would become of the business if he were to leave the scene. But now? After Rahella's death? He could no longer even say to himself, 'Well, Rahella needs me.'

His children, he knew, thought of him chiefly as a source of guilt and misgiving. (Except for the soldier, of course, who, if he was still alive, presumably thought of him not at all.) Kobus did not have any complaints against the two who were still living nearby; not at all. Both of them, in their different ways, wished to do more for him than they could, or than he would let them; they also wished that they had to do less for him than they did; then they reproached themselves for both sets of wishes. To his grandchildren, even the grown-up ones, he was a kindly stranger, hardly more: the gulf between the years he had lived and the years they still had to live was too great for either side to bridge. How could they really believe that one day they would be as old and shrivelled and bent as he was? And they were quite right to find the thought incredible, since (should they live long enough) they would then indeed no longer be the people they were when their grandfather had been alive.

As for his two tiny great-grandchildren: to them, so far as they were conscious of him at all, he surely made a bizarre and perhaps even frightening spectacle. A ten-year-old was in their eyes virtually an adult: what kind of creature, then, did they make him out to be?

All that was clear and coherent enough in his mind.

Though sometimes Kobus was not sure that his wife's name really had been Rahella. That was the name recollection offered him, the name his pen inscribed, without hesitation, with the same speed and self-assurance with which it produced any other word, when he sat at his desk, as he often did, trying to put his thoughts in order. But once the name stood there on the page, fixed, as if waiting for him to look at it, it seemed unfamiliar, even slightly menacing, difficult to associate with the silently breathing shape under the bedclothes which he had found, one morning, to be breathing no longer. 'Rahella! Rahella!' Is that what he had cried at it? At her? Is that what he said over and over again as he took her hand in his own and looked at the grey wasted face turned to one side on the pillow, with its eyes irrevocably closed? If so, why did he have no memory of the syllables on his tongue? If not, what name did she carry all the years that had gone before?

Well, setting that aside, he remained fairly sure of everything else: his name, and the name of the town he lived in, and his widowed state, and the fact that he had had three children who survived their childhood, and that he had five or possibly six grandchildren and definitely two great-grandchildren.

The real confusions in his mind began later; or began elsewhere. He could never separate the confusion that seemed to inhere in certain events from the confusions of his attempts to recollect them. He knew that an 'accident' had befallen him; but what form this accident had taken, how it happened, even when it happened—all that remained a mystery to him. He was told afterwards that he had been found on the floor, in the room downstairs, near the door to the street. How long was it after the accident that he had been found there? Nobody knew. He was unconscious. There was a gash on his forehead.

Later, when he put his hand to his brow, well above the left eye, he could touch the scar with his fingertips. Faintly tender still, it felt like a hard worm, if such an object could be imagined. What had produced it? Had he suffered an apoplexy of some kind, and cut his head in falling? Or had he merely stumbled over something? Or perhaps fought off an intruder?

Any guess was as good as any other. He had no recollection whatever of the mishap. Even the period after he had returned (more or less) to consciousness remained with him subsequently as a blur, for the most part. He remembered of it random noise; too much light; too much darkness; the presence of many strangers, or rather of people who claimed an intimacy with him he could not understand; something remorseless going on outside him and something feeble going on inside him. And of course the hideous cuppings and leechings to which he had been subjected, together with the evil-smelling and even fouler-tasting concoctions which he was compelled to swallow.

All these experiences ran promiscuously into one another and then departed, as if in a hurry, like a routed army, leaving him more or less where he had been. Recovered—ostensibly. In silence. Frailer than before. Even more distant from himself. Even more dependent than before on the ministrations of Elisabet.

Housekeeper, cook, cleaner, butt, object of pity and scorn, Elisabet was somewhat younger than her master but even less prepossessing. At least, Kobus hoped he was not deluding himself on that score. She was skinny but big-bottomed; splay-legged; bent forward at the hips and bent upwards at the neck. Denied a bridge to her nose, she had been endowed by way of compensation with exceptionally narrow, deep nostrils. The upward twist of her neck made it all the easier for the onlooker to gaze into these; as well as to take note of the limited yet exaggerated range of expressions which crossed her little face.

There was her scowl of unavailing concentration; her puffed-cheek, closed-eye acknowledgement of pain; her rare grin of pleasure, when both her elongated yellow teeth were revealed; her generalised wrinkling up from chin to forehead, which showed that respect and wonder were going on within. All these expressions were accompanied by more or less identical gasps. She spoke little, and when she did it was difficult to follow her. Her clothes were rags. Her smell was not sweet.

But Kobus was not really in a position to belittle her. (Though he did it of course; sometimes in his mind, occasionally with his pen, most often with his tongue, when she irritated him sufficiently.) She was the only person on earth to whom he remained a figure of power, even if one diminished from what he once had been. He could read, he could write, he owned many books, he had three rooms to himself, he had a son and a daughter to protect him, he had money and valuables concealed in a strong-box (she did not, he believed, know where under the floorboards it was concealed) and more money still deposited with the local Hanaper. Whereas she existed on sufferance in the hovel of her daughter and son-in-law. A paviour by trade, the latter used his fists on her, and on the daughter, and on his children too, whenever he felt particularly aggrieved about the disappointments life had brought him. Kobus had seen the marks on her.

What Elisabet longed for most in the world was for him to offer her a permanent place under his roof. No, not as his wife or mistress (her ambitions were not that elevated; and anyway she must have had a pretty good idea of his current capacities in that direction). It was promotion to the role of resident housekeeper for which she longed. So far he had not extended the invitation to her. Only when he had been confined to bed after the accident was she allowed to remain there constantly; once he had got up he banished her again. For days thereafter she went about her cooking and cleaning and other such tasks with a fierce look of injury fixed on her preposterous little face.

Bit by bit, as best he could, and with Elisabet's help, Kobus began to put together again the modest domesticities that had sustained him before the accident. He got up in the morning, ate the dishes she prepared for him, walked (a little), opened the shutters and stared out at the life (not very much of it) that passed in the street. There were plaster and lath houses like his own across the road, with tiled roofs and twisted chimney-pots; a bakery; an old woman who sold, directly from her doorway, cabbages and other greens (fresh in summer, pickled in winter) and sometimes more exotic fruits like oranges, figs, pomegranates. Though the town was considered to be quite large, farmyard as well as human smells were never far from his nostrils. There were dogs to be seen; small windows, some of them leaded and glazed, like the one Kobus looked out of; dim lights flickering here and there after dusk—that kind of thing. Occasionally he would visit his son who would bring him back in his 'carriage', as the son loved to call it, though to Kobus's eyes it was little more than a pony-trap. More often he would go to his daughter's for a meal. If time seemed to go by even more slowly than it had in the past, if he felt both more indifferent to himself and the world outside him, and yet always conscious of the sadness of the past, of the present, of the future he would never know— well, that too was merely an intensification of states long familiar to him. Stark or subdued dawns came up at his bedroom window; summer afternoons expanded as if they would never end and then contracted meekly, as they had to, into dusk; night produced its usual effects of faint gleams and isolated footsteps, sleep and wakefulness.

That he could hardly tell the events of the days apart from one another, even while he was going through them, did not worry him greatly. What he found himself incessantly puzzling over was something more trivial. Or so an outsider might have thought. It was the fact that he simply could not remember the *names* of those indistinguishable days. The Sabbath day was easy, and so was the Sabbath eve, when the whole town was hushed, and the town-guard wore their finery, or what passed as such among them, and men and boys in their best clothes could be seen going about the streets, on their way to and from the town's two places of worship. So that was the Sabbath: easy. But the next day? What was it *called?* And the day after that? Nothing should have been plainer; but in fact nothing proved more obscure to him—until the Sabbath eve would come round again, sometimes sooner than Kobus had expected it to, sometimes later.

The same problem arose with much else besides the names of days. All sorts of words, which had once seemed as firmly attached to particular things as his own name was to him, had drifted loose and would not be tethered down again. For instance, he might find himself turning over a spoon in his hand and wondering what it was called; on more than one occasion he even gazed in the same bemused fashion at his own fingers. Other appellations came readily enough, but seemed peculiarly indocile once they had arrived; they had a will of their own and led him into unfamiliar places. As with Rahella's name, they sounded strange in his own head; they made unconvincing shapes and patterns when he tried to write them down.

Ashkenaz. That was another case in point. It was, he was usually convinced, where he lived, where he had always lived; where his grandparents and (as far as he knew) their grandparents had lived; and yet, having written the word down, he would find himself staring at it as if it were the name of some foreign part he had never seen. Ashkenaz . . . Ashkenaz . . . Perhaps in the end it was nothing more than one of those mythical countries, supposedly visited by travellers of times long past, which he had read about in the books he had once made a habit of collecting. How could he tell?

There were many similar instances. When people repeated rumours about great public events (that the Muselmi had tried to put an army into the land of Pannonia and had been driven back with much loss of life; that the so-called Davidic Chief Priest of Yerusalaim had been taken prisoner by the Farasim, who had appointed their own candidate, an upstart Ectabani, in his place) he would sometimes nod wisely, as if the references they made were familiar to him. But they were not. Occasionally, in speaking to his son and daughter-in-law, he would see them exchange glances with one another: half-amused and half-alarmed. Then he would try to remember what word he had just used that might have provoked them to exchange such a look. Better, he would think, to have said something like, 'I can't remember the name,' or, 'What's it called,' or, 'Thing . . . thing,' than to have made a mincemeat of his own speech. But no, these words, whatever they were, would just fly off his tongue; apparently so right, and yet apparently so wrong.

Reading was another difficulty. He used to be a great reader. It went with the trade, he would say, by way of excuse. (Actually this was an untruth; some of the most skilled among his colleagues and competitors had been quite indifferent to the contents of what they dignified or even ennobled with their art.) He used to read all sorts of books, though never the Holy Scriptures which he had been compelled to study as a lad; nor the commentaries on these, and the commentaries which had proliferated on the commentaries. Other kinds of writing had seized his imagination—legends, histories (or what purported to be histories); above all, those travellers' tales about the sights they claimed to have seen in distant corners of the world. With them he had travelled to the land of Sinn, where the great teacher Buddh does not rule but waits eternally for men to follow him; to Hoddo, where they worship gods that have many arms and heads, many organs and many orifices to put them into; to Habbash, whence the Queen of Sheba had set out to pay tribute to the King Solomon and gone home again with his child and his

Law; to regions more remote still, where, it was said, even the Christer people had their own kings and queens; to places more fantastical than these. From such books he had become acquainted with amazing beasts, stones that spoke, rivers that flowed uphill, great cities of crystal, kingdoms without end, a copper-skinned people inhabiting a giant, unvisited continent far in the west . . .

Of all of these he had read in several languages: in the sacred tongue, in Ashkenazit, Spharadit, Latinit.

Oh yes, he had passed for a scholar, in this town at least, once upon a time.

Now he could read nothing. His eyes could no longer focus on a single line of type; not even in the narrowest of columns. His gaze constantly jumped above or below the line he was trying to read, turning everything into rubbish.

This was a further deprivation, of course. But if he were to admit the truth to himself, it was more like a deprivation remembered than felt as a present loss. It was, in the end, just another aspect of the emptiness he occupied, and which occupied him.

Into this emptiness, eventually, there came a change.

Somewhere within his mind, as if at the very corners of his brain, he became aware of movements and shifts, changes of pressure, flurries, cracks, creaks, small but decisive liftings and sinkings, as of animals stirring, or of tiles or timbers settling. What made all these nudges and tamperings more disturbing to him was precisely the fact that they seemed to be taking place not only inside his head, but also outside him, in the very fabric of the house he lived in.

Everyone who lives in solitude knows the feeling that (a) he is not alone; and (b) whatever is keeping him company is determined for its own reasons to elude him. Or rather determined both to elude him and to let him know that it is there.

So it was with him, or with whatever it was now intruding on him. Just when he wasn't looking, just when he wasn't listening, when his attention was diverted—it was then that apprehensions of this kind came to him. Quite sharp and clear, they were; and yet for all his vigilance, they always took him by surprise; he was always too late to catch the exact moment when they occurred.

Something or someone had been watching him, and he had not

known it was doing so until it was gone. A noise he had not been aware of was no longer audible; its cessation alone told him that he had missed it. Had not that door been closed when he had last looked at it? Surely that shutter or drape now hanging so still, so demurely still, had swelled forward and fallen back just a moment before. Hadn't it?

That's how it was.

Until, on an evening indistinguishable to his senses from any other, the source of the unease he had been feeling chose to make itself known.

There they were at last, made visible in front of him: the secret co-tenants of his living space.

A more innocent spectacle it would have been difficult to imagine.

It was a puzzle to Kobus, later, that he should never have doubted for a moment the connection between his visitors and all the starts and stirrings that had gone before. It was as if, from deep within a turmoil of fear and dismay, he wanted to say, 'Oh, so it was you all the time. Now I know.'

In the middle of the downstairs room, kneeling on the floor, their heads together, apparently engrossed in a game they were playing and which Kobus could not see, were two children, a boy and a girl. The girl was a year or two older, he would have guessed, than the boy. She must have been about nine years old. She was wearing a long, velvety dress, spotted with white flowers. The hem of it was spread copiously on the floor around her. The boy wore trousers and a sleeveless red jerkin; of wool, Kobus supposed. There was nothing misty or unclear about them. Kobus could see the freckles on the boy's ingenuous, chubby face; he could see the tips of the girl's little ears peeping through her hair, which hung down almost to her shoulders. She wore a small, white, close-fitting embroidered cap which was tied with ribbons beneath her chin; and her hair, which was straight and dark, seemed to spring out below the cap, as if to escape from the constraint of it. The boy's head was bare.

Their lips moved, the kneeling boy sat back on his heels, gazing downwards, the girl crouched lower over the floor, and not a sound came from them. Neither of them took the slightest notice of Kobus. He stood in the doorway, transfixed, unable to speak or to advance on them, or even to shut his eyes and so hide them from his gaze, or himself from them. All he could do was to stare. And to feel his heart banging away, as if it hung inside some empty space much larger than his breast.

Later they were gone. He did not know how much later. He did not know where they went, or how they went. He simply discovered that they were no longer there. He could move again.

His first thought was to go to the window, to see if they had somehow emerged into the street. Half of it was in sunlight, half in shadow. The vacancy of early afternoon held it in thrall. There was a tabby cat on a doorstep. A woman came out from one of the houses down the road; her face and gait were familiar to Kobus though he did not know her name. The wooden tray in which the baker's boy took around his wares every morning lay on the ground, with its heavy leather strap coiled on it.

This familiar scene was uncanny too: uncanny in its ordinariness, its ignorance of the encounter he had just been through.

Then Kobus said out aloud, 'What's the matter with you, you old fool? Why shouldn't your grandchildren come to play here? Their mother must have left them. Little Braam and . . . what's her name? . . . Thirza?'

But he heard in his own voice the falsity of what he was saying. Braam and Thirza, indeed! The children he had seen did not look like his recollection of Braam and Thirza. That he was certain of. Also that his grandchildren were older than these. And there was something else about them which was even stranger to him than their faces and figures.

Since when, he had to ask himself, did his grandchildren wear the clothes of the Christer—of the followers of Yeshua, Jesus, the Christus, the Natzerit, whatever they liked to call him? The one who had supposedly lived and died and lived again a thousand years before; or perhaps even more than that, for all bewildered Kobus could tell. The girl's cap; the boy's bare head; his red sleeveless jerkin: these were unmistakable signs. So were their little boots. For some reason, sunk beyond recall in an immemorial tradition or superstition, only they, the Christer, wore boots with buttons down the side; the God-Fearers never did. In his childhood Kobus and his friends had believed devoutly that the Christers' boots had to be buttoned in that style because of some quality peculiar to pig-leather.

Even then it surprised him that he should have remembered such a thing so clearly—the buttons, that is, and the childish tale about them—when he recollected how long it was since he had last actually seen any of the Christer in the flesh. When the Amar Yotam had driven them away he had told the people that he was also driving away all their troubles. Famines, plagues, poverty, even their own stupidity.

The first sight of the children was inevitably etched with its own particular sharpness in Kobus's mind. But the other visits they made eventually ran together indistinguishably. Having come once, the children came before him again and again. Soon they had come so many times it was impossible for him even to estimate how often he had seen them. There were single days when he found himself sharing moments of their lives on perhaps half-a-dozen separate occasions. There were also days, and days following on days, when he saw them not at all, and began to assume or to hope that they had gone for good.

They never behaved in a manner that was at all out of the ordinary—apart, of course, from the inexplicability of their very presence, of their mode of manifesting themselves and then vanishing. The apparent ordinariness of their demeanour was itself one of the strangest things about them. It might have been (to judge from the way they looked and acted) that they had just returned from a walk, or had just eaten a meal, or were waiting for their mother to finish a task before taking them out of the house. The gestures of the girl's slender hands and the quiver of her lively brown eyes became familiar to Kobus; so did the boy's slouching or dragging walk, which had worn down the outer sides of the heels of his wooden-soled boots. More than that: as in some ineluctable dream, Kobus felt that everything about them had always been familiar to him; he had an intimacy with them which it was impossible for him to explain. In the presence of the children there was no need to explain it: he simply knew them, and had always known them, and that was all.

Yet this too was a source of fear and bewilderment. From where did this conviction come? Where had he met them before? How was it that he knew the slender column of the girl's upright, unlined neck, every pale curve and hollow of it; that he was sure he would recognise her voice if only she would speak to him; that her dresses and the stockings that went with them were to his eyes just as they should have been? And the red scratch that suddenly appeared on the back of the boy's hand—that too was known to him. The next time he came Kobus looked for it; and yes, it was still there; only it had darkened slightly, as it had begun to heal.

Yet of him, their watcher, their knower, their host, they took not the slightest notice. They looked at him and beyond him; they walked towards him and through him; he saw them in front of him and turned to find them behind him. Never a word did they say to him. Then they were gone. He saw them wear expressions angry, playful, absorbed, thoughtful; they talked to each other (inaudibly), smiled (at he knew not what), held hands, gazed out of his window, looked (as incomprehendingly as Elisabet herself) at the backs of the books on his shelves. Not a sound from them ever managed to reach his ears; and not a sound from his full breast and contracted throat and dry mouth apparently reached theirs.

So vivid they were, full-fleshed, space-occupying, light-blocking, at one instant; nothing at all the next. Each time they had gone, he remained staring at an emptiness which now contained not the faintest remembrance of their presence. No rug or pillow was disarranged, there was no scent in the air, nothing they might have touched was ever out of place.

Gabriel Josipovici

was born in Nice in 1940 and educated at
Victoria College, Cairo, and at Oxford
University. Since 1963 he has been a member of the School of European Studies at
the University of Sussex where he is now
professor of English. In 1981 he gave the
Northcliffe Lectures at London University
and in 1996–97 he was the Lord Weidenfeld Visiting Professor of Comparative Literature at Oxford. He has published a
number of critical works, eleven novels,
and two volumes of short stories, and his
plays have been performed on stage and by
the BBC. In a Hotel Garden (1993) is a novel
about memory and, like many of Josipovici's novels, about the hold of the past
on the present. In the excerpt here Ben
relates to his skeptical English friends
the story of a prewar love affair between
Lily's grandmother and her Italian-Jew-
ish cousin, and gives vent to his growing
obsession with Lily.

Gabriel Josipovici

EXCERPT FROM **In a Hotel Garden**

IX Lots of People

Walking up Putney Hill with Rick and the dog, Ben says:—I tried
to phone this morning.

—I was in all the time.

—No no. Phone Lily.

—Lily who?

—The woman I told you about. From the Dolomites.

—Sit! Rick says.

The dog looks up at him pleadingly.

—Sit!

The dog, still looking at him, lowers his behind a few inches.

—Go on, Rick says. Sit!

The dog sighs, lowers his behind a little further.

—Now! Rick says.

Once across the road he lets the dog go and he disappears into
the bushes in a cloud of dust.

—Go on, Rick says to his friend.

—I just said I tried to phone her.

—And what happened?

—Happened?

—When you phoned.

—I got the chap.

—Oh? Rick says. He whistles for the dog, who comes scurrying
out of the bushes, his nose close to the ground, crosses their path
and disappears again on the other side.

—I thought you weren't going to phone her, Rick says. Isn't that
what you'd decided?

—Yes, Ben says.

Rick stops and whistles. Nothing happens. They begin to walk again, in the direction of the pond.

—What made you change your mind? Rick asks him after a while.

—I don't know.

—And so, Rick says. What happened?

—He went off to call her, Ben says. Then came back and said she didn't seem to be around.

—So?

—I think she may not be there anymore.

—But if he went to call her?

—He could have been pretending.

—Pretending what?

—To call.

—You mean for your benefit?

—I had the feeling there was nobody there.

—But why shouldn't he just say so?

—I don't know, Ben says. I just had the feeling.

The dog is suddenly at their heels. Ben pats his head and the dog licks his hand, leaving a web of saliva over his fingers.

—Do you think I should try again? he asks, bending to rub his hand on the dog's coat.

—What made you change your mind? Rick asks, as they enter the underpass.

—In what way?

—I thought you weren't going to phone her.

—I don't know, Ben says.

They emerge and head for the pond.

—I just decided, Ben says. It seemed silly not to. If I was curious.

—And now? Rick says.

—I don't know. I'd like to know if she's there.

—I thought you said she'd decided not to go back to him, Rick says.

—I don't know, Ben says. I thought so, yes.

They start to walk round the pond, the dog at their heels.

—I thought I'd just say hello, Ben says.

—Why not? Rick says.

—But now I don't know whether to phone again or not.

—Because you mean he might do the same thing again?

—Uhuh.

—Why not write?

—He might simply throw the letter away, Ben says. And then I wouldn't know if she'd got it and was deliberately not answering or had never got it and would have answered if she had.

—Well then phone, Rick says.

—The same thing could happen again.

The dog has disappeared. Ben whistles for him as they walk.

Rick looks at his watch.

The dog comes round a bend in the path ahead of them, his nose covered in dust.

—Good boy! Ben says, kneeling down and embracing him.

—Shall we go back? Rick says.

—I don't mind.

—Come on boy, Rick says.

They turn and begin to walk back. The dog doesn't move.

—Good boy! Rick says, stopping and looking back at him. Good boy! Food's waiting!

The dog stands still, looking at them.—Come! Rick says. Come Em, come! Good boy! Good boy!

—Good boy Em, Ben says, patting his knees encouragingly. Come on boy! Come!

—He'll come as soon as he loses sight of us, Rick says, setting off again.

—I suppose, Ben says, hurrying after him, I could just phone and ask for her again and then if he puts me off again ask if she really is still living there.

—Why not? Rick says, quickening his pace.

—As if I knew nothing about their relationship and just thought she had a room there or something, Ben says, hurrying to keep up with him.

—Why not? Rick says again. He stops and looks back.

—But he could say yes and then not do anything about it if I left a message, Ben says, stepping a yard or two ahead of him.

—You could go out there and see her, Rick says. See for yourself.

—Oh I couldn't do that, Ben says.

—Why not?

—I wouldn't want to spy on her.

—Who said anything about spying?

—Well, Ben says, if I was snooping around waiting to catch a glimpse of her . . .

There is a sound of thundering feet and the dog is upon them.— Good boy! Rick says, hugging him. Good boy.

He disentangles the lead from his neck and snaps it on the dog's collar.

—I suppose I could try phoning once more, Ben says. And then decide.

—Why should he try to hide her from you? Rick asks as they head for home.

—I don't know, Ben says. I just had the feeling he was calling out in an empty house.

—On the phone?

—How do you mean, on the phone?

—You were able to sense that on the phone?

—You know how it is. There was a sort of echo.

—But if she was out it would be empty, wouldn't it?

—I just felt he was pretending to call, Ben says. He knew there was no one there and just pretended to call.

—Sit, Rick says.

The dog sits at once. They wait for a break in the traffic.

—One can get an impression of something like that, Ben says. Even at a distance.

—Come, Rick says. He takes his friend's arm and the three of them quickly cross the road.

—It's to do with echo, Ben says as they set off down the hill. Even on the phone you can sense the echo if a house is empty.

—Only if it's really empty, Rick says. If there isn't any furniture or anything.

—You can sense if someone is only pretending to call, Ben says.

—Oh yes, Rick says, you can always sense that.

—It's to do with a lack of belief in the call itself, Ben says. You can sense that on the phone.

—Oh yes, Rick says. You can sense that on the phone. Come on boy! he says, as the dog drags him sideways across the pavement.

—Especially if you're looking out for something funny, Ben says.

The dog pulls them down the hill.

—She went because her mother had sat there years before with some man she didn't even marry? Francesca says.

—Grandmother, Ben says.

—Grandmother then, Francesca says. It makes even less sense.

—It was important to her, Ben says.

—Do you understand what it was all about? Francesca asks Rick.

—In a way, he says. But—

—Went where? Robert asks.

—Don't interrupt, his mother says.

—Went where?

—To a garden in Siena, Ben says.

—What garden?

—Eat your supper, his father says.

—I have.

—You've still got some on your plate.

—It's bad.

—What do you mean bad?

—It's bad. Look at it.

—There's nothing wrong with it.

—The potatoes are black.

—Come on, his father says. Eat up.

—I can't. Look at it. It's all black.

—If there's a black spot in it, cut it out.

—I can't. It's all black.

—Robert, his father says.

—Dad!

—I'll give you another, his mother says.

—I don't want another. I'm not hungry any more.

—All right, his mother says. You can go out and play if you want.

—I want my pudding.

—Then finish what's on your plate first.

—It's bad. I want my pudding.

—All right, his mother says. You'll have it when I serve it up for all of us.

Robert pushes his plate away from him and rubs his mouth furiously with his napkin.

—It meant something to her, Ben says to Francesca. When she told me about it I could see it meant something. I just haven't been able to convey it properly.

She clears away their plates and brings the pudding to the table.

—It seems, Ben says, that the whole family was killed by the Nazis. The old mother, that is, and the brother and his wife and their children and him and his wife and children.

—How did she find out? Rick asks.

—I don't know. She may have been told. They were quite a well-known family in Trieste.

Robert holds out his empty plate.

—You want a second helping? his mother asks him.

He nods.

—Don't you have a tongue?

He nods again.

—Well?

—Please.

She refills his plate.

—She never saw him again? Rick asks.

—No, Ben says. He actually went on writing to her for a while but she never replied and eventually he stopped.

Robert holds out his empty plate again.

—No, his mother says. You've had enough.

—Please.

—No.

—Please, Mum!

—Go on, Rick says. Give him a spoonful.

—I think a cousin survived, Ben says. It may have been through him she heard.

—There, Francesca says. But no more. Understand?

—She was in touch with this cousin? Rick asks.

—I don't know, Ben says. She didn't say.

Robert licks his spoon and puts it down on his empty plate.

—Can I go now? he asks.

—Yes dear, his mother says. Fold your napkin.

—I think that's what made such an impression on her, Ben says.

—What? Rick says.

—That it might have been her grandfather and he was killed like that.

—He couldn't have been her grandfather, Francesca says. If they'd married she wouldn't have existed.

—One doesn't think like that, does one? Ben says.

—I said fold your napkin, Francesca says to her son.

—One can't imagine not being, Ben says. Only being slightly different.

—I said fold it, Francesca says. Come on. Don't be silly.

—I think that's what she was trying to understand, Ben says. Why the garden was so important to her.

—Because they died like that? Francesca says, folding her son's napkin and putting it in its ring.

—Because of everything, Ben says.

—I still don't get it, Francesca says.

—I haven't explained it very well.

—No, no. I probably didn't understand.

And, later, when he has gone, she says to Rick:—I really can't see what the fuss is about. He wasn't even her grandfather.

—That's just the point, isn't it? Rick says.

—Lots of people died in the war, she says. If one started to get upset because of every single one of them there'd be no end to it. I mean it would be different if she'd actually known this chap.

And when he is silent she says:—Explain it to me then. Explain to me just what you think the point is.

—I can't really, he says. But I think I understand what he means.

—Well if you understand then explain it to me.

—I can't, Fran, he says. If you don't see it you don't see it.

—I'm fed up with people being obsessed by the Holocaust, she says. It's done and we've got to move on.

—It's different if you're Jewish, Rick says.

—I don't see why, she says. I don't say we must forget. Only not make it an excuse for all sorts of private hang-ups.

—How do you mean an excuse?

—Just an excuse.

—How do you mean?

—Oh never mind, she says. If you don't see it you don't see it.

—Come on, Fran, he says. That's no way to argue.

—He's always like that, she says. He can't have a simple affair based on sex or mutual interests or anything. It always has to be these odd-ball things nobody understands and he gets tired of before the year's out.

—I don't know what you mean, he says.

—Don't you?

—No.

—Well with Sand it was because he was curious about how anyone could work for something called the Egg Marketing Board and with Henrietta it was because she'd been raped and he was sorry for her and with Nancy it was because her mother had been a tightrope walker.

—Oh come on! he says.

—It's true, she says. Just think about it.

—And with you?

—That was just an adolescent crush, she says.

—Well, he says, we've all got our quirks.

—What's that supposed to mean?

—Nothing. Just what I said.

—Well, she says, all I can say is that some of us are a lot quirkier than others.

—I don't see why you say that.

—Don't you?

—No I don't, he says.

—Why do you always stand up for him like that? she says. You know basically you agree with me.

—I don't agree with you, he says. You always say that, as if I had to agree with you or be deliberately perverse.

—But you are, she says. You take the other side just to have an argument.

—You think I like arguing with you?

—I don't know why else you do it then.

—There you go again, he says.

—I go again?

—If what you say is true, he says, everybody would always be of the same opinion as everybody else. It's ridiculous.

—I didn't say everybody, she says. I said you and I.

—We always have to agree about everything?

—No. But we usually do. Only you won't admit it.

—That's ridiculous, Rick says.

And, later still, after he's walked the dog and they are putting out the lights downstairs, he says:—We've all got our quirks you know. You've got yours and I've got mine as much as he has his.

—All I can say then, she says, is that I'm glad I don't have his.

—So am I, he says. But there's no reason to be so dismissive of his.

—I wasn't dismissive, she says. I just said it didn't make sense to me.

—There's a lot of things about other people that don't make sense, he says. But that's no reason to dismiss them.

—What's the matter with you tonight? she says. I told you I wasn't dismissing him.

—I don't know what you were doing then, he says.

—I told you, she says. I just said I couldn't understand what all the fuss was about.

—It's not fuss, he says as he climbs into bed.

—All right, she says. I can't understand what this woman was on about or why he was so taken up by it.

—Perhaps she's beautiful, he says.

—I wouldn't get so upset for him if he fell for beautiful women, she says, putting out the light on her side of the bed. That would be understandable. But it's this other thing I find so peculiar.

—I don't see anything very seductive about working for the Egg Marketing Board, he says, putting out the light on his side and yawning.

—That's exactly it, she says. Don't you see? It intrigued him that anyone could work for something so unseductive.

—She was quite striking though, he says after a while.

—Who?

—Sand.

—Sand? You found her striking?

—She's a striking woman. Of course she is.

—Only a man could see her as striking, she says.

—I'm speaking as a man, he says, yawning again.

—I thought she was vulgar beyond belief, she says.

—Did you?

—Yes.

—Ah, he says, but this time the word is engulfed by a third, enormous yawn.

x Edmund Spencer

—I didn't think you'd come, he says.

—Why?

—I don't know. I just didn't.

She is silent, looking down at her feet.

—First, he says, I didn't think you'd call back. Then I didn't think you'd come.

—Why didn't you think I'd call back?

—I don't know. I wasn't even sure if you were still there. If you remember, the last time we spoke you said you might not go back.

—I couldn't leave Bess, she says. I really couldn't.

—So you're prepared to put up with Frank for the sake of the dog?

—Oh, she says, it's not like that.

They start to walk along the Embankment towards Westminster Bridge.

—Why didn't you think I'd call you back?

—I don't know.

—I was out at my Yoga. Then it was too late to call you that evening.

—Anyway, he says, here you are.

—Here I am, she says.

—Everything's back to where it was before.

She laughs.

—Did you ever finish *The Ambassadors*? she asks.

—No. I'll have to start again next year.

—You could always read it when you're not on holiday.

—No, he says. It's my holiday book. I'll finish it one day.

They walk.

—You told your mother? he asks.

—Told her what?

—About seeing the garden.

—No.

—But I thought—?

—I never talked about it with her, she says. I don't even know if Granny ever told her.

—I see, he says. But you never asked her if she knew? If they had talked about it?

—No, she says. She's a different kind of person altogether.

—Yes but still . . .

—She's mainly interested in her health.

They walk.

—And you? he says. Have you understood what you were looking for there?

She laughs.

—Have you?

—Not really, she says.

—I've been thinking about it, he says.

—You?

—It's as if you'd given me something to think about. Literally.

She laughs.

They climb the steps to the bridge, cross the road and go down the steps to the other side.

—To be honest, she says, a horrible suspicion has begun to dawn on me.

—Oh? he says.

—About the garden.

—What about it?

—I think it may not have been the right one.

—Not the right one?

—But it doesn't matter, she says. Does it?

—I don't know, he says. I . . .

—It was at the airport, she says. I was thinking about it all and I suddenly heard Granny's voice saying on the south side of town and this one was west.

—How do you know?

They draw aside to let a group of joggers pass.

—When the sun set it was between the sun and the town, she says, when they resume their walk.

—That's all very vague, he says.

—I looked at the map, she says. I found monuments in the guide book they said they were in the south part of town. It wasn't where the hotel was.

—You're sure she said south?

—I think so. Yes.

—You don't think she made a mistake.

—She could have. But why be so precise?

—But there couldn't be two hotels in Siena with that sort of garden, he says.

—If there was one, she says, why not two?

He is silent, at her side.

—That must have been the pattern, mustn't it? she says. In the old palazzos. Build them on the edge of the plateau with a garden stretching out at the back, looking out over the valley to the hills beyond.

Another group of joggers forces them up against the embankment wall.

—It doesn't matter though, does it? she says, when they are walking again. Even if it wasn't Siena but San Gimignano, say.

—But, he says, if you sat there and began to feel that you understood something about your life and why you . . . and then you . . .

—I don't think it matters, she says. But I felt I had to tell you.

—Why?

—Because you'd listened. Because you'd helped me to talk about it. I didn't want to think . . .

—I wouldn't ever have known, would I? he says.

—I just felt bad, she says. I felt like a fraud.

—So that's why you said you were glad I'd rung?

—Yes.

They walk on towards Lambeth Bridge.

—Is Sandra all right now? she asks.

—Sandra? I wouldn't know.

—Oh?

—I don't see her any more, he says.

—You mean . . . ?

—Yes.

She is silent.

They reach Lambeth Bridge and stop.

—So it *was* a mistake, she says. Going to the mountains.

—Why a mistake?

—Well if—. Oh, she says. I see.

—I feel a lot better myself, he says.

They lean against the embankment wall and look down at the river.

—What about your father? he asks.

—What about him?

—He's well?

—He's always well, she says. He likes to let you know it too.

They watch the driftwood glide past.

—They went walking in the Himalayas, she says.

—Who did?

—My father and his family.

—Really?

—Remarkable, he said it was.

—What was remarkable about it?

—Oh, she says, everything.

He is silent.

—You've seen him then? he says at last.

—Him?

—Your father.

—I go there for lunch on the first Sunday of every month, she says.

—I didn't realize it was that regular.

—My father likes regularity.

—And you?

—Me?

—I mean, how did it feel, seeing him after your experience in the garden and everything?

—It was interesting, she said. I tried to measure the distance between us. To see if it had made any difference.

—And had it?

—Yes, she says.

—In what way?

—I don't know, she says. I just feel more established in my difference now I've been there. Do you understand?

—Yes, he says. I think so. But if it wasn't even . . . ?

—I told you, she says. That doesn't matter. It was sitting there and feeling the place and feeling how it must have been all those years ago and feeling time sort of standing still before starting to flow again.

—And then you came back to the same life, he says.

—That's what made it possible, she says.

—How possible?

—I don't know how to explain, she says.

They watch the boats move slowly past them.

—I suppose it's to do with a past, she says. Having your own past and nobody else's. This is you. There isn't anyone else like that. There never was and never will be. So it's a responsibility.

He is silent.

—You remember when we talked about Absalom? she says. That first evening?

—Of course, he says.

—He had his hair, she says. No one else had hair like that.

—I had a look at that passage, he says. With a father like that what else could he do?

—He chose to act as he did, she says. He chose to do that with his hair.

—But that past, he says. What you told me about it. It has nothing to do with you, does it? It was just an episode in your grandmother's life. It may not even have happened as she told it.

—It doesn't matter, she says. That day was a turning point for her. And for me.

—But it didn't change anything.

—It did for me, she says.

He is silent.

—Shall we go back? she says.

They turn back in the direction of the Festival Hall.

—Not just that day as she told it, she says. But everything that happened afterwards.

—You mean his death?

—Everything, she says.

—You see, she says, it's the silence that's so frightening. This man who sent a donkey and then more and more letters, which she never answered. And then his life was snuffed out. And all that's left is what my grandmother told me about that garden.

—But what kind of a man was he? he says. First he's engaged and then he's rushing after your grandmother and promising to meet her when she comes back to Italy and then he's back with his fiancée but still writing to her. Does his death really make all that meaningful?

—What's meaningful? she says.

They climb the steps and recross Westminster Bridge.

—Anyway, she says, when something like that happens it makes you think not just about your own past but about that of Jews as a whole.

—Why not mankind? he says. Why stop at Jews?

—One can't think in those terms, she says. At least I can't. It's too vague. It doesn't mean anything.

—And the past of Jews means something?

—To me, yes, she says.

—But you told me you don't believe.

—Not in God, no.

—Well then.

—God has nothing to do with it.

—How can you talk about Jews without talking about God?

—It's easy, she says.

—You mean they were deluded?

—It doesn't matter to me whether they were or they weren't, she says. What happened to the Jews in the past and then in this century—that's alive for me. Through him.

—It came to me at the airport, she says. Why it was so important, that garden. It's as if that day their whole lives were present to them, their lives before and their lives after. Everything that would happen and not happen and all that would happen and not happen to their descendants. Everything. Enclosed in that garden. Held together by the trees and the wall and the silence. That's why I had to go there. To feel it for myself.

—Except that it was the wrong garden.

—It doesn't matter where it was, she says. The important thing is that everything came together in a single moment in a single enclosed spot. And if I could really feel it, really understand it, then perhaps I could understand why I was alive and what I had to do.

—And do you?

—Of course not, she says.

They walk in silence.

—One never does, she says, does one?

He points with his foot:—Look. They take the trouble to cut quotations into the concrete and then they can't even spell the names of the poets right. Sweet Thames run softly till I end my song. Edmund Spencer. With a cee. That's the nineteenth-century philosopher. And he was called Herbert, not Edmund.

—I'd never noticed, she says.

—It's new, he says. Part of the general refurbishment. But they're like bad imitators pretending to be part of a tradition. Everything's a little bit wrong.

—Of course, he says, the Elizabethans weren't too worried about spelling and Spenser may even sometimes have spelt his name with a cee, but somehow I don't think whoever did this was sophisticated enough to be trying to draw that to our attention.

They walk on.

—Isn't it strange, he says, that we should be walking here like this and talking about life and death and God as if we were talking about the weather.

—How else should one talk about it?

—I don't know, he says. It's just strange.

They draw level with the Festival Hall.

—So, he says, you've gone back after all.

—Back?

—To Frank. Your life.

—For the moment, she says. Yes.

—Just for the moment?

—The crisis comes, she says, and then it passes. And one just goes on. Nothing ever really clears up though one keeps thinking it will. And then the sense of crisis recedes. For a little while at least.

—I thought you said you'd found a new strength, he says. In your difference.

—From my father, she says. Yes.

They stop and look at the river.

—Anyway, she says, one says things like that. One even believes it. But it's the jargon of the time, isn't it?

—It doesn't correspond to anything?

—I don't know, she says. At moments I suppose one thinks it does. But one can never really step outside, can one, and really see things clearly?

She glances at her watch.

—I have to go, she says.

—Now? he says. I thought we might have a cup of coffee.

—No. I'm sorry. I have to go.

—Home?

—I've got some shopping to do.

—I see.

She stands beside him.

—Which way are you going? he asks her.

—I'll walk over Hungerford Bridge.

—I'll come with you.

—No. Please.

She holds out her hand:—Thank you. For agreeing to see me.

—Well it was you who . . .

—Goodbye.

He takes her hand:—Goodbye.

She turns and hurries up the stairs. He stands, watching her, waiting for her to turn at the top and wave to him.

Jonathan Wilson

was born in London in 1950 and educated at the University of Essex, Oxford University, and the Hebrew University of Jerusalem. He teaches English and American literature at Tufts University, Medford, Massachusetts, and was made a Guggenheim Fellow in fiction for 1994–95. Wilson's stories have been published in the *New Yorker* and *Tikkun* and have been collected in *Schoom* (1993). His novel *The Hiding Room* (1995), set in Jerusalem, was the runner-up for the Jewish Quarterly/ Wingate fiction prize. 'From Shanghai' (1993) characteristically combines a British-Jewish story with a more global perspective.

Jonathan Wilson

From Shanghai

The advice note, dropped on my father's desk in the first week of
September 1955, lay unread for a week. My father was away from
home, resolving a dispute over burial sites in Manchester. He was
a synagogue troubleshooter, the Red Adair of Anglo-Jewish internecine struggles, and it was his job to travel up and down the country,
mollifying rabbis and pacifying their sometimes rebellious congre-
gations. It was only when he returned to his office in Tavistock
Square that he learned that a package awaited him at London docks.
My father was a little confused. The note had come from the Office
of Refugee Affairs, a department, now almost defunct, that he had
little to do with. What could possibly be sent to him, and why?

During his lunch hour he travelled to Tilbury, emerging by the
loading dock on the river where bulky cargo vessels lined up beneath
towering cranes. It took him a long time to locate the appropriate
office, and even longer to find the right collection point. But my
father was used to bureaucrats, and patient with them, and he chat-
ted amiably while the papers he had brought with him were perused
and stamped.

In the warehouse, he was presented not with the brown paper
parcel that he had imagined but with two enormous crates, lowered
to his feet by a man on a forklift truck.

'What's in them?' asked my father.

'No idea, guv. They're in off the boat from Shanghai.'

'I see,' said my father, utterly bemused. After the usual delays
and indignation, a crowbar was provided, and my father, with the
reluctant aid of the forklift driver, pried open one of the wood slats
on the side of the crate. The driver, his inquisitiveness aroused,
tore through some thin paper wrapping.

'Looks like books,' he said.

'Books?'

'Yes, mate, books.'

'But who from?'

They searched the surface of the crate; the bill of lading indicated only 'P.O. Box 1308, Shanghai'.

'Well, I've got work to do,' the driver announced, remounting his forklift and starting the engine.

My father reached into the crate and dislodged one of the books. It was a German translation of *The Collected Tales of Hans Andersen*, strongly bound in blue linen. He took out another book: it was written in a language he couldn't understand, Japanese or Chinese. The third book was, again, the *Collected Tales*, but this time in English. He tugged out five more illustrated English-language versions of *The Fairy Tales of Hans Andersen*. My father returned to the Far Eastern text and flicked through the pages. Sure enough, there were the tell-tale drawings: a duckling, a nightingale, three dogs with eyes as big as saucers.

Over the next few months more and more crates arrived, each one adding to the Andersen collection. My father arranged to have them held in a warehouse near the docks. My mother was less than pleased with the extra expense imposed upon our family by this storage of books from nowhere. After all, we had only recently been freed from the restrictions of wartime rationing: filling the larder was her priority, not the unasked-for freight of a phantom dispatch agent. But my father reacted in his usual lighthearted manner, as if we had all entered a fairy tale. From out of the blue a gift had come our way. Who could possibly guess what the magical consequences might be?

By the end of the year we had some twenty thousand books in storage. One winter morning, under a cold blue sky, my father took me down to the warehouse with him to view the crates. It was like a trip to the pyramids. I ventured cautiously into the dark alleyways between the wood containers, piled three high, as if these mysterious monuments held an ancient power. What on earth had we come to possess? Of course, my father had written to the P.O. Box in Shanghai, but so far he had received no reply.

As we walked away from the docks, the ships grew smaller and smaller in the distance, until they looked like the curios at the fun fair that you could snatch up with the metal jaws of a miniature crane. I asked my father, as I had heard my mother ask him in a moment of frustration and anger, why we didn't sell the books. 'Because they are not ours to sell,' he replied.

It was Sunday, and we were both free, for the only day of the week, from the dual constraints of work (homework in my case) and synagogue. We walked all the way to Tower Bridge. A small crowd had gathered in an open area on the wharf. Nearby, on the river, a brightly painted houseboat, The Artful Dodger, had been moored.

A small, muscular man, with a shaved head and an ugly tattoo inscribed upon his forearm—barbed wire entwining a naked woman—was passing round a set of heavy chains for the crowd to inspect. Shortly he bound himself up. My father, who appeared more captivated than most, was selected to turn, and then pocket, the key of a massive padlock that secured our escapologist. The Artful Dodger then asked my father to gag him. After this a giggling woman from the audience helped the escapologist step into a burlap sack, laid out on the flagstone next to him. This accomplished, the woman waved to her cheering friends, and tightened the drawstring with a flourish.

Behind the writhing sack, the black Thames flowed hastily. Two swift Sunday-morning scullers, who had taken my attention, disappeared behind a chugging tugboat. By the time they emerged, our prisoner was free. I wasn't surprised. I knew his trick. I had read all about Houdini in a school library book. I knew that our man had swallowed a duplicate key before the show, and then regurgitated it while in the sack. But, to my astonishment, I found myself no less impressed. Escape, however it was accomplished, was the glittering thing.

In the spring, my Uncle Hugo arrived from Shanghai. He wasn't really my uncle but my father's second cousin. He brought with him his wife, Lotte, and nothing more than the clothes on their backs. At first, of course, he was simply a stranger who walked into my father's office one day in March, and announced that he had come to claim both the Andersen books and a relationship.

My father took Hugo for lunch, by which I mean that they went to a nearby park, sat on a bench, and shared sandwiches. It was one

of those transitional spring days, when it is warm enough in the
sun but still very cold in the shade. While they sat, side by side,
lifting their faces to the pale medallion in the sky, Hugo told his
story. He had been expelled from his home in the Austrian Burgen-
land in 1938. Like many others he had fled, in desperation, to the
International Settlement in Shanghai, the only city in the world he
could enter without a visa. A gentile friend, Artur Jelinek, a philate-
list, had forwarded the Andersen books to China with money left
for the purpose by Hugo. He had lived in Shanghai for fifteen years,
working as a technician in a hospital laboratory. By profession he
was a biologist, he had written a botanical treatise on mushrooms;
by inclination he was a bibliophile. In Austria, before the war,
through penny-pinching, perseverance and resourcefulness, he had
accumulated what he believed to be the world's second largest collection of Hans Andersen books, exceeded only by the corpus
owned by the Danish royal family.

My father listened. There had been, of course, a thousand refugee
stories in wide circulation in the London Jewish community in the
previous ten years; most reported greater hardship, some less. Hugo
had escaped early. He was lucky. Of course, his life had been terribly
disrupted, but he was alive, he was here, his collection was intact.

'But how did you get to me?' my father asked.

'Your cousin, Miki, the one who . . . '

My father nodded before Hugo could proceed. He already knew
the details, and wanted to spare himself the pain of hearing them
repeated.

'Well,' Hugo continued, 'before—that is, some months before—
he was taken, when I was about to leave, he gave me your name. He
told me that you were an administrator for Jews. The address of the
office I discovered in Shanghai.'

'But why,' my father continued, 'didn't you reply to my letters?'

'Arthritis,' Hugo replied, and held his misshapen hands out for
my father to inspect. 'I cannot hold a pen.'

'But surely . . . ' my father stopped. Sometimes, he told me later,
an excuse, given for whatever reason, simply has to be accepted.

Hugo had met Lotte in Shanghai. Like him she was a refugee
from Hitler's Europe. But, unlike him, she was vivacious and energetic. Partly this derived from the fact that she was twenty years

Hugo's junior. Although Hugo was only in his mid-fifties, he was, to my eyes, an old man, with his shock of white hair and deeply lined face. It was Lotte who enchanted me. She would arrive for Saturday-night dinner in a fox-fur stole (borrowed from her neighbour) and chain-smoke through a long cigarette holder. She liked to sing, and after supper she would call my father to the upright piano in our dining room. He would accompany her in feisty, throaty renditions of songs in German that I couldn't understand, but of which both Hugo and my mother appeared to disapprove. I would like to stand near Lotte, in the aura of her rich heavy perfume, and take deep breaths.

Lotte's family, miraculously, had survived the war and were now dispersed all over the world. Her parents were in America with her sister, Grete; one of her brothers was in Buenos Aires, the other in Israel. Sometimes she would bring me the latest postcards and letters that she had received, and together we would sit in the kitchen, soak the stamps off, and carefully catalogue them in my album. You might have thought that this kind of activity would have been more up Hugo's street, but he remained remarkably indifferent to me, almost cold, until the day that my father gave me the present.

Two evenings a week my father took art classes at the Adult Education programme of St Martin's School of Art. The works that he produced provoked a great deal of hilarity in our household. He generally painted nudes. The teacher, not rich in imagination, seemed to demand two poses of his models. The first a dull, straightforward, upright-seated position in a high-backed chair; the second, a 'sensual', provocative draping of the body over a velvet-backed chaise longue. My father, an admirer of Matisse but not a great colourist himself, would bring home to us strange light-brown figures, twisted, not altogether intentionally, into expressionist poses. He would line his canvases up against a wall in the hall. My brother and I would collapse in laughter. My mother, busy with supper, barely gave the works more than a passing glance. To his credit, my father took our cruel responses very well. For two nights a week he seemed to enjoy playing the part, not of the overburdened synagogue administrator, but of the lonely artist struggling in a hostile, philistine world.

Perhaps in order to establish for himself evidence of the duality of his personality, or perhaps, in some unconscious way, to sanctify the graven images that he created, my father initialled all his paintings in the bottom righthand corner, but with *Hebrew* letters: a serpentine *lamed* and squarish *vav* that served to represent the artist, Leslie Visser.

After the arrival of Hugo and Lotte, I thought I began to detect something new in 'Lamed Vav's' paintings (my brother and I had taken up the initials as sobriquet). I may have been mistaken, but it seemed to me that the faces of the nudes were coming more and more to carry Lotte's features: her full lips and unmistakable green eyes. But whether this was the result of my fantasies or those of 'Lamed Vav' has never been clear to me.

My father had a friend at the art class, a man named Joe Kline, who worked as a salesman for the publishing company of Eyre & Spottiswoode. One night, my father came home with a small cardboard box packed with four hardback books. 'More?' said my mother, who was suspicious of all transactions involving bound volumes. We were still defraying the costs of the Andersen storage until Hugo and Lotte could 'get on their feet'.

'These are a gift,' my father responded, 'from Joe. They're remainders, out of print, but in mint condition. It was really very nice of him. There's a book for every member of our family, including you.'

There was a novel for my mother, while my brother received a How-to guide to safe chemistry experiments in the home. My book was, well, a brand new, very nicely illustrated edition of *The Collected Tales of Hans Andersen*. 'Coals to Newcastle,' said my mother scornfully.

I was twelve, a little old for Hans Andersen, I thought, although secretly I still liked the stories and soon became quite attached to one lavish illustration in particular. It showed the beautiful princess from 'The Tinder Box', asleep on the giant dog's back, a low-cut dress revealing the cleavage of what the illustrator had decided would be disproportionately large breasts. This colour print fed into the fantasy connected to Evelyn, the fourteen-year-old girl whose bedroom window faced mine across the two postage-stamp-sized lawns that abutted our homes. Recently, I had removed a round mirror from my bicycle, bolted it to a long stick, and attached it to one of my bedposts. In this way I was able to watch Evelyn Boone undress in her room, without being observed myself. Unfortunately, most of the time, Evelyn took what was the conventional precaution in our enclosed neighbourhood of drawing the curtains before disrobing. So far, I had not seen any more in my magic mirror than had already been granted to me by Eyre & Spottiswoode's dubiously inspired illustrator.

From the first time he laid eyes upon it Uncle Hugo wanted my book. In the wide world of desire, there is little that exceeds the covetousness of the collector. From a distant, unconcerned relative, Hugo suddenly transformed into a charming, wily confrère. I was not immune to the bribery and seductiveness of adults, nor was I invulnerable to the parental cajoling that began when my father (my mild-mannered father!) decided to join in the fray and persuade me to hand over my book to Hugo. Indeed, I might have given in, were it not for the fact that what Hugo was asking for constituted, however bizarrely, a piece of the puzzle of my erotic life, one that I was unwilling to relinquish. Lotte, who seemed to have a sense that there was more than stubbornness and obstinacy to my refusal, took my side.

'You don't have enough books?' she asked her husband. 'So you have to steal from a child?'

'It's not stealing,' my father interposed. 'Hugo has offered Michael an extremely rare and valuable first edition in return for his book. We are talking about a swap here. An exchange in which Michael will come out the winner.'

The two men pressured me for a month, but I held my ground.

'Why can't he buy the book from someone else, if he wants it that badly?' I whined to my father, after Hugo had left the house one day.

'Because it is unavailable in bookshops, and Uncle Hugo does not steal from libraries. What is more, buying books costs money, and, at the moment, Hugo and Lotte are trying to *save* money. You're not too young to understand that. Joe Kline tells me that they only printed a thousand copies of your edition. It didn't do well. Too many competitors on the market. It isn't valuable, but Hugo would have an impossible job tracking one down. To you, it's virtually worthless, but to Hugo, as part of a collection, it means something.'

Has it sunk in what Hugo is offering you in return? You could own a book worth, maybe, fifty pounds!'

Fifty pounds to give up Evelyn Boone's breasts? For, yes, I could no longer distinguish her teenage bumps from the more developed forms that belonged to the princess in the illustration. Out of the question!

For reasons of domestic propriety (perhaps my mother had noticed the Lotte heads on the naked bodies too) the Wassermans had, some time during the summer, been switched from Saturday nights to Sunday afternoons. Hugo and Lotte had bought a car on the HP, an old Singer with seventy thousand miles on the clock. In this distinguished vehicle, Hugo at the wheel, Lotte making hand signals because the left indicator did not work, they negotiated a slow, careful way to our house each weekend. When they pulled up at the kerb my father would look out of the window and say, 'Here comes the Rolls Canardly, rolls down one side of a hill, can 'ardly get up the other.'

Hugo was now a fully incorporated member of something my father called the 'Cheese-Cake Club'. This organization now boasted four members, men from the neighbourhood who gathered weekly to overpraise my mother's pâtisserie and discuss the contemporary scene. One of the men, Sidney Oberman, would arrive with the week's newspapers under his arm. It was his responsibility to select and underline topics for further discussion. The group's heroes were Winston Churchill, the late Chaim Weizman, and Dr Armand Kalinowski, a brilliant Jewish panellist on the popular radio show Brains Trust. In deference to this invisible mentor, the members of the 'Cheese-Cake Club' each sported a bow-tie, symbol of decorum and high thought.

Six weeks after Hugo had first held my book in his hands for examination and quiet evaluation, the Wassermans arrived, as usual, late for Sunday tea, and, as usual, in the middle of an argument. The general cause of their altercations was 'The Collection'. The Wassermans were poor. They lived in a tiny two-room flat in Willesden Green. Hugo had looked for laboratory work, but, he said, his strong German accent made prospective employers uneasy. The Wassermans' small income accrued from Lotte's piano lessons offered to neighbourhood children in their own homes, and from piece-work (advice on fungus and fungicides) that Hugo performed as assistant to a local landscape gardener. According to Lotte, if Hugo were only to sell his books, they could live like royalty. On the other hand, if Hugo ever tried to unpack his books in her home, he would have to find another wife.

Lotte's scorn for Hans Christian Andersen and his work knew no limits. Fairy tales! What nonsense. A collection of Goethe or Tolstoy she might respect, although, in her present crisis, she would still want to sell it. But a grown man straining his eyes poring over 'The Emperor's New Clothes' in twenty different languages? What a terrible waste.

When Lotte spoke this way Hugo flushed deeply; he would look around to see if my brother or I were in earshot. When his eyes met ours we would try to look distracted and hard of hearing. On this particular occasion, their argument appeared to have peaked shortly before the ring on our doorbell, and what I overheard as I opened the door ('You want us to remain poor all our lives?'/'Is this all you care about, money?') were their last tired shots, the blows of a boxer whose arms are spent, and legs wobbly.

Lotte moved shakily toward the kitchen. 'I need a glass of water,' she said. Hugo carefully removed his jacket and searched our hall cupboard for a hanger. Were there tears in his eyes? I wasn't sure, but suddenly I felt sorry for him. Perhaps it was the look of deep exhaustion on his face (a look I had seen before but not really registered) that softened me, or maybe it was simply the fact that, for the first time since we had begun our battle of wills, he did not say to me, 'So, have you changed your mind?' Whatever the reason, I hovered around until Hugo had hung up his jacket, and then I said, 'I'll swap.'

The ceremonial exchange of books did not take place for more than a fortnight. It was mid-August, and time for our annual holiday. My parents would book us into some quiet, respectable boarding house in Margate or Swanage or Southbourne, making sure to order vegetarian meals in advance, in this way anticipating and surmounting problems that might arise with *kashrut*. Off we would go, packed snugly into our old Ford Prefect. After a long eighty miles or so of traffic jams, car-sickness and back-seat fights, we would arrive at someone else's house, not too different from our own, ready to read indoors while the rain fell in sheets; play crazy-golf in light drizzle; and venture out on the three or four fine, warm days that nature seemed to guarantee us, to swim in the cold sea and shiver.

This year, however, we were doing something different. We had rented a seaman's cottage on the beach in Folkestone. High, choppy waves thundered against the retaining wall behind the little dwelling. When I lay in bed at night I felt as if my bedroom were a ship's cabin, pitching and rolling in the summer winds. In the mornings, my brother and I explored the dunes near where the ferry came in from Boulogne. The sandy knolls and hillocks were still dotted with concrete pill-boxes. We clambered inside these dry chambers, peered through their narrow window slits, and pretended to be gunners scanning the Channel for approaching German aircraft.

At the end of the first week my father was suddenly and mysteriously called back to London. All we knew was that Lotte had phoned one day in a state of high excitement. My father had a few whispering sessions with my mother. But, after he had departed, she claimed, and she seemed to be telling the truth, that my father had told her only that Hugo and Lotte had a real emergency, not of a medical nature, but serious enough to warrant his returning home for a couple of days to help them out.

It rained for the duration of my father's three-day absence. We visited a shop that held demonstrations in toffee manufacture, went to the pictures to see Danny Kaye in *The Court Jester*, and attended a children's talent contest in the local town hall.

When he returned, late one night, my father appeared anxious and disturbed. In fact, he was so agitated that I allowed myself to imagine, for one brief flicker of a thought, that he and Lotte had perhaps, well . . . no, it was inconceivable.

The Prince of Denmark, we learned eventually, had sent an emissary to Hugo. The royal family's librarian wished to review the collection. There was genuine interest from Copenhagen. If Hugo would not agree to sell it whole, perhaps he would permit the collection to be split up?

Lotte had called on my father to help her persuade Hugo that this was a once-in-a-lifetime chance. They could escape their dreary lodgings and dead-end jobs. They could move to Golders Green, better, to Hampstead! If he wished to pursue his 'hobby', Hugo could open an antiquarian bookshop. My father had spoken to Hugo, but he was powerfully resistant to the idea of selling.

'Leslie, you don't understand,' he had said. 'I have to hold it together. The collection has to be protected.'

But then something happened. Here, my father paused in his narrative, as if to gather strength. My mother poured him a cup of tea. Hugo had received a letter in the post. He had not let Lotte see it, but after reading it he had rushed out of the house. He had gone missing for a day and a night, and when he returned in the early hours of this morning, hatless, soaked through, with his teeth chattering, he had simply slumped in a chair and refused to explain himself. My father had visited the Wassermans for lunch. Hugo had been polite, but withdrawn. He did not want to discuss the collection any more. Perhaps, after all, he would sell, he only wanted to be left alone and given a little more 'time to think'.

'Well,' said my mother testily, when my father had finished speaking. 'I think they've got a nerve. Interrupting a person's holiday, and then behaving in this outrageous fashion, when you—and only *you* would do this—went up there to help them.' My father didn't reply. Outside the sea swelled and surged, spraying droplets of surf against our kitchen windows. I thought, in my ignorance, that my mother had a point.

When we returned to London, my father immediately had to deal with a crisis at work: for the first time, a woman had been elected to the Board of Management of a North London synagogue, and now the entire spiritual staff, rabbi, cantor, beadle and choirmaster, were threatening to resign. 'This is the beginning of the end for Judaism,' the rabbi had written back to headquarters, and added in parentheses, ' "A foolish woman is clamorous: she is simple, and knoweth nothing." (Proverbs 9:13)' My father was dispatched to calm everybody down.

The school holidays were drawing to a close. I had to buy a new blazer, and stock up on those sweet-smelling essentials, an eraser, a new exercise book, blue-black ink, and a fountain pen. In the subdued excitements of anticipation before a new school year, I almost forgot about Hugo and Lotte.

One evening, when an autumn chill could already be felt in the air, they turned up on our doorstep. Lotte was transformed. She was wearing a white crepe de chine blouse, and a knee-length black satin skirt. Her hair was dressed in a chic new style. She was brimming over with joy. 'He's going to sell!' she announced even before she greeted us.

Hugo followed her sheepishly into the house. It seemed that Lotte had jumped the gun. Her emphatic expectation of great wealth had led her to spend, in one brave day, the little savings that they had managed to accumulate in the previous six months of struggle and hardship. 'Yes, I will sell,' said Hugo. 'But who knows what I will get?'

Late in the evening Hugo pulled me aside. 'Come in the other room', he said. 'We need to talk.' I had been expecting him to approach me, and wondering why he had delayed. 'Listen,' he whispered, pushing his face close to mine. I smelled alcohol on his heavy breath. 'I am going to give you a book. I don't want *them* to get it. It's very valuable, but it's worth nothing. I want you to keep it. You can't sell it.'

The bars of our electric fire, turned on for the first time in four months, glowed bright orange and gave off a pungent scent of burned dust. Hugo raked his white hair back with his fingers. 'You must,' he said, taking me by the shoulders, 'you, above all people, must forgive me.' Despite the heat that was moving in waves up my back, I felt a chill go through me. He was weeping now, sobbing, his shoulders heaving as if he could never stop. Suddenly, Lotte and my father appeared in the doorway. They rushed to Hugo, put their arms around him, and led him back into the kitchen.

That night, my parents sent my brother and me to bed early. But, as was our custom when this happened, we crept half-way down the stairs to eavesdrop on the grown-up conversation. We sat in our pyjamas, hugging the banister. In the brightly-lit kitchen, Hugo began to speak, in low tones, and with a halting voice. At first we only caught words and phrases: 'wife', 'son', 'arrangements', 'waited and waited', 'betrayed', 'not even Lotte'. Huddled on the stairs we heard, clear as train whistles in the night, sharp intakes of breath around the kitchen table. Soon we grew used to Hugo's broken, hoarse whisper.

If, at any point in Hugo's story, my brother and I could have returned to our beds, we would probably have done so. But curiosity had called us to listen, and now we were trapped.

After ten or fifteen minutes Hugo paused for a moment. My father got up and switched the lights off in the kitchen. It was a strange thing to do. Perhaps he wanted to take the harsh light of self-interrogation off Hugo. Now, Hugo's voice came up to us out of darkness. 'The collection,' he said, 'the collection came to Shanghai, but not my family.' There was a long silence. 'Soon after the war, I received a confirmation. My wife. Someone from the woman's camp who was there. I received a letter. But my son, of course, unlikely, all right impossible, but even so. Two weeks ago, a letter comes. You know. Sixteen years. An official letter; the place, the date.' Hugo began a muffled sob. 'My Hans, Hans Wasserman, Hans Wasserman.' He said the name again and again.

It was thirty years before I opened the edition of the *Collected Tales* that Hugo had given me. My nine-year-old son's teacher had invited parents to come to school and share their favourite children's story with the Nintendo-obsessed throng. I thought for a while before settling (of course!) on Andersen's 'The Tinder Box'. My old, illustrated copy of the tales had long since been lost in some chaotic transfer from home to home. But I had managed to hold onto Hugo's gift. It was an ordinary-looking book, with a slightly torn blue binding and faded gold lettering on the cover. The early pages were spotted with brown stains. The frontispiece proudly announced 'A New Translation, by Mrs H. B. Paull'. I flicked through the pages; they appeared unmarked. I turned to the Contents: a faint circle had been inscribed around 'The Brave Tin Soldier'. I found the story, and read it through. In the last sentence two phrases had been thinly underlined in pencil: 'instantly in flames', 'burnt to a cinder'.

Elena Lappin

was born in Moscow in 1954 and educated in Prague, in Germany, and at the University of Tel Aviv. She has also lived in Canada and the United States and has been resident in Britain since 1993. From 1994 to 1997 she was editor of the *Jewish Quarterly*, Britain's leading Jewish literary magazine. The *Culture Cube*, which she wrote, directed, and produced, was named 'Best Canadian Children's Cable Programme' in 1983. Lappin is the editor of two anthologies, *Jewish Voices, German Words: Growing Up Jewish in Postwar Germany and Austria* (1994) and *Daylight in Nightclub Inferno: New Czech Fiction from the Post-Kundera Generation* (1997). Her short story 'The Fraud' appeared in *Argo* (1982). 'Noa and Noah,' an original contribution to this anthology and her first British-Jewish story, will appear in her collection *Foreign Brides*.

Elena Lappin

Noa and Noah

Noa's decision to stop buying kosher meat, without letting her husband Noah know, was, on the face of it, a sudden impulse. One afternoon, on her way home from the park, she passed the butcher shop near her house, as she did almost every day. She had been thinking of the effort involved in making a special trip to her annoyingly talkative, nosey, and rude kosher butcher, the time it would take, the people she would have to 'bump into' while 'choosing' her usual cuts of lamb, chicken, and turkey (beef was no longer on the menu). The thought of it made her sick. Here, on the other hand, was a rosy-cheeked, cleanshaven JOE MCELLIGOTT (as the red-and-white lettering above the shop's awning cheerfully announced) who displayed various pink sections of dead pigs in his window with such pride and delight that it almost made Noa's mouth water. So, she thought, what if I just went in there, pretending to be one of *them*, what if I just asked for a couple of broilers and some minced turkey—it looks the same, Noah will never know the difference. And if he doesn't know, he's not sinning. I am, but fuck that.

Not only did Noah not notice the difference—he was terribly pleased with that Friday night meal. He actually loved the chicken, and asked Noa if she was finally using his mother's recipe. This was Noah's highest praise—he considered Noa's Israeli cooking unrefined. It used to upset her when he berated her culinary skills as if she were a kitchen apprentice trying to qualify for tenure as a wife. But now she thought, what can I expect from a debt collector.

When they first met, almost six years ago in Israel, Noah made Noa laugh by constantly referring to the similarity of their names. It didn't help that Noa pointed out the difference in the Hebrew spelling, and the fact that their names certainly didn't *sound* the same in Hebrew. His ended in a hard, guttural 'ch', which he liked to ignore; in his native North Londoner's English, 'Noah' dissolved in a nice soft vowel, and so did 'Noa', and therefore—he argued— they were meant for each other. It had been a funny joke until one night this red-haired British cousin of her best friend's stepsister took her to a decadent Tel Aviv disco, danced in a slightly drunken way, and then insisted on making love to her in his parents' empty summer penthouse.

Noa was intimidated by the chrome and glass everywhere. Her own parents' apartment in Ramat Gan contained mostly decrepit dark wood furniture, covered with dusty lace and musty-smelling polyester. Noah seemed sleek and intriguing to Noa. He talked incessantly in bed, which she found impressive; her Israeli boy-friends hardly ever uttered anything verbal except an occasional *ze tov?* She didn't understand half of what he was saying but it all sounded sweet, sexy, and somehow mysterious.

A few months later, she was starring in her own wedding video, though she didn't exactly remember signing the contract. His par-ents took over, there was a breeze of London in it all, her poor old Polish parents almost disappeared under the weight of so much chrome and glass and gold and diamonds. Finchley Gothic versus Ramat Gan Post-Holocaust Modern. Masses of dewy pale veiny legs on stiletto heels versus sun-devoured parched feet in sandals. Her friends didn't understand what she was up to, and neither did Noa—but it felt good. So she was giving up her life as she knew it, marrying a kippa-wearing accountant, moving to London. So what. She was twenty and he made her feel all grown up. And he sure didn't wear his kippa in bed.

The first two years were almost a success. Noa's English was so basic that she continued to be seduced by her image of Noah as a glamorous young businessman. Their home in East Finchley, a family-owned property, seemed like a palace to Noa—though she felt uncomfortable with the decor, which was an almost exact replica of the Tel Aviv penthouse. To Noah's surprise, his brand-new wife was spending more time in the bathroom than in any other part of the house; for there, she could close her eyes in the blue-green bathwater and picture herself on the Tel Aviv beach. She felt like a trapped mermaid, escaping to her natural habitat.

Then one day she noticed that her English had improved so dra-
matically that she could enter into arguments with Gerda, her
mother-in-law, and, although she didn't exactly win them, she
didn't lose them either. Even better, Noa's ear suddenly started
picking up occasional slip-ups in Noah's mother's accent; no matter
how hard Gerda tried, her East End vowels kept showing in her
unnaturally clipped speech, like the dark roots in her bleached hair.
Noa, who had wanted with all her heart to feel close to her new
family, was puzzled by so much unnecessary artifice, and now
thought of her parents' home as refreshingly warm and unpreten-
tious.

By the time she realized that Noah was actually employed in his
father's business as a junior *debt collector*, and that his life's aspiration
was to one day run the small Finchley office and become a *senior*
debt collector, Noa was already pregnant with Noah's child. She
had also by now finally deciphered and demystified her husband's
sexy mumblings which invariably accompanied their lovemaking:
the words Arsenal and Tottenham came up a lot, with very unsexy
adjectives describing various players and plaintive remarks about
their technique. When she had first grasped this incredible fact,
Noa simply asked Noah why he had to think and talk about football
during sex. He had answered, without the slightest hint of embarrassment, that he thought about football all the time, and saying
his thoughts out loud during sex helped him slow down. Noa was
so flabbergasted she forgot to ask which team he supported—
though she had a strong feeling it was Tottenham.

And what did Noa think about in bed? Initially, close to nothing.
She tried to slowly get to know Noah, whose way of life she had
accepted so blindly, without worrying about the fact that he was a
total stranger to her. So she did what she had done from the day
they met: watched him, watched his every movement, listened to
his every word. As long as Noah remained an enigma, he was worth
every boring minute of her boring life with him. He was safe. But
the minute she cracked his code, he was finished and didn't even
know it.

'Noah,' she said one evening after putting their son to bed. They
were lounging around in front of the TV, without really watching
anything. 'What does a debt collector actually do?'

Her husband of five years looked up from the sports page of the evening paper and stared at Noa. She repeated the question. 'We . . . we make people pay their debts,' he said slowly and gave her a hard look she knew well. It meant: shut up and leave me alone. Not this time; Noa was on a roll. 'But how? Are you some kind of police or something?'

Noah sighed. ''Course not. We just write letters and tell people what will happen if they don't pay up.' He was dying to go back to his paper. Noa's inquisitive mood was beginning to annoy him. And she was exposing her ignorance about things everyone knew and no one questioned. Thank God his parents weren't there to hear.

'So what are you?' Noa's next question startled him. 'Some kind of Mafia?'

Noah's eyes narrowed just a bit before he said, his voice louder than usual: 'No, we're not. Of course we're not. But we *are* licensed to send in the bailiffs and initiate court orders if the client doesn't cooperate.'

Noah knew how to keep cool, very cool. Even under a lot of stress. He knew how to sound menacing and detached at the same time. Maybe it went with that strange job of his. But Noa smelt defeat in the air, and it wasn't hers. 'So, Noah,' she persisted, emphasising the 'ch' sound which she knew he hated, 'I still don't see it. How do you get people to pay their debts? And why do you do it? Are you evil or something? I think you are. You and your father. But you're worse.'

Noah searched his wife's face for a trace of a smile. Anything to indicate that she was joking. Whenever Noa said something weird, which happened quite often, he made excuses for her on account of her underdeveloped Israeli idea of humour. Like her cooking, Noa's sense of what constituted an acceptable remark was frequently on the clumsy side. Noah was tired. He hated his job. He hated the life he had forced himself to lead. He was beginning to hate his gorgeous, awkward, crazy wife.

'If you're trying to be funny, give it up. You have nothing to say, as usual. And you can't hurt me. I'm going to sleep.'

Noa was a good aim. She had been a first-rate shot in the army. The remote control she threw hit Noah between the shoulderblades. He turned around, raving mad. The Armenian candlestick hit him in the balls. He doubled over, gasping for air and cursing. 'You bitch. You fuckin' bitch. Go to hell.'

Noa slid off the couch and reached for Noah's red mane, gingerly. He tried to bite her arm, but she gave him her mouth instead. For the first time ever, Noah forgot his football mantra.

Later, while he slept, Noa went to the bathroom to cry. But I did mean it, she thought. I meant everything I said, and I meant to hurt him. I need him to go back to being the stranger I fucked. But with me in control this time. You owe me, my little debt collector, she whispered almost tenderly, climbing back into bed. It's pay-up time.

After that night, their daily routine returned to normal, seemingly unchanged. Noah's life continued to revolve around his father's office, football, and dutiful socializing with his parents on weekends and holidays. Sometimes he craved Noa's body, though not her thoughts. Noa couldn't care less. She had a plan. Dressing their son mostly in red and white (Arsenal colours) was only a small part of it.

It began with that visit to Joe McElligott's butcher shop and her first purchase of *treyf* chicken. She had intended to be in and out of the shop as quickly as possible, to avoid being seen by a friend or acquaintance of Noah's family. But she was delayed by two things that caught her eye, almost simultaneously: Joe McElligott's attractively bulging biceps under his white, slightly bloodstained T-shirt, and the sign on the cash register saying WE DELIVER. He smiled at her and said something flattering about her lovely French accent. She smiled back without correcting him and made a mental note of the price list on the wall. She would save a lot of money by sticking to *treyf*. 'Yes, ma'am, I do the deliveries myself these days. No charge. Call us anytime.' His plump cheeks reminded her of her son's smooth round *tusik* . . . She took the business card he offered her and nodded. Joe McWhatever, she thought, pushing the stroller outside, guess what. This French customer wants your meat.

The phone rang as soon as she unlocked her door. 'Noale,' her mother said softly, as if she were in the same room. 'I don't know what to do. Your father . . .' 'What??! What happened to him?' Noa screamed. Does the punishment system work this fast?! She hadn't done anything so far except think about it! 'Nothing, nothing happened to him. It's what happened to me. He has another woman,

that's what.' Noa was numb. This didn't make sense. Her parents
were in their late sixties, and everything about them was as predict-
able as the pattern on her net curtains. They were both survivors,
from the same small Polish town. They've known each other since
they were almost children. Now they were old, wrinkled, their health
was precarious. Their lives had been unspeakably hard, and their
worn-out bodies showed it. They couldn't possibly feel desire for
other people and their bodies!

'I don't know what to do, Noale. You know the beach we drive to
every morning?' Noa's parents belonged to the daily contingent of
determined old men and women who exercised on the Tel Aviv
beach early each morning. She had watched them sometimes. Their
leathery skin shook in tiny ripples as they marched in and out of
the cold waves and performed old-fashioned calisthenics on the
sand. 'The Russian woman we befriended? The one that had those
bruises from her husband. The shikse! I invited her to my own home
and gave her my old dishes and a kitchen table! My own dishes! Call
me back, we can't afford this.' Noa called back and listened to her
mother weep, long distance. First quietly, like a little girl who lost
a precious toy, then louder and louder until her wail sounded like
an ear-piercing siren, or a mother mourning the loss of her child.
'Do you need me there? Do you want to come here?' Noa asked,
gently. 'I don't know yet. I have to think. Kiss the baby from me.
Call me next week.' She's not falling apart, Noa thought, amazed.
She wants him back!

For some reason, she decided not to tell Noah. She could just
hear his feeble jokes about her father the geriatric philanderer. As
she unwrapped the pale, moist chicken, spreading its juicy thighs,
a horrible image of her father humping a fleshy, hairy Russian lady
flashed through her mind. She could only picture his penis as a kind
of insemination syringe, not an instrument of pleasure. Come to
think of it, she couldn't picture it at all. She rubbed a thick layer of
spices and sauces into the skin of the cold chicken, to hide its true
identity, and shoved it in the oven. Don't let me down, she said to
the dead bird. Act kosher.

Noah's parents dropped in the next day on their way home from
shul. Gerda was stunned by her son's praise of Noa's chicken, and
insisted on tasting the leftovers. Noa was a bit worried but did not

resist. Gerda tasted, swallowed, approved. With a slight tinge of envy, she asked her uncouth daughter-in-law for the recipe. Go to Joe McElligott's in the High Street, Noa felt like saying. He'll inspire you.

After that, it was a cinch. She would call Joe with her order, and he would deliver. At first, only once a week. 'Thank you.' 'You're welcome, ma'am. What a cute baby.' He was a bit of a chef, and they started talking recipes. She discovered that Noah loved the food she prepared according to Joe's suggestions. There was the semblance of peace in their home. They were a happy dysfunctional family. Just like everybody else they knew.

Joe's biceps continued to intrigue her. Sometimes she watched him, unseen, through the shop window, chopping and slicing masses of bloody animal corpses, his muscular right arm a vigorous extension of his powerful body. At home, when she dug with her hands into the raw meat she had bought from him, she felt a wave of lust for her new butcher. One day she lingered a little longer than usual in the window, until he looked up and saw her. Their eyes interlocked for a brief moment, unsmiling. Two hours later, he brought her order, four days too soon. She dumped the meat on the kitchen floor and took him straight into her bedroom. Afterwards, Joe tried to thank her in basic French. Noa giggled and told him the truth.

Joe sat up in her and Noah's bed, which seemed to have shrunk in size. 'Ah. So *that's* why you never buy my pork. I've been wondering.' He gave Noa a great recipe for roast turkey and promised to bring an Arsenal hat for Noa's little boy. Next time.

Noah loved the turkey and failed to detect another man's scent in his bed. He did, however, object to the hat when it appeared on his son's head. 'Noa, Noa. Don't you know *we* support Spurs? Get rid of that thing.' But the baby screamed when he made an attempt to grab the hat, and so it stayed, to be followed by a little Arsenal T-shirt and jacket. Joe was a fan.

Noa loved what happened almost every time Joe came to her door. It never lasted long—it couldn't—but it was perfect. They were lying to the world, but not to each other. They were strangers outside, but not in her bed. The polar opposite of the life she led with Noah. She even loved Joe's work; she called him her butcher from heaven.

She had been expecting her mother's call, but not this: her mother wanted to come to London and stay with Noa until her husband came to his senses. How long? A week, a month, a year—as long as it takes. 'I'll show him, Noale. He can have her but he can't have me as well. I want to live too. Like you. Kiss the baby from me. See you Friday. Can't wait.'

Gerda's call a few minutes later gave her a chill. 'Noa, have you switched butchers? Mr. Meyerson has been asking for you. He said he hasn't seen you in ages! *Where* do you get your meat these days? Not Shmulik's, I hope? He's a real ganef. You should have asked me first!'

Noa lied, with great skill. No, Gerda. Not Shmulik's. And changed the subject, no less skillfully, to her mother's visit. 'This Friday. Well . . . it's my father. He's been cheating on her. Can you believe it?'

Gerda could hardly conceal the excitement in her voice. This was juicy. Didn't think the old Weinstock had it in him. She offered solicitous advice and said she'd come stay with the baby while Noa went to Heathrow to pick up her mother. Noa thanked her and accepted.

And so it happened that Joe knocked on Noa's door, his usual meat delivery in hand (with a few pork chops thrown in this time to introduce his favourite customer to a new delicacy), and found himself face to face with Gerda. She gave him a stern look and asked who he was. 'McElligott the butcher, ma'am,' said Joe, a bit taken aback but still smiling—and why not? As far as he knew, their affair was a sweet secret, and Noa had told him nothing about her subversive anti-kosher activity. He left the parcel with Gerda and went, a little surprised at Noa's absence, but not too worried.

Gerda carried the meat into the kitchen, moving very very slowly, like a stunned animal. Had she heard right? *Mc something?* A *goyishe* butcher? This could not be. She unwrapped the package and let out a primal scream. It had to be a mistake. But Noa's name and address was on the invoice she found attached inside. This Israeli parvenue was feeding her son *treyf*!! She had always known there was some-thing strange about her. And that father of hers! And her poor boy! Suddenly, Gerda remembered the delicious taste of Noa's chicken. She shuddered. She wanted to scream again, and call Noah, but instead she cried and cried, until she fell asleep, exhausted, on the living room couch.

On the way home from the airport, Noa listened to her mother's stories about 'that man' and 'that woman.' But he's still my father, she thought, how do I tell her that? And it seems I have more in common with him than I ever knew. Suddenly she saw her father's gentle face, remembered his shy smile and his kind eyes, his slow, awkward gestures when he tried to hug her. So what if his still barely erect body had a life of its own. Everything was so goddam complicated . . . 'Oh I love this English rain, Noale. I'll stay a while. Let them bake in the heat.'

When they arrived, Noah was already there, summoned by his mother. Gerda, without acknowledging Noa's mother's presence, grabbed Noa by the sleeve and pulled her into the kitchen. 'This!!' she screamed, pointing at the meat with a mixture of moral outrage and physical nausea, 'this you've been feeding us! Who are you, the devil? Noch?'

Noa was expecting some kind of explosion someday, but not so soon. Not today, not like this. Gerda wasn't supposed to have the upper hand. She looked around the living room. Noah's face was white, even more than usual. He was speechless. Noa's mother was confused. She didn't understand what this was about, but she did register Gerda's rudeness and barely contained violence. And the defiant look on her daughter's face.

Observing what was about to become a scene of carnage, Noa regained her courage just as quickly as she had lost it. Strengthened by months of cheerful lovemaking with Joe, she suddenly felt like facing the enemy instead of wallowing in hidden pain. She would leave the collecting of debts to these pitiful characters, she decided, with their ugly penthouses and their phoney accents.

'I've been meaning to tell you,' she said without a trace of hysteria, looking straight at Noah, 'I'm not staying. Not if it means living like this. Like your parents. You're an *efes* . . . A zero. And . . . and your team is crap.'

Gerda jumped up and offered to throw away the meat, but her son stopped her and asked both mothers to take a walk. When they were alone, Noah collapsed on the sofa and burst out laughing: 'Noa. Come here. You idiot. I never eat kosher away from home. I really don't give a shit. I do these things for their sake, but I don't give a shit. Didn't you know? Really and truly. You can buy any meat you want as far as I'm concerned. What's for dinner?'

He reached for her, but there was a knock on the door. Joe had come back, hoping to find Noa alone this time. Instead, she was with her pale-looking, panting husband. Noa made a step towards Joe, but her son preceded her. He ran to him, waving his little arms and shouting 'Ah-senal! Ah-senal!'

Some debts are not worth collecting, thought Noah, noticing the wistful look Joe gave his wife. 'Wait!' he said quietly as Joe turned to leave. He disappeared in the kitchen and came running out with the meat parcel. 'Please take this back. My wife and I are becoming vegetarians. As of tonight.'

'And I'm cooking,' he added when they were alone again. 'Do you feel like pasta?'

Noa nodded. She wasn't sure who had won this one, and she didn't care. It was over, and it felt good. She decided to buy little Gili a Tottenham hat.

Jonathan Treitel

was born in London in 1959 and educated at Oxford, Cambridge, Johns Hopkins, and Stanford, where he was awarded a doctorate. Treitel has worked in Japan and California as a physicist. His poetry has been published extensively, including in *Poetry Introduction 7* (1990), a Faber & Faber anthology of new poets in Britain. Treitel is the author of two acclaimed novels, *The Red Cabbage Café* (1990) and *Emma Smart* (1992). His stories 'Selflessness; or Alexander and His Electric Wok' and 'Shaking Hands with Theodor Herzl,' the former of which is an original contribution to this anthology, are characterized by his restless and unsettling narrative technique.

Jonathan Treitel

Selflessness; or Alexander and His Electric Wok

Before he died, Uncle Alexander told me the wok anecdote. I call him Uncle because he was my uncle: the brother of my father; sometimes men who aren't the uncle of anyone in particular are awarded the title on account of their bearing and white hairs and the way they tell jokes—a kind of affable seniority, in short—but this didn't apply to Alexander: he wasn't the type to accept any nickname or adjective or designation whatsoever which didn't belong to him by right. He was high and stiff on the high stiff hospital bed. Once old men used to be allowed to die at home, surrounded by soft pillows stuffed with goose down, and fringed lampshades, and beloved nephews, and a favourite watercolour of wildfowl passing above a frozen lake . . . but now they are spread out in a clean place: declarative as the first proposition in a syllogism: the 'given' axiom from which everything else must be deduced.

The story is that his white blood cell count was down. So he was going to die soon. Some five years ago already he'd had a laryngotomy and had learned to speak in a new voice issuing from deep inside: the kind of breathy bubbling used by Venusians addressing earthlings. I bent my ear closer. Definitely he was trying to say something. (We come in peace . . . Take me to your leader . . .) The oxygen cylinder was hissing in the background: his whisper seemed composed of pieces of that hiss. And so I knew, even before I understood a word, that whatever fraction of his life he wanted to impart to me, whatever message or moral or tittle-tattle, the conclusion was going to be this: this hiss; this silence.

To appreciate the significance of his tale, you must know first of all that Alexander was an unremarkable man. He had a profound sense of his own unremarkableness. He wasn't even remarkably unremarkable: just unremarkably unremarkable. He was always known as Alexander, for one thing; another man might have mutated into an Alex or an Al; I knew a Xander once, in a Philadelphia suburb; Sasha is not at all an impossibility; any Alexander might be known to at least one other human being (scoffingly, sure, but not wholly so) as The Great . . . but my uncle didn't budge a syllable from his given name. Nor did he grow a beard (in the decade when beards were possible), nor take up a passion for Thai restaurants or cloisonné snuffboxes, and he didn't marry either. He didn't feel entitled. He was as selfless as anybody can be—almost to the verge of saintliness—and this is often considered a virtue, but is it? Unless you have an idea of your own worth and what the world owes you, how can you ever relate to humanity? (And that wasn't a rhetorical question: I don't know the answer myself, so I'm just leaving it hanging. Teku—as my father used to say, quoting my grandfather quoting the Talmud. When the ancient rabbis came across some enigma they couldn't crack despite their best mental exertions, they stated this disyllable: an acronym meaning that the problem won't be solved until Elijah the Prophet returns, heralding the Messiah. I'm told that the same expression is used today in Israel when a basketball or soccer game ends in a tie. It's the hardest lesson: sometimes nobody wins.)

If we've learned anything from Freud, it is that all our grief is the fault of our parents; and our parents' of their parents; and so on back to the beginning. So what was the original sin? Freud himself cooked up some crazy myth about a murderous tribe in the Paleolithic Era; other people blame it on a Serpent in a Garden; me, I can go back no farther than my grandfather. My grandfather was brought up in Warsaw at the last moment: he described himself as the flea on the tip of the tail of the Enlightenment. On the one hand he studied Talmud in the traditional manner; on the other hand he also studied Kant in precisely the same manner. I mean that literally: he shokeled to and fro in front of the lectern, chanting a passage from the Critique of Pure Reason, analysing it word by word by syllable by punctuation mark. His critique of the Critique was articulated with Talmudic rhetorical flourishes such as, 'this comes to teach us . . .' and, 'but the wise men say . . .' When I knew him he was an old man with a habit of using 'to learn' as an intransitive verb—a tic which has passed down to me. (When strangers enquire with formulaic politeness: 'What do you do?' I reply, 'I learn.') Grandfather peppered his speech with aphorisms: I was never too sure if he was quoting Rabbi Judah the Prince or Immanuel of Königsberg. Double whammy! To believe in abstract ethical principles and to believe these can govern a real life. To suppose the Categorical Imperative is addressed to you. His children had something big to blame their own failings on.

Grandfather used to spread the fingers on his right hand and say, 'These are my five sons.' He brought them up effectively on his own, since his wife was always sickly. He would name them in order of seniority, ending at the pinkie: 'Philip, Julius, Alexander, Anthony, Cincinnatus.' It is hard these days, when families are small or non-existent, to imagine his love—too many children to hug all at once. Once large families were the rage—the stuff of three-volume sagas; there was an assumption that quantity implied quality; nowadays stern muttering takes place concerning overpopulation and family planning. His family was planned also, but on a moral dimension. He parceled out an equal quantum of love to each of his sons (or gave that impression, at least) in his absolute determination to avoid playing favourites. It is hard to sympathise with him: since we can identify more easily with the child rebelling against the parent—staging a revolution or writing a sonnet cycle—than the other way round. I'm reminded of a riddle my father teased me with when I was a boy: if every person has two parents, four grandparents, eight great-grandparents . . . one thousand and twenty-four great-great-great-great-great-great-great-great-great-grandparents, et cetera, then the world was vastly more populous in the past!?

Of course the sons did become differentiated. They each were 'special' in some way: Philip was the eldest; Julius (my father) the cleverest; Anthony had a portwine stain on his forehead; Cincinnatus was named Cincinnatus. This gave them a core of identity which was elaborated on to become their adult personality. Only Alexander remained no more than a representative son and brother and citizen and homo sapiens: the x in the equation: the individual who is duty bound to obey the Principle of Sufficient Reason. Kant's great edifice is built on this Principle: an individual should do that which, if everybody were to do it, would be good. It sounds plausible on first read-through, but it leaves no room for moral quirkiness, for moral individuation. I am acquainted with a Mrs. Fishbein (I see her many afternoons by the park railings) who feeds the pigeons with crumbled raisin bagels. If everybody in the city copied her, the mess would be terrible; but let's grant she is warmhearted, all the same. And the Principle excludes love as an ethical force: you can save either your beloved or two strangers, who has priority? Kant's answer isn't yours or mine.

Uncle Alexander had attachments of duty but none of love, so far as anyone knew. He was always uncomfortable in his own or anybody's company. There should have been a square hole to fit his square peg, but he overlooked it somehow. He was, when all is said and done, an American: and America is built on a myth of democracy, an exaltation of Joe Anybody. (The only qualification needed to declare Civis Americanus Sum is Latin 001 taken in sophomore year to satisfy a distribution requirement.) Had he been born a notch lower on the social ladder, he could have identified himself as 'just a regular guy'—but his collar was too white for that. And nor was he classy or wealthy enough to share the assurance of the elite that America is theirs. He was a member of the middle class, sure, but nobody wears a T-shirt printed PROUD TO BE MIDDLE CLASS. And Jewishness isn't sufficient on its own; if he could have identified the Jewish with the American sense of moral destiny (as did many American Jews of his generation) he would have been home and dry; but he was pessimistic when America was optimistic; he came across as a touch intellectual, a touch 'European.' All he had to call his own was a body, of a standard type, and a death, at more or less the median age for such a thing, of a disease which carries off many of us.

Maybe he was a saint, after all. If so, he was unaware of it, for in the ethics which he assumed, there is no such thing as a saint.

And he had an anecdote about a wok. He communicated it to me in his eery pre-death voice: a series of gulps and whispers. I was reminded of the line from Coleridge's Xanadu: ' . . . As if this earth in fast thick pants were breathing.' Unintentionally comic: you imagine a plump globe clad in too-tight knickerbockers. Well, Xanadu is a Utopian vision: Coleridge's private heaven—and surely Coleridge would not be surprised to find Fancy as well as Imagination there. This sickroom also was a heaven: its aesthetic and moral simplicity was my grandfather's Rabbinico-Kantian idea of perfection.

The story. Uncle Alexander had seen an electric wok on markdown at Neumann & Schwartz; he didn't even like Chinese food especially, but he bought it. He took it home to his kitchen. Attached it in its proper place. Switched it on. Some internal electronics exploded with reasonable gentleness, giving off brown fumes. A stink of burning electrical insulation. He threw the wok in the trash . . . And my uncle closed his eyes and lay on his high bed, smiling.

Then, and often after his death, I wondered why he had chosen to tell me the story. The obvious explanation is that the wok is a blatant metaphor. It could happen to anyone—imagine the richesse on the kitchen work surface: soy sauce, sesame oil, fresh ginger, a packet of egg noodles, a bag of bean sprouts . . . Bang—smoke—stink—trash. (Hiss from the oxygen cylinder; silence.) But, in fact, I think he meant it literally. The wok episode had been his one mad hope. Suppose the gizmo had operated perfectly: he might well have acquired an oriental recipe book; imagine him flourishing his chopsticks. In due course—and this is not beyond belief—he would have produced fabulous stirfries, or at least distinctive ones; henceforth he would be acclaimed as Alexander and His Electric Wok.

I sorted out my uncle's belongings, and dealt with his financial affairs. I guess nobody else in the family wanted the responsibility, and I had experience of this, having coped after my own father died (six years earlier; still with his own teeth and hair; suddenly), and besides I couldn't think of a reason for saying no. Squirreled away in my uncle's wallet, tucked behind his many decades out-of-date service ID, was a lock of brown hair scotchtaped onto a pink card on which was written: *For my AlexXXX.*

I threw it away, of course. Well, not exactly. His belongings were waiting for me at the hospital in a black plastic trash bag. I transferred what was valuable or interesting into the trunk of my car, and returned the trash bag to the hospital receptionist. I think she was surprised but she didn't let it show. She must see so many strange reactions. Let some orderly dispose of the lock and the XXX on my and my family's behalf.

I recognised the hair and the handwriting. My mother's. I was shocked but only briefly. As I drove out into the traffic (the fumes, the clamour, the red lights and the green lights) I tut-tutted like a grandfather: I felt I had been pushed into a false position. Let's be rational about this. Let's be adult. We are all mature individuals here. So my mother and my uncle had had some kind of affair or let's call it an 'incident.' It might have amounted to very little: a single tipsy kiss; a snipped lock of hair; a sly, shy smile. 'Love' would be too strong a word. I appreciate that Pope had written a whole mock-epic in heroic couplets over a comparable hair-theft, and Hamlet under a similar provocation had gotten more than a little distraught, but on due reflection I was touched: these two old folk having a sprinkle of romance in their lives. Not that they had been so very old at the time, necessarily: there was no way to date the card. It couldn't have been within the last four years of course, not least because my mother's hair had been white ever since she'd stopped dyeing it once the symptoms had come on. Many times over the years she'd had patches of distractedness and forgetfulness, sometimes a weepy spell. After her Alzheimer's had been diag-nosed, I had reinterpreted the past, explaining these as early signs or (since the physician assured me the symptoms wouldn't have shown up so early) as prefigurations. And now I had to reinterpret again: let these be the outward marks of a secret amour.

And maybe this was the meaning of the wok anecdote: it was a declaration of love—a recounting of his frustrated intention. My mother wasn't available (in her condition she couldn't visit the hos-pital, and if she did she wouldn't understand: she can comprehend things happening in front of her, here and now—not an exploding wok in another decade) so I was chosen as the next best thing . . . Or maybe it was intended as a consolation: 'See how lucky you are not to have loved me: a man who can't even operate an electric wok.'

We always assume an allegorical meaning is hiding behind the literal one like Polonius behind the arras; stab it hard enough and the allegory falls bleeding on the stage. My mother's condition feels like it ought to stand for something grander. Ditto the wok. But here's another explanation why my uncle told me that then: it was chance. Socrates remarked that he owed a cock to Asclepius, not thinking he was going to die and this casual mutter would go down to posterity. Goethe's sight was fading so he requested Mehr Licht: if he'd tried to come up with a Famous Last Word I'm sure he could have thought of something more profound and zingier. So Alexander happened to be in a mood for Chinese cuisine (the dying have weird food cravings, just like the pregnant) and by a train of thought this reminded him of the wok business: he mentioned it; and then he wasn't.

I read an article by a psychologist which proved that any two individuals will fall in love provided the following six conditions are satisfied. (I forget the six conditions.) But there has to be something more subtle and individual going on: please, why: why did they do it—given that my father was handsome and interesting while my uncle was a plain bore? Let's test this for plausibility: she wanted to commit adultery (I can understand the urge, even or especially if her husband was impeccable) and she didn't want to commit adultery (I can understand this also), so she chose a man who didn't really count. And he consented for much the same reason: he wanted to have a romance; he wanted to desire someone, to put his own desire before moral principles, to commit seduction . . . but since he lacked the urge, he made do with a woman who was available yet not available. (The demon in the overstretched knickerbockers chuckles.)

And am I one hundred percent sure the handwriting and the hair was my mother's? Ninety-nine point nine nine. Not that it matters now . . . No way can I ask her: she remembers nothing coherent. My mother is in the last stage. She needs to be cared for, twenty-four hours a day.

Here is a not very illuminating ethical question: should the only son personally take on the care of his decrepit parent, or should he store her in a nursing home? Certainly, had she been asked when young and sane, she'd have urged me not to 'sacrifice myself' for her. And yet I do look after her (except when the night nurse is taking charge). Certain individuals (my cousins, my nieces . . .) pucker their mouths and call me 'selfless'; they imply: 'What makes you so special, so smalltown Mother Teresa? You want to show the rest of us up? You want to flaunt your goody-goody soul? Oh sure, you're "good"—but is "good" good?'

Fact: I'm selfish. I'd stuff that lock of hair down my mother's throat to stop her crying, if I thought it would stop her crying. I'd fly off to Bermuda, abandoning her, if I could convince myself I had a desire to be in Bermuda. I tend her because I simply cannot think of anything else to do.

Rabbi Hillel, when asked by a gentile to explain the Law while standing on one leg, replied: 'Do not do unto others that which you would not wish them do unto you.' The injunction works both ways: if you favour self-interest, you can deduce you should help others also; and vice-versa. And Hillel said: 'If I am not for myself, who am I for? And if only for myself, what am I? And if not now, when?'

I know the old doctrine that selfishness is the natural human state. I know the arguments for it. Selfishness is innate, they say. A capitalist society works best if everybody is selfish, they say. Selfishness is justified on the strength of ignorance: one never really knows what others want: one's own desires are what one is sure of, they say.

And there's another argument in the Talmud. (I have it from my father who has it from my grandfather who has it from . . . The Talmud itself is often written like this: a long list of attributions and one tiny saying at the end.) Two people are in the desert with a single waterskin, enough for only one person to survive. Is X duty bound to give it to Y? The answer is no: for if so, then Y would equally be bound to give it to X, and they would spend their last hours on earth tossing the waterskin to and fro like a volleyball. Ergo, by logical elimination, X should drink it himself. And so should Y.

What interests me is that we should feel the need to find this argument for selfishness, this chink, this ethical cranny. It's so much easier and comfier to help others: children, parents; society, the future . . . And I begin to understand what my uncle meant in his Parable of the Electric Wok. He recognised me as a fellow sufferer. He was urging me to break loose for once in my life: to find some desire, however fleeting and slight, and seek to satisfy it. Buy an electric wok and explode it. It's better than nothing.

Jonathan Treitel

Shaking Hands with
Theodor Herzl

Although it is November, Jerusalem is hot. There is a white dust on
the hills and alleys and the Homburg hat of the notable writer and
thinker Dr. Theodor Herzl. His black beard is itching. It is 1898.
Two miniscule flunkeys in canary-yellow livery lean back on the
Byzanto-Romanesque double doors of the Grand Levantine Hotel
on Jaffa Road. Herzl enters. The doors swing shut and bang his
shoulder blades. 'Ahem,' says Herzl. The clerk at the reception desk
says, 'One minute, sir.' The clerk's head is bent over the acrosticon
puzzle in the overseas edition of *The Chicago Clarion and Puzzler.* The
clerk considers solutions; he angles his skull; his ultra-straight hair-
parting teeters like the needle on a weighing machine. 'And what
can I do for you, sir?' 'I have reserved a room. The name is Dr.
Herzl.' 'It is very difficult. We have little space. The German Kaiser
is paying a state visit to the Pasha so most of our suites are—' 'Yes,
yes. That in fact is precisely why I myself am in—' 'What was the
name, sir?' The clerk glances up; he peers at Herzl's nose through
pince-nez. 'I am afraid we have nothing suitable, Mr. Cohen—' 'Dr.
Herzl.' 'Perhaps, on some future occasion, Mr. Levy.' 'Dr. Herzl.'
'Next year, possibly, or in the new century . . . ' 'But I insist!' Herzl
drums his fist on the counter. 'I have come all the way from Vienna
to Jerusalem expressly to meet the—!' 7 Down is WAN GERMAN
STONE (cryptic). Herzl flings up an arm in a theatrical gesture. The
clerk blinks. Herzl orates, 'Do you expect me to sleep in the gutter?!'
'That,' says the clerk, neatly pencilling in PALESTINE, 'is entirely
your own decision, sir.'

Whom should Herzl bump into as he stumbles backwards out of
the Grand Levantine Hotel but his old chum Siegfried Perl. 'Good
to see you, Tancred!' says Perl, slapping Herzl on the back. 'Tan-

cred?' says Herzl, slapping back. 'My name is Dr. Theodor Herzl.'
'Don't you remember? Vienna University? The Alba Club? Your nickname?' 'Of course I remember . . . er . . . Galahad. But what are
you doing in Palestine?' 'I live here. I am a Zionist. Zionism is the
name of a political movement headed by a certain Dr. Theodor . . .
Surely not?' Herzl blushes and nods. Perl says, 'Then you must come
round for pastries and coffee! Where are you staying?' 'Well, actually . . .' 'Then you must stay at my house. No, I insist!'

Perl guides Herzl through the narrow rutted alleys. 'I live at 19
Mehmet Ali Street,' says Perl. 'It is quite easy to find. You just follow
the Stations of the Via Dolorosa. Here you are flagellated. Here you
slip and fall. Just before you are crucified, make a sharp left.'

As Herzl follows his friend along the winding route, he smells
an odd, nasty but richly nostalgic smell. He cannot quite place it.

Herzl is made welcome at 19 Mehmet Ali Street. He likes the look
of the place at once: it has such a reassuringly cluttered Central
European air. Here is a brilliant Turkish carpet on the floor, here is
another one on the table. Here is the mantelpiece, weighed down
with Meissen shepherdesses and Byzantine oil lamps. The walls are
hung with lots of little German oil paintings in the 'Levantine
Mode': an odalisque leans against a palm tree; a Bedouin warrior
sits upright on his camel; a bejewelled Sultan decapitates a negro
slave. 'Which reminds me,' says Herzl, 'I am to be received by the
Kaiser tomorrow. I must make a good impression. He has influence
with the Ottomans. I will persuade him to favour a Jewish State in
Palestine!' 'Bravo!' says Perl. The other members of Perl's family
also express their admiration. Perl introduces them. 'Here is my
son, Karl-Heinz.' A thin spotty youth, clapping very softly. 'And this
is my daughter, Brunhilde.' An aproned girl with floury fingers; she
claps, and the white powder rises in a shaft of sunshine. 'And last
but not least, my dear lady wife. Her name is—' A dark plump
woman, pearl-earringed; she pouts at Herzl. 'You may call her Frau
Perl.'

So Herzl is settled down, in the master bedroom, of course. Herr
and Frau Perl move temporarily into Brunhilde's room. Brunhilde
is assigned a camp bed in the kitchen. One effect of these
manoeuvrings and shiftings is to displace four chamberpots; these

are lined up against a wall of the sitting room. At this point, Karl-Heinz, a shy serious young man, makes the first and only joke of his life. In years to come, at dinner parties and soirées, he will tell of Herzl's visit and repeat this witticism. Since the pun translates poorly from German into Hebrew, he will have to explain the punch line at length. 'Ach,' says Karl-Heinz, 'This house was so *commode* and now it is full of commodes!'

Coffee and cakes are to be served shortly in the sitting room. Frau Perl grinds the coffee beans in a cylindrical copper device which resembles a land mine. Herzl offers to assist. Frau Perl narrows her eyes at Herzl and says, 'Such a gentleman!' Herzl knocks over the grinder and the beans scatter on the floor. Herzl gets down on hands and knees and retrieves them. Frau Perl joins him, crawling alongside, and panting, 'Such a gentleman! Such a gentleman!' Herzl and Frau Perl simultaneously grab the same bean; their hands touch. 'The Hegelian synthesis of the nation-state, pace Zionism, is the instantiation of the ethnos, would you not agree, Dr. Herzl?' says Perl, who was sitting on the sofa all along. 'Yes,' says Herzl, rising to his feet.

Turkish coffee is ground and percolated and poured into the best Rosenthal china coffeecups. Brunhilde enters from the kitchen bearing a silver platter loaded with a massive chocolate cake topped with whipped cream. 'Tell me, Dr. Herzl,' Brunhilde says, presenting Herzl with a generous slice, 'is my Sachertorte as scrumptious as the Sachertorte at Sacher in Vienna?' Herzl tastes the offering. He chews a mouthful, slowly. In his considered opinion, the cake is overbaked and too sweet. 'Certainly, Brunhilde.' Throughout Brunhilde's prolonged old age, whenever she has the opportunity to feed her children and grandchildren her favourite dry sugary Sachertorte, she will mutter, 'So aristocratic! Such Kultur! As good as in Sacher, he said, better even!' And her family will nod. And she will mumble to herself: ' "Delicious, Brunhilde," he said, "Mmm, Brunhilde," he said. "Yum yum, Brunhilde," he said. Nobody calls me Brunhilde, now. I have a new Israeli name. I know it begins with B . . . Bracha? . . . Beruria? . . . Bilha? Oh, I'll forget my own name next.' Herzl also samples Linztorte and Apfelstrudel. He makes appropriate comments. Everybody is satisfied.

*   *   *

It is bedtime. Herzl is lying on his back between the sheets of the double bed. His neck is pressing on the hard bolster. He is reviewing his tactics for the forthcoming meeting with the Kaiser. He is sucking his beard. He blows out the candle. He cannot rest comfortably in this strange bed. He turns on his right side; he smells Perl's male odour. He rolls over onto the other half of the bed; he is disturbed by the faintest hint of Frau Perl's Nuit d'Amour. He falls asleep.

An odalisque, leaning against a palm tree, is waving to a tall turbaned Bedouin seated on a cream-coloured camel on top of a pile of shiny brown camel droppings. The odalisque, who is Brunhilde, assures Herzl the droppings are at least as delicious as those made in Vienna. A Sultan, waving a bloody sword, commands Herzl to eat the stuff. Delicious, says Herzl compliantly; though in fact it tastes dry and sugary. The Bedouin, who is Perl, informs Herzl that he will have to stay in this position forever to demonstrate his Zionist commitment. The camel licks Herzl's beard; the camel is Frau Perl. The camel caresses Herzl's ribcage with a bony ankle; or the Sultan's sword is poking his heart; or the Kaiser himself is posing heroically with his jackboot on the recumbent Herzl.

Herzl awakes. He is lying on the very edge of the double bed. Some complex hard object is digging into his side. He rolls over and pulls back the sheets. He was sleeping on Frau Perl's whalebone corset.

It is morning. A harsh sun angles through a gap in the shutter and hits Herzl's head. A muezzin calls all good men to prayer and awakens Herzl. Herzl arranges himself with care. He brushes his hair, beard, teeth and tailcoat. He fastens his starched collar with a pearl collar stud, and, for double security, holds it in place with a safety pin at the back.

Herzl strolls into the sitting room. Perl greets him with a firm handshake and a cry of, 'Long live the Zionist Ideal!' Herzl says, 'Ah, good morning.' Frau Perl rises from the sofa; her hair is done up in a chignon and she is wearing a low-cut dress; she looks at Herzl and says nothing. At last, she says, 'Did you sleep well?' Herzl considers how to reply. She says, 'Isn't that muezzin drone simply awful?' Herzl says, 'Very well, thank you. And you?' She says, 'My! you look smart.' Herzl says, 'Yes, quite dreadful.' She says, 'Would you like a little music?' Herzl says, 'You're attractively dressed yourself.' 'A Jewish state or a state for Jews, that is the question, is it not?' says Perl loudly. 'Do you want some coffee?' Herzl nods. Perl shouts at the kitchen door, 'Karl-Heinz! Make the coffee for my old friend. Brunhilde! Bring on the strudel.' Frau Perl repeats, 'Would you like a little music?' Perl says, 'Surely you're not going to the Kaiser without a top hat? He'll have your head chopped off if you don't wear a top hat. Top people are very keen on top hats. Not to worry, I've got a top hat upstairs somewhere, you can borrow mine.' Perl goes in search of his top hat. Whenever the name of Herzl will crop up in political discussions in years to come, Perl will always refer to him as 'What'shisname-I-lent-my-top-hat-to.'

In contrast, Frau Perl will refuse to mention Herzl. She will say, 'Ach, men, always talking this boring politics.' Now, she is alone in the sitting room with Herzl. She walks over to a window niche, where there is a high shelf set with Dresden figurines and half a Philistine saucer. Underneath it is Frau Perl's prize possession: the Symphonion: a cross between a pianola and a phonograph. Frau Perl turns the handle to crank the machine. She selects a shiny metal disc pierced with slots in a spiral pattern. She places it on the turntable. The Symphonion emits a tinny music-box sound; it is playing *Deutschland über Alles*. Frau Perl turns to face Herzl. She says, 'Ah, music, it is my soul!' She walks towards him. 'There is little good music in Jerusalem. How I miss it. My husband doesn't like music. Have you been to the latest Strauss in Vienna?' 'No,' says Herzl. 'How I envy you! We must talk about music in the twilight.' 'I won't be here this evening. After meeting the Kaiser, I will catch the train to Haifa, and then the ship. Thank you for your kind hospitality.' 'Farewell!' Frau Perl opens her arms wide to embrace Herzl and bursts into tears.

At this point, Karl-Heinz and Brunhilde enter from the kitchen bearing a jug of coffee and a plate of strudel smothered in whipped cream, and Perl comes down the stairs carrying a large candy-striped box which he opens to reveal a dusty, slightly moth-eaten top hat. Herzl smells four smells: the aroma of coffee, the odour of strudel, the stink of mothballs, and Nuit d'Amour. Herzl will shortly be received by the Kaiser who will listen to Herzl's plea for a Jewish National Home in Palestine and turn the request down flat. And

Herzl will deliver a speech at the World Zionist Congress in which he will argue there is nothing special about Palestine and why should the Jews not settle in, oh, say, Uganda. Now Herzl sees the four members of the Perl family advancing on him from every direction. Suddenly, he recognises that strange nostalgic stench which had troubled him earlier. It is the Jewish Smell. He backs towards the door. 'Go away!' he cries. 'Go away, you Jews!'

Acknowledgments

'A Birthday in London' reprinted from *Like Birds, Like Fishes and Other Stories* (London: John Murray), copyright © 1963 by Ruth Prawer Jhabvala. Used by permission of the author.

Excerpt reprinted from *The Elected Member* (London: Abacus), copyright © 1969 by Bernice Rubens. Used by permission of the author.

'Fanya' reprinted from *Journey through a Small Planet* (London: Michael Joseph), copyright © 1972 by Emanuel Litvinoff. Used by permission of the author.

Excerpt reprinted from *Little Eden: A Child at War* (London: Faber & Faber), copyright © 1978 by Eva Figes. Used by permission of the author c/o Rogers, Coleridge & White Ltd., 20 Powis Mews, London WII IJN.

'Another Survivor' (1978) and 'A Wizard's Robe Patterned with Stars and Moons' reprinted from *Dr Clock's Last Case* (London: Virago), copyright © 1994 by Ruth Fainlight. Used by permission of the author.

'Wingate Football Club' and 'Bedbugs' reprinted from *For Good or Evil* (London: Penguin), copyright © 1991 by Clive Sinclair. Used by permission of the author.

'Inge Wendler's Diary' reprinted from *The Border* (London: Hutchinson), copyright © 1984 by Elaine Feinstein. Used by permission of the author.

'Prologue' reprinted from *Peeping Tom* (London: Chatto & Windus), copyright © 1984 by Howard Jacobson. Used by permission of the author.

Excerpt reprinted from *The Therapy of Avram Blok* (London: Heinemann), copyright © 1985 by Simon Louvish, and 'Guilty as Charged' reprinted from *The Days of Miracles and Wonders* (Toronto: Somerville House; Edinburgh: Canongate), copyright © 1997 by Simon Louvish. Used by permission of the author.